1992 Supplement
To Seventh Editions

MODERN CRIMINAL PROCEDURE

Cases — Comments — Questions

and

BASIC CRIMINAL PROCEDURE

Cases — Comments — Questions

By

Yale Kamisar

*Clarence Darrow Distinguished University Professor of Law,
University of Michigan*

Wayne R. LaFave

*David C. Baum Professor of Law,
University of Illinois*

Jerold H. Israel

*Alene and Allan F. Smith Professor of Law,
University of Michigan*

AMERICAN CASEBOOK SERIES®

WEST PUBLISHING CO.
ST. PAUL, MINN.
1992

Preface

This supplement contains all significant United States Supreme Court cases since the end of the 1988–89 Term—the cut-off date for the principal books. This volume also contains selected provisions of the U.S. Constitution (App. A); selected federal statutory provisions, e.g., the Bail Reform Act, the Speedy Trial Act and the recently amended Wire and Electronic Communications Interception Act (App. B); the Federal Rules of Criminal Procedure (App. C); and proposed amendments to the Rules (App. D).

YALE KAMISAR
WAYNE LaFAVE
JEROLD H. ISRAEL

July, 1992

*

Table of Contents

PART THREE

THE COMMENCEMENT OF FORMAL PROCEEDINGS

PART FIVE

APPEALS, POST–CONVICTION REVIEW

APPENDIX

Table of Cases

The principal cases are in bold type. Cases cited or discussed in the text are roman type. References are to pages. Cases cited in principal cases and within other quoted materials are not included.

1992 Supplement
To Seventh Editions

MODERN CRIMINAL PROCEDURE

Cases — Comments — Questions

and

BASIC CRIMINAL PROCEDURE

Cases — Comments — Questions

*

Part One

INTRODUCTION

Chapter 3

THE RIGHT TO COUNSEL, TRANSCRIPTS AND OTHER AIDS; POVERTY, EQUALITY AND THE ADVERSARY SYSTEM

SECTION 1. THE RIGHT TO APPOINTED COUNSEL AND RELATED PROBLEMS

7th ed., p. 64; before Argersinger, add new Note 4:

4. *Gideon a quarter-century later.* For the transcript of remarks made at a conference commemorating the twenty-fifth anniversary of *Gideon,* see 10 Pace L.Rev. 327–426 (1990). Contributors include Abe Krash (co-author of the brief on Gideon's behalf), Anthony Lewis (author of *Gideon's Trumpet*), Ronald Tabak (an attorney with extensive experience litigating death penalty cases), Judges Judith Kaye and Jack Weinstein, and Professors Yale Kamisar, Michael Mushlin, Charles Ogletree and Barbara Underwood.

SECTION 3. THE RIGHT TO APPOINTED COUNSEL IN PROCEEDINGS OTHER THAN CRIMINAL PROSECUTIONS

7th ed., p. 100; after Note 2, add:

3. Where state law holds that a claim of ineffective assistance of counsel at trial cannot be raised on an appeal from the conviction, but must be presented through state habeas corpus, is there a constitutional right to the assistance of counsel in presenting that claim in the habeas proceeding (as there would have been on first appeal if it could have been raised there)? Consider the treatment of this issue in *Coleman v. Thompson*, discussed at Supp. p. 161.

Part Two
POLICE PRACTICES

Chapter 5
ARREST, SEARCH AND SEIZURE

SECTION 1. THE EXCLUSIONARY RULE

7th ed., p. 145; end of Note 6, add:

Even if there has been direct U.S. involvement in the foreign search, the Fourth Amendment may be inapplicable for yet another reason. In *United States v. Verdugo–Urquidez,* 494 U.S. 259, 110 S.Ct. 1056, 108 L.Ed.2d 222 (1990), the opinion of the Court, per Rehnquist, C.J., declares that the phrase "the people" in the Fourth Amendment (and the First, Second, Ninth and Tenth Amendments) "refers to a class of persons who are part of a national community or who have otherwise developed sufficient connection with this community to be considered part of that community." The defendant in the instant case was deemed not to be such a person; he was a Mexican citizen and resident who, to be sure, just two days before the search of his residence in Mexico had been turned over to U.S. authorities by Mexican police, but "this sort of presence—lawful but involuntary—is not the sort to indicate any substantial connection with our country." (The Court added it was an open question whether even the illegal aliens in *Lopez–Mendoza,* 7th ed., p. 143, were such persons, though their situation was different from the defendant's here because they "were in the United States voluntarily and presumably

had accepted some societal obligations.") The three dissenters agreed, as Blackmun, J., put it, "that when a foreign national is held accountable for purported violations of United States criminal laws, he has effectively been treated as one of 'the governed' and therefore is entitled to Fourth Amendment protections." Because the two concurring Justices placed great emphasis upon the inapplicability of the Fourth Amendment's warrant clause to the search in the instant case (Kennedy, J., stressing this was not a case in which "the full protections of the Fourth Amendment would apply" because of the "absence of local judges or magistrates available to issue warrants"; Stevens, J., that "American magistrates have no power to authorize such searches"), the application of *Verdugo–Urquidez* to a foreign search of an alien's property made even without probable cause is not entirely clear.

7th ed., p. 148; end of Note 3, add:

In *United States v. Alvarez–Machain,* ___ U.S. ___, 112 S.Ct. 2188, ___ L.Ed.2d ___ (1992), the Court held that *Ker,* involving forcible abduction from a foreign country, was "fully applicable to this case" despite the fact that here the abduction was from Mexico, with whom the U.S. has an extradition treaty. "The Treaty says nothing about the obligations of the [parties] to refrain from forcible abductions of people from the territory of the other nation, or the consequences under the Treaty if such an abduction occurs."

SECTION 2. PROTECTED AREAS AND INTERESTS

7th ed., p. 161; add fn. gg after "item," col. 2, line 12:

gg. Sometimes a drug dog alert will lead to nothing but currency. See, e.g., *United States v. Trayer*, 898 F.2d 805 (D.C.Cir.1990). It has been estimated that most of the cash in circulation (the estimates range from 70% to 97% of all bills) contains sufficient quantities of cocaine to alert a trained dog, so that "a court considering whether a dog sniff provides probable cause • • • • may have to take into account the possibility that the dog signalled only the presence of money, not drugs." *United States v. Six Hundred Thirty–Nine Thousand Five Hundred and Fifty–Eight Dollars In U.S. Currency*, 955 F.2d 712 (D.C.Cir. 1992).

7th ed., p. 161; end of fn. i, add:

Thomas was questioned and distinguished in *United States v. Colyer*, 878 F.2d 469 (D.C.Cir. 1989), holding there was no search where a drug dog in the public corridor of a train "alerted" to a particular sleeper compartment.

SECTION 4. SEARCH WARRANTS

7th ed., p. 206; in lieu of first paragraph of Note 6, add:

6. *Seizure of items not named in the search warrant.* In HORTON v. CALIFORNIA, 496 U.S. 128, 110 S.Ct. 2301, 110 L.Ed. 2d 112 (1990), a police officer's affidavit established probable cause to search defendant's home for the proceeds of a robbery (including three specified rings) and for the weapons used in that robbery, but the magistrate issued a warrant only for the proceeds. They were not found in execution of the warrant, but the guns were; they were seized. The defendant claimed this seizure did not come within Justice Stewart's plurality decision in *Coolidge v. New Hampshire*, 403 U.S. 443, 91 S.Ct. 2022, 29 L.Ed.2d 564 (1971), that items found in "plain view" may be seized "where it is immediately apparent to the police that they have evidence before them," because he also required "that the discovery of evidence in plain view must

be inadvertent." The Court in *Horton*, 7–2, disagreed. STEVENS, J., explained:

"Justice Stewart concluded that the inadvertence requirement was necessary to avoid a violation of the express constitutional requirement that a valid warrant must particularly describe the things to be seized. He explained:

'The rationale of the exception to the warrant requirement, as just stated, is that a plain-view seizure will not turn an initially valid (and therefore limited) search into a "general" one, while the inconvenience of procuring a warrant to cover an inadvertent discovery is great. But where the discovery is anticipated, where the police know in advance the location of the evidence and intend to seize it, the situation is altogether different. The requirement of a warrant to seize imposes no inconvenience whatever, or at least none which is constitutionally cognizable in a legal system that regards warrantless searches as "*per se* unreasonable" in the absence of "exigent circumstances."

'If the initial intrusion is bottomed upon a warrant that fails to mention a particular object, though the police know its location and intend to seize it, then there is a violation of the express constitutional requirement of "Warrants . . . particularly describing . . . [the] things to be seized." '

"We find two flaws in this reasoning. First, evenhanded law enforcement is best achieved by the application of objective standards of conduct, rather than standards that depend upon the subjective state of mind of the officer. The fact that an officer is interested in an item of evidence and fully expects to find it in the course of a search should not invalidate its seizure if the search is confined in area and duration by the terms of a warrant or a valid exception to the warrant requirement. If the officer has knowledge approaching certainty that the item will be found, we see no reason why he or she would deliberately om it a particular description of the item to be seized from the application for a search warrant. Specification of the additional items could only permit the officer to expand the scope of the search. On the other hand, if he or she has a valid warrant to search for one item and merely a suspicion concerning the second, whether or not it amounts to probable cause, we fail to see why that suspicion should immunize the second item from seizure if it is found during a lawful search for the first. The hypothetical case put by Justice White in his dissenting opinion in *Coolidge* is instructive:

'Let us suppose officers secure a warrant to search a house for a rifle. While staying well within the range of a rifle search, they discover two photographs of the murder victim, both in plain sight in the bedroom. Assume also that the discovery of the one photograph was inadvertent but finding the other was anticipated. The Court would permit the seizure of only one of the photographs. But in terms of the "minor" peril to Fourth Amendment values there is surely no difference between these two photographs: the interference with possession is the same in each case and the officers' appraisal of the photograph they expected to see is no less reliable than their judgment about the other. And in both situations the actual inconvenience and danger to evidence remain identical if the officers must depart and secure a warrant.'

"Second, the suggestion that the inadvertence requirement is necessary to prevent the police from conducting general searches, or from converting specific warrants into general warrants, is not persuasive because that interest is already served by the requirements that no warrant issue unless it 'particularly describ[es] the place to be searched and the persons or things to be seized,' and that a warrantless search be circumscribed by the exigencies which justify its initiation. Scrupulous adherence to these requirements serves the interests in limiting the area and duration of the search that the inadvertence requirement inadequately protects. Once those commands have been satisfied and the officer has a lawful right of access, however, no additional Fourth Amendment interest is furthered by requiring that the discovery of evidence be inadvertent. If the scope of the search exceeds that permitted by the terms of a validly issued warrant or the character of the relevant exception from the warrant requirement, the subsequent seizure is unconstitutional without more."

BRENNAN, J., joined by Marshall, J. dissenting, responded that "these flaws are illusory. First, the majority explains that it can see no reason why an officer who 'has knowledge approaching certainty' that an item will be found in a particular location 'would deliberately omit a particular description of the item to be seized from the application for a search warrant.' But to the individual whose possessory interest has been invaded, it matters not *why* the police officer decided to omit a particular item from his application for a search warrant. When an officer with probable cause to seize an item fails to mention that item in his application for a search warrant—for whatever reason—and then seizes the item anyway, his conduct is *per se* unreasonable. Suppression of the evidence so seized will encourage officers to be more precise and complete in future warrant applications.

"Furthermore, there are a number of instances in which a law enforcement officer might deliberately choose to omit certain items from a warrant application even though he has probable cause to seize them, knows they are on the premises, and intends to seize them when they are discovered in plain view. For example, the warrant application process can often be time-consuming, especially when the police attempt to seize a large number of items. An officer interested in conducting a search as soon as possible might decide to save time by listing only one or two hard-to-find items, such as the stolen rings in this case, confident that he will find in plain view all of the other evidence he is looking for before he discovers the listed items. Because rings could be located almost anywhere inside or outside a house, it is unlikely that a warrant to search for and seize the rings would restrict the scope of the search. An officer might rationally find the risk of immediately discovering the items listed in the warrant—thereby forcing him to conclude the search immediately—outweighed by the time saved in the application process.

"The majority also contends that, once an officer is lawfully in a house and the scope of his search is adequately circumscribed by a warrant, 'no additional Fourth Amendment interest is furthered by requiring that the discovery of evidence be inadvertent.' Put another way, ' "the inadvertence rule will in no way reduce the number of places into which [law enforcement officers] may lawfully look." ' The majority is correct, but it has asked the wrong question. It is true that the inadvertent discovery requirement furthers no privacy interests. The requirement in no way reduces the scope of a search or the number of places into which officers may look. But it does protect possessory interests. Cf. *Illinois v. Andreas*, [7th ed., p. 256] ('The plain-view doctrine is grounded on the proposition that once police are lawfully in a position to observe an item first-hand, its owner's privacy interest in that item is lost; *the owner may retain the incidents of title and possession* but not privacy') (emphasis added). The inadvertent discovery requirement is essential if we are to take seriously the Fourth Amendment's protection of possessory interests as well as privacy interests. The Court today eliminates a rule designed to further possessory interests on the ground that it fails to further privacy interests. I cannot countenance such constitutional legerdemain."

7th ed., p. 207; in lieu of first 7 lines of Note 2, add:

2. The preference for the warrant process is commonly explained on the ground that it, more so than the post-search suppression process, *prevents* illegal searches. Compare Stuntz, *Warrants and Fourth Amendment Remedies,* 77 Va.L.Rev. 881, 893 (1991): "Unfortunately, given our existing system, warrants may not have the desired preventive effect. Police officers are not the only ones who can get the relevant legal standards wrong; other actors in the system make mistakes as well. And while requiring warrants does reduce the odds of police mistake in applying the relevant legal standards, it also creates additional opportunities for error by magistrates. This is no small problem. Magistrates (1) may do a bad job of applying the probable cause standard because of deficiencies in the warrant process (review is ex parte and cursory), and (2) nevertheless receive a great deal of deference by judges after the fact. Requiring warrants therefore may lead to many *more* bad searches than would a simple system of police decisionmaking followed by after-the-fact review.

"And even if warrants do prevent bad searches, so do after-the-fact sanctions. An ounce of prevention may indeed be worth a pound of cure, but the pound of cure—after-the-fact sanctions—is itself a preventive device, since the threat of ex post penalties affects behavior ex ante. This is a simple point, but an important one. Police officers, like other regulated actors, respond to legal signals and alter their behavior in order to avoid after-the-fact sanctions. In most other contexts, that is thought to be the cheapest means of achieving a given level of deterrence * * *. Thus, to defend warrants, one must point to some reason why after-the-fact deterrence will work unusually poorly in the search and seizure context—some argument that explains why search and seizure law should be treated *differently* than most other regulatory regimes."

Stuntz, id. at 884, suggests some other reasons—that "the exclusionary rule generates an additional pair of problems for fourth amendment law, problems that warrants might plausibly help solve. Exclusion * * * may bias judges' after-the-fact probable cause determinations by requiring that they be made in cases where the officer actually found incriminating evidence. Similarly, the lack of a credible opponent (the defendant has, after all, been found with incriminating evidence) invites the police to subvert the governing legal standard by testifying falsely at suppression hearings. Warrants can reduce both problems by forcing the necessary judicial decision to be made, and the police officer's account of the facts to be given, before the evidence is found."

3. Compare Bradley, *Two Models of the Fourth Amendment*, 83 Mich.L.Rev. 1468, 1471–72 (1985), who suggests "that current fourth amendment law, complete with [see 7th Ed. for continuation of sentence].

SECTION 5. WARRANTLESS ARRESTS

7th ed., p. 218; in lieu of Note 10, add:

10. In COUNTY OF RIVERSIDE v. McLAUGHLIN, ___ U.S. ___, 111 S.Ct. 1661, 114 L.Ed.2d 49 (1991), the Court confronted the question of "what is 'prompt' under *Gerstein*" and concluded, 5–4, per O'CONNOR, J.:

"Our task in this case is to articulate more clearly the boundaries of what is permissible under the Fourth Amendment. Although we hesitate to announce that the Constitution compels a specific time limit, it is important to provide some degree of certainty so that States and counties may establish procedures with confidence that they fall within constitutional bounds. Taking into account the competing interests articulated in *Gerstein*, we believe that a jurisdiction that provides judicial determinations of probable cause within 48 hours of arrest will, as a general matter, comply with the promptness requirement of *Ger-*

stein. For this reason, such jurisdictions will be immune from systemic challenges.

"This is not to say that the probable cause determination in a particular case passes constitutional muster simply because it is provided within 48 hours. Such a hearing may nonetheless violate *Gerstein* if the arrested individual can prove that his or her probable cause determination was delayed unreasonably. Examples of unreasonable delay are delays for the purpose of gathering additional evidence to justify the arrest, a delay motivated by ill will against the arrested individual, or delay for delay's sake. In evaluating whether the delay in a particular case is unreasonable, however, courts must allow a substantial degree of flexibility. Courts cannot ignore the often unavoidable delays in transporting arrested persons from one facility to another, handling late-night bookings where no magistrate is readily available, obtaining the presence of an arresting officer who may be busy processing other suspects or securing the premises of an arrest, and other practical realities.

"Where an arrested individual does not receive a probable cause determination within 48 hours, the calculus changes. In such a case, the arrested individual does not bear the burden of proving an unreasonable delay. Rather, the burden shifts to the government to demonstrate the existence of a bona fide emergency or other extraordinary circumstance. The fact that in a particular case it may take longer than 48 hours to consolidate pretrial proceedings does not qualify as an extraordinary circumstance. Nor, for that matter, do intervening weekends. A jurisdiction that chooses to offer combined proceedings must do so as soon as is reasonably feasible, but in no event later than 48 hours after arrest. * * *

"Everyone agrees that the police should make every attempt to minimize the time a presumptively innocent individual spends in jail. One way to do so is to provide a judicial determination of probable cause immediately upon completing the administrative steps incident to arrest—*i.e.*, as soon as the suspect has been booked, photographed, and fingerprinted. As the dissent explains, several States, laudably, have adopted this approach. The Constitution does not compel so rigid a schedule, however. Under *Gerstein,* jurisdictions may choose to combine probable cause determinations with other pretrial proceedings, so long as they do so promptly. This necessarily means that only certain proceedings are candidates for combination. Only those proceedings that arise very early in the pretrial process—such as bail hearings and arraignments—may be chosen. Even then, every effort must be made to expedite the combined proceedings."

SCALIA, J., dissenting, reasoned that the Fourth Amendment "preserves for our citizens the traditional protections against unlawful arrest afforded by the common law"; that one such protection is the right of prompt production before a magistrate, as to which "the only element bearing upon the reasonableness of delay was * * * the arresting officer's ability, once the prisoner had been secured, to reach a magistrate who could issue the needed warrant for further detention"; that consequently the majority had erred in concluding "that combining the [probable cause] determination with other proceedings justifies a delay"; and that without such an invalid consideration the time at which the presumption should shift ought to be only 24 hours.

SECTION 6. WARRANTLESS SEARCHES OF PREMISES, VEHICLES, AND CONTAINERS

7th ed., p. 224; in lieu of Note 3(b), add:

(b) *When the officers are acting for their own protection.* The question of when a "protective sweep" is permissible reached the Court in MARYLAND v. BUIE, 494 U.S. 325, 110 S.Ct. 1093, 108 L.Ed.2d 276 (1990), where the state court had

required full probable cause of a dangerous situation. By analogy to *Terry v. Ohio,* 7th ed., p. 269, and *Michigan v. Long,* 7th ed., p. 291, the Court opted for a less demanding reasonable suspicion test. The state had argued for a "bright-line rule" to the effect that "police should be permitted to conduct a protective sweep whenever they make an in-home arrest for a violent crime"; the Court responded that *Terry* requires individualized suspicion, but then adopted a two-part sweep rule which included another kind of bright line. Specifically, the Court (7–2), per WHITE, J., concluded:

"We agree with the State, as did the court below, that a warrant was not required. We also hold that as an incident to the arrest the officers could, as a precautionary matter and without probable cause or reasonable suspicion, look in closets and other spaces immediately adjoining the place of arrest from which an attack could be immediately launched. Beyond that, however, we hold that there must be articulable facts which, taken together with the rational inferences from those facts, would warrant a reasonable prudent officer in believing that the area to be swept harbors an individual posing a danger to those on the arrest scene. * * *

"We should emphasize that such a protective sweep, aimed at protecting the arresting officers, if justified by the circumstances, is nevertheless not a full search of the premises, but may extend only to a cursory inspection of those spaces where a person may be found. The sweep lasts no longer than is necessary to dispel the reasonable suspicion of danger and in any event no longer than it takes to complete the arrest and depart the premises."

The Court remanded for application of this test. The facts, as stated in the Supreme Court opinions, are these: Two men (one wearing a red running suit) committed an armed robbery of a restaurant on Feb. 3; warrants for them (Buie and Allen) were issued that day, and

Buie's home was immediately placed under surveillance. On Feb. 5, after a police department secretary called the residence and verified that Buie was there, 6 or 7 officers proceeded to the house and fanned out through the first and second floors. Officer Rozar said he would "freeze" the basement so that no one could come up; he drew his weapon and twice shouted into the basement for anyone there to come out, and Buie then emerged from the basement. He was arrested, searched and handcuffed by Rozar. Once Buie was outside the house, Officer Frolich entered the basement, noticed a red running suit in plain view and seized it. Rozar testified he was not worried about any possible danger when he arrested Buie; Frolich said he entered the basement "in case there was someone else" down there, though he "had no idea who lived there." What should the result be on remand?

7th ed., pp. 226–227; delete Notes 3 and 4:
7th ed., p. 231; before Note 4, add:

3a. Assuming no such exigent circumstances, is it permissible for police to engage in a subterfuge which causes an occupant to remove the evidence to another place where warrantless search is permissible? See *State v. Hendrix,* 782 S.W.2d 833 (Tenn.1989) (proper for police to telephone residence with anonymous false "tip" that police were on their way there with search warrant, causing defendant to leave with drugs in car, which was then stopped and searched). What if the telephoning police had falsely reported a gas leak and likely explosion?

7th ed., p. 239, before Note 4, add:

Would the result in *Welsh* have been different if the police were in immediate hot pursuit? See *State v. Bolte,* 560 A.2d 644 (N.J.1989) (rejecting state's argument answer is yes because "citizens should not be encouraged to elude arrest by retreating into their homes").

3a. MINNESOTA v. OLSON, 495 U.S. 91, 110 S.Ct. 1684, 109 L.Ed.2d 85 (1990) (also discussed at Supp., p. 81), another warrantless entry to arrest case, involved these facts: "Shortly before 6 a.m. on Saturday, July 18, 1987, a lone gunman robbed an Amoco gasoline station in Minneapolis, Minnesota, and fatally shot the station manager. A police officer heard the police dispatcher report and suspected Joseph Ecker. The officer and his partner drove immediately to Ecker's home, arriving at about the same time that an Oldsmobile arrived. The Oldsmobile took evasive action, spun out of control, and came to a stop. Two men fled the car on foot. Ecker, who was later identified as the gunman, was captured shortly thereafter inside his home. The second man escaped.

"Inside the abandoned Oldsmobile, police found a sack of money and the murder weapon. They also found a title certificate with the name Rob Olson crossed out as a secured party, a letter addressed to a Roger R. Olson of 3151 Johnson Street, and a videotape rental receipt made out to Rob Olson and dated two days earlier. The police verified that a Robert Olson lived at 3151 Johnson Street.

"The next morning, Sunday, July 19, a woman identifying herself as Dianna Murphy called the police and said that a man by the name of Rob drove the car in which the gas-station killer left the scene and that Rob was planning to leave town by bus. About noon, the same woman called again, gave her address and phone number, and said that a man named Rob had told a Maria and two other women, Louanne and Julie, that he was the driver in the Amoco robbery. The caller stated that Louanne was Julie's mother and that the two women lived at 2406 Fillmore Northeast. The detective-in-charge who took the second phone call sent police officers to 2406 Fillmore to check out Louanne and Julie. When police arrived they determined that the dwelling was a duplex and that Louanne Bergstrom and her daughter Julie lived in the upper unit but were not home. Police spoke to Louanne's mother, Helen Niederhoffer, who lived in the lower unit. She confirmed that a Rob Olson had been staying upstairs but was not then in the unit. She promised to call the police when Olson returned. At 2 p.m., a pickup order, or 'probable cause arrest bulletin,' was issued for Olson's arrest. The police were instructed to stay away from the duplex.

"At approximately 2:45 p.m., Niederhoffer called police and said Olson had returned. The detective-in-charge instructed police officers to go to the house and surround it. He then telephoned Julie from headquarters and told her Rob should come out of the house. The detective heard a male voice say 'tell them I left.' Julie stated that Rob had left, whereupon at 3 p.m. the detective ordered the police to enter the house. Without seeking permission and with weapons drawn, the police entered the upper unit and found respondent hiding in a closet."

The Court, per WHITE, J., determined that "the Minnesota Supreme Court was correct in holding that there were no exigent circumstances that justified the warrantless entry into the house to make the arrest.

"The Minnesota Supreme Court applied essentially the correct standard in determining whether exigent circumstances existed. The court observed that 'a warrantless intrusion may be justified by hot pursuit of a fleeing felon, or imminent destruction of evidence, or the need to prevent a suspect's escape, or the risk of danger to the police or to other persons inside or outside the dwelling.' The court also apparently thought that in the absence of hot pursuit there must be at least probable cause to believe that one or more of the other factors justifying the entry were present and that in assessing the risk of danger, the gravity of the crime and likelihood that the suspect is armed should be considered. Applying this standard, the

state court determined that exigent circumstances did not exist.

"We are not inclined to disagree with this fact-specific application of the proper legal standard. The court pointed out that although a grave crime was involved, respondent 'was known not to be the murderer but thought to be the driver of the getaway car,' and that the police had already recovered the murder weapon. 'The police knew that Louanne and Julie were with the suspect in the upstairs duplex with no suggestion of danger to them. Three or four Minneapolis police squads surrounded the house. The time was 3 p.m., Sunday. . . . It was evident the suspect was going nowhere. If he came out of the house he would have been promptly apprehended.' We do not disturb the state court's judgment that these facts do not add up to exigent circumstances."

7th ed., p. 246; delete *Ross* and Notes and Questions following.

7th ed., p. 263; before *Bertine*, add:

CALIFORNIA v. ACEVEDO

___ U.S. ___, 111 S.Ct. 1982, 114 L.Ed.2d 619 (1991).

JUSTICE BLACKMUN delivered the opinion of the Court.

[One Daza picked up a package the police knew contained marijuana from a Federal Express office and took it to his apartment. About two hours later, Acevedo entered that apartment and shortly thereafter left carrying a brown paper bag the size of one of the wrapped marijuana packages. He placed the bag in the trunk of his car and drove off; the police then stopped him, opened the trunk and bag, and found marijuana. The California Court of Appeal held the marijuana should have been suppressed, the state supreme court denied review, and the Supreme Court then granted certiorari.]

In *United States v. Ross,* 456 U.S. 798, 102 S.Ct. 2157, 72 L.Ed.2d 572, decided in 1982, we held that a warrantless search of an automobile under the *Carroll* doctrine could include a search of a container or package found inside the car when such a search was supported by probable cause. The warrantless search of Ross' car occurred after an informant told the police that he had seen Ross complete a drug transaction using drugs stored in the trunk of his car. The police stopped the car, searched it, and discovered in the trunk a brown paper bag containing drugs. We decided that the search of Ross' car was not unreasonable under the Fourth Amendment: "The scope of a warrantless search based on probable cause is no narrower—and no broader—than the scope of a search authorized by a warrant supported by probable cause." Thus, "[i]f probable cause justifies the search of a lawfully stopped vehicle, it justifies the search of every part of the vehicle and its contents that may conceal the object of the search." In *Ross,* therefore, we clarified the scope of the *Carroll* doctrine as properly including a "probing search" of compartments and containers within the automobile so long as the search is supported by probable cause.

In addition to this clarification, *Ross* distinguished the *Carroll* doctrine from the separate rule that governed the search of closed containers. The Court had announced this separate rule, unique to luggage and other closed packages, bags, and containers, in *United States v. Chadwick,* 433 U.S. 1, 97 S.Ct. 2476, 53 L.Ed.2d 538 (1977). In *Chadwick,* federal narcotics agents had probable cause to believe that a 200–pound double-locked footlocker contained marijuana. The agents tracked the locker as the defendants removed it from a train and carried it through the station to a waiting car. As soon as the defendants lifted the locker into the trunk of the car, the agents arrested them, seized the locker, and searched it. In this Court, the United States did not contend that the locker's brief contact with the automobile's trunk sufficed to make the *Carroll* doctrine applicable. Rather,

the United States urged that the search of movable luggage could be considered analogous to the search of an automobile.

The Court rejected this argument because, it reasoned, a person expects more privacy in his luggage and personal effects than he does in his automobile. Moreover, it concluded that as "may often not be the case when automobiles are seized," secure storage facilities are usually available when the police seize luggage.

In *Arkansas v. Sanders,* 442 U.S. 753, 99 S.Ct. 2586, 61 L.Ed.2d 235 (1979), the Court extended *Chadwick*'s rule to apply to a suitcase actually being transported in the trunk of a car. In *Sanders,* the police had probable cause to believe a suitcase contained marijuana. They watched as the defendant placed the suitcase in the trunk of a taxi and was driven away. The police pursued the taxi for several blocks, stopped it, found the suitcase in the trunk, and searched it. Although the Court had applied the *Carroll* doctrine to searches of integral parts of the automobile itself, (indeed, in *Carroll,* contraband whiskey was in the upholstery of the seats), it did not extend the doctrine to the warrantless search of personal luggage "merely because it was located in an automobile lawfully stopped by the police." Again, the *Sanders* majority stressed the heightened privacy expectation in personal luggage and concluded that the presence of luggage in an automobile did not diminish the owner's expectation of privacy in his personal items.

In *Ross,* the Court endeavored to distinguish between *Carroll,* which governed the *Ross* automobile search, and *Chadwick,* which governed the *Sanders* automobile search. It held that the *Carroll* doctrine covered searches of automobiles when the police had probable cause to search an entire vehicle but that the *Chadwick* doctrine governed searches of luggage when the officers had probable cause to search only a container within the vehicle. Thus, in a *Ross* situation, the police could conduct a reasonable search under the Fourth Amendment without obtaining a warrant, whereas in a *Sanders* situation, the police had to obtain a warrant before they searched.

The dissent is correct, of course, that *Ross* involved the scope of an automobile search. *Ross* held that closed containers encountered by the police during a warrantless search of a car pursuant to the automobile exception could also be searched. Thus, this Court in *Ross* took the critical step of saying that closed containers in cars could be searched without a warrant because of their presence within the automobile. Despite the protection that *Sanders* purported to extend to closed containers, the privacy interest in those closed containers yielded to the broad scope of an automobile search. * * *

This Court in *Ross* rejected *Chadwick*'s distinction between containers and cars. It concluded that the expectation of privacy in one's vehicle is equal to one's expectation of privacy in the container, and noted that "the privacy interests in a car's trunk or glove compartment may be no less than those in a movable container." It also recognized that it was arguable that the same exigent circumstances that permit a warrantless search of an automobile would justify the warrantless search of a movable container. In deference to the rule of *Chadwick* and *Sanders,* however, the Court put that question to one side. It concluded that the time and expense of the warrant process would be misdirected if the police could search every cubic inch of an automobile until they discovered a paper sack, at which point the Fourth Amendment required them to take the sack to a magistrate for permission to look inside. We now must decide the question deferred in *Ross:* whether the Fourth Amendment requires the police to obtain a warrant to open the sack in a movable vehicle simply because they lack probable cause to search the entire car. We conclude that it does not.

Dissenters in *Ross* asked why the suitcase in *Sanders* was "more private, less difficult for police to seize and store, or in any other relevant respect more properly subject to the warrant requirement, than a container that police discover in a probable-cause search of an entire automobile?" We now agree that a container found after a general search of the automobile and a container found in a car after a limited search for the container are equally easy for the police to store and for the suspect to hide or destroy. In fact, we see no principled distinction in terms of either the privacy expectation or the exigent circumstances between the paper bag found by the police in *Ross* and the paper bag found by the police here. Furthermore, by attempting to distinguish between a container for which the police are specifically searching and a container which they come across in a car, we have provided only minimal protection for privacy and have impeded effective law enforcement.

The line between probable cause to search a vehicle and probable cause to search a package in that vehicle is not always clear, and separate rules that govern the two objects to be searched may enable the police to broaden their power to make warrantless searches and disserve privacy interests. * * * At the moment when officers stop an automobile, it may be less than clear whether they suspect with a high degree of certainty that the vehicle contains drugs in a bag or simply contains drugs. If the police know that they may open a bag only if they are actually searching the entire car, they may search more extensively than they otherwise would in order to establish the general probable cause required by *Ross.*

Such a situation is not far fetched. In *United States v. Johns,* 469 U.S. 478, 105 S.Ct. 881, 83 L.Ed.2d 890 (1985), customs agents saw two trucks drive to a private airstrip and approach two small planes. The agents drew near the trucks, smelled marijuana, and then saw in the backs of the trucks packages wrapped in a manner that marijuana smugglers customarily employed. The agents took the trucks to headquarters and searched the packages without a warrant. Relying on *Chadwick,* the defendants argued that the search was unlawful. The defendants contended that *Ross* was inapplicable because the agents lacked probable cause to search anything but the packages themselves and supported this contention by noting that a search of the entire vehicle never occurred. We rejected that argument and found *Chadwick* and *Sanders* inapposite because the agents had probable cause to search the entire body of each truck, although they had chosen not to do so. We cannot see the benefit of a rule that requires law enforcement officers to conduct a more intrusive search in order to justify a less intrusive one.

To the extent that the *Chadwick–Sanders* rule protects privacy, its protection is minimal. Law enforcement officers may seize a container and hold it until they obtain a search warrant. "Since the police, by hypothesis, have probable cause to seize the property, we can assume that a warrant will be routinely forthcoming in the overwhelming majority of cases." And the police often will be able to search containers without a warrant, despite the *Chadwick–Sanders* rule, as a search incident to a lawful arrest [under] *Belton.* * * *

Finally, the search of a paper bag intrudes far less on individual privacy than does the incursion sanctioned long ago in *Carroll.* In that case, prohibition agents slashed the upholstery of the automobile. This Court nonetheless found their search to be reasonable under the Fourth Amendment. If destroying the interior of an automobile is not unreasonable, we cannot conclude that looking inside a closed container is. In light of the minimal protection to privacy afforded by the *Chadwick–Sanders* rule, and our serious doubt whether that rule substantially serves privacy interests, we now hold that the Fourth Amendment does not compel separate treatment for an automobile search that extends only to a container within the vehicle.

The *Chadwick–Sanders* rule not only has failed to protect privacy but it has also confused courts and police officers and impeded effective law enforcement. * * *

The discrepancy between the two rules has led to confusion for law enforcement officers. For example, when an officer, who has developed probable cause to believe that a vehicle contains drugs, begins to search the vehicle and immediately discovers a closed container, which rule applies? The defendant will argue that the fact that the officer first chose to search the container indicates that his probable cause extended only to the container and that *Chadwick* and *Sanders* therefore require a warrant. On the other hand, the fact that the officer first chose to search in the most obvious location should not restrict the propriety of the search. The *Chadwick* rule, as applied in *Sanders,* has devolved into an anomaly such that the more likely the police are to discover drugs in a container, the less authority they have to search it. * * *

Although we have recognized firmly that the doctrine of *stare decisis* serves profoundly important purposes in our legal system, this Court has overruled a prior case on the comparatively rare occasion when it has bred confusion or been a derelict or led to anomalous results. *Sanders* was explicitly undermined in *Ross,* and the existence of the dual regimes for automobile searches that uncover containers has proved as confusing as the *Chadwick* and *Sanders* dissenters predicted. We conclude that it is better to adopt one clear-cut rule to govern automobile searches and eliminate the warrant requirement for closed containers set forth in *Sanders.*

The interpretation of the *Carroll* doctrine set forth in *Ross* now applies to all searches of containers found in an automobile. In other words, the police may search without a warrant if their search is supported by probable cause. The Court in *Ross* put it this way:

> "The scope of a warrantless search of an automobile . . . is not defined by the nature of the container in which the contraband is secreted. Rather, it is defined by the object of the search and the places in which there is probable cause to believe that it may be found."

It went on to note: "Probable cause to believe that a container placed in the trunk of a taxi contains contraband or evidence does not justify a search of the entire cab." We reaffirm that principle. In the case before us, the police had probable cause to believe that the paper bag in the automobile's trunk contained marijuana. That probable cause now allows a warrantless search of the paper bag. The facts in the record reveal that the police did not have probable cause to believe that contraband was hidden in any other part of the automobile and a search of the entire vehicle would have been without probable cause and unreasonable under the Fourth Amendment.

Our holding today neither extends the *Carroll* doctrine nor broadens the scope of the permissible automobile search delineated in *Carroll, Chambers,* and *Ross.* It remains a "cardinal principle that 'searches conducted outside the judicial process, without prior approval by judge or magistrate, are *per se* unreasonable under the Fourth Amendment—subject only to a few specifically established and well-delineated exceptions.' " We held in *Ross:* "The exception recognized in *Carroll* is unquestionably one that is 'specifically established and well delineated.' "

Until today, this Court has drawn a curious line between the search of an automobile that coincidentally turns up a container and the search of a container that coincidentally turns up in an automobile. The protections of the Fourth Amendment must not turn on such coincidences. We therefore interpret *Carroll* as providing one rule to govern all automobile search-

es. The police may search an automobile and the containers within it where they have probable cause to believe contraband or evidence is contained. * * *

JUSTICE SCALIA, concurring in the judgment.

I agree with the dissent that it is anomalous for a briefcase to be protected by the "general requirement" of a prior warrant when it is being carried along the street, but for that same briefcase to become unprotected as soon as it is carried into an automobile. On the other hand, I agree with the Court that it would be anomalous for a locked compartment in an automobile to be unprotected by the "general requirement" of a prior warrant, but for an unlocked briefcase within the automobile to be protected. I join in the judgment of the Court because I think its holding is more faithful to the text and tradition of the Fourth Amendment, and if these anomalies in our jurisprudence are ever to be eliminated that is the direction in which we should travel. * * *

Although the Fourth Amendment does not explicitly impose the requirement of a warrant, it is of course textually possible to consider that implicit within the requirement of reasonableness. For some years after the (still continuing) explosion in Fourth Amendment litigation that followed our announcement of the exclusionary rule in *Weeks v. United States,* [7th ed., p. 118], our jurisprudence lurched back and forth between imposing a categorical warrant requirement and looking to reasonableness alone. * * *

The victory was illusory. Even before today's decision, the "warrant requirement" had become so riddled with exceptions that it was basically unrecognizable. In 1985, one commentator cataloged nearly 20 such exceptions, including "searches incident to arrest . . . automobile searches . . . border searches . . . administrative searches of regulated businesses . . . exigent circumstances . . . search[es] incident to nonarrest when there is probable cause to arrest . . . boat boarding for document checks . . . welfare searches . . . inventory searches . . . airport searches . . . school search[es]. . . ." Bradley, *Two Models of the Fourth Amendment,* 83 Mich.L.Rev. 1468, 1473–1474 (1985) (footnotes omitted). Since then, we have added at least two more. *California v. Carney* [7th ed., p. 240] (searches of mobile homes); *O'Connor v. Ortega* [7th ed., p. 155] (searches of offices of government employees). Our intricate body of law regarding "reasonable expectation of privacy" has been developed largely as a means of creating these exceptions, enabling a search to be denominated not a Fourth Amendment "search" and therefore not subject to the general warrant requirement.

Unlike the dissent, therefore, I do not regard today's holding as some momentous departure, but rather as merely the continuation of an inconsistent jurisprudence that has been with us for years. There can be no clarity in this area unless we make up our minds, and unless the principles we express comport with the actions we take.

In my view, the path out of this confusion should be sought by returning to the first principle that the "reasonableness" requirement of the Fourth Amendment affords the protection that the common law afforded. I have no difficulty with the proposition that that includes the requirement of a warrant, where the common law required a warrant; and it may even be that changes in the surrounding legal rules (for example, elimination of the common-law rule that reasonable, good-faith belief was no defense to absolute liability for trespass), may make a warrant indispensable to reasonableness where it once was not. But the supposed "general rule" that a warrant is always required does not appear to have any basis in the common law, and confuses rather than facilitates any attempt to develop rules of reasonableness in light of changed legal circumstances, as the anomaly eliminated and the anomaly

created by today's holding both demonstrate.

And there are more anomalies still. Under our precedents (as at common law), a person may be arrested outside the home on the basis of probable cause, without an arrest warrant. *United States v. Watson* [7th ed., p. 208]. Upon arrest, the person, as well as the area within his grasp, may be searched for evidence related to the crime. *Chimel v. California* [7th ed., p. 219]. Under these principles, if a known drug dealer is carrying a briefcase reasonably believed to contain marijuana (the unauthorized possession of which is a crime), the police may arrest him and search his person on the basis of probable cause alone. And, under our precedents, upon arrival at the station house, the police may inventory his possessions, including the briefcase, even if there is no reason to suspect that they contain contraband. *Illinois v. Lafayette* [7th ed., p. 303]. According to our current law, however, the police may not, on the basis of the same probable cause, take the less intrusive step of stopping the individual on the street and demanding to see the contents of his briefcase. That makes no sense *a priori,* and in the absence of any common-law tradition supporting such a distinction, I see no reason to continue it.

I would reverse the judgment in the present case, not because a closed container carried inside a car becomes subject to the "automobile" exception to the general warrant requirement, but because the search of a closed container, outside a privately owned building, with probable cause to believe that the container contains contraband, and when it in fact does contain contraband, is not one of those searches whose Fourth Amendment reasonableness depends upon a warrant. For that reason I concur in the judgment of the Court.

JUSTICE WHITE, dissenting.

Agreeing as I do with most of Justice Stevens' opinion and with the result he reaches, I dissent and would affirm the judgment below.

JUSTICE STEVENS, with whom JUSTICE MARSHALL joins, dissenting.

At the end of its opinion, the Court pays lip service to the proposition that should provide the basis for a correct analysis of the legal question presented by this case: It is " 'a cardinal principle that "searches conducted outside the judicial process, without prior approval by judge or magistrate, are *per se* unreasonable under the Fourth Amendment—subject only to a few specifically established and well-delineated exceptions." ' * * *"

The Fourth Amendment is a restraint on Executive power. The Amendment constitutes the Framers' direct constitutional response to the unreasonable law enforcement practices employed by agents of the British Crown. Over the years—particularly in the period immediately after World War II and particularly in opinions authored by Justice Jackson after his service as a special prosecutor at the Nuremburg trials—the Court has recognized the importance of this restraint as a bulwark against police practices that prevail in totalitarian regimes.

This history is, however, only part of the explanation for the warrant requirement. The requirement also reflects the sound policy judgment that, absent exceptional circumstances, the decision to invade the privacy of an individual's personal effects should be made by a neutral magistrate rather than an agent of the Executive. In his opinion for the Court in *Johnson v. United States* [7th ed., p. 209], Justice Jackson explained:

"The point of the Fourth Amendment, which often is not grasped by zealous officers, is not that it denies law enforcement the support of the usual inferences which reasonable men draw from evidence. Its protection consists in requiring that those inferences be drawn by a neutral and detached magistrate instead of being judged by the

officer engaged in the often competitive enterprise of ferreting out crime."

Our decisions have always acknowledged that the warrant requirement imposes a burden on law enforcement. And our cases have not questioned that trained professionals normally make reliable assessments of the existence of probable cause to conduct a search. We have repeatedly held, however, that these factors are outweighed by the individual interest in privacy that is protected by advance judicial approval. The Fourth Amendment dictates that the privacy interest is paramount, no matter how marginal the risk of error might be if the legality of warrantless searches were judged only after the fact. * * *

In *Chadwick,* the Department of Justice had mounted a frontal attack on the warrant requirement. The Government's principal contention was that "the Fourth Amendment Warrant Clause protects only interests traditionally identified with the home." We categorically rejected that contention, relying on the history and text of the amendment, the policy underlying the warrant requirement, and a line of cases spanning over a century of our jurisprudence. We also rejected the Government's alternative argument that the rationale of our automobile search cases demonstrated the reasonableness of permitting warrantless searches of luggage.

We concluded that neither of the justifications for the automobile exception could support a similar exception for luggage. We first held that the privacy interest in luggage is "substantially greater than in an automobile." Unlike automobiles and their contents, we reasoned, "[l]uggage contents are not open to public view, except as a condition to a border entry or common carrier travel; nor is luggage subject to regular inspections and official scrutiny on a continuing basis." Indeed, luggage is specifically intended to safeguard the privacy of personal effects, unlike an automobile, "whose primary function is transportation."

We then held that the mobility of luggage did not justify creating an additional exception to the Warrant Clause. Unlike an automobile, luggage can easily be seized and detained pending judicial approval of a search. Once the police have luggage "under their exclusive control, there [i]s not the slightest danger that the [luggage] or its contents could [be] removed before a valid search warrant could be obtained. . . . With the [luggage] safely immobilized, it [i]s unreasonable to undertake the additional and greater intrusion of a search without a warrant" (footnote omitted). * * *

[W]e recognized in *Ross* that *Chadwick* and *Sanders* had not created a special rule for container searches, but rather had merely applied the cardinal principle that warrantless searches are per se unreasonable unless justified by an exception to the general rule. *Ross* dealt with the scope of the automobile exception; *Chadwick* and *Sanders* were cases in which the exception simply did not apply.

In its opinion today, the Court recognizes that the police did not have probable cause to search respondent's vehicle and that a search of anything but the paper bag that respondent had carried from Daza's apartment and placed in the trunk of his car would have been unconstitutional. Moreover, as I read the opinion, the Court assumes that the police could not have made a warrantless inspection of the bag before it was placed in the car. Finally, the Court also does not question the fact that, under our prior cases, it would have been lawful for the police to seize the container and detain it (and respondent) until they obtained a search warrant. Thus, all of the relevant facts that governed our decisions in *Chadwick* and *Sanders* are present here whereas the relevant fact that justified the vehicle search in *Ross* is not present.

The Court does not attempt to identify any exigent circumstances that would justify its refusal to apply the general rule against warrantless searches. Instead, it advances these three arguments: First, the rules identified in the foregoing cases are confusing and anomalous. Second, the rules do not protect any significant interest in privacy. And, third, the rules impede effective law enforcement. None of these arguments withstands scrutiny. * * *

The Court summarizes the alleged "anomaly" created by the coexistence of *Ross, Chadwick,* and *Sanders* with the statement that "the more likely the police are to discover drugs in a container, the less authority they have to search it." This juxtaposition is only anomalous, however, if one accepts the flawed premise that the degree to which the police are likely to discover contraband is correlated with their authority to search *without a warrant.* Yet, even proof beyond a reasonable doubt will not justify a warrantless search that is not supported by one of the exceptions to the warrant requirement. And, even when the police have a warrant or an exception applies, once the police possess probable cause, the extent to which they are more or less certain of the contents of a container has no bearing on their authority to search it.

To the extent there was any "anomaly" in our prior jurisprudence, the Court has "cured" it at the expense of creating a more serious paradox. For, surely it is anomalous to prohibit a search of a briefcase while the owner is carrying it exposed on a public street yet to permit a search once the owner has placed the briefcase in the locked trunk of his car. One's privacy interest in one's luggage can certainly not be diminished by one's removing it from a public thoroughfare and placing it—out of sight—in a privately owned vehicle. Nor is the danger that evidence will escape increased if the luggage is in a car rather than on the street. In either location, if the police have probable cause, they are authorized to seize the luggage and to detain it until they obtain judicial approval for a search. Any line demarking an exception to the warrant requirement will appear blurred at the edges, but the Court has certainly erred if it believes that, by erasing one line and drawing another, it has drawn a clearer boundary.

The Court's statement that *Chadwick* and *Sanders* provide only "minimal protection to privacy" is also unpersuasive. Every citizen clearly has an interest in the privacy of the contents of his or her luggage, briefcase, handbag or any other container that conceals private papers and effects from public scrutiny. That privacy interest has been recognized repeatedly in cases spanning more than a century.

Under the Court's holding today, the privacy interest that protects the contents of a suitcase or a briefcase from a warrantless search when it is in public view simply vanishes when its owner climbs into a taxicab. Unquestionably the rejection of the *Sanders* line of cases by today's decision will result in a significant loss of individual privacy.

To support its argument that today's holding works only a minimal intrusion on privacy, the Court suggests that "[i]f the police know that they may open a bag only if they are actually searching the entire car, they may search more extensively than they otherwise would in order to establish the general probable cause required by *Ross*." As I have already noted, this fear is unexplained and inexplicable. Neither evidence uncovered in the course of a search nor the scope of the search conducted can be used to provide *post hoc* justification for a search unsupported by probable cause at its inception.

The Court also justifies its claim that its holding inflicts only minor damage by suggesting that, under *New York v. Belton*, the police could have arrested respondent and searched his bag if respondent had placed the bag in the passenger compartment of the automobile instead of the trunk. In *Belton*, however, the justification for stopping the car and arresting the driver had nothing to do with the subsequent search, which was based on the potential danger to the arresting officer. The holding in *Belton* was supportable under a straightforward application of the automobile exception. I would not extend *Belton*'s holding to this case, in which the container—which was protected from a warrantless search before it was placed in the car—provided the only justification for the arrest. Even accepting *Belton*'s application to a case like this one, however, the Court's logic extends its holding to a container placed in the *trunk* of a vehicle, rather than in the passenger compartment. And the Court makes this extension without any justification whatsoever other than convenience to law enforcement.

The Court's suggestion that *Chadwick* and *Sanders* have created a significant burden on effective law enforcement is unsupported, inaccurate, and, in any event, an insufficient reason for creating a new exception to the warrant requirement.

Despite repeated claims that *Chadwick* and *Sanders* have "impeded effective law enforcement," the Court cites no authority for its contentions. * * *

Ever if the warrant requirement does inconvenience the police to some extent, that fact does not distinguish this constitutional requirements from any other procedural protection secured by the Bill of Rights. It is merely a part of the price that our society must pay in order to preserve its freedom. Thus, in a unanimous opinion that relied on both *Johnson* and *Chadwick*, Justice Stewart wrote:

> "Moreover, the mere fact that law enforcement may be made more efficient can never by itself justify disregard of the Fourth Amendment. The investigation of crime would always be simplified if warrants were unnecessary. But the Fourth Amendment reflects the view of those who wrote the Bill of Rights that the privacy of a person's home and property may not be totally sacrificed in

the name of maximum simplicity in enforcement of the criminal law." *Mincey v. Arizona,* [7th ed., p. 231].

It is too early to know how much freedom America has lost today. The magnitude of the loss is, however, not nearly as significant as the Court's willingness to inflict it without even a colorable basis for its rejection of prior law.

I respectfully dissent.

Notes and Questions

[Consider here notes 3 and 4, 7th ed., pp. 256–257.]

7th ed., p. 269; after Note 3, add:

4. In *Florida v. Wells,* 495 U.S. 1, 110 S.Ct. 1632, 109 L.Ed.2d 1 (1990), all members of the Court agreed that the inventory of a locked suitcase found in an impounded vehicle was unlawful under *Bertine* because "the Florida Highway Patrol had no policy whatever with respect to the opening of closed containers encountered during an inventory search." The Chief Justice, for five members of the Court, went on to say that the state court erred in saying *Bertine* requires a policy either mandating or barring inventory of all containers:

"But in forbidding uncanalized discretion to police officers conducting inventory searches, there is no reason to insist that they be conducted in a totally mechanical 'all or nothing' fashion. * * * A police officer may be allowed sufficient latitude to determine whether a particular container should or should not be opened in light of the nature of the search and characteristics of the container itself. Thus, while policies of opening all containers or of opening no containers are unquestionably permissible, it would be equally permissible, for example, to allow the opening of closed containers whose contents officers determine they are unable to ascertain from examing the containers' exteriors. The allowance of the exercise of judgment based on concerns related to the purposes

of an inventory search does not violate the Fourth Amendment."

Brennan and Marshall, JJ., concurring, declined to join the majority opinion because, in "pure dictum given the disposition of the case," it "goes on to suggest that a State may adopt an inventory policy that vests individual police officers with *some* discretion to decide whether to open such containers." Blackmun, J., concurring, agreed that the Fourth Amendment did not impose an "all or nothing" requirement, so that a state "probably could adopt a policy which requires the opening of all containers that are not locked, or a policy which requires the opening of all containers over or under a certain size, even though these policies do not call for the opening of all or no containers," but objected it was "an entirely different matter, however, to say, as this majority does, that an individual policeman may be afforded discretion in conducting an inventory search." Stevens, J., concurring separately, agreed with the Blackmun opinion.

5. Consider *Ex parte Boyd,* 542 So.2d 1276 (Ala.1989): "We are unaware of any case, federal or state, that presents the issue of whether a search can be valid as an inventory notwithstanding a four-day lapse of time between the impoundment and the inventory. We are of the opinion that the Fourth Amendment requires that, without a demonstrable justification based upon exigent circumstances other than the mere nature of automobiles, the inventory be conducted either contemporaneously with the impoundment or as soon thereafter as would be safe, practical, *and* satisfactory in light of the objectives for which this exception to the Fourth Amendment warrant requirement was created. In other words, to be valid, there must be a sufficient temporal proximity between the impoundment and the inventory. * * * The justifications for the intrusion—protecting the owner's property, protecting the police from false claims or disputes, and protecting the police from danger—are simply not served, however,

when the inventory is inexcusably post-poned; in that circumstance, the inventory becomes unreasonable."

SECTION 7. STOP AND FRISK

7th ed., pp. 277–280; in lieu of Notes 1–4, add:

1. FLORIDA v. BOSTICK, ___ U.S. ___, 111 S.Ct. 2382, 115 L.Ed.2d 389 (1991), involved these facts, as stated by the state supreme court: "Two officers, complete with badges, insignia and one of them holding a recognizable zipper pouch, containing a pistol, boarded a bus bound from Miami to Atlanta during a stopover in Fort Lauderdale. Eyeing the passen-gers, the officers admittedly without ar-ticulable suspicion, picked out the defen-dant passenger and asked to inspect his ticket and identification. The ticket, from Miami to Atlanta, matched the defendant's identification and both were immediately returned to him as unremarkable. How-ever, the two police officers persisted and explained their presence as narcotics agents on the lookout for illegal drugs. In pursuit of that aim, they then requested the defendant's consent to search his lug-gage. Needless to say, there is a conflict in the evidence about whether the defen-dant consented to the search of the second bag in which the contraband was found and as to whether he was informed of his right to refuse consent. However, any conflict must be resolved in favor of the state, it being a question of fact decided by the trial judge." That court ruled that "an impermissible seizure result[s] when police mount a drug search on buses during scheduled stops and question boarded pas-sengers without articulable reasons for do-ing so, thereby obtaining consent to search the passengers' luggage." The Supreme Court reversed; O'CONNOR, J., for the majority, stated:

"Our cases make it clear that a seizure does not occur simply because a police officer approaches an individual and asks a few questions. So long as a reasonable person would feel free 'to disregard the police and go about his business,' the en-counter is consensual and no reasonable suspicion is required. The encounter will not trigger Fourth Amendment scrutiny unless it loses its consensual nature.

* * *

"There is no doubt that if this same encounter had taken place before Bostick boarded the bus or in the lobby of the bus terminal, it would not rise to the level of a seizure. The Court has dealt with similar encounters in airports and has found them to be 'the sort of consensual encounter[s] that implicat[e] no Fourth Amendment in-terest.' We have stated that even when officers have no basis for suspecting a par-ticular individual, they may generally ask questions of that individual, ask to ex-amine the individual's identification, and request consent to search his or her lug-gage—as long as the police do not convey a message that compliance with their re-quests is required.

"Bostick insists that this case is different because it took place in the cramped con-fines of a bus. A police encounter is much more intimidating in this setting, he ar-gues, because police tower over a seated passenger and there is little room to move around. Bostick claims to find support in cases indicating that a seizure occurs when a reasonable person would believe that he or she is not 'free to leave.' Bostick main-tains that a reasonable bus passenger would not have felt free to leave under the circumstances of this case because there is nowhere to go on a bus. Also, the bus was about to depart. Had Bostick dis-embarked, he would have risked being stranded and losing whatever baggage he had locked away in the luggage compart-ment.

"The Florida Supreme Court found this argument persuasive, so much so that it adopted a *per se* rule prohibiting the police from randomly boarding buses as a means of drug interdiction. The state court erred, however, in focusing on whether Bostick was 'free to leave', rather than on the principle that those words were intended to capture. When police attempt to question a person who is walking down the street or through an airport lobby, it makes sense to inquire whether a reasonable person would feel free to continue walking. But when the person is seated on a bus and has no desire to leave, the degree to which a reasonable person would feel that he or she could leave is not an accurate measure of the coercive effect of the encounter.

"Here, for example, the mere fact that Bostick did not feel free to leave the bus does not mean that the police seized him. Bostick was a passenger on a bus that was scheduled to depart. He would not have felt free to leave the bus even if the police had not been present. Bostick's movements were 'confined' in a sense, but this was the natural result of his decision to take the bus; it says nothing about whether or not the police conduct at issue was coercive.

"In this respect, the Court's decision in *INS v. Delgado*, [466 U.S. 210, 104 S.Ct. 1758, 80 L.Ed.2d 247 (1984)] is dispositive. At issue there was the INS' practice of visiting factories at random and questioning employees to determine whether any were illegal aliens. Several INS agents would stand near the building's exits, while other agents walked through the factory questioning workers. The Court acknowledged that the workers may not have been free to leave their worksite, but explained that this was not the result of police activity: 'Ordinarily, when people are at work their freedom to move about has been meaningfully restricted, not by the actions of law enforcement officials, but by the workers' voluntary obligations to their employers.' We concluded that there was no seizure because, even though the workers were not free to leave the building without being questioned, the agents' conduct should have given employees 'no reason to believe that they would be detained if they gave truthful answers

to the questions put to them or if they simply refused to answer.'

"The present case is analytically indistinguishable from *Delgado*. Like the workers in that case, Bostick's freedom of movement was restricted by a factor independent of police conduct—*i.e.*, by his being a passenger on a bus. Accordingly, the 'free to leave' analysis on which Bostick relies is inapplicable. In such a situation, the appropriate inquiry is whether a reasonable person would feel free to decline the officers' requests or otherwise terminate the encounter. This formulation follows logically from prior cases and breaks no new ground. We have said before that the crucial test is whether, taking into account all of the circumstances surrounding the encounter, the police conduct would 'have communicated to a reasonable person that he was not at liberty to ignore the police presence and go about his business.' Where the encounter takes place is one factor, but it is not the only one. And, as the Solicitor General correctly observes, an individual may decline an officer's request without fearing prosecution. We have consistently held that a refusal to cooperate, without more, does not furnish the minimal level of objective justification needed for a detention or seizure.

"The facts of this case, as described by the Florida Supreme Court, leave some doubt whether a seizure occurred. Two officers walked up to Bostick on the bus, asked him a few questions, and asked if they could search his bags. As we have explained, no seizure occurs when police ask questions of an individual, ask to examine the individual's identification, and request consent to search his or her luggage—so long as the officers do not convey a message that compliance with their requests is required. Here, the facts recited by the Florida Supreme Court indicate that the officers did not point guns at Bostick or otherwise threaten him and that they specifically advised Bostick that he could refuse consent.

"Nevertheless, we refrain from deciding whether or not a seizure occurred in this case. The trial court made no express findings of fact, and the Florida Supreme Court rested its decision on a single fact—that the encounter took place on a bus—rather than on the totality of the circumstances. We remand so that the Florida courts may evaluate the seizure question under the correct legal standard. We do reject, however, Bostick's argument that he must have been seized because no reasonable person would freely consent to a search of luggage that he or she knows contains drugs. This argument cannot prevail because the 'reasonable person' test presupposes an *innocent* person. * * *

"The dissent also attempts to characterize our decision as applying a lesser degree of constitutional protection to those individuals who travel by bus, rather than by other forms of transportation. This, too, is an erroneous characterization. Our Fourth Amendment inquiry in this case—whether a reasonable person would have felt free to decline the officers' requests or otherwise terminate the encounter—applies equally to police encounters that take place on trains, planes, and city streets. It is the dissent that would single out this particular mode of travel for differential treatment by adopting a *per se* rule that random bus searches are unconstitutional."

MARSHALL, J., for the three dissenters, interpreted the state court holding as not a "*per se* rule" but rather as a decision based on all the facts, but then added that in any event the Supreme Court could determine the "question of law" of whether *all* the facts set forth in the state court opinion add up to a Fourth Amendment seizure. Accepting the majority's "free to decline" test, Marshall continued:

"Unlike the majority, I have no doubt that the answer to this question is no. Apart from trying to accommodate the officers, respondent had only two options. First, he could have remained seated while obstinately refusing to respond to the officers' questioning. But in light of the intimidating show of authority that the officers made upon boarding the bus, respondent reasonably could have believed that such behavior would only arouse the officers' suspicions and intensify their interrogation. Indeed, officers who carry out bus sweeps like the one at issue here frequently admit that this is the effect of a passenger's refusal to cooperate. The majority's observation that a mere refusal to answer questions, 'without more,' does not give rise to a reasonable basis for seizing a passenger, is utterly beside the point, because a passenger unadvised of his rights and otherwise unversed in constitutional law *has no reason to know* that the police cannot hold his refusal to cooperate against him.

"Second, respondent could have tried to escape the officers' presence by leaving the bus altogether. But because doing so would have required respondent to squeeze past the gun-wielding inquisitor who was blocking the aisle of the bus, this hardly seems like a course that respondent reasonably would have viewed as available to him. The majority lamely protests that nothing in the stipulated facts shows that the questioning officer 'point[ed] [his] gu[n] at [respondent] or otherwise *threatened* him' with the weapon. Our decisions recognize the obvious point, however, that the choice of the police to 'display' their weapons during an encounter exerts significant coercive pressure on the confronted citizen. We have never suggested that the police must go so far as to put a citizen in immediate apprehension of *being shot* before a court can take account of the intimidating effect of being questioned by an officer with weapon in hand.

"Even if respondent had perceived that the officers would *let* him leave the bus, moreover, he could not reasonably have been expected to resort to this means of evading their intrusive questioning. For so far as respondent knew, the bus' departure from the terminal was imminent. Unlike a person approached by the police on the street or at a bus or airport terminal after reaching his destination, a passenger approached by the police at an intermediate point in a long bus journey cannot simply leave the scene and repair to a safe haven to avoid unwanted probing by law-enforcement officials. The vulnerability that an intrastate or interstate traveler experiences when confronted by the police outside of his 'own familiar territory' surely aggravates the coercive quality of such an encounter.

"The case on which the majority primarily relies, *INS v. Delgado,* is distinguishable in every relevant respect. In *Delgado,* this Court held that workers approached by law-enforcement officials inside of a factory were not 'seized' for purposes of the Fourth Amendment. The Court was careful to point out, however, that the presence of the agents did not furnish the workers with a reasonable basis for believing that they were not free to leave the factory, as at least some of them did. Unlike passengers confronted by law-enforcement officials on a bus stopped temporarily at an intermediate point in its journey, workers approached by law-enforcement officials at their workplace need not abandon personal belongings and venture into unfamiliar environs in order to avoid unwanted questioning. Moreover, the workers who did not leave the building in *Delgado* remained free to move about the entire factory, a considerably less confining environment than a bus. Finally, contrary to the officer who confronted respondent, the law-enforcement officials in *Delgado* did not conduct their interviews with guns in hand.

"Rather than requiring the police to justify the coercive tactics employed here, the majority blames respondent for his own sensation of constraint. The majority concedes that respondent 'did not feel free to leave the bus' as a means of breaking off the interrogation by the Broward County officers. But this experience of confinement, the majority explains, 'was the natural result of *his* decision to take the

bus.' Thus, in the majority's view, because respondent's 'freedom of movement was restricted by a factor independent of police conduct—*i.e.,* by his being a passenger on a bus,' respondent was not seized for purposes of the Fourth Amendment.

"This reasoning borders on sophism and trivializes the values that underlie the Fourth Amendment. Obviously, a person's 'voluntary decision' to place himself in a room with only one exit does not authorize the police to force an encounter upon him by placing themselves in front of the exit. It is no more acceptable for the police to force an encounter on a person by exploiting his 'voluntary decision' to expose himself to perfectly legitimate personal or social constraints. By consciously deciding to single out persons who have undertaken interstate or intrastate travel, officers who conduct suspicionless, dragnet-style sweeps put passengers to the choice of cooperating or of exiting their buses and possibly being stranded in unfamiliar locations. It is exactly because this 'choice' is no 'choice' at all that police engage this technique."

2. In CALIFORNIA v. HODARI D., ___ U.S. ___, 111 S.Ct. 1547, 113 L.Ed. 2d 690 (1991), Hodari fled upon seeing an approaching police car, only to be pursued on foot by Officer Pertoso, after which Hodari tossed away what appeared to be a small rock but which when retrieved by the police proved to be crack cocaine. The state court suppressed the cocaine as the fruit of a seizure made without reasonable suspicion, but the Supreme Court, per SCALIA, J., reversed:

"To say [as the common law authorities do] that an arrest is effected by the slightest application of physical force, despite the arrestee's escape, is not to say that for Fourth Amendment purposes there is a *continuing* arrest during the period of fugitivity. If, for example, Pertoso had laid his hands upon Hodari to arrest him, but Hodari had broken away and had *then* cast away the cocaine, it would hardly be realistic to say that that disclosure had been made during the course of an arrest. Cf. *Thompson v. Whitman*, 18 Wall. 457, 471 (1874) ('A seizure is a single act, and not a continuous fact'). The present case, however, is even one step further removed. It does not involve the application of any physical force; Hodari was untouched by Officer Pertoso at the time he discarded the cocaine. His defense relies instead upon the proposition that a seizure occurs 'when the officer, by means of physical force *or show of authority*, has in some way restrained the liberty of a citizen.' *Terry v. Ohio*, [7th ed., p. 269]. Hodari contends (and we accept as true for purposes of this decision) that Pertoso's pursuit qualified as a 'show of authority' calling upon Hodari to halt. The narrow question before us is whether, with respect to a show of authority as with respect to application of physical force, a seizure occurs even though the subject does not yield. We hold that it does not.

"The language of the Fourth Amendment, of course, cannot sustain respondent's contention. The word 'seizure' readily bears the meaning of a laying on of hands or application of physical force to restrain movement, even when it is ultimately unsuccessful. ('She seized the purse-snatcher, but he broke out of her grasp.') It does not remotely apply, however, to the prospect of a policeman yelling 'Stop, in the name of the law!' at a fleeing form that continues to flee. That is no seizure. Nor can the result respondent wishes to achieve be produced—indirectly, as it were—by suggesting that Pertoso's uncomplied-with show of authority was a common-law arrest, and then appealing to the principle that all common-law arrests are seizures. An arrest requires *either* physical force (as described above) *or*, where that is absent, *submission* to the assertion of authority. * * *

"We do not think it desirable, even as a policy matter, to stretch the Fourth Amendment beyond its words and beyond the meaning of arrest, as respondent urges.

Street pursuits always place the public at some risk, and compliance with police orders to stop should therefore be encouraged. Only a few of those orders, we must presume, will be without adequate basis, and since the addressee has no ready means of identifying the deficient ones it almost invariably is the responsible course to comply. Unlawful orders will not be deterred, moreover, by sanctioning through the exclusionary rule those of them that are *not* obeyed. Since policemen do not command 'Stop!' expecting to be ignored, or give chase hoping to be outrun, it fully suffices to apply the deterrent to their genuine, successful seizures.

STEVENS, J., for the two dissenters, objected: "The deterrent purposes of the exclusionary rule focus on the conduct of law enforcement officers, and on discouraging improper behavior on their part, and not on the reaction of the citizen to the show of force. In the present case, if Officer Pertoso had succeeded in tackling respondent before he dropped the rock of cocaine, the rock unquestionably would have been excluded as the fruit of the officer's unlawful seizure. Instead, under the Court's logic-chopping analysis, the exclusionary rule has no application because an attempt to make an unconstitutional seizure is beyond the coverage of the Fourth Amendment, no matter how outrageous or unreasonable the officer's conduct may be.

"It is too early to know the consequences of the Court's holding. If carried to its logical conclusion, it will encourage unlawful displays of force that will frighten countless innocent citizens into surrendering whatever privacy rights they may still have. It is not too soon, however, to note the irony in the fact that the Court's own justification for its result is its analysis of the rules of the common law of arrest that antedated our decisions in *Katz* [7th ed., p. 148] and *Terry*. Yet, even in those days the common law provided the citizen with protection against an attempt to make an unlawful arrest. The central message of

Katz and *Terry* was that the protection the Fourth Amendment provides to the average citizen is not rigidly confined by ancient common-law precept. The message that today's literal-minded majority conveys is that the common law, rather than our understanding of the Fourth Amendment as it has developed over the last quarter of a century, defines, and limits, the scope of a seizure. The Court today defines a seizure as commencing, not with egregious police conduct, but rather, with submission by the citizen. Thus, it both delays the point at which 'the Fourth Amendment becomes relevant' to an encounter and limits the range of encounters that will come under the heading of 'seizure.' Today's qualification of the Fourth Amendment means that innocent citizens may remain 'secure in their persons . . . against unreasonable searches and seizures' only at the discretion of the police."

What result would the Court have reached if, before Hodari threw away the cocaine, Officer Pertoso had (a) fired his pistol at Hodari, barely missing him; (b) fired his pistol at Hodari, causing a wound which slowed down but did not stop him; (c) cornered Hodari in a dead-end alley; or (d) grabbed the collar of Hodari's jacket, only to have him slip out of the garment?

3. In *Bostick* and *Hodari D.* the defendants were black. Is that relevant? Consider Maclin, *"Black and Blue Encounters"—Some Preliminary Thoughts About Fourth Amendment Seizures: Should Race Matter?*, 26 Val.U.L.Rev. 243, 250 (1991): "I submit that the dynamics surrounding an encounter between a police officer and a black male are quite different from those that surround an encounter between an officer and the so-called average, reasonable person. My tentative proposal is that the Court should disregard the notion that there is an average, hypothetical, reasonable person out there by which to judge the constitutionality of police encounters. When assessing the coercive nature of an

encounter, the Court should consider the race of the person confronted by the police, and how that person's race might have influenced his attitude toward the encounter."

4. In *United States v. Wilson*, 953 F.2d 116 (4th Cir.1991), involving an airport encounter between a DEA agent and a drug courier suspect, Wilson granted the agent's request to speak with him and submitted to questioning, produced identification upon request, and allowed the agent and an associate to search his bag and his person. But when the agent asked to search the two coats Wilson was carrying, Wilson angrily refused and walked away. The agent stayed with him, repeatedly requesting that Wilson consent to search of the coats and repeatedly asking Wilson to explain why he would not allow the search. Wilson continued walking through the terminal and then outside on the sidewalk, objecting the entire time to the harassment, but he finally consented to the search, which uncovered a bag of cocaine. If Wilson claims his consent to the search was the fruit of an illegal seizure, what result under *Bostick* and *Hodari D.*?

7th ed., p. 283; in lieu of Note 3, but incorporating fns. h and i (all but first sentence), add:

3. ALABAMA v. WHITE, 496 U.S. 325, 110 S.Ct. 2412, 110 L.Ed.2d 301 (1990), involved these facts: "On April 22, 1987, at approximately 3 p.m., Corporal B.H. Davis of the Montgomery Police Department received a telephone call from an anonymous person, stating that Vanessa White would be leaving 235–C Lynwood Terrace Apartments at a particular time in a brown Plymouth station wagon with the right taillight lens broken, that she would be going to Dobey's Motel, and that she would be in possession of about an ounce of cocaine inside a brown attaché case. Corporal Davis and his partner, Corporal P.A. Reynolds, proceeded to the Lynwood Terrace Apartments. The officers saw a brown Plymouth station wagon with a broken right taillight in the parking lot in

facts

front of the 235 building. The officers observed respondent leave the 235 building, carrying nothing in her hands, and enter the station wagon. They followed the vehicle as it drove the most direct route to Dobey's Motel. When the vehicle reached the Mobile Highway, on which Dobey's Motel is located, Corporal Reynolds requested a patrol unit to stop the vehicle. The vehicle was stopped at approximately 4:18 p.m., just short of Dobey's Motel. Corporal Davis asked respondent to step to the rear of her car, where he informed her that she had been stopped because she was suspected of carrying cocaine in the vehicle. He asked if they could look for cocaine and respondent said they could look. The officers found a locked brown attaché case in the car and, upon request, respondent provided the combination to the lock." In upholding the stop, the Court, per WHITE, J., reasoned:

"The opinion in [*Illinois v.*] *Gates* [7th ed., p. 175] recognized that an anonymous tip alone seldom demonstrates the informant's basis of knowledge or veracity inasmuch as ordinary citizens generally do not provide extensive recitations of the basis of their everyday observations and given that the veracity of persons supplying anonymous tips is 'by hypothesis largely unknown, and unknowable.' This is not to say that an anonymous caller could never provide the reasonable suspicion necessary for a *Terry* stop.[h] But the tip in *Gates* was not an exception to the general rule, and the anonymous tip in this case is like the one in *Gates:* '[it] provides virtually nothing from which one might conclude that [the caller] is either honest or his information reliable; likewise, the [tip] gives absolutely no indication of the basis for the [caller's] predictions regarding [Vanessa White's] criminal activities.' * * *

"As there was in *Gates,* however, in this case there is more than the tip itself. The tip was not as detailed, and the corroboration was not as complete, as in *Gates,* but

the required degree of suspicion was likewise not as high. * * *

"Reasonable suspicion is a less demanding standard than probable cause not only in the sense that reasonable suspicion can be established with information that is different in quantity or content than that required to establish probable cause, but also in the sense that reasonable suspicion can arise from information that is less reliable than that required to show probable cause.[i] * * * Reasonable suspicion, like probable cause, is dependent upon both the content of information possessed by police and its degree of reliability. Both factors—quantity and quality—are considered in the 'totality of the circumstances—the whole picture' that must be taken into account when evaluating whether there is reasonable suspicion. Thus, if a tip has a relatively low degree of reliability, more information will be required to establish the requisite quantum of suspicion than would be required if the tip were more reliable. The *Gates* Court applied its totality of the circumstances approach in this manner, taking into account the facts known to the officers from personal observation, and giving the anonymous tip the weight it deserved in light of its indicia of reliability as established through independent police work. The same approach applies in the reasonable suspicion context, the only difference being the level of suspicion that must be established. Contrary to the court below, we conclude that when the officers stopped respondent, the anonymous tip had been sufficiently corroborated to furnish reasonable suspicion that respondent was engaged in criminal activity and that the investigative stop therefore did not violate the Fourth Amendment.

"It is true that not every detail mentioned by the tipster was verified, such as the name of the woman leaving the building or the precise apartment from which she left; but the officers did corroborate that a woman left the 235 building and got into the particular vehicle that was described by the caller. With respect to the time of departure predicted by the informant, Corporal Davis testified that the caller gave a particular time when the woman would be leaving, but he did not state what that time was. He did testify that, after the call, he and his partner proceeded to the Lynwood Terrace Apartments to put the 235 building under surveillance. Given the fact that the officers proceeded to the indicated address immediately after the call and that respondent emerged not too long thereafter, it appears from the record before us that respondent's departure from the building was within the time frame predicted by the caller. As for the caller's prediction of respondent's destination, it is true that the officers stopped her just short of Dobey's Motel and did not know whether she would have pulled in or continued on past it. But given that the four-mile route driven by respondent was the most direct route possible to Dobey's Motel, but nevertheless involved several turns, we think respondent's destination was significantly corroborated.

"The Court's opinion in *Gates* gave credit to the proposition that because an informant is shown to be right about some things, he is probably right about other facts that he has alleged, including the claim that the object of the tip is engaged in criminal activity. Thus, it is not unreasonable to conclude in this case that the independent corroboration by the police of significant aspects of the informer's predictions imparted some degree of reliability to the other allegations made by the caller.

"We think it also important that, as in *Gates,* 'the anonymous [tip] contained a range of details relating not just to easily obtained facts and conditions existing at the time of the tip, but to future actions of third parties ordinarily not easily predicted.' The fact that the officers found a car precisely matching the caller's description in front of the 235 building is an example of the former. Anyone could have 'predicted' that fact because it was a condition presumably existing at the time of the call. What was important was the caller's ability to predict respondent's *future behavior,* because it demonstrated inside information—a special familiarity with respondent's affairs. The general public would have had no way of knowing that respondent would shortly leave the building, get in the described car, and drive the most direct route to Dobey's Motel. Because only a small number of people are generally privy to an individual's itinerary, it is reasonable for police to believe that a person with access to such information is likely to also have access to reliable information about that individual's illegal activities. When significant aspects of the caller's predictions were verified, there was reason to believe not only that the caller was honest but also that he was well informed, at least well enough to justify the stop."

STEVENS, J., for the three dissenters, objected: "Anybody with enough knowledge about a given person to make her the target of a prank, or to harbor a grudge against her, will certainly be able to formulate a tip about her like the one predicting Vanessa White's excursion. In addition, under the Court's holding, every citizen is subject to being seized and questioned by any officer who is prepared to testify that the warrantless stop was based on an anonymous tip predicting whatever conduct the officer just observed. Fortunately, the vast majority of those in our law enforcement community would not adopt such a practice. But the Fourth Amendment was intended to protect the citizen from the overzealous and unscrupulous officer as well as from those who are conscientious and truthful. This decision makes a mockery of that protection."

7th ed., p. 292; end of Note 5, add:

Cf. *Arizona v. Hicks,* 7th ed., p. 225; and *Ybarra v. Illinois,* 7th ed., p. 203.

SECTION 9. ADMINISTRATIVE INSPECTIONS AND REGULATORY SEARCHES: MORE ON BALANCING THE NEED AGAINST THE INVASION OF PRIVACY

7th ed., p. 312; In lieu of Notes 6–7, add:

6. *Interior checkpoints.*

MICHIGAN DEP'T OF STATE POLICE v. SITZ

496 U.S. 444, 110 S.Ct. 2481, 110 L.Ed.2d 412 (1990).

CHIEF JUSTICE REHNQUIST delivered the opinion of the Court. * * *

Under the guidelines, [for a sobriety checkpoint pilot program established by the Department], checkpoints would be set up at selected sites along state roads. All vehicles passing through a checkpoint would be stopped and their drivers briefly examined for signs of intoxication. In cases where a checkpoint officer detected signs of intoxication, the motorist would be directed to a location out of the traffic flow where an officer would check the motorist's driver's license and car registration and, if warranted, conduct further sobriety tests. Should the field tests and the officer's observations suggest that the driver was intoxicated, an arrest would be made. All other drivers would be permitted to resume their journey immediately.

The first—and to date the only—sobriety checkpoint operated under the program was conducted in Saginaw County with the assistance of the Saginaw County Sheriff's Department. During the hour-and-fifteen-minute duration of the checkpoint's operation, 126 vehicles passed through the checkpoint. The average delay for each vehicle was approximately 25 seconds. Two drivers were detained for field sobriety testing, and one of the two was arrested for driving under the influence of alcohol. A third driver who drove through without stopping was pulled over by an officer in an observation vehicle and arrested for driving under the influence.

On the day before the operation of the Saginaw County checkpoint, respondents filed a complaint in the Circuit Court of Wayne County seeking declaratory and injunctive relief from potential subjection to the checkpoints. Each of the respondents "is a licensed driver in the State of Michigan . . . who regularly travels throughout the State in his automobile." During pretrial proceedings, petitioners agreed to delay further implementation of the checkpoint program pending the outcome of this litigation.

After the trial, [the] court ruled that the Michigan program violated the Fourth Amendment * * *. On appeal, the Michigan Court of Appeals affirmed * * *.

To decide this case the trial court performed a balancing test derived from our opinion in *Brown v. Texas* [7th ed., p. 285]. * * *

As characterized by the Court of Appeals, the trial court's findings with respect to the balancing factors were that the State has "a grave and legitimate" interest in curbing drunken driving; that sobriety checkpoint programs are generally "ineffective" and, therefore, do not significantly further that interest; and that the checkpoints' "subjective intrusion" on individual liberties is substantial. * * *

In this Court respondents seek to defend the judgment in their favor by insisting that the balancing test derived from *Brown v. Texas* was not the proper method of analysis. Respondents maintain that the analysis must proceed from a basis of probable cause or reasonable suspicion and rely for support on language from our decision last Term in *Treasury Employees v. Von Raab,* [7th ed., p. 319]. We said in *Von Raab:*

"Where a Fourth Amendment intrusion serves special governmental needs, beyond the normal need for law enforcement, it is necessary to balance the individual's privacy expectations against the Government's interests to determine whether it is impractical to require a warrant or some level of individualized suspicion in the particular context."

Respondents argue that there must be a showing of some special governmental need "beyond the normal need" for criminal law enforcement before a balancing analysis is appropriate, and that petitioners have demonstrated no such special need.

But it is perfectly plain from a reading of *Von Raab*, which cited and discussed with approval our earlier decision in *United States v. Martinez–Fuerte*, 428 U.S. 543, 96 S.Ct. 3074, 49 L.Ed.2d 1116 (1976), that it was in no way designed to repudiate our prior cases dealing with police stops of motorists on public highways. *Martinez–Fuerte*, which utilized a balancing analysis in approving highway checkpoints for detecting illegal aliens, and *Brown v. Texas*, are the relevant authorities here.

Petitioners concede, correctly in our view, that a Fourth Amendment "seizure" occurs when a vehicle is stopped at a checkpoint. * * * The question thus becomes whether such seizures are "reasonable" under the Fourth Amendment.

It is important to recognize what our inquiry is *not* about. No allegations are before us of unreasonable treatment of any person after an actual detention at a particular checkpoint. See *Martinez–Fuerte* ("claim that a particular exercise of discretion in locating or operating a checkpoint is unreasonable is subject to post-stop judicial review"). As pursued in the lower courts, the instant action challenges only the use of sobriety checkpoints generally. We address only the initial stop of each motorist passing through a checkpoint and the associated preliminary questioning and observation by checkpoint officers. Detention of particular motorists for more extensive field sobriety testing may require satisfaction of an individualized suspicion standard.

No one can seriously dispute the magnitude of the drunken driving problem or the States' interest in eradicating it. Media reports of alcohol-related death and mutilation on the Nation's roads are legion. The anecdotal is confirmed by the statistical. "Drunk drivers cause an annual death toll of over 25,000 and in the same time span cause nearly one million personal injuries and more than five billion dollars in property damage." * * *

Conversely, the weight bearing on the other scale—the measure of the intrusion on motorists stopped briefly at sobriety checkpoints—is slight. We reached a similar conclusion as to the intrusion on motorists subjected to a brief stop at a highway checkpoint for detecting illegal aliens. See *Martinez–Fuerte*. We see virtually no difference between the levels of intrusion on law-abiding motorists from the brief stops necessary to the effectuation of these two types of checkpoints, which to the average motorist would seem identical save for the nature of the questions the checkpoint officers might ask. The trial court and the Court of Appeals, thus, accurately gauged the "objective" intrusion, measured by the duration of the seizure and the intensity of the investigation, as minimal.

With respect to what it perceived to be the "subjective" intrusion on motorists, however, the Court of Appeals found such intrusion substantial. The court first affirmed the trial court's finding that the guidelines governing checkpoint operation minimize the discretion of the officers on the scene. But the court also agreed with the trial court's conclusion that the checkpoints have the potential to generate fear and surprise in motorists. This was so because the record failed to demonstrate that approaching motorists would be aware of their option to make U-turns or turnoffs to avoid the checkpoints. On that basis, the court deemed the subjective intrusion from the checkpoints unreasonable.

We believe the Michigan courts misread our cases concerning the degree of "subjective intrusion" and the potential for generating fear and surprise. The "fear and surprise" to be considered are not the natural fear of one who has been drinking over the prospect of being stopped at a sobriety checkpoint but, rather, the fear and surprise engendered in law abiding motorists by the nature of the stop. This was made clear in *Martinez–Fuerte*. Comparing checkpoint stops to roving patrol stops considered in prior cases, we said,

> "we view checkpoint stops in a different light because the subjective intrusion—the generating of concern or even fright on the part of lawful travelers—is appreciably less in the case of a checkpoint stop. In [*United States v.*] *Ortiz*, [422 U.S. 891, 95 S.Ct. 2585, 45 L.Ed.2d 623 (1975),] we noted:

> " '[T]he circumstances surrounding a checkpoint stop and search are far less intrusive than those attending a roving-patrol stop. Roving patrols often operate at night on seldom-traveled roads, and their approach may frighten motorists. At traffic checkpoints the motorist can see that other vehicles are being stopped, he can see visible signs of the officers' authority, and he is much less likely to be frightened or annoyed by the intrusion.' " [a]

Here, checkpoints are selected pursuant to the guidelines, and uniformed police officers stop every approaching vehicle. The intrusion resulting from the brief stop at the sobriety checkpoint is for constitutional purposes indistinguishable from the checkpoint stops we upheld in *Martinez–Fuerte.*

The Court of Appeals went on to consider as part of the balancing analysis the "effectiveness" of the proposed checkpoint program. Based on extensive testimony in the trial record, the court concluded that the checkpoint program failed the "effectiveness" part of the test, and that this failure materially discounted petitioners' strong interest in implementing the pro-

gram. We think the Court of Appeals was wrong on this point as well.

The actual language from *Brown v. Texas,* upon which the Michigan courts based their evaluation of "effectiveness," describes the balancing factor as "the degree to which the seizure advances the public interest." This passage from *Brown* was not meant to transfer from politically accountable officials to the courts the decision as to which among reasonable alternative law enforcement techniques should be employed to deal with a serious public danger. Experts in police science might disagree over which of several methods of apprehending drunken drivers is preferrable as an ideal. But for purposes of Fourth Amendment analysis, the choice among such reasonable alternatives remains with the governmental officials who have a unique understanding of, and a responsibility for, limited public resources, including a finite number of police officers. *Brown*'s rather general reference to "the degree to which the seizure advances the public interest" was derived, as the opinion makes clear, from the line of cases culminating in *Martinez–Fuerte*. Neither *Martinez–Fuerte* nor *Delaware v. Prouse,* 440 U.S. 648, 99 S.Ct. 1391, 59 L.Ed.2d 660 (1979), however, the two cases cited by the Court of Appeals as providing the basis for its "effectiveness" review, supports the searching examination of "effectiveness" undertaken by the Michigan court.

In *Delaware v. Prouse,* we disapproved random stops made by Delaware Highway Patrol officers in an effort to apprehend unlicensed drivers and unsafe vehicles. We observed that *no* empirical evidence indicated that such stops would be an effective means of promoting roadway safety and said that "[i]t seems common sense that the percentage of all drivers on the road who are driving without a license is very small and that the number of licensed drivers who will be stopped in order to

a. However, the Court held in *Ortiz* that vehicle *searches* at a permanent checkpoint could be undertaken only upon probable cause.

find one unlicensed operator will be large indeed." We observed that the random stops involved the "kind of standardless and unconstrained discretion [which] is the evil the Court has discerned when in previous cases it has insisted that the discretion of the official in the field be circumscribed, at least to some extent." We went on to state that our holding did not "cast doubt on the permissibility of roadside truck weigh-stations and inspection checkpoints, at which some vehicles may be subject to further detention for safety and regulatory inspection than are others." [b]

Unlike *Prouse,* this case involves neither a complete absence of empirical data nor a challenge to random highway stops. During the operation of the Saginaw County checkpoint, the detention of each of the 126 vehicles that entered the checkpoint resulted in the arrest of two drunken drivers. Stated as a percentage, approximately 1.5 percent of the drivers passing through the checkpoint were arrested for alcohol impairment. In addition, an expert witness testified at the trial that experience in other States demonstrated that, on the whole, sobriety checkpoints resulted in drunken driving arrests of around 1 percent of all motorists stopped. By way of comparison, the record from one of the consolidated cases in *Martinez–Fuerte,* showed that in the associated checkpoint, illegal aliens were found in only 0.12 percent of the vehicles passing through the checkpoint. The ratio of illegal aliens detected to vehicles stopped (considering that on occasion two or more illegal aliens were found in a single vehicle) was approximately 0.5 percent. We concluded that this "record . . . provides a rather complete picture of the effectiveness of the San Clemente checkpoint", and we sustained its constitutionality. We see no

justification for a different conclusion here.

In sum, the balance of the State's interest in preventing drunken driving, the extent to which this system can reasonably be said to advance that interest, and the degree of intrusion upon individual motorists who are briefly stopped, weighs in favor of the state program. We therefore hold that it is consistent with the Fourth Amendment. The judgment of the Michigan Court of Appeals is accordingly reversed, and the cause is remanded for further proceedings not inconsistent with this opinion.[c]

JUSTICE STEVENS, with whom JUSTICE BRENNAN and JUSTICE MARSHALL join as to Parts I and II, dissenting. * * *

I

There is a critical difference between a seizure that is preceded by fair notice and one that is effected by surprise. That is one reason why a border search, or indeed any search at a permanent and fixed checkpoint, is much less intrusive than a random stop. A motorist with advance notice of the location of a permanent checkpoint has an opportunity to avoid the search entirely, or at least to prepare for, and limit, the intrusion on her privacy.

No such opportunity is available in the case of a random stop or a temporary checkpoint, which both depend for their effectiveness on the element of surprise. A driver who discovers an unexpected checkpoint on a familiar local road will be startled and distressed. She may infer, correctly, that the checkpoint is not simply "business as usual," and may likewise infer, again correctly, that the police have made a discretionary decision to focus their law enforcement efforts upon her and others who pass the chosen point.

b. The Court in *Prouse* also said it was not prohibiting driver's license checks by methods "that involve less intrusion or that do not involve the unconstrained exercise of discretion," and listed as "one possible alternative" the "question-

ing of all oncoming traffic at roadblock-type stops."

c. The concurring opinion of Blackmun, J., and the dissenting opinion of Brennan, J., joined by Marshall, J., are omitted.

This element of surprise is the most obvious distinction between the sobriety checkpoints permitted by today's majority and the interior border checkpoints approved by this Court in *Martinez–Fuerte.* The distinction casts immediate doubt upon the majority's argument, for *Martinez–Fuerte* is the only case in which we have upheld suspicionless seizures of motorists. But the difference between notice and surprise is only one of the important reasons for distinguishing between permanent and mobile checkpoints. With respect to the former, there is no room for discretion in either the timing or the location of the stop—it is a permanent part of the landscape. In the latter case, however, although the checkpoint is most frequently employed during the hours of darkness on weekends (because that is when drivers with alcohol in their blood are most apt to be found on the road), the police have extremely broad discretion in determining the exact timing and placement of the roadblock.

There is also a significant difference between the kind of discretion that the officer exercises after the stop is made. A check for a driver's license, or for identification papers at an immigration checkpoint, is far more easily standardized than is a search for evidence of intoxication. A Michigan officer who questions a motorist at a sobriety checkpoint has virtually unlimited discretion to detain the driver on the basis of the slightest suspicion. A ruddy complexion, an unbuttoned shirt, bloodshot eyes or a speech impediment may suffice to prolong the detention. Any driver who had just consumed a glass of beer, or even a sip of wine, would almost certainly have the burden of demonstrating to the officer that her driving ability was not impaired.

Finally, it is significant that many of the stops at permanent checkpoints occur during daylight hours, whereas the sobriety checkpoints are almost invariably operated at night. A seizure followed by interrogation and even a cursory search at night is surely more offensive than a daytime stop that is almost as routine as going through a toll gate. Thus we thought it important to point out that the random stops at issue in *Ortiz* frequently occurred at night.

These fears are not, as the Court would have it, solely the lot of the guilty. To be law abiding is not necessarily to be spotless, and even the most virtuous can be unlucky. Unwanted attention from the local police need not be less discomforting simply because one's secrets are not the stuff of criminal prosecutions. Moreover, those who have found—by reason of prejudice or misfortune—that encounters with the police may become adversarial or unpleasant without good cause will have grounds for worrying at any stop designed to elicit signs of suspicious behavior. Being stopped by the police is distressing even when it should not be terrifying, and what begins mildly may by happenstance turn severe.

For all these reasons, I do not believe that this case is analogous to *Martinez–Fuerte.* In my opinion, the sobriety checkpoints are instead similar to—and in some respects more intrusive than—the random investigative stops that the Court held unconstitutional in [*United States v.*] *Brignone–Ponce*[, 422 U.S. 873, 95 S.Ct. 2574, 45 L.Ed.2d 607 (1975),] [d] and *Prouse.* In the latter case the Court explained:

"We cannot agree that stopping or detaining a vehicle on an ordinary city street is less intrusive than a roving-patrol stop on a major highway and that it bears greater resemblance to a permissible stop and secondary detention at a checkpoint near the border. In this regard, we note that *Brignoni–Ponce* was not limited to roving-patrol stops on limited-access roads, but applied to any roving-patrol stop by Border Patrol

d. Holding that a roving patrol could stop motorists near the border for brief inquiry into

their residential status only upon individualized reasonable suspicion.

agents on any type of roadway on less than reasonable suspicion. We cannot assume that the physical and psychological intrusion visited upon the occupants of a vehicle by a random stop to check documents is of any less moment than that occasioned by a stop by border agents on roving patrol. Both of these stops generally entail law enforcement officers signaling a moving automobile to pull over to the side of the roadway, by means of a possibly unsettling show of authority. Both interfere with freedom of movement, are inconvenient, and consume time. Both may create substantial anxiety."

We accordingly held that the State must produce evidence comparing the challenged seizure to other means of law enforcement, so as to show that the seizure

"is a sufficiently productive mechanism to justify the intrusion upon Fourth Amendment interests which such stops entail. On the record before us, that question must be answered in the negative. Given the alternative mechanisms available, both those in use and those that might be adopted, we are unconvinced that the incremental contribution to highway safety of the random spot check justifies the practice under the Fourth Amendment."

II

* * *

The Court's analysis of [the degree to which the sobriety checkpoint seizures advance the public interest] resembles a business decision that measures profits by counting gross receipts and ignoring expenses. The evidence in this case indicates that sobriety checkpoints result in the arrest of a fraction of one percent of the drivers who are stopped, but there is abso-

lutely no evidence that this figure represents an increase over the number of arrests that would have been made by using the same law enforcement resources in conventional patrols. Thus, although the *gross* number of arrests is more than zero, there is a complete failure of proof on the question whether the wholesale seizures have produced any *net* advance in the public interest in arresting intoxicated drivers.

Indeed, the position adopted today by the Court is not one endorsed by any of the law enforcement authorities to whom the Court purports to defer. The Michigan police do not rely, as the Court does, on the *arrest rate* at sobriety checkpoints to justify the stops made there. Colonel Hough, the commander of the Michigan State Police and a leading proponent of the checkpoints, admitted at trial that the arrest rate at the checkpoints was "very low." Instead, Colonel Hough and the State have maintained that the mere *threat* of such arrests is sufficient to deter drunk driving and so to reduce the accident rate. * * * There is, obviously, nothing wrong with a law enforcement technique that reduces crime by pure deterrence without punishing anybody; on the contrary, such an approach is highly commendable. One cannot, however, prove its efficacy by counting the arrests that were made. One must instead measure the number of crimes that were avoided. Perhaps because the record is wanting, the Court simply ignores this point.

The Court's sparse analysis of this issue differs markedly from Justice Powell's opinion for the Court in *Martinez–Fuerte.* He did not merely count the 17,000 arrests made at the San Clemente checkpoint in 1973; he also carefully explained why those arrests represented a net benefit to the law enforcement interest at stake.[15]

---

15. "Our previous cases have recognized that maintenance of a traffic-checking program in the interior is necessary because the flow of illegal aliens cannot be controlled effectively at the border. We note here only the substantiality of the public interest in the practice of routine stops for

inquiry at permanent checkpoints, a practice which the Government identifies as the most important of the traffic-checking operations. These checkpoints are located on important highways; in their absence such highways would offer illegal aliens a quick and safe route into the

Common sense, moreover, suggests that immigration checkpoints are more necessary than sobriety checkpoints: there is no reason why smuggling illegal aliens should impair a motorist's driving ability, but if intoxication did not noticeably affect driving ability it would not be unlawful. Drunk driving, unlike smuggling, may thus be detected absent any checkpoints. A program that produces thousands of otherwise impossible arrests is not a relevant precedent for a program that produces only a handful of arrests which would be more easily obtained without resort to suspicionless seizures of hundreds of innocent citizens.

III

[M]y objections to random seizures or temporary checkpoints do not apply to a host of other investigatory procedures that do not depend upon surprise and are unquestionably permissible. These procedures have been used to address other threats to human life no less pressing than the threat posed by drunken drivers. It is, for example, common practice to require every prospective airline passenger, or every visitor to a public building, to pass through a metal detector that will reveal the presence of a firearm or an explosive. Permanent, nondiscretionary checkpoints could be used to control serious dangers at other publicly operated facilities. Because concealed weapons obviously represent one such substantial threat to public safety, I would suppose that all subway passengers could be required to pass through metal detectors, so long as the detectors were permanent and every passenger was subjected to the same search. Likewise, I would suppose that a State could condition

interior. Routine checkpoint inquiries apprehend many smugglers and illegal aliens who succumb to the lure of such highways. And the prospect of such inquiries forces others onto less efficient roads that are less heavily traveled, slowing their movement and making them more vulnerable to detection by roving patrols.

"A requirement that stops on major routes inland always be based on reasonable suspicion

access to its toll roads upon not only paying the toll but also taking a uniformly administered breathalyzer test. That requirement might well keep all drunken drivers off the highways that serve the fastest and most dangerous traffic. This procedure would not be subject to the constitutional objections that control this case: the checkpoints would be permanently fixed, the stopping procedure would apply to all users of the toll road in precisely the same way, and police officers would not be free to make arbitrary choices about which neighborhoods should be targeted or about which individuals should be more thoroughly searched.

* * *

7th ed., p. 316; end of Note 8, add:

But see *United States v. $124,570 U.S. Currency*, 873 F.2d 1240 (9th Cir.1989) (*Davis* rationale unavailable where airport detection system significantly "distorted" by customs officials offering inspectors rewards for discovery of large amounts of cash).

Compare *People v. Heimel*, 812 P.2d 1177 (Colo.1991) (right to refuse inspection and to withdraw exists only "prior to the actual commencement of the screening process," as "airport security personnel have a duty to discover firearms and explosive devices that pose a risk to air travelers, including airport occupants who have not yet entered the sterile area of the airport," which "cannot be fulfilled if a potential passenger, after electing to undergo security screening and participating in the initial stage of the screening process, is permitted to prohibit a physical search of a carry-on item by removing himself from the checkpoint station and sterile area").

would be impractical because the flow of traffic tends to be too heavy to allow the particularized study of a given car that would enable it to be identified as a possible carrier of illegal aliens. In particular, such a requirement would largely eliminate any deterrent to the conduct of well-disguised smuggling operations, even though smugglers are known to use these highways regularly."

7th ed., p. 319; end of Note 10, add:

Relying upon the "special needs" analysis in *Griffin,* the court in *State v. Guzman,* 480 N.W.2d 446 (Wis.1992), held "that when a convicted defendant is awaiting sentencing for a drug related offense and probation is a sentencing alternative, a judge may in his or her discretion order such defendant to submit to urinalysis or other appropriate tests to determine the presence of illegal drugs in his or her system." The majority concluded that in such circumstances *neither* probable cause *nor* any individualized suspicion is needed, and that consequently no warrant is necessary. The dissenters objected (i) that sentencing, "part of the 'normal' operation of the criminal justice system," is not attended by needs any more special than at the earlier guilt-determination stage; and (ii) that under the majority's balancing approach nothing would "prevent future courts from ordering all manner of searches of a defendant's person, home, car or effects if any information relevant to sentencing is arguably ascertainable."

SECTION 10. CONSENT SEARCHES

7th ed., 329; end of Note 6, add:

In *Florida v. Bostick,* Supp. p. 19, in response to the defendant's contention that "no reasonable person would freely consent to a search of language that he or she knows contains drugs," the Court responded that such an "argument cannot prevail because the 'reasonable person' test presupposes an *innocent* person."

7th ed., p. 331; in lieu of first paragraph in Note 11, add:

The standard for measuring the scope of a suspect's consent, the Court concluded in *Florida v. Jimeno,* ___ U.S. ___, 111 S.Ct. 1801, 114 L.Ed.2d 297 (1991), is neither the suspect's intent nor the officer's perception thereof but rather "that of 'objective' reasonableness—what would the typical reasonable person have understood by the exchange between the officer and the suspect?" Given the officer's statement in *Jimeno* that he would be looking for narcotics, "it was objectively reasonable for the police to conclude that the general consent to search respondent's car included consent to search containers within that car which might bear drugs." But, the nature of the container is also relevant. "It is very unreasonable to think that a suspect, by consenting to the search of his trunk, has agreed to the breaking open of a locked briefcase within the trunk, but it is otherwise with respect to a closed paper bag."

Does the *Jimeno* principle, that "the scope of the search is generally defined by its expressed object," suffice as to consent searches of the person? Consider *United States v. Rodney,* 956 F.2d 295 (D.C.Cir. 1992) (sweeping motion over crotch area during consent search for drugs lawful, as it no more intrusive than a *Terry* frisk; court distinguishes *United States v. Blake,* 888 F.2d 795 (11th Cir.1989), suppressing drugs found on person, as that case involved "a direct ' "frontal touching" ' of the defendant's private parts").

In *United States v. Mines,* 883 F.2d 801 (9th Cir.1989), the defendant consented to search of his luggage upon being told the agents were conducting a narcotics investigation. Inside defendant's bag the police found a machine gun, which they turned over to reveal it was without serial numbers, a fact which led to a determination the gun was illegally possessed because not registered. In response to defendant's reliance on *Arizona v. Hicks,* 7th ed., p. 225, the court asserted the instant case was distinguishable because (i) consent searches, unlike the warrantless search on exigent circumstances in *Hicks,* need not be "strictly circumscribed by the exigencies," and (ii) the search here "occurred not in a private apartment but in a public place—an airport—where expectations of privacy are sharply reduced." Are these reasons convincing? Is the result correct?

7th ed., p. 331; in lieu of *Matlock* case and Note 6 following, add:

ILLINOIS v. RODRIGUEZ

497 U.S. 177, 110 S.Ct. 2793, 111 L.Ed.2d 148 (1990).

JUSTICE SCALIA delivered the opinion of the Court. * * *

On July 26, 1985, police were summoned to the residence of Dorothy Jackson on South Wolcott in Chicago. They were met by Ms. Jackson's daughter, Gail Fischer, who showed signs of a severe beating. She told the officers that she had been assaulted by respondent Edward Rodriguez earlier that day in an apartment on South California. Fischer stated that Rodriguez was then asleep in the apartment, and she consented to travel there with the police in order to unlock the door with her key so that the officers could enter and arrest him. During this conversation, Fischer several times referred to the apartment on South California as "our" apartment, and said that she had clothes and furniture there. It is unclear whether she indicated that she currently lived at the apartment, or only that she used to live there.

The police officers drove to the apartment on South California, accompanied by Fischer. They did not obtain an arrest warrant for Rodriguez, nor did they seek a search warrant for the apartment. At the apartment, Fischer unlocked the door with her key and gave the officers permission to enter. They moved through the door into the living room, where they observed in plain view drug paraphernalia and containers filled with white powder that they believed (correctly, as later analysis showed) to be cocaine. They proceeded to the bedroom, where they found Rodriguez asleep and discovered additional containers of white powder in two open attaché cases. The officers arrested Rodriguez and seized the drugs and related paraphernalia.

Rodriguez was charged with possession of a controlled substance with intent to deliver. He moved to suppress all evidence seized at the time of his arrest, claiming that Fischer had vacated the apartment several weeks earlier and had no authority to consent to the entry. The Cook County Circuit Court granted the motion, holding that at the time she consented to the entry Fischer did not have common authority over the apartment. The Court concluded that Fischer was not a "usual resident" but rather an "infrequent visitor" at the apartment on South California, based upon its findings that Fischer's name was not on the lease, that she did not contribute to the rent, that she was not allowed to invite others to the apartment on her own, that she did not have access to the apartment when respondent was away, and that she had moved some of her possessions from the apartment. The Circuit Court also rejected the State's contention that, even if Fischer did not possess common authority over the premises, there was no Fourth Amendment violation if the police *reasonably believed* at the time of their entry that Fischer possessed the authority to consent. * * *

The Fourth Amendment generally prohibits the warrantless entry of a person's home, whether to make an arrest or to search for specific objects. The prohibition does not apply, however, to situations in which voluntary consent has been obtained, either from the individual whose property is searched, or from a third party who possesses common authority over the premises, see *United States v. Matlock,* [415 U.S. 164, 94 S.Ct. 988, 39 L.Ed.2d 242 (1974)]. The State of Illinois contends that that exception applies in the present case.

As we stated in *Matlock*, "[c]ommon authority" rests "on mutual use of the property by persons generally having joint

access or control for most purposes." [a]
The burden of establishing that common
authority rests upon the State. On the
basis of this record, it is clear that burden
was not sustained. The evidence showed
that although Fischer, with her two small
children, had lived with Rodriguez beginning in December 1984, she had moved
out on July 1, 1985, almost a month before the search at issue here, and had gone
to live with her mother. She took her and
her children's clothing with her, though
leaving behind some furniture and household effects. During the period after July
1 she sometimes spent the night at Rodriguez's apartment, but never invited her
friends there, and never went there herself
when he was not home. Her name was
not on the lease nor did she contribute to
the rent. She had a key to the apartment,
which she said at trial she had taken without Rodriguez's knowledge (though she
testified at the preliminary hearing that
Rodriguez had given her the key). On
these facts the State has not established
that, with respect to the South California
apartment, Fischer had "joint access or
control for most purposes." To the contrary, the Appellate Court's determination
of no common authority over the apartment was obviously correct.

[R]espondent asserts that permitting a
reasonable belief of common authority to
validate an entry would cause a defendant's Fourth Amendment rights to be "vi-
cariously waived." We disagree.

We have been unyielding in our insistence that a defendant's waiver of his trial
rights cannot be given effect unless it is
"knowing" and "intelligent." We would
assuredly not permit, therefore, evidence

seized in violation of the Fourth Amendment to be introduced on the basis of a
trial court's mere "reasonable belief"—
derived from statements by unauthorized
persons—that the defendant has waived his
objection. But one must make a distinction between, on the one hand, trial rights
that *derive* from the violation of constitutional guarantees and, on the other hand,
the nature of those constitutional guarantees themselves. * * *

What Rodriguez is assured by the trial
right of the exclusionary rule, where it
applies, is that no evidence seized in violation of the Fourth Amendment will be
introduced at his trial unless he consents.
What he is assured by the Fourth Amendment itself, however, is not that no government search of his house will occur
unless he consents; but that no such search
will occur that is "unreasonable." There
are various elements, of course, that can
make a search of a person's house "reasonable"—one of which is the consent of the
person or his cotenant. The essence of
respondent's argument is that we should
impose upon this element a requirement
that we have not imposed upon other elements that regularly compel government
officers to exercise judgment regarding the
facts: namely, the requirement that their
judgment be not only responsible but correct. [b]

[I]n order to satisfy the "reasonableness" requirement of the Fourth Amendment, what is generally demanded of the
many factual determinations that must regularly be made by agents of the government—whether the magistrate issuing a
warrant, the police officer executing a warrant, or the police officer conducting a

a. Where there is such "common authority,"
the Court went on to say in *Matlock*, "it is
reasonable to recognize that any of the co-inhabi-
tants has the right to permit the inspection in his
own right and that the others have assumed the
risk that one of their number might permit the
common area to be searched."

b. In an omitted portion of the opinion, illustrations were given: (i) the probable cause requirement for a warrant, as to which the magis-

trate may act on "seemingly reliable but
factually inaccurate information"; (ii) the warrant requirement, as to which the officer may be
reasonably mistaken as to the warrant's scope,
Maryland v. Garrison, 7th ed., p. 200; and (iii)
the search incident to arrest doctrine, where the
officer may be reasonably mistaken as to the
person to be arrested, *Hill v. California*, 7th ed.,
p. 325.

search or seizure under one of the exceptions to the warrant requirement—is not that they always be correct, but that they always be reasonable. As we put it in *Brinegar v. United States,* [7th ed., p. 178]:

> "Because many situations which confront officers in the course of executing their duties are more or less ambiguous, room must be allowed for some mistakes on their part. But the mistakes must be those of reasonable men, acting on facts leading sensibly to their conclusions of probability."

We see no reason to depart from this general rule with respect to facts bearing upon the authority to consent to a search. Whether the basis for such authority exists is the sort of recurring factual question to which law enforcement officials must be expected to apply their judgment; and all the Fourth Amendment requires is that they answer it reasonably. The Constitution is no more violated when officers enter without a warrant because they reasonably (though erroneously) believe that the person who has consented to their entry is a resident of the premises, than it is violated when they enter without a warrant because they reasonably (though erroneously) believe they are in pursuit of a violent felon who is about to escape.

Stoner v. California, [7th ed., p. 332] is in our view not to the contrary. There, in holding that police had improperly entered the defendant's hotel room based on the consent of a hotel clerk, we stated that "the rights protected by the Fourth Amendment are not to be eroded . . . by unrealistic doctrines of 'apparent authority.'" It is ambiguous, of course, whether the word "unrealistic" is descriptive or limiting—that is, whether we were condemning as unrealistic all reliance upon apparent authority, or whether we were condemning only such reliance upon apparent authority as is unrealistic. Similarly ambiguous is the opinion's earlier statement that "there [is no] substance to the

claim that the search was reasonable because the police, relying upon the night clerk's expressions of consent, had a reasonable basis for the belief that the clerk had authority to consent to the search." Was there no substance to it because it failed as a matter of law, or because the facts could not possibly support it? At one point the opinion does seem to speak clearly:

> "It is important to bear in mind that it was the petitioner's constitutional right which was at stake here, and not the night clerk's nor the hotel's. It was a right, therefore, which only the petitioner could waive by word or deed, either directly or through an agent."

But as we have discussed, what is at issue when a claim of apparent consent is raised is not whether the right to be free of searches has been *waived,* but whether the right to be free of *unreasonable* searches has been *violated.* Even if one does not think the *Stoner* opinion had this subtlety in mind, the supposed clarity of its foregoing statement is immediately compromised, as follows:

> "It is true that the night clerk clearly and unambiguously consented to the search. But there is nothing in the record to indicate that *the police had any basis whatsoever to believe that* the night clerk had been authorized by the petitioner to permit the police to search the petitioner's room."

The italicized language should have been deleted, of course, if the statement two sentences earlier meant that an appearance of authority could never validate a search. In the last analysis, one must admit that the rationale of *Stoner* was ambiguous—and perhaps deliberately so. It is at least a reasonable reading of the case, and perhaps a preferable one, that the police could not rely upon the obtained consent because they knew it came from a hotel clerk, knew that the room was rented and exclusively occupied by the defendant, and could not reasonably have believed that the former had general access to or control over the latter. * * *

As *Stoner* demonstrates, what we hold today does not suggest that law enforcement officers may always accept a person's invitation to enter premises. Even when the invitation is accompanied by an explicit assertion that the person lives there, the surrounding circumstances could conceivably be such that a reasonable person would doubt its truth and not act upon it without further inquiry. As with other factual determinations bearing upon search and seizure, determination of consent to enter must "be judged against an objective standard: would the facts available to the officer at the moment . . . 'warrant a man of reasonable caution in the belief'" that the consenting party had authority over the premises? If not, then warrantless entry without further inquiry is unlawful unless authority actually exists. But if so, the search is valid.

In the present case, the Appellate Court found it unnecessary to determine whether the officers reasonably believed that Fischer had the authority to consent, because it ruled as a matter of law that a reasonable belief could not validate the entry. Since we find that ruling to be in error, we remand for consideration of that question. The judgment of the Illinois Appellate Court is reversed and remanded for further proceedings not inconsistent with this opinion.

Justice Marshall, with whom Justice Brennan and Justice Stevens join, dissenting. * * *

Unlike searches conducted pursuant to the recognized exceptions to the warrant requirement, third-party consent searches are not based on an exigency and therefore serve no compelling social goal. Police officers, when faced with the choice of relying on consent by a third party or securing a warrant, should secure a warrant, and must therefore accept the risk of

error should they instead choose to rely on consent. * * *

Acknowledging that the third party in this case lacked authority to consent, the majority seeks to rely on cases suggesting that reasonable but mistaken factual judgments by police will not invalidate otherwise reasonable searches. The majority reads these cases as establishing a "general rule" that "what is generally demanded of the many factual determinations that must regularly be made by agents of the government—whether the magistrate issuing a warrant, the police officer executing a warrant, or the police officer conducting a search or seizure under one of the exceptions to the warrant requirement—is not that they always be correct, but that they always be reasonable."

The majority's assertion, however, is premised on the erroneous assumption that third-party consent searches are generally reasonable. The cases the majority cites thus provide no support for its holding. In *Brinegar v. United States,* for example, the Court confirmed the unremarkable proposition that police need only probable cause, not absolute certainty, to justify the arrest of a suspect on a highway. As *Brinegar* makes clear, the possibility of factual error is built into the probable cause standard, and such a standard, by its very definition, will in some cases result in the arrest of a suspect who has not actually committed a crime. Because probable cause defines the reasonableness of searches and seizures outside of the home, a search is reasonable under the Fourth Amendment whenever that standard is met, notwithstanding the possibility of "mistakes" on the part of police. In contrast, our cases have already struck the balance against warrantless home intrusions in the absence of an exigency. Because reasonable factual errors by law enforcement officers will not validate unreasonable searches, the reasonableness of the officer's mistaken belief that the third party had authority to consent is irrelevant. * * *[c]

7th ed., p. 332; in lieu of Note 1, add:

1. *Husband-wife.* In *United States v. Duran,* 957 F.2d 499 (7th Cir.1992), holding defendant's wife could consent to search of a separate building on their farm which he used as a gym, the court concluded the requisite access was established by the wife's testimony that she could have entered that building at any time, though the wife had not theretofore done so and had none of her personal effects there. This is not to say, the court cautioned, that there is "a per se rule that common spousal authority extends to every square inch of property upon which a couple's residence is built"; such an approach "presumes that spouses, in forging a marital bond, remove any and all boundaries between them," which "does not reflect reality, either in practice or in the eyes of the law." The *Duran* court thus opted for this position: "In the context of a more intimate marital relationship [as compared to other co-occupants], the burden upon

c. As for the other illustrations given by the majority, the dissenters explained that "*Hill* should be understood no less than *Brinegar* as simply a gloss on the meaning of 'probable cause,'" while *Garrison* "was premised on the

the government should be lighter. We hold that a spouse presumptively has authority to consent to a search of all areas of the homestead; the nonconsenting spouse may rebut this presumption only by showing that the consenting spouse was denied access to the particular area searched." Query, what is the effect of the rebuttal in light of *Rodriguez?*

7th ed., p. 334; in lieu of all of Note 4 in column 2, add:

State v. Leach, 782 P.2d 1035 (Wash.1989) (co-owner's prior consent to search of travel agency not effective against defendant, who was arrested there but remained present during the search, as where "the police have obtained consent to search from an individual possessing, at best, equal control over the premises, that consent remains valid against a cohabitant, who also possesses equal control, only while the cohabitant is absent," and "should the cohabitant be present and able to object, the police must also obtain the cohabitant's consent").

[fact that] searches based on warrants are generally reasonable," and "like *Brinegar,* thus tells us nothing about the reasonableness under the Fourth Amendment of a warrantless arrest."

Chapter 7

POLICE "ENCOURAGEMENT" AND THE DEFENSE OF ENTRAPMENT

7th ed., 411; end of chapter, add new section:

SECTION 4. CONTINUING CONTROVERSY OVER THE ENTRAPMENT DEFENSE

In *Jacobson v. United States,* set forth below, the Court purports to be applying the "subjective" test for entrapment. To what extent, however, did the result in *Jacobson* turn on the fact that the 5–4 majority was offended by the tactics used by the government to induce defendant to commit the crime? Does *Jacobson* illustrate that it is much easier to keep the "subjective" and "objective" tests separate and distinct in theory than to do so in practice? (Cf. the discussion of the *DeLorean* case, 7th ed., p. 396, Note 5.)

JACOBSON v. UNITED STATES

___ U.S. ___, 112 S.Ct. 1535, 118 L.Ed.2d 147 (1992).

JUSTICE WHITE delivered the opinion of the Court.

On September 24, 1987, [petitioner] was indicted for violating a provision of the Child Protection Act of 1984, which criminalizes the knowing receipt through the mails of a "visual depiction [that] involves the use of a minor engaging in sexually explicit conduct. . . ." Petitioner defended on the ground that the Government entrapped him into committing the crime through a series of communications from undercover agents that spanned the 26 months preceding his arrest. Petitioner was found guilty after a jury trial. The Court of Appeals affirmed his conviction, holding that the Government had carried its burden of proving beyond reasonable doubt that petitioner was predisposed to break the law and hence was not entrapped.

Because the Government overstepped the line between setting a trap for the "unwary innocent" and the "unwary criminal," and as a matter of law failed to establish that petitioner was independently predisposed to commit the crime for which he was arrested, we reverse * * *.

* * *

In February 1984, petitioner, a 56-year-old veteran-turned-farmer who supported his elderly father in Nebraska, ordered two magazines and a brochure from a California adult bookstore. The magazines, entitled *Bare Boys I* and *Bare Boys II,* contained photographs of nude preteen and teenage boys. The contents of the magazines startled petitioner, who testified that he had expected to receive photographs of "young men 18 years or older."

[The] young men depicted in the magazines were not engaged in sexual activity, and petitioner's receipt of the magazines was legal under both federal and Nebraska law. Within three months, the law with respect to child pornography changed; Congress passed the Act illegalizing the receipt through the mails of sexually explicit depictions of children. In the very month that the new provision became law, postal inspectors found petitioner's name on the mailing list of the California bookstore that had mailed him *Bare Boys I* and *II*. There followed over the next 2½ years, repeated efforts by two Government agencies, through five fictitious organizations and a bogus pen pal, to explore petitioner's willingness to break the new law by ordering sexually explicit photographs of children through the mail.

The Government began its efforts in January 1985 when a postal inspector sent petitioner a letter supposedly from the American Hedonist Society, which in fact was a fictitious organization. The letter included a membership application and stated the Society's doctrine: that members had the "right to read what we desire, the right to discuss similar interests with those who share our philosophy, and finally that we have the right to seek pleasure without restrictions being placed on us by outdated puritan morality." Petitioner enrolled in the organization and returned a sexual attitude questionnaire that asked him to rank on a scale of one to four his enjoyment of various sexual materials, with one being "really enjoy," two being "enjoy," three being "somewhat enjoy," and four being "do not enjoy." Petitioner ranked the entry "[p]reteen sex" as a two, but indicated that he was opposed to pedophilia.

For a time, the Government left petitioner alone. But then a new "prohibited mail specialist" in the Postal Service found petitioner's name in a file and in May 1986 petitioner received a solicitation from a second fictitious consumer research company, "Midlands Data Research," seeking a response from those who "believe in the joys of sex and the complete awareness of those lusty and youthful lads and lasses of the neophite [*sic*] age." The letter never explained whether "neophite" referred to minors or young adults. Petitioner responded: "Please feel free to send me more information, I am interested in teenage sexuality. Please keep my name confidential."

Petitioner then heard from yet another Government creation, "Heartland Institute for a New Tomorrow" (HINT), which proclaimed that it was "an organization founded to protect and promote sexual freedom and freedom of choice. We believe that arbitrarily imposed legislative sanctions restricting your sexual freedom should be rescinded through the legislative process." The letter also enclosed a second survey. Petitioner indicated that his interest in "[p]reteen sex-homosexual" material was above average, but not high. In response to another question, petitioner wrote: "Not only sexual expression but freedom of the press is under attack. We must be ever vigilant to counter attack right wing fundamentalists who are determined to curtail our freedoms."

"HINT" replied, portraying itself as a lobbying organization seeking to repeal "all statutes which regulate sexual activities, except those laws which deal with violent behavior, such as rape. HINT is also lobbying to eliminate any legal definition of 'the age of consent'." These lobbying efforts were to be funded by sales from a catalog to be published in the future "offering the sale of various items which we believe you will find to be both interesting and stimulating." HINT also provided computer matching of group members with similar survey responses; and, although petitioner was supplied with a list of potential "pen pals," he did not initiate any correspondence.

Nevertheless, the Government's "prohibited mail specialist" began writing to petitioner, using the pseudonym "Carl Long." The letters employed a tactic known as "mirroring," which the inspector described as "reflect[ing] whatever the interests are of the person we are writing to." Petitioner responded at first, indicating that his interest was primarily in "male-male items." Inspector "Long" wrote back:

"My interests too are primarily male-male items. Are you satisfied with the type of VCR tapes available? Personally, I like the amateur stuff better if its [sic] well produced as it can get more kinky and also seems more real. I think the actors enjoy it more."

Petitioner responded:

"As far as my likes are concerned, I like good looking young guys (in their late teens and early 20's) doing their thing together."

Petitioner's letters to "Long" made no reference to child pornography. After writing two letters, petitioner discontinued the correspondence.

By March 1987, 34 months had passed since the Government obtained petitioner's name from the mailing list of the California bookstore, and 26 months had passed since the Postal Service had commenced its mailings to petitioner. Although petitioner had responded to surveys and letters, the Government had no evidence that petitioner had ever intentionally possessed or been exposed to child pornography. The Postal Service had not checked petitioner's mail to determine whether he was receiving questionable mailings from persons—other than the Government—involved in the child pornography industry.

At this point, a second Government agency, the Customs Service, included petitioner in its own child pornography sting, "Operation Borderline," after receiving his name on lists submitted by the Postal Service. Using the name of a fictitious Canadian company called "Produit Outaouais," the Customs Service mailed petitioner a brochure advertising photographs of young boys engaging in sex. Petitioner placed an order that was never filled.

The Postal Service also continued its efforts in the Jacobson case, writing to petitioner as the "Far Eastern Trading Company Ltd." The letter began:

"As many of you know, much hysterical nonsense has appeared in the American media concerning 'pornography' and what must be done to stop it from coming across your borders. This brief letter does not allow us to give much comments; however, why is your government spending millions of dollars to exercise international censorship while tons of drugs, which makes yours the world's most crime ridden country are passed through easily."

The letter went on to say:

"[W]e have devised a method of getting these to you without prying eyes of U.S. Customs seizing your mail. . . . After consultations with American solicitors, we have been advised that once we have posted our material through your system, it cannot be opened for any inspection without authorization of a judge."

The letter invited petitioner to send for more information. [He] responded. A catalogue was sent and petitioner ordered *Boys Who Love Boys,* a pornographic magazine depicting young boys engaged in various sexual activities. Petitioner was arrested after a controlled delivery of a photocopy of the magazine.

When petitioner was asked at trial why he placed such an order, he explained that the Government had succeeded in piquing his curiosity:

"Well, the statement was made of all the trouble and the hysteria over pornography and I wanted to see what the material was. * * * I didn't know for sure what kind of sexual action they were referring to in the Canadian letter. . . . ."

In petitioner's home, the Government found the *Bare Boys* magazines and materials that the Government had sent to him in the course of its protracted investigation, but no other materials that would indicate that petitioner collected or was actively interested in child pornography.

Petitioner was indicted for [receiving child pornography through the mails.]

The trial court instructed the jury on the petitioner's entrapment defense,[1] petitioner was convicted, and a divided Court of Appeals for the Eighth Circuit, sitting *en banc,* affirmed, concluding that "Jacobson was not entrapped as a matter of law."

* * *

II

[In] their zeal to enforce the law [the Government] may not originate a criminal design, implant in an innocent person's mind the disposition to commit a criminal act, and then induce commission of the crime so that the Government may prosecute. Where the Government has induced an individual to break the law and the defense of entrapment is at issue, as it was in this case, the prosecution must prove beyond reasonable doubt that the defendant was disposed to commit the criminal act prior to first being approached by Government agents.[2]

Thus, an agent deployed to stop the traffic in illegal drugs may offer the opportunity to buy or sell drugs, and, if the offer is accepted, make an arrest on the spot or

1. The jury was instructed:

"As mentioned, one of the issues in this case is whether the defendant was entrapped. If the defendant was entrapped he must be found not guilty. The government has the burden of proving beyond a reasonable doubt that the defendant was not entrapped.

"If the defendant before contact with law-enforcement officers or their agents did not have any intent or disposition to commit the crime charged and was induced or persuaded by law-enforcement officers o[r] their agents to commit that crime, then he was entrapped. On the other hand, if the defendant before contact with law-enforcement officers or their agents did have an intent or disposition to commit the crime charged, then he was not entrapped even though law-enforcement officers or their agents provided a favorable opportunity to commit the crime or made committing the crime easier or even participated in acts essential to the crime."

2. Inducement is not at issue in this case. The Government does not dispute that it induced petitioner to commit the crime. The sole issue is whether the Government carried its burden of proving that petitioner was predisposed to violate the law *before* the Government intervened. The dissent is mistaken in claiming that this is an innovation in entrapment law and in suggesting

later. In such a typical case, or in a more elaborate "sting" operation involving government-sponsored fencing where the defendant is simply provided with the opportunity to commit a crime, the entrapment defense is of little use because the ready commission of the criminal act amply demonstrates the defendant's predisposition. Had the agents in this case simply offered petitioner the opportunity to order child pornography through the mails, and petitioner—who must be presumed to know the law—had promptly availed himself of this criminal opportunity, it is unlikely that his entrapment defense would have warranted a jury instruction.

But that is not what happened here. By the time petitioner finally placed his order, he had already been the target of 26 months of repeated mailings and communications from Government agents and fictitious organizations. Therefore, although he had become predisposed to break the law by May 1987, it is our view that the Government did not prove that this predisposition was independent and not the product of the attention that the Govern-

that the Government's conduct prior to the moment of solicitation is irrelevant. * * * Indeed, the proposition that the accused must be predisposed prior to contact with law enforcement officers is so firmly established that the Government conceded the point at oral argument, submitting that the evidence it developed during the course of its investigation was probative because it indicated petitioner's state of mind *prior* to the commencement of the Government's investigation.

This long-established standard in no way encroaches upon Government investigatory activities. Indeed, the Government's internal guidelines for undercover operations provide that an inducement to commit a crime should not be offered unless:

"(a) there is a reasonable indication, based on information developed through informants or other means, that the subject is engaging, has engaged, or is likely to engage in illegal activity of a similar type; *or*

"(b) The opportunity for illegal activity has been structured so that there is reason for believing that persons drawn to the opportunity, or brought to it, are predisposed to engage in the contemplated illegal activity." *Attorney General's Guidelines on FBI Undercover Operations* (Dec. 31, 1980).

ment had directed at petitioner since January 1985.

The prosecution's evidence of predisposition falls into two categories: evidence developed prior to the Postal Service's mail campaign, and that developed during the course of the investigation. The sole piece of preinvestigation evidence is petitioner's 1984 order and receipt of the Bare Boys magazines. But this is scant if any proof of petitioner's predisposition to commit an illegal act, the criminal character of which a defendant is presumed to know. It may indicate a predisposition to view sexually-oriented photographs that are responsive to his sexual tastes; but evidence that merely indicates a generic inclination to act within a broad range, not all of which is criminal, is of little probative value in establishing predisposition.

Furthermore, petitioner was acting within the law at the time he received these magazines. * * * Evidence of predisposition to do what once was lawful is not, by itself, sufficient to show predisposition to do what is now illegal, for there is a common understanding that most people obey the law even when they disapprove of it. [Hence,] the fact that petitioner legally ordered and received the *Bare Boys* magazines does little to further the Government's burden of proving that petitioner was predisposed to commit a criminal act. This is particularly true given petitioner's unchallenged testimony was that he did not know until they arrived that the magazines would depict minors.

The prosecution's evidence gathered during the investigation also fails to carry the Government's burden. Petitioner's responses to the many communications prior to the ultimate criminal act were at most indicative of certain personal inclinations, including a predisposition to view photographs of preteen sex and a willing-

ness to promote a given agenda by supporting lobbying organizations. Even so, petitioner's responses hardly support an inference that he would commit the crime of receiving child pornography through the mails.[3]

[On] the other hand, the strong arguable inference is that, by waving the banner of individual rights and disparaging the legitimacy and constitutionality of efforts to restrict the availability of sexually explicit materials, the Government not only excited petitioner's interest in sexually explicit materials banned by law but also exerted substantial pressure on petitioner to obtain and read such material as part of a fight against censorship and the infringement of individual rights. * * *

Petitioner's ready response to these solicitations cannot be enough to establish beyond reasonable doubt that he was predisposed, prior to the Government acts intended to create predisposition, to commit the crime of receiving child pornography through the mails. The evidence that petitioner was ready and willing to commit the offense came only after the Government had devoted $2\frac{1}{2}$ years to convincing him that he had or should have the right to engage in the very behavior proscribed by law. Rational jurors could not say beyond a reasonable doubt that petitioner possessed the requisite predisposition prior to the Government's investigation and that it existed independent of the Government's many and varied approaches to petitioner. As was explained in *Sherman*, where entrapment was found as a matter of law, "the Government [may not] pla[y] on the weaknesses of an innocent party and beguil[e] him into committing crimes which he otherwise would not have attempted."

Law enforcement officials go too far when they "implant in the mind of an

3. We do not hold, as the dissent suggests, that the Government was required to prove that petitioner knowingly violated the law. We simply conclude that proof that petitioner engaged in legal conduct and possessed certain generalized personal inclinations is not sufficient evidence to prove beyond a reasonable doubt that he would have been predisposed to commit the crime charged independent of the Government's coaxing.

innocent person the *disposition* to commit the alleged offense and induce its commission in order that they may prosecute." *Sorrells* (emphasis added). [When] the Government's quest for convictions leads to the apprehension of an otherwise law-abiding citizen who, if left to his own devices, likely would have never run afoul of the law, the courts should intervene.

* * *

JUSTICE O'CONNOR, with whom THE CHIEF JUSTICE and JUSTICE KENNEDY join, and with whom JUSTICE SCALIA joins except as to Part II, dissenting.

Keith Jacobson was offered only two opportunities to buy child pornography through the mail. Both times, he ordered. Both times, he asked for opportunities to buy more. He needed no Government agent to coax, threaten, or persuade him; no one played on his sympathies, friendship, or suggested that his committing the crime would further a greater good. In fact, no Government agent even contacted him face-to-face. The Government contends that from the enthusiasm with which Mr. Jacobson responded to the chance to commit a crime, a reasonable jury could permissibly infer beyond a reasonable doubt that he was predisposed to commit the crime. I agree.

[The] first time the Government sent Mr. Jacobson a catalog of illegal materials, he ordered a set of photographs advertised as picturing "young boys in sex action fun." He enclosed the following note with his order: "I received your brochure and decided to place an order. If I like your product, I will order more later." For reasons undisclosed in the record, Mr. Jacobson's order was never delivered.

The second time the Government sent a catalog of illegal materials, Mr. Jacobson ordered a magazine called "Boys Who Love Boys," described as: "11 year old and 14 year old boys get it on in every way possible. Oral, anal sex and heavy masturbation. If you love boys, you will be delighted with this." Along with his order, Mr. Jacobson sent the following note: "Will order other items later. I want to be discreet in order to protect you and me."

Government agents admittedly did not offer Mr. Jacobson the chance to buy child pornography right away. Instead, they first sent questionnaires in order to make sure that he was generally interested in the subject matter. Indeed, a "cold call" in such a business would not only risk rebuff and suspicion, but might also shock and offend the uninitiated, or expose minors to suggestive materials. Mr. Jacobson's responses to the questionnaires gave the investigators reason to think he would be interested in photographs depicting preteen sex.

The Court, however, concludes that a reasonable jury could not have found Mr. Jacobson to be predisposed beyond a reasonable doubt on the basis of his responses to the Government's catalogs, even though it admits that, by that time, he was predisposed to commit the crime. The Government, the Court holds, failed to provide evidence that Mr. Jacobson's obvious predisposition at the time of the crime "was independent and not the product of the attention that the Government had directed at petitioner." In so holding, I believe the Court fails to acknowledge the reasonableness of the jury's inference from the evidence, redefines "predisposition," and introduces a new requirement that Government sting operations have a reasonable suspicion of illegal activity before contacting a suspect.

I

This Court has held previously that a defendant's predisposition is to be assessed as of the time the Government agent first suggested the crime, not when the Government agent first became involved. * * * Even in *Sherman,* in which the Court held that the defendant had been entrapped as a matter of law, the Government agent had repeatedly and unsuccessfully coaxed the defendant to buy drugs, ultimately succeeding only by playing on the defendant's sympathy. The Court found lack of predisposition based on the Government's numerous unsuccessful attempts to induce the crime, not on the basis of preliminary contacts with the defendant.

Today, the Court holds that Government conduct may be considered to create a predisposition to commit a crime, even before any Government action to induce the commission of the crime. In my view, this holding changes entrapment doctrine. Generally, the inquiry is whether a suspect is predisposed before the Government induces the commission of the crime, not before the Government makes initial contact with him. There is no dispute here that the Government's questionnaires and letters were not sufficient to establish inducement; they did not even suggest that Mr. Jacobson should engage in any illegal activity. If all the Government had done was to send these materials, Mr. Jacobson's entrapment defense would fail. Yet the Court holds that the Government must prove not only that a suspect was predisposed to commit the crime before the opportunity to commit it arose, but also before the Government came on the scene.

The rule that preliminary Government contact can create a predisposition has the potential to be misread by lower courts as well as criminal investigators as requiring that the Government must have sufficient evidence of a defendant's predisposition *before it ever seeks to contact him.* Surely the Court cannot intend to impose such a requirement, for it would mean that the Government must have a reasonable suspicion of criminal activity before it begins an investigation, a condition that we have never before imposed. The Court denies that its new rule will affect run-of-the-mill sting operations and one hopes that it means what it says. Nonetheless, after this case, every defendant will claim that something the Government agent did before soliciting the crime "created" a predisposi-

tion that was not there before. For example, a bribe taker will claim that the description of the amount of money available was so enticing that it implanted a disposition to accept the bribe later offered. A drug buyer will claim that the description of the drug's purity and effects was so tempting that it created the urge to try it for the first time. In short, the Court's opinion could be read to prohibit the Government from advertising the seductions of criminal activity as part of its sting operation, for fear of creating a predisposition in its suspects. That limitation would be especially likely to hamper sting operations such as this one, which mimic the advertising done by genuine purveyors of pornography. No doubt the Court would protest that its opinion does not stand for so broad a proposition, but the apparent lack of a principled basis for distinguishing these scenarios exposes a flaw in the more limited rule the Court today adopts.

The Court's rule is all the more troubling because it does not distinguish between Government conduct that merely highlights the temptation of the crime itself, and Government conduct that threatens, coerces, or leads a suspect to commit a crime in order to fulfill some other obligation. For example, in *Sorrells,* the Government agent repeatedly asked for illegal liquor, coaxing the defendant to accede on the ground that "one former war buddy would get liquor for another." In *Sherman,* the Government agent played on the defendant's sympathies, pretending to be going through drug withdrawal and begging the defendant to relieve his distress by helping him buy drugs.

The Government conduct in this case is not comparable. While the Court states that the Government "exerted substantial pressure on petitioner to obtain and read such material as part of a fight against censorship and the infringement of individual rights," one looks at the record in vain for evidence of such "substantial pressure." The most one finds is letters advocating legislative action to liberalize obscenity laws, letters which could easily be ignored or thrown away. Much later, the Government sent separate mailings of catalogs of illegal materials. Nowhere did the Government suggest that the proceeds of the sale of the illegal materials would be used to support legislative reforms. * * * Mr. Jacobson's curiosity to see what " 'all the trouble and the hysteria' " was about is certainly susceptible of more than one interpretation. And it is the jury that is charged with the obligation of interpreting it. In sum, the Court fails to construe the evidence in the light most favorable to the Government, and fails to draw all reasonable inferences in the Government's favor. It was surely reasonable for the jury to infer that Mr. Jacobson was predisposed beyond a reasonable doubt, even if other inferences from the evidence were also possible.

II

The second puzzling thing about the Court's opinion is its redefinition of predisposition. The Court acknowledges that "[p]etitioner's responses to the many communications prior to the ultimate criminal act [were] indicative of certain personal inclinations, including a predisposition to view photographs of preteen sex. . . ." If true, this should have settled the matter; Mr. Jacobson was predisposed to engage in the illegal conduct. Yet, the Court concludes, "petitioner's responses hardly support an inference that he would commit the crime of receiving child pornography through the mails."

The Court seems to add something new to the burden of proving predisposition. Not only must the Government show that a defendant was predisposed to engage in the illegal conduct, here, receiving photographs of minors engaged in sex, but also that the defendant was predisposed to break the law knowingly in order to do so. The statute violated here, however, does not require proof of specific intent to break the law; it requires only knowing

receipt of visual depictions produced by using minors engaged in sexually explicit conduct. Under the Court's analysis, however, the Government must prove *more* to show predisposition than it need prove in order to convict.

The Court ignores the judgment of Congress that specific intent is not an element of the crime of receiving sexually explicit photographs of minors. The elements of predisposition should track the elements of the crime. The predisposition requirement is meant to eliminate the entrapment defense for those defendants who would have committed the crime anyway, even absent Government inducement. Because a defendant might very well be convicted of the crime here absent Government inducement even though he did not know his conduct was illegal, a specific intent requirement does little to distinguish between those who would commit the crime without the inducement and those who would not. In sum, although the fact that Mr. Jacobson's purchases of *Bare Boys I* and *Bare Boys II* were legal at the time may have some relevance to the question of predisposition, it is not, as the Court suggests, dispositive.

The crux of the Court's concern in this case is that the Government went too far and "abused" the "processes of detection and enforcement" by luring an innocent person to violate the law. Consequently, the Court holds that the Government failed to prove beyond a reasonable doubt that Mr. Jacobson was predisposed to commit the crime. It was, however, the jury's task, as the conscience of the community, to decide whether or not Mr. Jacobson was a willing participant in the criminal activity here or an innocent dupe. [There] is no dispute that the jury in this case was fully and accurately instructed on the law of entrapment, and nonetheless found Mr. Jacobson guilty. Because I believe there was sufficient evidence to uphold the jury's verdict, I respectfully dissent.

Chapter 8

POLICE INTERROGATION AND CONFESSIONS

SECTION 2. HISTORICAL BACKGROUND

D. THE RIGHT TO COUNSEL AND THE ANALOGY TO THE ACCUSATORIAL, ADVERSARY TRIAL

7th ed., 430; after 2nd full ¶ add:

Although rejected in the 1960s, the *Crooker–Cicenia* approach to the admissibility of confessions is still a matter of debate. Compare Grano, *Introduction—The Changed and Changing World of Constitutional Criminal Procedure: The Contribution of the Department of Justice's Office of Legal Policy,* 22 U.Mich.J.L.Ref. 395, 397–98 (1989) with Kamisar, *Remembering the "Old World" of Criminal Procedure: A Reply to Professor Grano,* 23 U.Mich.J.L.Ref. 537, 569–75 (1990).

SECTION 3. THE *MIRANDA* "REVOLUTION"

Applying and Explaining *Miranda*

7th ed., p. 498; add to Note 8:

ILLINOIS v. PERKINS, 496 U.S. 292, 110 S.Ct. 2394, 110 L.Ed.2d 243 (1990), resolved the controversy described in Note 8 over whether the use of "jail plants" to elicit incriminating statements from incarcerated suspects constitutes "custodial interrogation" within the meaning of *Miranda.* "The interests protected by *Miranda* are not implicated in these cases," held the Court, per KENNEDY, J.; "*Mi-*

randa warnings are not required when the suspect is unaware that he is speaking to a law enforcement officer and gives a voluntary statement."

The case arose as follows: Respondent Perkins, who was suspected of committing the Stephenson murder, was incarcerated on charges unrelated to the murder. The police placed Charlton (who had been a fellow inmate of Perkins in another prison) and Parisi (an undercover officer) in the same cellblock with Perkins. The secret government agents were instructed to engage Perkins in casual conversation and to report anything he said about the Stephenson murder. The cellblock consisted of 12 separate cells that opened onto a common room. When Charlton met Perkins in the prison he introduced Parisi by his alias. Parisi suggested that the three of them escape. There was further conversation. Parisi asked Perkins if he had ever "done" anybody. Perkins replied that he had and proceeded to describe his involvement in the Stephenson murder in detail.

In an opinion joined by six other Justices, Kennedy, J., explained why Perkins' statements were not barred by *Miranda*:

"The essential ingredients of a 'police-dominated atmosphere' and compulsion are not present when an incarcerated person speaks freely to someone that he believes to be a fellow inmate. Coercion is determined from the perspective of the suspect. [When] a suspect considers himself in the company of cellmates and not officers, the coercive atmosphere is lacking. * * *

"It is the premise of *Miranda* that the danger of coercion results from the interaction of custody and official interrogation. We reject the argument that *Miranda* warnings are required whenever a suspect is in custody in a technical sense and converses with someone who happens to be a government agent. [When] the suspect has no reason to think that the listeners have official power over him, it should not be assumed that his words are motivated by the reaction he expects from his listeners. '[W]hen the agent carries neither badge nor gun and wears not "police blue," but the same prison gray' as the suspect, there is no 'interplay between police interrogation and police custody.' Kamisar, *Brewer v. Williams, Massiah and Miranda: What is 'Interrogation?' When Does it Matter?,* 67 Geo.L.J. 1, 67, 63 (1978). [The] only difference between this case and *Hoffa* [7th ed., p. 369] is that the suspect here was incarcerated, but detention, whether or not for the crime in question, does not warrant a presumption that the use of an undercover agent to speak with an incarcerated suspect makes any confession thus obtained involuntary.

* * *

"This Court's Sixth Amendment decisions in [the *Massiah* line of cases, see 7th ed. at pp. 431, 575–95] also do not avail respondent. We held in those cases that the government may not use an undercover agent to circumvent the Sixth Amendment right to counsel once a suspect has been charged with the crime. After charges have been filed, the Sixth Amendment prevents the government from interfering with the accused's right to counsel.

In the instant case no charges had been filed on the subject of the interrogation, and our Sixth Amendment precedents are not applicable." [a]

Only MARSHALL, J., dissented, maintaining that "[t]he conditions that require the police to apprise a defendant of his constitutional rights—custodial interrogation conducted by an agent of the police—were present in this case. Because [respondent] received no *Miranda* warnings before he was subjected to custodial interrogation, his confession was not admissible." Continued Justice Marshall:

"Because Perkins was interrogated by police while he was in custody, *Miranda* required that the officer inform him of his rights. In rejecting that conclusion, the Court finds that 'conversations' between undercover agents and suspects are devoid of the coercion inherent in stationhouse interrogations conducted by law enforcement officials who openly represent the State. *Miranda* was not, however, concerned solely with police *coercion*. It dealt with *any* police tactics that may operate to compel a suspect in custody to make incriminating statements without full awareness of his constitutional rights. [Thus,] when a law enforcement agent structures a custodial interrogation so that a suspect feels compelled to reveal incriminating information, he must inform the suspect of his constitutional rights and give him an opportunity to decide whether or not to talk. * * *

"Custody works to the State's advantage in obtaining incriminating information. The psychological pressures inherent in confinement increase the suspect's anxiety, making him likely to seek relief by talking with others. Dix, *Undercover Investigations*

---

a. Brennan, J., concurred in the judgment of the Court, "agree[ing] that when a suspect does not know that his questioner is a police agent, such questioning does not amount to 'interrogation' in an 'inherently coercive' environment so as to require application of *Miranda* "—"the only issue raised at this stage of the litigation." But he went on to say that "the deception and manipulation practiced on respondent raise a substan-

tial claim that the confession was obtained in violation of the Due Process Clause." For "the deliberate use of deception and manipulation by the police appears to be incompatible 'with a system that presumes innocence and assures that a conviction will not be secured by inquisitional means' and raises serious concerns that respondent's will was overborne."

and Police Rulemaking, 53 Texas L.Rev. 203, 230 (1975). The inmate is thus more susceptible to efforts by undercover agents to elicit information from him. Similarly, where the suspect is incarcerated, the constant threat of physical danger peculiar to the prison environment may make him demonstrate his toughness to other inmates by recounting or inventing past violent acts. 'Because the suspect's ability to select people with whom he can confide is completely within their control, the police have a unique opportunity to exploit the suspect's vulnerability. In short, the police can insure that if the pressures of confinement lead the suspects to confide in anyone, it will be a police agent.' W. White, *Police Trickery in Inducing Confessions,* 127 U.Pa.L.Rev. 581, 605 (1979). In this case, the police deceptively took advantage of Perkins' psychological vulnerability by including him in a sham escape plot, a situation in which he would feel compelled to demonstrate his willingness to shoot a prison guard by revealing his past involvement in a murder. See App. 49 (agent stressed that a killing might be necessary in the escape and then asked Perkins if he had ever murdered someone).

"Thus, the pressures unique to custody allow the police to use deceptive interrogation tactics to compel a suspect to make an incriminating statement. The compulsion is not eliminated by the suspect's ignorance of his interrogator's true identity. The Court therefore need not inquire past the bare facts of custody and interrogation to determine whether *Miranda* warnings are required. * * *

"Even if *Miranda,* as interpreted by the Court, would not permit such obviously compelled confessions, the ramifications of today's opinion are still disturbing. The exception carved out of the *Miranda* doctrine today may well result in a proliferation of departmental policies to encourage police officers to conduct interrogations of confined suspects through undercover agents, thereby circumventing the need to administer *Miranda* warnings. Indeed, if *Miranda* now requires a police officer to issue warnings only in those situations in which the suspect might feel compelled 'to speak by the fear of reprisal for remaining silent or in the hope of more lenient treatment should he confess,' presumably it allows custodial interrogation by an undercover officer posing as a member of the clergy or a suspect's defense attorney. Although such abhorrent tricks would play on a suspect's need to confide in a trusted adviser, neither would cause the suspect to 'think that the listeners have official power over him.' The Court's adoption of the 'undercover agent' exception to the *Miranda* rule thus is necessarily also the adoption of a substantial loophole in our jurisprudence protecting suspects' Fifth Amendment rights."

———

7th ed., p. 498; after Note 8, add new Note:

8(a). *More on "custodial interrogation" and the "booking question exception" to Miranda.* Consider PENNSYLVANIA v. MUNIZ, 496 U.S. 582, 110 S.Ct. 2638, 110 L.Ed.2d 528 (1990) (also discussed at Supp., p. 79. The case arose as follows:

Respondent Muniz was arrested for driving while intoxicated. Without advising him of his *Miranda* rights, Officer Hosterman asked Muniz to perform three standard field sobriety tests. Muniz performed poorly and then admitted that he had been drinking. Muniz was taken to a Booking Center. Following its routine practice for receiving persons suspected of driving under the influence, the Booking Center videotaped the ensuing proceedings. Muniz was told that his action and voice were being recorded, but again he was not advised of his *Miranda* rights. Officer Hosterman first asked Muniz his name, address, height, weight, eye color, date of birth, and current age (the "first seven questions" or the seven "booking" questions). Both the delivery and content of his answers were incriminating. Next the officer asked Muniz what the Court called "the sixth birthday question": "Do you know what the date was of your sixth birthday?" Muniz responded, "No, I don't."

The officer then requested Muniz to perform the same sobriety tests that he had been asked to do earlier during the initial roadside stop. While performing the tests, Muniz made several audible and incriminating statements. Finally, Muniz was asked to submit to a breathalyzer test. He refused. At this point, for the first time, Muniz was advised of his *Miranda* rights. Both the video and audio portions of the videotape were admitted into evidence, along with the arresting officer's testimony that Muniz failed the roadside sobriety tests and made incriminating statements at the time. Muniz was convicted of driving while intoxicated.

The Court excluded only Muniz's response to the "sixth birthday question" (by a 5–4 vote). BRENNAN, J., wrote the opinion of the Court, except as to the grounds for admitting Muniz's answers to the first seven questions or "booking" questions.

Some of the issues raised by the case were relatively easy. Muniz's answers to direct questions were not barred by *Miranda* "merely because the slurred nature of his speech was incriminating." Under *Schmerber v. California* (discussed at pp. 37, 597, 692–93 & 697–98 of the 7th ed.) and its progeny, "any slurring of speech and other evidence of lack of muscular coordination revealed by Muniz's responses * * * constitute nontestimonial components of those responses." Muniz's incriminating utterances during the physi-

cal sobriety tests were also admissible because "not prompted by an interrogation within the meaning of *Miranda.*" Officer Hosterman's conversation with Muniz concerning the tests "consisted primarily of carefully scripted instructions as to how the tests were to be performed," instructions "not likely to be perceived as calling for any verbal response" and thus "not 'words or actions' constituting custodial interrogation." [a]

More difficult issues were whether Muniz's response to the sixth birthday question should be allowed into evidence and whether Muniz's answers to the first seven questions asked him at the Booking Center (the seven "booking" questions) were admissible—and if not, *why* not.

In contrast to a number of other questions Muniz was asked, the sixth birthday question, observed the Court, per Brennan, J., "required a testimonial response. When Officer Hosterman asked Muniz if he knew the date of his sixth birthday and Muniz, for whatever reason, could not remember or calculate that date, he was [placed in a predicament the self-incrimination clause was designed to prevent]. By hypothesis, the inherently coercive environment created by the custodial interrogation precluded the option of remaining silent. Muniz was left with the choice of incriminating himself by admitting that he did not then know the date of his sixth birthday, or answering untruthfully by reporting a date that he did not then believe to be accurate (an incorrect guess would be incriminating as well as truthful). [The] incriminating inference of impaired mental facilities stemmed, not just from the fact that Muniz slurred his response,

a. "Similarly," added the Court, "*Miranda* does not require suppression of the statements Muniz made when asked to submit to a breathalyzer examination." The officer who requested Muniz to take the breathalyzer test "carefully limited her role to providing Muniz with relevant information about [the] test and the implied consent law. She questioned Muniz only as to whether he understood her instructions and wished to submit to the test. These

limited and focused inquiries were necessarily 'attendant to' the legitimate police procedure [and] not likely to be perceived as calling for any incriminating response."

The Court noted that "Muniz does not and cannot challenge the introduction into evidence of his refusal to submit to the breathalyzer test." See *South Dakota v. Neville* (fn. a, 7th ed., p. 489).

but also from a testimonial aspect of that response."

REHNQUIST, C.J., joined by White, Blackmun and Stevens, JJ., disagreed:

"The sixth birthday question here was an effort on the part of the police to check how well Muniz was able to do a simple mathematical exercise. Indeed, had the question related only to the date of his birthday, it presumably would have come under the 'booking exception' to *Miranda* to which the Court refers elsewhere in its opinion. [See discussion below.] [If] the police may require Muniz to use his body in order to demonstrate the level of his physical coordination, there is no reason why they should not be able to require him to speak or write in order to determine his mental coordination. That was all that was sought here. Since it was permissible for the police to extract and examine a sample of Schmerber's blood to determine how much that part of his system had been affected by alcohol, I see no reason why they may not examine the functioning of Muniz's mental processes for the same purpose."

Eight members of the Court agreed that the answers to the "booking" questions were admissible, but they differed as to the reason. Four Justices (Rehnquist, C.J., joined by White, Blackmun and Stevens, JJ.) did not consider the questions "testimonial." Thus, they did not address the issue whether, even if the questions were "testimonial," they came under a "booking exception" to *Miranda*. The other four Justices (Brennan, J., joined by O'Connor, Scalia and Kennedy, JJ.,) believed the first seven questions were "testimonial" and did amount to "custodial interrogation" within the meaning of *Miranda*. Nonetheless, they concluded that Muniz's answers were admissible because of a "routine booking question" exception to *Miranda* —one that permits questions "to secure the 'biographical data necessary to complete booking or pretrial services.'" The state court had found that

the first seven questions were "requested for record-keeping purposes only"; thus, "the questions appear reasonably related to the police's administrative concerns."

Only MARSHALL, J., would have kept out the answers to the first seven questions. He rejected both the Brennan group's and the Rehnquist group's rationales for admitting Muniz's answers to these questions;

"[The questions] sought 'testimonial' responses for the same reason the sixth birthday question did: because the content of the answers would indicate Muniz's state of mind. The booking questions, like the sixth birthday question, required Muniz to (1) answer correctly, indicating lucidity, (2) answer incorrectly, implying that his mental facilities were impaired, or (3) state that he did not know the answer, also indicating impairment. Muniz's initial incorrect response to the question about his age and his inability to give his address without looking at his license, like his inability to answer the sixth birthday question, in fact gave rise to the incriminating inference that his mental facilities were impaired."

As for the Brennan group's rationale for admitting Muniz's answers—the questions fell within a "routine booking question" exception to *Miranda*—even if such an exception was appropriate in some instances, responded Marshall, J., the exception "should not extend to booking questions [asked in circumstances, such as the instant case, which] the police should know are reasonably likely to elicit incriminating responses."

More generally, Justice Marshall balked at creating "yet another exception" to *Miranda* because "[s]uch exceptions undermine *Miranda*'s fundamental principle that the doctrine should be clear so that it can be easily applied by both police and courts." Continued Marshall:

"The plurality's position, were it adopted by a majority of the Court, would necessitate difficult, time-consuming litigation over whether particular questions asked during booking are 'routine,' whether they are necessary to secure biographical information, whether that information is itself necessary for recordkeeping purposes, and whether the questions are—despite their routine nature—designed to elicit incriminating testimony. The far better course would be to maintain the clarity of the doctrine by requiring police to preface all direct questioning of a suspect with *Miranda* warnings if they want his responses to be admissible at trial."

7th ed., pp. 505–06; end of first fn. a, add:

As pointed out in M. Berger *Legislating Confession Law in Great Britain: A Statutory Approach to Police Interrogation*, 24 U.Mich.J.L.Ref. 1, 56 (1990), the British Code of Practice on Tape Recording, issued in 1988 after a series of field trials assessing the impact and feasibility of tape recording, "describes procedures for the open recording of stationhouse interviews, with suspects specifically informed that the interview will be recorded. If the suspect objects, the police should record the objections before turning off the tape machine; the Tape Recording Code does not provide for surreptitious taping." Continues Professor Berger, id. at 56–57:

"If tape recording is otherwise required, the custody officer can approve a decision not to tape record the questioning in the limited cases in which the equipment is unavailable or has failed and there are reasonable grounds for not delaying the questioning, or where it is clear that there will be no prosecution. When tape recording is required, '[t]he whole of each interview shall be tape recorded, including the taking and reading back of any statement.' Police are warned in the guidance notes that '[a] decision not to tape record . . . may be the subject of comment in court' and they 'should therefore be prepared to justify [the] decision in each case.'

"Even though the Tape Recording Code envisions recording interviews, it does not provide for transcribing all of the resulting tapes. One of the concerns in a system with universal taping of interviews is that it will entail much unnecessary cost and time in preparing transcripts or monitoring the tapes. The Code's solution to this has been to direct police to prepare a written (but not verbatim) record of the interview. The defense can then accept or reject the police version, and if accepted it can 'be used for the conduct of the case by the prosecution, the defence, and the court.' On this basis, '[t]he record shall, therefore, comprise a balanced account of the interview including points in mitigation and/or defence made by the suspect.'"

7th ed., p. 512; in lieu of the *Roberson* case, add the *Minnick* case, set forth below:

15. *Resumption of questioning following the exercise of rights; the distinction between asserting the right to remain silent and the right to counsel.*

MINNICK v. MISSISSIPPI

__ U.S. __, 111 S.Ct. 486, 112 L.Ed.2d 489 (1990).

JUSTICE KENNEDY delivered the opinion of the Court.

* * * The issue in the case before us is whether *Edwards'* protection ceases once the suspect has consulted with an attorney.

[Petitioner Minnick and fellow prisoner Dykes escaped from a Mississippi jail and broke into a trailer in search of weapons. In the course of the burglary, they killed two people. Minnick and Dykes fled to Mexico, where they fought, and Minnick then proceeded alone to California where, some four months after the murders, he was arrested by local police and placed in a San Diego jail. The day following his arrest, Saturday, two FBI agents came to the jail to interview him. After being advised of his rights and acknowledging that he understood them, Minnick refused to sign a rights waiver form, but agreed to answer some questions. He maintained that Dykes had killed one victim and forced him to shoot the other, but otherwise he hesitated to discuss what happened at the trailer.]

[At this point] the [FBI] agents reminded him he did not have to answer questions without a lawyer present. According to the [FBI] report, "Minnick stated that he would make a more complete statement then with his lawyer present." The FBI interview ended.

After the FBI interview, an appointed attorney met with petitioner. [He] spoke with the lawyer on two or three occasions, though it is not clear from the record whether all of these conferences were in person.

On Monday [Denham, a Mississippi deputy sheriff,] came to the San Diego jail to question Minnick. Minnick testified that his jailers * * * told him he would "have to talk" to Denham and that he "could not refuse." Denham advised petitioner of his rights, and petitioner again declined to sign a rights waiver form. [However, Minnick agreed to answer some questions and made a number of incriminating statements].

Minnick was tried for murder in Mississippi. He moved to suppress all statements given to the FBI or other police officers, including Denham. The trial court denied the motion with respect to petitioner's statements to Denham, but suppressed his other statements. Petitioner was convicted on two counts of capital murder and sentenced to death.

On appeal, petitioner argued that the confession to Denham was taken in violation of his rights to counsel under the Fifth and Sixth Amendments. The Mississippi Supreme Court rejected the claims. With respect to the Fifth Amendment aspect of the case, the court [concluded that the *Edwards* rule did not apply, since counsel had been made available to petitioner.] The court also rejected the Sixth Amendment claim, finding that petitioner waived his Sixth Amendment right to counsel when he spoke with Denham. [W]ithout reaching any Sixth Amendment implications in the case, we decide that the Fifth Amendment protection of *Edwards* is not terminated or suspended by consultation with counsel. * * *

Edwards is "designed to prevent police from badgering a defendant into waiving his previously asserted *Miranda* rights." *Michigan v. Harvey* [Supp., p. 92.] The rule ensures that any statement made in subsequent interrogation is not the result of coercive pressures. *Edwards* conserves judicial resources which would otherwise be expended in making difficult determinations of voluntariness, and implements the protections of *Miranda* in practical and straightforward terms.

The merit of the *Edwards* decision lies in the clarity of its command and the certainty of its application. We have confirmed that the *Edwards* rule provides " 'clear and unequivocal' guidelines to the law enforcement profession." Even before *Edwards,* we noted that *Miranda*'s "relatively rigid requirement that interrogation must cease upon the accused's request for an attorney . . . has the virtue of informing police and prosecutors with specificity as to what they may do in conducting custodial interrogation, and of informing courts under what circumstances statements obtained during such interrogation are not admissible. This gain in specificity, which benefits the accused and the State alike, has been thought to outweigh the burdens that the decision in *Miranda* imposes on law enforcement agencies and the courts by requiring the suppression of trustworthy and highly probative evidence even though the confession might be voluntary under traditional Fifth Amendment analysis." *Fare v. Michael C.* This pre-*Edwards* explanation applies as well to *Edwards* and its progeny.

The Mississippi Supreme Court relied on our statement in *Edwards* that an accused who invokes his right to counsel "is not subject to further interrogation by the authorities until counsel has been made available to him. . . ." We do not interpret this language to mean, as the Mississippi court thought, that the protection of *Edwards* terminates once counsel has consulted with the suspect. In context, the requirement that counsel be "made available" to the accused refers to more than an opportunity to consult with an attorney outside the interrogation room.

In *Edwards,* we focused on *Miranda*'s instruction that when the accused invokes his right to counsel, "the interrogation must cease until an attorney is *present*" (emphasis added), agreeing with Edwards' contention that he had not waived his right "to have counsel *present* during custodial interrogation" (emphasis added). In the sentence preceding the language quoted by the Mississippi Supreme Court, we referred to the "right to have counsel *present* during custodial interrogation," and in the sentence following, we again quoted the phrase " 'interrogation must cease until an attorney is *present* ' " from *Miranda* (emphasis added). The full sentence relied on by the Mississippi Supreme Court, moreover, says: "We further hold that an accused, such as Edwards, *having expressed his desire to deal with the police only through counsel*, is not subject to further interrogation by the authorities until counsel has been made available to him, unless the accused himself initiates further communication, exchanges, or conversations with the police" (emphasis added).

Our emphasis on counsel's *presence* at interrogation is not unique to *Edwards*. It derives from *Miranda*, where we said that in the cases before us "[t]he presence of counsel . . . would be the adequate protective device necessary to make the process of police interrogation conform to the dictates of the [Fifth Amendment] privilege. His presence would insure that statements made in the government-established atmosphere are not the product of compulsion." Our cases following *Edwards* have interpreted the decision to mean that the authorities may not initiate questioning of the accused in counsel's absence. Writing for a plurality of the Court, for instance, then Justice Rehnquist described the holding of *Edwards* to be "that subsequent incriminating statements made *without [Edwards'] attorney present* violated the rights secured to the defendant by the Fifth and Fourteenth Amendments to the United States Constitution." *Oregon v. Bradshaw* [7th ed., p. 518] (emphasis added). [In] our view, a fair reading of *Edwards* and subsequent cases demonstrates that we have interpreted the rule to bar police-initiated interrogation unless the accused has counsel with him at the time of questioning. Whatever the ambiguities

of our earlier cases on this point, we now hold that when counsel is requested, interrogation must cease, and officials may not reinitiate interrogation without counsel present, whether or not the accused has consulted with his attorney.

We consider our ruling to be an appropriate and necessary application of the *Edwards* rule. A single consultation with an attorney does not remove the suspect from persistent attempts by officials to persuade him to waive his rights, or from the coercive pressures that accompany custody and that may increase as custody is prolonged. The case before us well illustrates the pressures, and abuses, that may be concomitants of custody. Petitioner testified that though he resisted, he was required to submit to both the FBI and the Denham interviews. In the latter instance, the compulsion to submit to interrogation followed petitioner's unequivocal request during the FBI interview that questioning cease until counsel was present. The case illustrates also that consultation is not always effective in instructing the suspect of his rights. One plausible interpretation of the record is that petitioner thought he could keep his admissions out of evidence by refusing to sign a formal waiver of rights. If the authorities had complied with Minnick's request to have counsel present during interrogation, the attorney could have corrected Minnick's misunderstanding, or indeed counseled him that he need not make a statement at all. We decline to remove protection from police-initiated questioning based on isolated consultations with counsel who is absent when the interrogation resumes.

The exception to *Edwards* here proposed is inconsistent with *Edwards'* purpose to protect the suspect's right to have counsel present at custodial interrogation. It is inconsistent as well with *Miranda*, where we specifically rejected respondent's theory that the opportunity to consult with one's attorney would substantially counteract the compulsion created by custodial interrogation. We noted in *Miranda* that "[e]ven preliminary advice given to the accused by his own attorney can be swiftly overcome by the secret interrogation process. Thus the need for counsel to protect the Fifth Amendment privilege comprehends not merely a right to consult with counsel prior to questioning, but also to have counsel present during any questioning if the defendant so desires."

The exception proposed, furthermore, would undermine the advantages flowing from *Edwards'* "clear and unequivocal" character. Respondent concedes that even after consultation with counsel, a second request for counsel should reinstate the *Edwards* protection. We are invited by this formulation to adopt a regime in which *Edwards'* protection could pass in and out of existence multiple times prior to arraignment, at which point the same protection might reattach by virtue of our Sixth Amendment jurisprudence, see *Michigan v. Jackson* [7th ed., pp. 522–23]. Vagaries of this sort spread confusion through the justice system and lead to a consequent loss of respect for the underlying constitutional principle.

In addition, adopting the rule proposed would leave far from certain the sort of consultation required to displace *Edwards*. Consultation is not a precise concept, for it may encompass variations from a telephone call to say that the attorney is in route, to a hurried interchange between the attorney and client in a detention facility corridor, to a lengthy in-person conference in which the attorney gives full and adequate advice respecting all matters that might be covered in further interrogations. And even with the necessary scope of consultation settled, the officials in charge of the case would have to confirm the occurrence and, possibly, the extent of consultation to determine whether further interrogation is permissible. The necessary inquiries could interfere with the attorney-client privilege.

Added to these difficulties in definition and application of the proposed rule is our concern over its consequence that the suspect whose counsel is prompt would lose the protection of *Edwards,* while the one whose counsel is dilatory would not. There is more than irony to this result. There is a strong possibility that it would distort the proper conception of the attorney's duty to the client and set us on a course at odds with what ought to be effective representation.

Both waiver of rights and admission of guilt are consistent with the affirmation of individual responsibility that is a principle of the criminal justice system. It does not detract from this principle, however, to insist that neither admissions nor waivers are effective unless there are both particular and systemic assurances that the coercive pressures of custody were not the inducing cause. The *Edwards* rule sets forth a specific standard to fulfill these purposes, and we have declined to confine it in other instances. See *Arizona v. Roberson,* 486 U.S. 675, 108 S.Ct. 2093, 100 L.Ed.2d 704 (1988) [*Edwards* applies even when the police want to question a suspect about an offense unrelated to the subject of their initial interrogation.] It would detract from the efficacy of the rule to remove its protections based on consultation with counsel.

Edwards does not foreclose finding a waiver of Fifth Amendment protections after counsel has been requested, provided the accused has initiated the conversation or discussions with the authorities; but that is not the case before us. There can be no doubt that the interrogation in question was initiated by the police; it was a formal interview which petitioner was compelled to attend. Since petitioner made a specific request for counsel before the interview, the police-initiated interrogation was impermissible. Petitioner's statement to Denham was not admissible at trial. * * *[a]

---

a. Justice Souter took no part in the consideration or decision of this case.

JUSTICE SCALIA, with whom THE CHIEF JUSTICE joins, dissenting.

The Court today establishes an irrebuttable presumption that a criminal suspect, after invoking his *Miranda* right to counsel, can *never* validly waive that right during any police-initiated encounter, even after the suspect has been provided multiple *Miranda* warnings and has actually consulted his attorney. This holding builds on foundations already established in *Edwards*, but "the rule of *Edwards* is our rule, not a constitutional command; and it is our obligation to justify its expansion." *Arizona v. Roberson* (Kennedy, J., dissenting). Because I see no justification for applying the *Edwards* irrebuttable presumption when a criminal suspect has actually consulted with his attorney, I respectfully dissent.

[The Court] holds that, because Minnick had asked for counsel during the interview with the FBI agents, he could not—as a matter of law—validly waive the right to have counsel present during the conversation initiated by Denham. That Minnick's original request to see an attorney had been honored, that Minnick had consulted with his attorney on several occasions, and that the attorney had specifically warned Minnick not to speak to the authorities, are irrelevant. That Minnick was familiar with the criminal justice system in general or *Miranda* warnings in particular (he had previously been convicted of robbery in Mississippi and assault with a deadly weapon in California) is also beside the point. The confession must be suppressed, not because it was "compelled," nor even because it was obtained from an individual who could realistically be assumed to be unaware of his rights, but simply because this Court sees fit to prescribe as a "systemic assuranc[e]" that a person in custody who has once asked for counsel cannot thereafter be approached by the police unless counsel is present. Of course the Constitution's proscription of compelled testimony does not remotely authorize this incursion upon state practices; and even

our recent precedents are not a valid excuse.

[The *Miranda* Court] expressly adopted the "high standar[d] of proof for the waiver of constitutional rights" set forth in *Johnson v. Zerbst* [see 7th ed. at 58, 454].

* * *

Notwithstanding our acknowledgment that *Miranda* rights are "not themselves rights protected by the Constitution but . . . instead measures to insure that the right against compulsory self-incrimination [is] protected," *Michigan v. Tucker*, we have adhered to the principle that nothing less than the *Zerbst* standard for the waiver of constitutional rights applies to the waiver of *Miranda* rights. Until *Edwards*, however, we refrained from imposing on the States a *higher* standard for the waiver of *Miranda* rights. For example, in *Michigan v. Mosley*, we rejected a proposed irrebuttable presumption that a criminal suspect, after invoking the *Miranda* right to remain silent, could not validly waive the right during any subsequent questioning by the police. In *North Carolina v. Butler*, we rejected a proposed rule that waivers of *Miranda* rights must be deemed involuntary absent an explicit assertion of waiver by the suspect. And in *Fare v. Michael C.*, we declined to hold that waivers of *Miranda* rights by juveniles are *per se* involuntary.

Edwards, however, broke with this approach, holding that a defendant's waiver of his *Miranda* right to counsel, made in the course of a police-initiated encounter after he had requested counsel but before counsel had been provided, was *per se* involuntary. The case stands as a solitary exception to our waiver jurisprudence. It does, to be sure, have the desirable consequences described in today's opinion. In the narrow context in which it applies, it provides 100% assurance against confessions that are "the result of coercive pressures"; it " 'prevent[s] police from badgering a defendant' "; it "conserves judicial resources which would otherwise be expended in making difficult determinations of voluntariness"; and it provides " ' "clear and unequivocal" guidelines to the law enforcement profession.' " But so would a rule that simply excludes all confessions by all persons in police custody. The value of any prophylactic rule (assuming the authority to adopt a prophylactic rule) must be assessed not only on the basis of what is gained, but also on the basis of what is lost. In all other contexts we have thought the above-described consequences of abandoning *Zerbst* outweighed by " 'the need for police questioning as a tool for effective enforcement of criminal laws,' " *Moran v. Burbine* [7th ed., p. 523]. "Admissions of guilt," we have said, "are more than merely 'desirable'; they are essential to society's compelling interest in finding, convicting, and punishing those who violate the law." Ibid.

In this case, of course, we have not been called upon to reconsider *Edwards,* but simply to determine whether its irrebuttable presumption should continue after a suspect has actually consulted with his attorney. Whatever justifications might support *Edwards* are even less convincing in this context.

Most of the Court's discussion of *Edwards*—which stresses repeatedly, in various formulations, the case's emphasis upon "the 'right to have counsel *present* during custodial interrogation' " (emphasis added by the Court)—is beside the point. The existence and the importance of the *Miranda*-created right "to have counsel *present* " are unquestioned here. What *is* questioned is why a State should not be given the opportunity to prove (under *Zerbst*) that the right was *voluntarily waived* by a suspect who, after having been read his *Miranda* rights twice and having consulted with counsel at least twice, chose to speak to a police officer (and to admit his involvement in two murders) without counsel present.

Edwards did not assert the principle that no waiver of the *Miranda* right "to have

counsel *present* " is possible. It simply adopted the presumption that no waiver is *voluntary* in certain circumstances, and the issue before us today is how broadly those circumstances are to be defined. They should not, in my view, extend beyond the circumstances present in *Edwards* itself— where the suspect in custody asked to consult an attorney, and was interrogated before that attorney had ever been provided. In those circumstances, the *Edwards* rule rests upon an assumption similar to that of *Miranda* itself: that when a suspect in police custody is first questioned he is likely to be ignorant of his rights and to feel isolated in a hostile environment. This likelihood is thought to justify special protection against unknowing or coerced waiver of rights. After a suspect has seen his request for an attorney honored, however, and has actually spoken with that attorney, the probabilities change. The suspect then knows that he has an advocate on his side, and that the police will permit him to consult that advocate. He almost certainly also has a heightened awareness (above what the *Miranda* warning itself will provide) of his right to remain silent—since at the earliest opportunity "any lawyer worth his salt will tell the suspect in no uncertain terms to make no statement to the police under any circumstances."

Under these circumstances, an irrebuttable presumption that any police-prompted confession is the result of ignorance of rights, or of coercion, has no genuine basis in fact. After the first consultation, therefore, the *Edwards* exclusionary rule should cease to apply. Does this mean, as the Court implies, that the police will thereafter have license to "badger" the suspect? Only if all one means by "badger" is asking, without such insistence or frequency as would constitute coercion, whether he would like to reconsider his decision not to confess. Nothing in the Constitution (the only basis for our intervention here) prohibits such inquiry, which may often produce the desirable result of a voluntary confession. If and when post-consultation police inquiry becomes so protracted or threatening as to constitute coercion, the *Zerbst* standard will afford the needed protection.

One should not underestimate the extent to which the Court's expansion of *Edwards* constricts law enforcement. Today's ruling, that the invocation of a right to counsel permanently prevents a police-initiated waiver, makes it largely impossible for the police to urge a prisoner who has initially declined to confess to change his mind—or indeed, even to ask whether he has changed his mind. Many persons in custody will invoke the *Miranda* right to counsel during the first interrogation, so that the permanent prohibition will attach at once. Those who do not do so will almost certainly request or obtain counsel at arraignment. We have held that a general request for counsel, after the Sixth Amendment right has attached, also triggers the *Edwards* prohibition of police-solicited confessions, see *Michigan v. Jackson* [7th ed., pp. 522–23], and I presume that the perpetuality of prohibition announced in today's opinion applies in that context as well. "Perpetuality" is not too strong a term, since, although the Court rejects one logical moment at which the *Edwards* presumption might end, it suggests no alternative. In this case Minnick was reapproached by the police three days after he requested counsel, but the result would presumably be the same if it had been three months, or three years, or even three decades. This perpetual irrebuttable presumption will apply, I might add, not merely to interrogations involving the original crime but to those involving other subjects as well. See *Arizona v. Roberson.*

Besides repeating the uncontroverted proposition that the suspect has a "right to have counsel *present*," the Court stresses the clarity and simplicity that are achieved by today's holding. Clear and simple rules are desirable, but only in pursuance of authority that we possess. We are authorized by the Fifth Amendment to exclude confessions that are "compelled," which we have interpreted to include confessions that the police obtain from a suspect in custody without a knowing and voluntary waiver of his right to remain silent. Undoubtedly some bright-line rules can be adopted to implement that principle, marking out the situations in which knowledge or voluntariness cannot possibly be established—for example, a rule excluding confessions obtained after five hours of continuous interrogation. But a rule excluding all confessions that follow upon even the slightest police inquiry cannot conceivably be justified on this basis. It does not rest upon a reasonable prediction that all such confessions, or even most such confessions, will be unaccompanied by a knowing and voluntary waiver.

It can be argued that the same is true of the category of confessions excluded by the *Edwards* rule itself. I think that is so, but, as I have discussed above, the presumption of involuntariness is at least more plausible for that category. There is, in any event, a clear and rational line between that category and the present one, and I see nothing to be said for expanding upon a past mistake. Drawing a distinction between police-initiated inquiry before consultation with counsel and police-initiated inquiry after consultation with counsel is assuredly more reasonable than other distinctions *Edwards* has already led us into—such as the distinction between police-initiated inquiry after assertion of the *Miranda* right to remain silent, and police-initiated inquiry after assertion of the *Miranda* right to counsel, see Kamisar, The *Edwards* and *Bradshaw* Cases: The Court Giveth and the Court Taketh Away, in 5 The Supreme Court: Trends and Developments 157 (J. Choper, Y. Kamisar, & L. Tribe eds. 1984) ("[E]ither *Mosley* was wrongly decided or *Edwards* was"); or the distinction between what is needed to prove waiver of the *Miranda* right to have counsel present and what is needed to prove waiver of rights found in the Constitution.

The rest of the Court's arguments can be answered briefly. The suggestion that it will either be impossible or ethically impermissible to determine whether a "consultation" between the suspect and his attorney has occurred is alarmist. Since, as I have described above, the main purpose of the consultation requirement is to eliminate the suspect's feeling of isolation and to assure him the presence of legal assistance, any discussion between him and an attorney whom he asks to contact, or who is provided to him, in connection with his arrest, will suffice. The precise content of the discussion is irrelevant.

As for the "irony" that "the suspect whose counsel is prompt would lose the protection of *Edwards,* while the one whose counsel is dilatory would not": There seems to me no irony in applying a special protection only when it is needed. The *Edwards* rule is premised on an (already tenuous) assumption about the suspect's psychological state, and when the event of consultation renders that assumption invalid the rule should no longer apply. One searching for ironies in the state of our law should consider, first, the irony created by *Edwards* itself: The suspect in custody who says categorically "I do not wish to discuss this matter" can be asked to change his mind; but if he should say, more tentatively, "I do not think I should discuss this matter without my attorney present" he can no longer be approached. To that there is added, by today's decision, the irony that it will be far harder for the state to establish a knowing and voluntary waiver of Fifth Amendment rights by a prisoner who has already consulted with counsel than by a newly arrested suspect.

Finally, the Court's concern that "*Edwards'* protection could pass in and out of existence multiple times" does not apply to the resolution of the matter I have proposed. *Edwards* would cease to apply, permanently, once consultation with counsel has occurred.

* * *

Today's extension of the *Edwards* prohibition is the latest stage of prophylaxis built upon prophylaxis, producing a veritable fairyland castle of imagined constitutional restriction upon law enforcement. This newest tower, according to the Court, is needed to avoid "inconsisten[cy] with [the] purpose" of *Edwards'* prophylactic rule, which was needed to protect *Miranda*'s prophylactic right to have counsel present, which was needed to protect the right against *compelled self-incrimination* found (at last!) in the Constitution.

It seems obvious to me that, even in *Edwards* itself but surely in today's decision, we have gone far beyond any genuine concern about suspects who do not *know* their right to remain silent, or who have been *coerced* to abandon it. Both holdings are explicable, in my view, only as an effort to protect suspects against what is regarded as their own folly. The sharp-witted criminal would know better than to confess; why should the dull-witted suffer for his lack of mental endowment? Providing him an attorney at every stage where he might be induced or persuaded (though not coerced) to incriminate himself will even the odds. Apart from the fact that this protective enterprise is beyond our authority under the Fifth Amendment or any other provision of the Constitution, it is unwise. The procedural protections of the Constitution protect the guilty as well as the innocent, but it is not their objective to set the guilty free. That some clever criminals may employ those protections to their advantage is poor reason to allow criminals who have not done so to escape justice.

Thus, even if I were to concede that an honest confession is a foolish mistake, I would welcome rather than reject it; a rule that foolish mistakes do not count would leave most offenders not only unconvicted but undetected. More fundamentally, however, it is wrong, and subtly corrosive of our criminal justice system, to regard an honest confession as a "mistake." While every person is entitled to stand silent, it is more virtuous for the wrongdoer to admit his offense and accept the punishment he deserves. Not only for society, but for the wrongdoer himself, "admissio[n] of guilt [if] not coerced, [is] inherently desirable," because it advances the goals of both "justice *and* rehabilitation." *Michigan v. Tucker* (emphasis added). A confession is rightly regarded by the sentencing guidelines as warranting a reduction of sentence, because it "demonstrates a recognition and affirmative acceptance of personal responsibility [for] criminal conduct," U.S. Sentencing Commission, Guidelines Manual § 3E1.1 (1988), which is the beginning of reform. We should, then, rejoice at an honest confession, rather than pity the "poor fool" who has made it; and we should regret the attempted retraction of that good act, rather than seek to facilitate and encourage it. To design our laws on premises contrary to these is to abandon belief in either personal responsibility or the moral claim of just government to obedience. Cf. Caplan, Questioning *Miranda*, 38 Vand.L. Rev. 1417, 1471–1473 (1985). Today's decision is misguided, it seems to me, in so readily exchanging, for marginal, *super-Zerbst* protection against genuinely compelled testimony, investigators' ability to urge, or even ask, a person in custody to do what is right.

7th ed., p. 523; add to Note 16(d):

16(d). *Application of Edwards rule to Sixth Amendment right to counsel.* In Mc-NEIL v. WISCONSIN, ___ U.S. ___, 111 S.Ct. 2204, 115 L.Ed.2d 158 (1991), a 6–3 majority held that a suspect's assertion of his Sixth Amendment right to counsel, by his appearance with counsel at a bail hearing concerning an offense with which he had been charged, does not serve as an invocation of the Fifth Amendment-based *Miranda–Edwards–Roberson* right to have counsel present during custodial interrogation. Thus, assertion of the Sixth Amendment right does not prevent the police from initiating counselless interrogation

about unrelated and uncharged crimes. The Sixth Amendment right is "offense specific" and the *Michigan v. Jackson* ban on counselless interrogation—unlike the *Edwards–Roberson* rule—is similarly limited.

The case arose as follows: After his arrest, pursuant to a warrant charging him with an armed robbery in West Allis (the West Allis crime), McNeil was represented by a public defender at a bail hearing. The commissioner set bail and scheduled a preliminary examination. Later that evening, a deputy sheriff, who had been investigating a murder, attempted murder and burglary in Caledonia (the Caledonia crimes), visited McNeil in jail. McNeil waived his *Miranda* rights, but said he had not been involved in the Caledonia crimes (although he did not deny knowledge of them). The deputy sheriff returned two days later with Caledonia detectives. McNeil again waived his rights and, this time, admitted his involvement in the Caledonia crimes. Two days later, the deputy sheriff returned for the third time, again with the Caledonia police. McNeil waived his rights again, and made additional incriminating statements. The following day, McNeil was formally charged with the Caledonia crimes. After his pretrial motion to suppress the incriminating statements was denied, McNeil was convicted, *inter alia*, of murder and attempted murder. The Court, per SCALIA, J., rejected his contention that his appearance at the bail hearing for the West Allis crime constituted an invocation of the *Miranda–Edwards–Roberson* right to counsel:

"The Sixth Amendment [right to counsel] is offense-specific. It cannot be invoked once for all future prosecutions, for it does not attach until a prosecution is commenced * * *. And just as the right is offense-specific, so also its *Michigan v. Jackson* effect of invalidating subsequent waivers in police-initiated interviews is offense-specific. * * * Because petitioner provided the statements at issue here before his Sixth Amendment right to counsel with respect to the *Caledonia* offenses had been (or even could have been) invoked, the right poses no bar to the admission of the statements in this case.

" * * * Petitioner seeks to prevail by combining the [*Miranda–Edwards* right to counsel and the Sixth Amendment right]. He contends that, although he expressly waived his *Miranda* right to counsel on every occasion he was interrogated, those waivers were the invalid product of impermissible approaches, because his prior invocation of the offense-specific right with regard to the West Allis burglary was also an invocation of the non-offense-West Allis burglary was also an invocation of the non-offense-specific *Miranda–Edwards* right. We think that is false as a matter of fact and inadvisable (even if permissible) as a contrary-to-fact presumption of policy.

"As to the former: The purpose of the Sixth Amendment counsel guarantee—and hence the purpose of invoking it—is to 'protec[t] the unaided layman at critical confrontations' with his 'expert adversary,' the government, *after* 'the adverse positions of government and defendant have solidified' with respect to a particular alleged crime. The purpose of the *Miranda–Edwards* guarantee, on the other hand—and hence the purpose of invoking it—is to protect a quite different interest: the suspect's 'desire to deal with the police only through counsel,' *Edwards.* [To] invoke the Sixth Amendment interest is, as a matter of *fact, not* to invoke the *Miranda–Edwards* interest. One might be quite willing to speak to the police without counsel present concerning many matters, but not the matter under prosecution. It can be said, perhaps, that it is *likely* that one who has asked for counsel's assistance in defending against a prosecution would want counsel present for all custodial interrogation, even interrogation unrelated to the charge. That is not necessarily true, since suspects often believe that they can avoid the laying of charges by demonstrating an assurance of innocence through frank and unassisted answers to questions. But even if it were true, the *likelihood* that

a suspect would wish counsel to be present is not the test for applicability of *Edwards.* The rule of that case applies only when the suspect 'ha[s] *expressed*' his wish for the particular sort of lawyerly assistance that is the subject of *Miranda. Edwards* (emphasis added). It requires, at a minimum, some statement that can reasonably be construed to be expression of a desire for the assistance of an attorney *in dealing with custodial interrogation by the police.* Requesting the assistance of an attorney at a bail hearing does not bear that construction.

* * *

"There remains to be considered the possibility that, even though the assertion of the Sixth Amendment right to counsel does not *in fact* imply an assertion of the *Miranda* 'Fifth Amendment' right, we should declare it to be such as a matter of sound policy. Assuming we have such an expansive power under the Constitution, it would not wisely be exercised. Petitioner's proposed rule has only insignificant advantages. If a suspect does not wish to communicate with the police except through an attorney, he can simply tell them that when they give him the *Miranda* warnings. There is not the remotest chance that he will feel 'badgered' by their asking to talk to him without counsel present, since the subject will not be the charge on which he has already requested counsel's assistance (for in that event *Jackson* would preclude initiation of the interview) and he will not have rejected uncounseled interrogation on *any* subject before (for in that event *Edwards* would preclude initiation of the interview). The proposed rule would, however, seriously impede effective law enforcement. The Sixth Amendment right to counsel attaches at the first formal proceeding against an accused, and in most States, at least with respect to serious offenses, free counsel is made available at that time and ordinarily requested. Thus, if we were to adopt petitioner's rule, most persons in pretrial custody for serious offenses would be *unapproachable* by police officers suspecting them of involvement in other crimes, *even though they have never expressed any unwillingness to be questioned.* Since the ready ability to obtain uncoerced confessions is not an evil but an unmitigated good, society would be the loser. * * * [2]

"Petitioner urges upon us the desirability of providing a 'clear and unequivocal' guideline for the police: no police-initiated questioning of any person in custody who has requested counsel to assist him in defense or in interrogation. But the police do not need our assistance to establish such a guideline; they are free, if they wish, to adopt it on their own. Of course it *is* our task to establish guidelines for judicial review. We like *them* to be 'clear and unequivocal,' but only when they guide sensibly, and in a direction we are authorized to go. Petitioner's proposal would in our view do much more harm than good, and is not contained within, or

even in furtherance of, the Sixth Amendment's right to counsel or the Fifth Amendment's right against compelled self-incrimination.[3]

* * *

" 'This Court is forever adding new stories to the temples of constitutional law, and the temples have a way of collapsing when one story too many is added.' We decline to add yet another story to *Miranda.*" [a]

Dissenting JUSTICE STEVENS, joined by Marshall and Blackmun, JJ., protested:

"The Court's opinion demeans the importance of the right to counsel. As a practical matter, the opinion probably will have only a slight impact on current custodial interrogation procedures. As a theoretical matter, the Court's innovative development of an 'offense-specific' limitation on the scope of the attorney-client relationship can only generate confu-

---

2. The dissent condemns these sentiments as "revealing a preference for an inquisitorial system of justice." We cannot imagine what this means. What makes a system adversarial rather than inquisitorial is not the presence of counsel, much less the presence of counsel where the defendant has not requested it; but rather, the presence of a judge who does not (as an inquisitor does) conduct the factual and legal investigation himself, but instead decides on the basis of facts and arguments pro and con adduced by the parties. In the inquisitorial criminal process of the civil law, the defendant ordinarily has counsel; and in the adversarial criminal process of the common law, he sometimes does not. Our system of justice is, and has always been, an inquisitorial one at the investigatory stage (even the grand jury is an inquisitorial body), and no other disposition is conceivable. Even if detectives were to bring impartial magistrates around with them to all interrogations, there would be no decision for the impartial magistrate to umpire. If all the dissent means by a "preference for an inquisitorial system" is a preference not to require the presence of counsel during an investigatory interview where the interviewee has not requested it—that is a strange way to put it, but we are guilty.

3. The dissent predicts that the result in this case will routinely be circumvented when, "[i]n future preliminary hearings, competent counsel . . . make sure that they, or their clients, make a statement on the record" invoking the *Miranda* right to counsel. We have in fact never held that a person can invoke his *Miranda* rights anticipatorily, in a context other than "custodial interro-

gation"—which a preliminary hearing will not always, or even usually, involve, cf. *Pennsylvania v. Muniz* [Supp., p. 40] (plurality opinion); *Rhode Island v. Innis.* If the *Miranda* right to counsel can be invoked at a preliminary hearing, it could be argued, there is no logical reason why it could not be invoked by a letter prior to arrest, or indeed even prior to identification as a suspect. Most rights must be asserted when the government seeks to take the action they protect against. The fact that we have allowed the *Miranda* right to counsel, once asserted, to be effective with respect to future custodial interrogation does not necessarily mean that we will allow it to be asserted initially outside the context of custodial interrogation, with similar future effect. Assuming, however, that an assertion at arraignment would be effective, and would be routinely made, the mere fact that adherence to the principle of our decisions will not have substantial consequences is no reason to abandon that principle. It would remain intolerable that a person in custody who had expressed *no* objection to being questioned would be unapproachable.

a. Justice Kennedy joined the majority opinion, but maintained, as he had in his *Roberson* dissent, that the Court's "sensible recognition that invocation of the Sixth Amendment right to counsel is specific to the offense in question should apply as well to requests for counsel under the Fifth Amendment." Thus, even if McNeil had invoked his *Miranda–Edwards* right with respect to the West Allis robbery, he would have allowed the police to question him about the Caledonia offenses.

sion in the law and undermine the protections that undergird our adversarial system of justice. As a symbolic matter, today's decision is ominous because it reflects a preference for an inquisitorial system that regards the defense lawyer as an impediment rather than a servant to the cause of justice.

"The predicate for the Court's entire analysis is the failure of the defendant at the preliminary hearing to make a 'statement that can reasonably be construed to be expression of a desire for the assistance of an attorney *in dealing with custodial interrogation by the police.*' If petitioner in this case had made such a statement indicating that he was invoking his Fifth Amendment right to counsel as well as his Sixth Amendment right to counsel, the entire offense-specific house of cards that the Court has erected today would collapse, pursuant to our holding in *Roberson,* that a defendant who invokes the right to counsel for interrogation on one offense may not be reapproached regarding any offense unless counsel is present.

"In future preliminary hearings, competent counsel can be expected to make sure that they, or their clients, make a statement on the record that will obviate the consequences of today's holding. That is why I think this decision will have little, if any, practical effect on police practices.

* * *

"[The] Court's 'offense-specific' characterization of the constitutional right to counsel ignores the substance of the attorney-client relationship that the legal profession has developed over the years. The scope of the relationship between an individual accused of crime and his attorney is as broad as the subject matter that might reasonably be encompassed by negotiations for a plea bargain or the contents of a presentence investigation report. Any notion that a constitutional right to counsel is, or should be, narrowly defined by the elements of a pending charge is both unrealistic and invidious. Particularly given

the implication that McNeil would be given favorable treatment if he told 'his side of the story' as to either or both crimes to the Milwaukee County officers, I find the Court's restricted construal of McNeil's relationship with his appointed attorney at the arraignment on the armed robbery charges to be unsupported.

"In any case, the offense-specific limitation on the Sixth Amendment right to counsel can only generate confusion in the law. The parties and the Court have assumed in this case, for the purposes of analyzing the legal issues, that the custodial interrogation of McNeil involved an offense (murder) that was completely unrelated to the pending charge of armed robbery. The Court therefore does not flesh out the precise boundaries of its newly created 'offense-specific' limitation on a venerable constitutional right. I trust its boundaries will not be patterned after the Court's double jeopardy jurisprudence, and I can only wonder how much leeway it will accord the police to file charges selectively in order to preserve opportunities for custodial interrogation, particularly if the Court is so unquestioningly willing to treat the offenses in this case as separate even though the investigations were concurrent and conducted by overlapping personnel. Whatever the future may portend, the Court's new rule can only dim the 'bright-line' quality of prior cases such as *Edwards* [and] *Michigan v. Jackson.*

"In the final analysis, the Court's decision is explained by its fear that making counsel available to persons held in custody would 'seriously impede effective law enforcement.' The magnitude of the Court's alarm is illuminated by its use of italics:

'Thus, if we were to adopt petitioner's rule, most persons in pretrial custody for serious offenses would be *unapproachable* by police officers suspecting them of involvement in other crimes, *even though they have never expressed any unwillingness to be questioned.*'

"Of course, the Court is quite wrong and its fears are grossly exaggerated. The fears are exaggerated because, as I have explained, today's holding will probably affect very few cases in the future. The fears are misguided because a contrary rule would not make all pretrial detainees 'unapproachable'; it would merely serve to ensure that a suspect's statements during custodial interrogation are truly voluntary.

"A contrary rule would also comport with respect to tradition. Undergirding our entire line of cases requiring the police to follow fair procedures when they interrogate presumptively innocent citizens suspected of criminal wrongdoing is the longstanding recognition that an adversarial system of justice can function effectively only when the adversaries communicate with one another through counsel and when laypersons are protected from overreaching by more experienced and skilled professionals. Whenever the Court ignores the importance of fair procedure in this context and describes the societal interest in obtaining 'uncoerced confessions' from pretrial detainees as an 'unmitigated good,' the Court is revealing a preference for an inquisitorial system of justice. As I suggested in *Moran v. Burbine:*

'This case turns on a proper appraisal of the role of the lawyer in our society. If a lawyer is seen as a nettlesome obstacle to the pursuit of wrongdoers—as in an inquisitorial society—then the Court's decision today makes a good deal of sense. If a lawyer is seen as an aid to the understanding and protection of constitutional rights—as in an accusatorial society—then today's decision makes

2. In his opinion dissenting for himself and two other members of the Wisconsin Supreme Court, Chief Justice Heffernan wrote:

"It is apparent that there is danger of 'subtle compulsion' when a defendant requests the assistance of an attorney at an initial appearance and is nevertheless subjected to further interrogation while custody continues. Whether a request for an attorney is made to a police officer or to a judge, whether in the jail or during an initial

no sense at all.' (Stevens, J., dissenting).

"The Court's refusal to acknowledge any 'danger of "subtle compulsion" ' [2] in a case of this kind evidences an inability to recognize the difference between an inquisitorial and an adversarial system of justice."

SECTION 4. THE "DUE PROCESS"—"VOLUNTARINESS" TEST REVISITED

7th ed., p. 560; revise first full ¶:

The statement that "improper use of an involuntary confession seems to require automatic reversal on appeal" is no longer accurate. In *Arizona v. Fulminante,* Supp., p. 146, the Court held that the harmless-error rule applies to the erroneous admission of a coerced confession.

A. *Miller v. Fenton:* WHAT KINDS OF TRICKERY OR DECEPTION, IF ANY, MAY THE POLICE EMPLOY AFTER A SUSPECT HAS WAIVED HIS RIGHTS?

7th ed., p. 570; before Sec. B, add new Note 6;

6. *Offering to protect a prisoner from physical harm at the hands of other inmates.* Consider ARIZONA v. FULMINANTE, ——— U.S. ———, 111 S.Ct. 1246, 113 L.Ed.2d 302 (1991) (other aspects of which are discussed at Supp., p. 146). The case arose as follows: After defendant Fulminante's 11–year–old stepdaughter, Jeneane, was murdered, he was convicted of an unrelated federal crime and incarcerated in a federal prison. There he was befriended by another inmate, Sarivola, who was a paid informant for the FBI masquerading as an organized crime figure. Upon hear-

Facts

appearance, the dangers of the inherent pressure of custodial interrogation when not having an attorney present are the same. Just as the *Edwards* protection is not dependent upon the subject matter of the interrogation, neither is this protection dependent upon whether the request for assistance of counsel is made to a police officer while in custody or to a magistrate at an initial appearance before the defendant is interrogated."

ing a rumor that defendant had killed his stepdaughter, Sarivola brought up the subject several times, but defendant repeatedly denied any involvement in the murder. Then Sarivola told defendant that he knew he was "starting to get some tough treatment" from other inmates because of the rumor that he had killed his stepdaughter but that he, Sarivola, would protect defendant from his fellow inmates if he told him the truth about the murder. Defendant then confessed to Sarivola that he had sexually molested and killed Jeneane. The confession was admitted at defendant's trial and he was convicted of murder and sentenced to death. On appeal, the state supreme court held that the confession was coerced. Although it considered the question "a close one," a 5–4 majority of the Supreme Court, per WHITE, J., agreed with the state supreme court:

PP

holding

"In applying the totality of the circumstances test to determine that the confession to Sarivola was coerced, the Arizona Supreme Court focused on a number of relevant facts. First, the court noted that 'because [Fulminante] was an alleged child murderer, he was in physical harm at the hands of other inmates.' In addition, Sarivola was aware that Fulminante was receiving 'rough treatment from the guys.' Using his knowledge of these threats, Sarivola offered to protect Fulminante in exchange for a confession to Jeneane's murder and 'in response to Sarivola's offer of protection [Fulminante] confessed.' Agreeing with Fulminante that 'Sarivola's promise was "extremely coercive,"' the Arizona Court declared: '[T]he confession was obtained as a direct result of extreme coercion and was tendered in the belief that the defendant's life was in jeopardy if he did not confess. * * * '

"We normally give great deference to the factual findings of the state court. Nevertheless, 'the ultimate issue of "voluntariness" is a legal question requiring independent federal determination.'

"Although the question is a close one, we agree [that] Fulminante's confession was coerced. The Arizona Supreme Court found a credible threat of physical violence unless Fulminante confessed. Our cases have made clear that a finding of coercion need not depend upon actual violence by a government agent; a credible threat is sufficient. * * * As in [*Payne v. Arkansas*, 356 U.S. 560, 78 S.Ct. 844, 2 L.Ed.2d 975 (1958)], where the Court found that a confession was coerced because the interrogating police officer had promised that if the accused confessed, the officer would protect the accused from an angry mob outside the jailhouse door, so too here, the Arizona Supreme Court found that it was fear of physical violence, absent protection from his friend (and Government agent) Sarivola, which motivated Fulminante to confess. Accepting the Arizona court's finding, permissible on this record, that there was a credible threat of physical violence, we agree with its conclusion that Fulminante's will was overborne in such a way as to render his confession the product of coercion."

Dissenting on this issue, REHNQUIST, C.J., joined by O'Connor, Kennedy and Souter, JJ., was "at a loss to see how the Supreme Court of Arizona reached the conclusion that it did":

"Fulminante offered no evidence that he believed his life was in danger or that he in fact confessed to Sarivola in order to obtain the proffered protection. Indeed, he had stipulated that '[a]t no time did the defendant indicate he was in fear of other inmates nor did he ever seek Mr. Sarivola's "protection."' Sarivola's testimony that he told Fulminante that 'if [he] would tell the truth, he could be protected,' adds little if anything to the substance of the parties' stipulation. The decision of the Supreme Court of Arizona rests on an assumption that is squarely contrary to this stipulation, and one that is not supported by any testimony of Fulminante.

"The facts of record in the present case are quite different from those present in cases where we have found confessions to be coerced and involuntary. Since Fulminante was unaware that Sarivola was an FBI informant, there existed none of 'the danger of coercion result[ing] from the interaction of custody and official interrogation.' *Illinois v. Perkins* [Supp., p. 48]. [The] conversations between Sarivola and Fulminante were not lengthy, and the defendant was free at all times to leave Sarivola's company. Sarivola at no time threatened him or demanded that he confess; he simply requested that he speak the truth about the matter. Fulminante was an experienced habitue of prisons, and presumably able to fend for himself. In concluding on these facts that Fulminante's confession was involuntary, the Court today embraces a more expansive definition of that term than is warranted by any of our decided cases."

Chapter 10

GRAND JURY INVESTIGATIONS

SECTION 1. THE ROLE OF THE INVESTIGATIVE GRAND JURY

7th ed., p. 639; end of fn. b, add:

In *Butterworth v. Smith*, 494 U.S. 624, 110 S.Ct. 1376, 108 L.Ed.2d 572 (1990), the Court sustained a First Amendment challenge to a state statute that imposed a secrecy obligation upon a grand jury witness (extending to the "content, gist, or import" of his testimony) insofar as that obligation extended beyond the point of discharge of the grand jury. The Court reasoned that several of the traditional functions of grand jury secrecy were no longer served by a witness-secrecy requirement following the end of the grand jury's investigation, and those that remained were "not sufficient to overcome [the witness'] First Amendment right to make a truthful statement of information he acquired on his own."

7th ed., p. 646; add at the end of Note 5:

Consider also the discussion in *United States v. Williams*, Supp. p. 96.

SECTION 2. CHALLENGES TO THE INVESTIGATION

7th ed., p. 678, end of Note 5, add:

Compare the position taken by the Supreme Court in UNITED STATES v. R. ENTERPRISES, INC., ___ U.S. ___, 111 S.Ct. 722, 112 L.Ed.2d 795 (1991). Federal Rule 17(c) authorizes a federal district court to quash or modify subpoenas duces tecum "if compliance would be unreasonable or oppressive." *United States v. Nixon*, 418 U.S. 683, 94 S.Ct. 3090, 41 L.Ed.2d 1039 (1974), dealing with a trial subpoena, established pursuant to Rule 17(c) three prerequisites for enforcement of a subpoena. The court below had held that the same three prerequisites—requiring a showing of "relevancy, admissibility, and specificity" as to the material being subpoenaed—also applied to a grand jury subpoena. The Supreme Court unanimously rejected this position. Speaking for six justices, Justice O'CONNOR noted in the opinion for the Court:

"This Court has emphasized on numerous occasions that many of the rules and restrictions that apply at a trial do not apply in grand jury proceedings. This is especially true of evidentiary restrictions. The same rules that, in an adversary hearing on the merits, may increase the likelihood of accurate determinations of guilt or innocence do not necessarily advance the mission of a grand jury, whose task is to conduct an *ex parte* investigation to determine whether or not there is probable cause to prosecute a particular defendant. * * * The teaching of the Court's decision is clear: A grand jury 'may compel the production of evidence or the testimony of witnesses as it considers appropriate, and its operation generally is unrestrained by the technical procedural and evidentiary rules governing the conduct of criminal trials.' *United States v. Calandra*.

"This guiding principle renders suspect the Court of Appeals' holding that the standards announced in *Nixon* as to subpoenas issued in anticipation of trial apply equally in the grand jury context. The multifactor test announced in *Nixon* would invite procedural delays and detours while courts evaluate the relevancy and admissibility of documents sought by a particular subpoena. We have expressly stated that grand jury proceedings should be free of such delays. * * * *United States v. Dionisio*. Additionally, application of the *Nixon* test in this context ignores that grand jury

68

proceedings are subject to strict secrecy requirements. See Fed.Rule Crim.Proc. 6(e). Requiring the Government to explain in too much detail the particular reasons underlying a subpoena threatens to compromise 'the indispensable secrecy of grand jury proceedings.' Broad disclosure also affords the targets of investigation far more information about the grand jury's internal workings than the Federal Rules of Criminal Procedure appear to contemplate.

"The investigatory powers of the grand jury are nevertheless not unlimited. Grand juries are not licensed to engage in arbitrary fishing expeditions, nor may they select targets of investigation out of malice or an intent to harass. In this case, the focus of our inquiry is the limit imposed on a grand jury by Federal Rule of Criminal Procedure 17(c), which governs the issuance of subpoenas *duces tecum* in federal criminal proceedings. The Rule provides that 'the court on motion made promptly may quash or modify the subpoena if compliance would be unreasonable or oppressive.' This standard is not self-explanatory. As we have observed, 'what is reasonable depends on the context.' * * * In the grand jury context, the decision as to what offense will be charged is routinely not made until after the grand jury has concluded its investigation. One simply cannot know in advance whether information sought during the investigation will be relevant and admissible in a prosecution for a particular offense.

"To the extent that Rule 17(c) imposes some reasonableness limitation on grand jury subpoenas, however, our task is to define it. In doing so, we recognize that a party to whom a grand jury subpoena is issued faces a difficult situation. As a rule, grand juries, do not announce publicly the subjects of their investigations. A party who desires to challenge a grand jury subpoena thus may have no conception of the Government's purpose in seeking production of the requested information. Indeed, the party will often not know wheth-

er he or she is a primary target of the investigation or merely a peripheral witness. Absent even minimal information, the subpoena recipient is likely to find it exceedingly difficult to persuade a court that 'compliance would be unreasonable.' As one pair of commentators has summarized it, the challenging party's 'unenviable task is to seek to persuade the court that the subpoena that has been served on [him or her] could not possibly serve any investigative purpose that the grand jury could legitimately be pursuing.' S. Beale & W. Bryson, *Grand Jury Law and Practice* § 6:28 (1986).

"Our task is to fashion an appropriate standard of reasonableness, one that gives due weight to the difficult position of subpoena recipients but does not impair the strong governmental interests in affording grand juries wide latitude, avoiding minitrials on peripheral matters, and preserving a necessary level of secrecy. We begin by reiterating that the law presumes, absent a strong showing to the contrary, that a grand jury acts within the legitimate scope of its authority. * * * Consequently, a grand jury subpoena issued through normal channels is presumed to be reasonable, and the burden of showing unreasonableness must be on the recipient who seeks to avoid compliance. * * * To the extent that the Court of Appeals placed an initial burden on the Government, it committed error. Drawing on the principles articulated above, we conclude that where, as here, a subpoena is challenged on relevancy grounds, the motion to quash must be denied unless the district court determines that there is no reasonable possibility that the category of materials the Government seeks will produce information relevant to the general subject of the grand jury's investigation. Respondents did not challenge the subpoenas as being too indefinite nor did they claim that compliance would be overly burdensome. The Court of Appeals accordingly did not consider these aspects of the subpoenas, nor do we.

"It seems unlikely, of course, that a challenging party who does not know the general subject matter of the grand jury's investigation, no matter how valid that party's claim, will be able to make the necessary showing that compliance would be unreasonable. After all, a subpoena recipient 'cannot put his whole life before the court in order to show that there is no crime to be investigated.' Consequently, a court may be justified in a case where unreasonableness is alleged in requiring the Government to reveal the general subject of the grand jury's investigation before requiring the challenging party to carry its burden of persuasion. We need not resolve this question in the present case, however, as there is no doubt that respondents knew the subject of the grand jury investigation pursuant to which the business records subpoenas were issued. In cases where the recipient of the subpoena does not know the nature of the investigation, we are confident that district courts will be able to craft appropriate procedures that balance the interests of the subpoena recipient against the strong governmental interests in maintaining secrecy, preserving investigatory flexibility, and avoiding procedural delays. For example, to ensure that subpoenas are not routinely challenged as a form of discovery, a district court may require that the Government reveal the subject of the investigation to the trial court *in camera,* so that the court may determine whether the motion to quash has a reasonable prospect for success before it discloses the subject matter to the challenging party." [a]

Justice STEVENS, joined by Marshall and Blackmun, J.J., joined that portion of the Court's opinion that rejected the application of the *Nixon* prerequisites. His concurring opinion added:

a. Justice Scalia did not join in this paragraph.

b. The investigation in question related to interstate transportation of obscene materials, and the subpoena sought copies of 93 videotapes

"This rule [17(c)] requires the district court to balance the burden of compliance, on the one hand, against the governmental interest in obtaining the documents on the other. A more burdensome subpoena should be justified by a somewhat higher degree of probable relevance than a subpoena that imposes a minimal or nonexistent burden. Against the procedural history of this case, the Court has attempted to define the term 'reasonable' in the abstract, looking only at the relevance side of the balance. Because I believe that this truncated approach to the Rule will neither provide adequate guidance to the district court nor place any meaningful constraint on the overzealous prosecutor, I add these comments. * * * The moving party has the initial task of demonstrating to the Court that he has some valid objection to compliance. This showing might be made in various ways. Depending on the volume and location of the requested materials, the mere cost in terms of time, money, and effort of responding to a dragnet subpoena could satisfy the initial hurdle. Similarly, if a witness showed that compliance with the subpoena would intrude significantly on his privacy interests, or call for the disclosure of trade secrets or other confidential information, further inquiry would be required. Or, as in this case, the movant might demonstrate that compliance would have First Amendment implications. [b]

"The trial court need inquire into the relevance of subpoenaed materials only after the moving party has made this initial showing. And, as is true in the parallel context of pretrial civil discovery, a matter also committed to the sound discretion of the trial judge, the degree of need sufficient to justify denial of the motion to quash will vary to some extent with the burden of producing the requested infor-

that had been shipped to various retailers. The lower court had relied solely on Rule 17(c) in quashing the subpoenas and had not reached the First Amendment claim.

mation. For the reasons stated by the Court, in the grand jury context the law enforcement interest will almost always prevail, and the documents must be produced. I stress, however, that the Court's opinion should not be read to suggest that the deferential relevance standard the Court has formulated will govern decision in every case, no matter how intrusive or burdensome the request."

SECTION 3. APPLICATION OF THE PRIVILEGE AGAINST SELF–INCRIMINATION

7th ed., p. 687; in lieu of Notes 4 and 5, add:

4. *Subsequent prosecution and the problem of "taint."* How extensive is the *Kastigar* prohibition against derivative use? What showing must the government make to establish that the prosecution of a previously immunized witness is "untainted"? Consider the discussion of these issues in UNITED STATES v. NORTH, 910 F.2d 843 (D.C.Cir.1990). The defendant North had been granted immunity by Congress in the course of highly publicized hearings on what came to be known as the Iran–Contra affair. At the time of the Congressional hearings, a grand jury investigation of the same activities, directed by a specially appointed Independent Counsel, had been well underway. Defendant raised a *Kastigar* challenge both to his subsequent indictment and conviction. A divided Court of Appeals (2–1) held that the district court had erred in the treatment of those claims and remanded for further proceedings. The per curiam opinion for the majority (SILBERMAN and SENTELLE, JJ.) reasoned:

"When the government proceeds to prosecute a previously immunized witness, it has 'the heavy burden of proving that all of the evidence it proposes to use was derived from legitimate independent sources.' *Kastigar.* Most courts following *Kastigar* have imposed a 'preponderance of the evidence' evidentiary burden on the government. * * * A trial court must

normally hold a hearing (a '*Kastigar* hearing') for the purpose of allowing the government to demonstrate that it obtained all of the evidence it proposes to use from sources independent of the compelled testimony. As this court [has noted previously], a trial court may hold a *Kastigar* hearing pre-trial, post-trial mid-trial (as evidence is offered) or it may employ some combination of these methods. A pre-trial hearing is the most common choice. * * * Whenever the hearing is held, the failure of the government to meet its burden can have most drastic consequences. * * * Dismissal of the indictment or vacation of the conviction is not necessary [only] where the use is found to be harmless beyond a reasonable doubt. * * *

"Before North's trial, the District Court held a 'preliminary' *Kastigar* inquiry and issued an order based thereon which it subsequently adopted as final (with certain changes) without benefit of further proceedings or hearings. * * * North's primary *Kastigar* complaint is that the District Court failed to require the Independent Counsel ('IC') to demonstrate an independent source for each item of evidence or testimony presented to the grand jury and the petit jury, and that the District Court erred in focusing almost wholly on the IC's leads to witnesses, rather than on the content of the witnesses' testimony. North also claims that the IC made an improper nonevidentiary use of the immunized testimony (as by employing it for purposes of trial strategy), or at least that the District Court failed to make a sufficient inquiry into the question. North also protests that his immunized testimony was improperly used to refresh the recollection of witnesses before the grand jury and at trial, that this refreshment caused them to alter their testimony, and that the District Court failed to give this question the careful examination it deserved. In our discussion here, we first consider alleged nonevidentiary use of immunized testimony by the IC. We will then proceed to consider the use of immunized testimony to refresh witnesses' recollections. Finally, we will address the distinction between use of immunized testimony as a lead to procure witnesses and use insofar as it affects the substantive content of witnesses' testimony. * * *

"1. *'Nonevidentiary' Use.* The District Court briefly discussed the problem of nonevidentiary use of immunized testimony through witnesses and through the IC's staff. The District Court found that witnesses had their memories refreshed with immunized testimony by 'hearing the testimony, reading about it, being questioned about aspects of it before the Select Committees and, to some extent, by exposure to it in the course of responding to inquiries within their respective agencies.' This exposure was not motivated, the Court found, by a desire 'to harm a defendant or help the prosecution.' The District Court concluded that in such a circumstance a 'trial before the trial' was not necessary because '[n]o court has ever so required, nor did *Kastigar* suggest anything of the kind.' The District Court was similarly untroubled by allegations of prosecutorial exposure to immunized testimony through a grand juror or a witness: * * * As a matter of 'common sense,' the District Court determined that a 'prosecutor who inadvertently overhears mention of a fact already confirmed by his own independent investigation' cannot be said to have used immunized testimony; similarly, a defendant's 'Fifth Amendment rights are not infringed if a witness hears immunized testimony yet testifies solely to facts personally known to the witness.' The District Court concluded that '[t]he good faith of Independent Counsel cannot be questioned on this record.'

"This Circuit has never squarely addressed the question of whether or not *Kastigar* encompasses so-called nonevidentiary use of immunized testimony. The federal use immunity statute does not speak in terms of 'evidence,' but rather provides that 'no testimony *or other infor-*

mation compelled under the order (*or any information directly or indirectly derived from such testimony or other information*) may be used against the witness in any criminal case' 18 U.S.C. § 6002 (emphasis supplied). *Kastigar* does not define, except perhaps by implication, what nonevidentiary use of compelled testimony might be nor does it expressly discuss the permissible scope of such use. [Courts in other Circuits] have differed on this question. * * *

"An initial difficulty is that a precise definition of the term nonevidentiary use is elusive. * * * Thus, we follow the lead of other courts and delineate nonevidentiary use by example rather than definition: 'One court has described such nonevidentiary use as "conceivably includ[ing] assistance in focusing the investigation, deciding to initiate prosecution, refusing to plea bargain, interpreting evidence, planning cross-examination, and otherwise generally planning trial strategy." ' * * * Prosecutorial knowledge of the immunized testimony may help explicate evidence theretofore unintelligible, and it may expose as significant facts once thought irrelevant (or vice versa). Compelled testimony could indicate which witnesses to call, and in what order. Compelled testimony may be helpful in developing opening and closing arguments. * * *

"Construing *Kastigar* in *United States v. McDaniel,* 482 F.2d 305 (8th Cir.1973), the Eighth Circuit forbade 'all prosecutorial use of the testimony, not merely that which results in the presentation of evidence before the jury.' Through a misunderstanding of North Dakota law, the United States Attorney read three transcript volumes of McDaniel's immunized state grand jury testimony before he obtained the indictment from the federal grand jury. He did not know that McDaniel was immunized, so 'he therefore could have perceived no reason to segregate McDaniel's testimony from his other sources of information.' Similarly, the court could not 'escape the conclusion that the testimony could not be wholly obliterated from the prosecutor's mind in his preparation and trial of the case.' The court concluded that 'if the immunity protection is to be coextensive with the Fifth Amendment privilege, as it must to be constitutionally sufficient, then it must forbid all prosecutorial use of the testimony, not merely that which results in the presentation of evidence before the jury.'

"The *McDaniel* rule has been criticized or rejected by *United States v. Serrano*, 870 F.2d 1 (1st Cir.1989), *United States v. Mariani*, 851 F.2d 595 (2d Cir.1988), and *United States v. Crownson*, 828 F.2d 1427 (9th Cir.1987). * * * [T]he First Circuit [in *Serrano*] disagreed with the *McDaniel* standard in dicta, stating that '[s]uch an approach amounts to a per se rule that would in effect grant a defendant *transactional* immunity once it is shown that government attorneys or investigators involved in the prosecution were exposed to the immunized testimony.' * * * In *Byrd*, the Eleventh Circuit [stated that] * * * '[t]he privilege against self-incrimination is concerned with direct and indirect *evidentiary* uses of compelled testimony and not with the exercise of prosecutorial discretion.' * * * We note that in a case following *Byrd*, the Eleventh Circuit continued to insist that *Kastigar* is concerned with evidentiary use only, but the court included as 'evidentiary' certain 'investigatory' uses that could reasonably be considered to be nonevidentiary.

* * * [Also], in language which places in some doubt the Second Circuit's apparent rejection in *Mariani* of the *McDaniel* approach, *United States v. Schwimmer*, 882 F.2d 22 (2d Cir.1989), * * * points out the danger of use that 'might assist the prosecutor in focusing additional investigation, planning, cross-examination, or otherwise generally mapping a strategy for retrial,' and suggests that the prosecutors, in the event of a retrial, should establish a Chinese wall.

" * * * Insofar as *Serrano, Mariani*, and *Byrd* may be read as establishing a rule that *Kastigar* allows nonevidentiary use of compelled testimony under all circumstances, we find those cases troubling. We are not unsympathetic, nevertheless, to the concerns voiced by the First, Second and Eleventh Circuits * * *. In the present appeal, the record is extensive and the District Court's findings are thorough as to precautions taken by the IC to prevent untoward exposure or use by his staff.[a] The record is clear and the findings are not clearly erroneous. Without significant exposure, the IC could not have made significant nonevidentiary use, permissible or impermissible. Thus, even assuming without deciding that a prosecutor cannot make nonevidentiary use of immunized testimony, in the case before us the IC did not do so. We do not reach the precise question, therefore, of the permissible quantum of nonevidentiary use by prosecutors, or indeed whether such use is per-

a. The district court had pointed to "several administrative steps which were taken by Independent Counsel from an early date to prevent exposure of himself and his associate counsel to any immunized testimony." Prosecuting personnel "were sealed off from exposure to the immunized testimony itself and publicity concerning it." "Nonprosecuting 'tainted' personnel" redacted all newspaper clippings, transcripts and similar material made available to the prosecuting personnel. The prosecuting personnel also was "instructed to shut off television or radio broadcasts that even approached discussion of the immunized testimony." All "inadvertent exposures were to be reported for review of their possible significance by an attorney, Douglass, who played no other role in the prosecution after

the immunized testimony started." An in camera review of his files, covering roughly 75 reports of inadvertent exposure, revealed that only 2 or 3 "had any semblance of meaningful significance." The district court also cited "written materials from Independent Counsel demonstrating that all the prosecutor's substantive witnesses were known to him before the first immunity grant." As a further safeguard, "all documents obtained by or subpoenaed by Independent Counsel, as well as interviews and leads already obtained before [that date] * * * [were] separated and sealed to ensure a full record of his independent development of acts and witnesses should that be necessary in more detail at a further post-trial *Kastigar* hearing." See 698 F.Supp. 300.

missible at all. Our concern is the use of immunized testimony by witnesses before the grand jury and at trial.

"We cannot agree with the District Court that the use of immunized testimony to refresh the memories of witnesses is a nonevidentiary matter and that therefore refreshment should not be subject to a *Kastigar* hearing * * *. In our view, the use of immunized testimony by witnesses to refresh their memories, or otherwise to focus their thoughts, organize their testimony, or alter their prior or contemporaneous statements, constitutes *indirect evidentiary* not *nonevidentiary use*. This observation also applies to witnesses who studied, reviewed, or were exposed to the immunized testimony in order to prepare themselves or others as witnesses. * * * The stern language of *Kastigar* does not become lenient because the compelled testimony is used to form and alter evidence in oblique ways exclusively, or at a slight distance from the chair of the immunized witness. Such a looming constitutional infirmity cannot be dismissed as merely nonevidentiary. This type of use by witnesses is not only evidentiary in any meaningful sense of the term; it is at the core of the criminal proceeding.

"2. *Refreshment.* Both the trial and the grand jury proceedings involved 'a considerable number' of witnesses who had 'their memories refreshed by the immunized testimony,' * * *. The District Court stated that '[t]here is no way a trier of fact can determine whether the memories of these witnesses would be substantially different if it had not been stimulated by a bit of the immunized testimony itself' and that 'there is no way of determining, except possibly by a trial before the trial, whether or not any defendant was placed in a substantially worse position by the possible refreshment of a witness' memory through such exposure.' The District Court found that such taint occurs in the 'natural course of events' because '[m]emory is a mysterious thing that can be stirred by a shaggy dog or a broken promise.'

"This observation, while likely true, is not dispositive of the searching inquiry *Kastigar* requires. The fact that a sizable number of grand jury witnesses, trial witnesses, and their aides apparently immersed themselves in North's immunized testimony leads us to doubt whether what is in question here is simply 'stimulation' of memory by 'a bit' of compelled testimony. * * * *Kastigar* does not prohibit simply 'a whole lot of use,' or 'excessive use,' or 'primary use' of compelled testimony. It prohibits '*any* use,' direct or indirect. From a prosecutor's standpoint, an unhappy byproduct of the Fifth Amendment is that *Kastigar* may very well require a trial within a trial (or a trial before, during, or after the trial) if such a proceeding is necessary for the court to determine whether or not the government has in any fashion used compelled testimony to indict or convict a defendant.

"If the government uses immunized testimony to refresh the recollection of a witness (or to sharpen his memory or focus his thought) when the witness testifies * * *, then the government clearly has *used* the immunized testimony. * * * [The IC argues, however,] that 'the testimony of witnesses about matters they had personally heard or observed is the product of their own memory, not of immunized testimony they might have seen or read.' * * * The following hypothetical illustrates the weakness of the IC's argument. A prosecutor locates a witness known to have observed certain events, seemingly inconsequential at the time but later critical to a criminal prosecution. The witness has absolutely no recollection of those events. The prosecution then arranges to procure the immunized testimony of the defendant. The forgetful witness sits in the gallery and listens to that immunized testimony. Under the IC's theory, that witness could then be brought forward to relate the events he had previously forgotten. It would require a curiously strained use of language and learning to hold that in such a case no 'use' of the immunized testimony had been made against the defendant. * * * 'The IC offers no logical distinction between that hypothetical and the dangers of use in the case at bar. It may be that it is possible in the present case to separate the wheat of the witnesses' unspoiled memory from the chaff of North's immunized testimony, but it may not. There at least should be a *Kastigar* hearing and specific findings on that question. * * *

"3. '*Identity of Witness*' v. '*Content of Testimony*.' The refreshment of witnesses' recollections is indicative, but not exhaustive, of the *Kastigar* questions left unanswered on the present record. The District Court's disposition of the 'identity-of-witness' issue, [see fn. a supra] does not dispose of the 'content-of-testimony' *Kastigar* problem: the District Court inquired as to whether the names of witnesses were derived independently of the immunized testimony, but it made no determination of the extent to which the substantive content of the witnesses' testimony may have been shaped, altered, or affected by the immunized testimony. * * * A central prob-

lem in this case is that many grand jury and trial witnesses were thoroughly soaked in North's immunized testimony, but no effort was made to determine what effect, if any, this extensive exposure had on their testimony. Papers filed under seal indicate that officials and attorneys from the Department of Justice, the Central Intelligence Agency, the White House, and the Department of State gathered, studies, and summarized North's immunized testimony in order to prepare themselves or their superiors and colleagues for their testimony before the investigating committees and the grand jury. * * *

"Our dissenting colleague asserts that she examined the grand jury transcripts, determined which witnesses testified as to matters touching upon Counts 6, 9 and 10, and then compared the substance of those witnesses' testimony both with their prior statements to the FBI and with North's trial testimony.[b] Although we do not doubt our colleague's thoroughness and perseverance, her review cannot substitute for the hearing required under *Kastigar* for at least three reasons. First, the dissent

b. Chief Judge Wald, in dissent, concluded that there had been a satisfactory showing of the absence of taint as to both the grand jury testimony and the trial testimony. As to the former, she noted that: (1) the trial judge's conclusion that none of the witnesses had become known to the government through immunized testimony was based, in part, on "substantive summaries of FBI interviews that mirrored subsequent grand jury testimony"; (2) "nearly all of the grand jury witnesses testifying with regards to Counts 6, 9 and 10 appeared before North presented his immunized testimony"; (3) a "reading of the relevant grand jury transcripts reveals that only the testimony of two highly placed Justice Department officials, relevant to Count 6 alone, could possibly raise *Kastigar* difficulties"; (4) as to those witnesses, one had "already described" the actions of North that were the heart of that witness' testimony, and "each witness' testimony was essentially cumulative of the other." Chief Judge Wald agreed that "the trial judge improperly suggested that refreshment of a witness' memory is not an evidentiary problem," but concluded that "refreshment of grand jury witnesses could have violated North's Fifth Amendment rights in only two possible scenarios, neither of which ever actually occurred." These were (1) "if North's immunized testimony triggered a witness' recollection of events that he had otherwise

forgotten" (a possibility that "defies credibility" as to the only two witnesses of concern), and (2) "if the IC would have violated *Kastigar* by directly presenting North's immunized testimony to grand jury witnesses to refresh their testimony" (which was contrary to the district judge's finding that prosecuting personnel was "sealed off from exposure as to the immunized testimony and publicity concerning it").

As to the "trial stage," Chief Judge Wald concluded that the district judge had acted within his discretion in deciding not to hold a post-trial *Kastigar* hearing. She noted that: (1) the district judge "took vigorous precautions to ensure that the IC carried his burden of showing lack of taint at trial," including the instruction of trial witnesses "either to testify from personal knowledge or, if they were unsure of the source of their recollection, not to answer the questions put to them"; (2) the district judge "reasonably concluded that the trial testimony of witnesses substantially mirrored their grand jury testimony"; and (3) "while North, of course, did not bear the burden of proof on the *Kastigar* issue, it is striking that his counsel does not cite to even a single line of trial testimony that indicates either a change from the grand jury testimony or any other evidence of taint."

does not determine that *trial* witnesses in no way incorporated, used or relied upon North's testimony in giving their own; rather, it relies on the District Court's legally erroneous finding concerning grand jury testimony, an approach that is flawed for the reasons noted above. Second, even by the dissent's lights, two Justice Department officials were substantially exposed to North's testimony and subsequently testified before the grand jury on matters concerning Count 6.[c] Even if we were to accept the dissent's conclusion that one of those witnesses testified consistently with a prior FBI interview, we are still left with the other witness. * * * Finally, and most importantly, an *ex parte* review in appellate chambers is not the equivalent of the open adversary hearing contemplated by *Kastigar*.[d] * * *

"In giving the IC a *Kastigar* clean bill of health, the District Court emphasized the warnings that were given to witnesses who appeared before the grand jury: 'Beginning in July, 1987, the lawyers and investigators began instructing potential witnesses during interviews not to repeat any of the immunized testimony they may have been exposed to.' The District Court went on to note that 'a limited number of cooperating witnesses agreed to avoid exposing themselves to any of the immunized testimony elicited by Congress' and

that Associate Independent Counsel 'were apparently careful to avoid broad, rambling questions that might inadvertently invite generalized answers that comprehended facts not personally known to the witness but learned from immunized testimony.' * * * We conclude that the District Court's reliance on warnings to witnesses (to avoid testifying as to anything they had learned from North's immunized testimony) was not sufficient to ensure that North's testimony was not used. As North argues, 'witnesses could not possibly filter each answer through the court's hypothetical "prior knowledge" test.' The fact that the District Court reviewed transcripts of testimony before the grand jury *in camera* would have alerted the Court to the presence of North's immunized testimony only if it were clearly identified as such. Such a review could not have disclosed the unattributed inclusion of immunized testimony in other evidence and is defective. The only proper remedy is the searching *Kastigar* inquiry prescribed [below]. * * *

"The convictions are vacated and the case is remanded to the District Court. On remand, if the prosecution is to continue, the District Court must hold a full *Kastigar* hearing that will inquire into the *content* as well as the *sources* of the grand jury and trial witnesses' testimony. That

---

c. The majority added in a footnote: "[W]e are not convinced by the dissent's belief that the *Kastigar* inquiry should be limited to witnesses who testified about the events underlying the counts on which North was eventually convicted. We do not doubt that North's *credibility* could have been compromised by a witness who used the immunized testimony but who happened to testify concerning matters not directly related to the conviction counts. Similarly, such testimony could have influenced North's decision to waive his right not to testify. The harmfulness of such use is, of course, a question for the District Court to determine on remand."

d. In its subsequent opinion on the application for rehearing, discussed infra, the majority added the following comments: "[T]he district judge (as did our colleague) relied on an in-chambers review, a sort of 'self-directed . . . inquiry,' to satisfy himself that there was no taint. Of course, this 'review' neatly avoided any cross-

examination of witnesses who were admittedly exposed to the immunized testimony (which, coupled with the switch in testimony of one key witness, may be at the core of this dispute). * * * The IC (and the district court) obviously wished to avoid cross-examination of the exposed witnesses. Some might convincingly testify that their exposure had no effect on their trial or grand jury testimony. Others might well testify that they simply were unable to determine just how much exposure affected their testimony, in which case that uncertainty would surely be a grave problem for the party with the burden of proof—the prosecutor. In this case, however, we know that at least one crucial witness changed his testimony before Congress after hearing the immunized testimony, and then presumably told the modified version to the trial jury. * * * When all is said and done, the district judge denied the defendant a hearing to which the Constitution entitled him."

inquiry must proceed witness-by-witness; if necessary, it will proceed line-by-line and item-by-item. For each grand jury and trial witness, the prosecution must show by a preponderance of the evidence that no use whatsoever was made of any of the immunized testimony either by the witness or by the Office of Independent Counsel in questioning the witness. This burden may be met by establishing that the witness was never exposed to North's immunized testimony, or that the allegedly tainted testimony contains no evidence not 'canned' by the prosecution before such exposure occurred. Unless the District Court can make express findings that the government has carried this heavy burden as to the content of all of the testimony of each witness, that testimony cannot survive the *Kastigar* test. We remind the prosecution that the *Kastigar* burden is 'heavy' not because of the evidentiary standard, but because of the constitutional standard: the government has to meet its proof only by a preponderance of the evidence, but *any* failure to meet that standard must result in exclusion of the testimony. * * * If the District Court finds that the government has failed to carry its burden with respect to any item or part of the testimony of any grand jury or trial witness, it should then consider whether that failure is harmless beyond a reasonable doubt."

On application for rehearing in the *North* case, the Court of Appeals denied a rehearing as to the taint issue. See 920 F.2d 940 (D.C.Cir.1990). Speaking to that issue the per curiam opinion for the same 2–1 majority noted:

"[The IC argues] that 'the prosecution's freedom from taint establishes that its evidence was necessarily derived independently' and therefore that the inquiry mandated by [our original opinion] would be 'superfluous.' This bold proposition, however, would convert *Kastigar*'s total prohibition on use * * * to a mere ban on significant prosecutorial exposure to the immunized testimony. * * * *Kastigar* is instead violated whenever the prosecution puts on a witness whose testimony is shaped, directly or indirectly, by compelled testimony, regardless of *how or by whom* he was exposed to that compelled testimony. Were the rule otherwise, a private lawyer for a witness sympathetic to the government could listen to the compelled testimony and use it to prepare the witness for trial. The government would presumably thereby gain the advantage of use of the immunized testimony so long as it did not actually cooperate in that effort. This interpretation of *Kastigar* ('Look ma, no hands') pressed by the IC, if accepted, would enormously increase the risk of providing immunized testimony. To reject it, it is unnecessary to decide whether, as North asserts, particular significance should be placed on the fact that other government personnel in the legislative and executive branches outside the Independent Counsel's office were, after exposure to immunized testimony, actively involved in preparing witnesses. * * *

"Our dissenting colleague does not disagree with us on this central point so vigorously disputed by the IC—that the content and circumstances of testimony given by a witness exposed to the defendant's immunized testimony may constitute 'use' of the immunized testimony in violation of a defendant's constitutional rights regardless of the prosecutor's 'fault.' But she does contend that we have extended [prior precedent] by insisting that the testimony of any witness exposed to the immunized testimony be 'pre-recorded' in much the same way as prosecutors memorialize their investigative material, including witnesses' statements, so as to be able to prove in a *Kastigar* hearing that the government has obtained no leads from the immunized testimony. We did not, however, set forth such a requirement; we only said this burden 'may' be met by 'cann[ing]' the testimony beforehand, just as wise prosecutors meet their burden of showing independent investigation by 'canning' the results of the investigation before the defendant gives immunized testimony. To be sure, if such steps are not taken, it may well be extremely difficult for the prosecutor to sustain its burden of proof that a witness exposed to immunized testimony has not shaped his or her testimony in light of the exposure, or * * * been motivated to come forward and testify in light of the immunized testimony. But we surely did not mean to preclude the use of any techniques of which we are not aware, nor did we mean to even suggest that the prosecutor was barred from trying to show in any fashion that a witness' testimony was not influenced by the immunized testimony.

"The premise of the Chief Judge's position is that the federal courts must treat the issue of *witness* exposure quite differently from prosecution staff exposure because a federal prosecutor can control only the latter. We think it is a mistaken premise because, as we have noted, it does not matter to a defendant if his immunized testimony is used against him by a key witness (and his lawyer) rather than by the prosecutor. The damage to the defendant—which is the focus of *Kastigar*—is the same in either case. In any event, although it is not an insignificant problem, we think the dissent exaggerates a prosecutor's difficulties. We can think of a number of ways that a federal prosecutor could seek to prevent exposure of witnesses he or she may intend to use, and even more ways to memorialize a witness' testimony before exposure. The dissent is apparent-

e. In its earlier opinion the majority had rejected the suggestion that executive officials, "from the same Administration as North himself," had purposefully "soaked themselves" in the immunized testimony, in "preparing for their own or their colleagues grand jury appearance," with improper motives. The majority noted:

"As an initial matter, there is absolutely nothing in the voluminous record that would even begin to support [such a] conspiracy theory * * *. In this heavily lawyered and professionally argued appeal, this notion appeared neither in the briefs nor at oral argument. * * * The more important point, however, is that such a conspiracy—even if it existed—would be entirely irrelevant to the issue before us, which is whether or not North's Fifth Amendment right was

ly concerned about a witness *hostile* to the prosecution who deliberately exposes himself to the immunized testimony in order to destroy the value of his testimony. There is, of course, not a shred of evidence that the IC encountered this problem in this case. * * * If a prosecutor had such a concern about a particular witness, that witness would be at the very top of the list of those whose testimony should be prerecorded. And if at a *Kastigar* hearing such a witness should seek to undermine the case, the prosecutor would be entitled to bring out such a motivation in his examination of the witness.

"Our dissenting colleague points also to the particular problem faced by an Independent Counsel whose investigation is targeted against one or more executive branch officials. She suggests that other officials in the executive branch who could be called as witnesses might seek to frustrate the conviction of a target by exposing themselves to immunized testimony.[e] That is actually less of a problem than it would be for an ordinary United States attorney targeting a non-government official. Government officials are subject to greater restraints on their behavior than private individuals. The Ethics in Government Act requires the Department of Justice to cooperate with an Independent Counsel. Other executive departments are expected to cooperate with the Department of Justice, the chief law enforcement arm of the executive. Moreover, the IC

violated. The Department of Justice could have held evening classes in 'The Parsing and Deconstruction of *Kastigar*' for the very purpose of 'derailing' the IC's prosecution, and such a curriculum would have been simply irrelevant to the question of whether or not the prosecution's case made *use* of North's compelled testimony. As the District Court aptly observed, we do not countenance political trials in this country, and this matter is not styled *Independent Counsel v. Executive Branch*, or even *Congress v. Executive Branch*. Rather, this is an individual's appeal from his criminal conviction, an appeal based on his contention that the government has violated his fundamental, enumerated constitutional right not to incriminate himself."

presumably has the power to bring charges of obstruction of justice against anyone who attempts to sabotage the investigation. We are not aware that the Independent Counsel made any efforts to prevent government officials who were to testify or who had already testified from exposing themselves to immunized testimony. The IC's position, unlike the dissent's, seems to have been that the matter was irrelevant or perhaps, after the exposure of the key witness and his modification of his testimony, that the horse was out of the barn.

"Finally, and perhaps at the heart of the dissent's concerns, is the argument that a straightforward application of *Kastigar* in cases where a witness testifies before Congress, after Congress grants immunity under section 6005, unduly restricts Congress' role—including wrongdoing in the executive branch. She even contends that witnesses who wished to frustrate prosecutors would 'line up to testify before Congress[ ] in exchange for . . . immunity.' We do not think Congress would be so naive as lightly to grant use immunity to such prospective defendants. Surely Congress does so only when its perception of the national interest justifies this extraordinary step. When Congress grants immunity before the prosecution has completed preparing its 'case,' the prosecutor, whoever that may be, can warn that the grant of immunity has its institutional costs; in this case, the IC indeed warned Congress that 'any grant of use and derivative use immunity would create serious—and perhaps insurmountable—barriers to the prosecution of the immunized witness.' Memorandum of the Independent Counsel Concerning Use Immunity (Submitted to the Joint Congressional Iran/Contra Committees). The decision as to whether the national interest justifies that institutional cost in the enforcement of the criminal laws is, of course, a political one to be made by Congress. Once made, however, that cost cannot be paid in the coin of a defendant's constitutional rights. That is simply not the way our system works."

7th ed., p. 702; after Note 5, add:

6. Consider in light of *Doe II* and *Schmerber* (fn. b, 7th ed., p. 692), *Pennsylvania v. Muniz*, 496 U.S. 582, 110 S.Ct. 2638, 110 L.Ed.2d 528 (1990) (more comprehensively discussed at Supp., p. 50). In *Muniz*, all but Justice Marshall agreed that a drunk-driving arrestee's slurring of his speech in responding to a series of sobriety-test questions was not in itself a "testimonial" communication. Justice Brennan's opinion for the Court noted that the arrestee's slurred speech reveals no more than the "physical manner in which he articulates words," analogous to revealing "the physical properties of the sound of one's voice" through a voiceprint. It accordingly constituted "real or physical evidence" under the doctrine of *Schmerber,* as did other evidence of lack of muscular coordination.

The Court was sharply divided (5–4), however, in the characterization of the arrestee's answer to the question, "Do you know what was the date of your sixth birthday"? The majority held that the answer to that question was testimonial "because of its content." "The trier of fact," Justice Brennan noted, "could infer from Muniz's answer (that he did not *know* the proper date) that his mental state was confused." Justice Brennan rejected as "addressing the wrong question" the state's contention that this inference concerns "the physiological function of the brain," no different than the "physiological makeup of his blood." He noted: "That the fact to be inferred * * * concern[s] the physical status of Muniz's brain merely describes the way in which the inference is incriminating. The correct question * * * is whether the incriminating inference of mental confusion is drawn from a testimonial act * * * [as defined in *Doe II*]." Here, the suspect clearly was "asked for a response requiring him to communicate an express or implied assertion of fact or belief," and he give such a response as to his knowledge of a particular fact. "The Commonwealth's protest that it had no investigatory interest in the actual date of Muniz's sixth birthday is inappropriate. The critical point is that the Commonwealth had an investigatory interest in Muniz's assertion of belief that was communicated by his answer to the question."

The four dissenters viewed the state's contention as well taken. "The sixth birthday question," Chief Justice Rehnquist noted, "was an effort on the part of the police to check how well Muniz was able to do a simple mathematical exercise." The Court does not question the police authority to require Muniz to perform a series of physical-dexterity tests. "If the police may thus require Muniz to use his body in order to demonstrate the level of physical coordination, there is no reason why they should not be able to require him to speak or write in order to determine his mental coordination." Just as *Schmerber* held it to be permissible under the Fifth Amendment to extract blood to "determine how much of that part of [the body's] system had been affected by alcohol," it should be held permissible here "to examine the functioning of Muniz's mental processes for the same purpose."

7th ed., p. 727; after Note 7, add:

8. The implications of the several doctrines discussed in this section were brought together in an unusual setting in *Baltimore City Department of Social Services v. Bouknight*, 493 U.S. 549, 110 S.Ct. 900, 107 L.Ed.2d 992 (1990). The Supreme Court there rejected a self-incrimination objection to a subpoena directing respondent Bouknight to produce her infant son, an abused child who had previously been declared a ward of the court. The Court noted that the respondent could not claim the privilege based upon "anything an examination of the [child] might reveal," as that would be a claim based upon "the contents or nature of the thing demanded." However, the mother could conceivably claim the privilege because "the act of production would amount to testimony regarding her control over and possession of [the child]." While the state could "readily introduce [other] evidence of Bouknight's continuing control over the child" (including the court order giving her limited custody and her previous statements reflecting control), her "implicit communication of control over [the child] at the moment of production might aid the state in prosecuting Bouknight [for child abuse]." The Court had no need to decide, however, whether "this limited testimonial assertion is sufficiently incriminating and sufficiently testimonial for purposes of the privilege." In receiving conditional custody from the juvenile court, the mother had "assumed custodial duties related to production" (analogous to that of an entity agent) and had done so as part of noncriminal regulatory scheme which included a production component (analogous to regulations sustained under the required records doctrine). The Court added that it had no need in the case before it "to define the precise limitations that may exist upon the State's ability to use the testimonial aspects of Bouknight's act of production in subsequent criminal proceedings," but the "imposition of such limitations," as done in *Braswell,* was not "foreclosed."

Chapter 11
THE SCOPE OF THE EXCLUSIONARY RULES

SECTION 1. "STANDING" TO OBJECT TO THE ADMISSION OF EVIDENCE

B. The Current Approach

ON THE MEANING OF *RAKAS*

7th ed., p. 741; after Note 1, add new Note 1(a):

1(a). *Overnight guests.* In MINNESOTA v. OLSON, 495 U.S. 91, 110 S.Ct. 1684, 109 L.Ed.2d 85 (1990) (also discussed at Supp., p. 8), finding the distinctions relied on by the prosecution between this case and *Jones v. United States* (7th ed., p. 732) "not legally determinative," the Court held that defendant's "status as an overnight guest" at the home of two women gave him a sufficient interest in the home to challenge the legality of the warrantless arrest there.

The case arose as follows: The police had reason to believe that Olson, a suspect in a recent robbery-murder, was staying at the home of two women. (He had, with the permission of the women, spent the previous night sleeping on the floor of their apartment and had a change of clothes with him.) Without seeking permission and with weapons drawn, the police entered the home, found Olson in a closet, and arrested him. Shortly thereafter, Olson made an incriminating statement at police headquarters. The statement was admitted at Olson's trial and he was convicted of murder and armed robbery. The state supreme court ruled that Olson had a sufficient connection with the premises to challenge the legality of his arrest, that the arrest was illegal because there were no exigent circumstances to justify a warrantless entry, and that Olson's statement was fatally tainted by that illegality. A 7–2 majority, per White, J., agreed.[a] As for the standing issue—

"We need go no further than to conclude, as we do, that Olson's status as an overnight guest is alone enough to show that he had an expectation of privacy in the home that society is prepared to recognize as reasonable.

"[In 1960, the *Jones* Court ruled that defendant] could challenge the search of the apartment, because he was 'legitimately on [the] premises.' Although [this standard] was rejected in *Rakas* as too broad, the *Rakas* Court explicitly reaffirmed the factual holding in *Jones*. [The *Rakas* case] thus recognized that, as an overnight guest, Jones was much more than just legitimately on the premises.

"The distinctions relied on by the State between this case and *Jones* are not legally determinative. The State emphasizes that in this case Olson was never left alone in the duplex or given a key, whereas in *Jones* the owner of the apartment was away and Jones had a key with which he could come and go and admit and exclude others. * * * We do not understand *Rakas*, [to] hold that an overnight guest can never

---

a. The court noted that the state had expressly disavowed any claim that the statement was not a fruit of the arrest and that therefore it would not consider the applicability of *New York v. Harris* (Supp., p. 83) to the facts of this case.

have a legitimate expectation of privacy except when his host is away and he has a key or that only when those facts are present may an overnight guest assert the 'unremarkable proposition,' *Rakas,* that a person may have a sufficient interest in a place other than his home to enable him to be free in that place from unreasonable searches and seizures.

"To hold that an overnight guest has a legitimate expectation of privacy in his host's home merely recognizes the everyday expectations of privacy that we all share. Staying overnight in another's home is a longstanding social custom that serves functions recognized as valuable by society. We stay in others' homes when we travel to a strange city for business or pleasure, when we visit our parents, children, or more distant relatives out of town, when we are in between jobs or homes, or when we house-sit for a friend. We will all be hosts and we will all be guests many times in our lives. From either perspective, we think that society recognizes that a houseguest has a legitimate expectation of privacy in his host's home.

"From the overnight guest's perspective, he seeks shelter in another's home precisely because it provides him with privacy, a place where he and his possessions will not be disturbed by anyone but his host and those his host allows inside. We are at our most vulnerable when we are asleep because we cannot monitor our own safety or the security of our belongings. It is for this reason that, although we may spend all day in public places, when we cannot sleep in our own home we seek out another private place to sleep, whether it be a hotel room, or the home of a friend. Society expects at least as much privacy in these places as in a telephone booth—'a temporarily private place whose momenta-

ry occupants' expectations of freedom from intrusion are recognized as reasonable,' *Katz* (Harlan, J., concurring).

"That the guest has a host who has ultimate control of the house is not inconsistent with the guest having a legitimate expectation of privacy. The houseguest is there with the permission of his host, who is willing to share his house and his privacy with his guest. It is unlikely that the guest will be confined to a restricted area of the house; and when the host is away or asleep, the guest will have a measure of control over the premises. The host may admit or exclude from the house as he prefers, but it is unlikely that he will admit someone who wants to see or meet with the guest over the objection of the guest. On the other hand, few houseguests will invite others to visit them while they are guests without consulting their hosts; but the latter, who have the authority to exclude despite the wishes of the guest, will often be accommodating. The point is that hosts will more likely than not respect the privacy interests of their guests, who are entitled to a legitimate expectation of privacy despite the fact that they have no legal interest in the premises and do not have the legal authority to determine who may or may not enter the household. If the untrammeled power to admit and exclude were essential to Fourth Amendment protection, an adult daughter temporarily living in the home of her parents would have no legitimate expectation of privacy because her right to admit or exclude would be subject to her parents' veto.

"Because respondent's expectation of privacy in the home was rooted in 'understandings that are recognized and permitted by society,' *Rakas,* it was legitimate, and respondent can claim the protection of the Fourth Amendment." [a]

a. Rehnquist, C.J., and Blackmun, J., dissented without opinion.

SECTION 2. THE "FRUIT OF THE POISONOUS TREE"

A. HISTORICAL BACKGROUND AND OVERVIEW

7th ed., p. 753; after Note 5, add new Note 5(a):

5(a). *Confession as the "fruit" of a Payton violation.* In NEW YORK v. HARRIS, 495 U.S. 14, 110 S.Ct. 1640, 109 L.Ed.2d 13 (1990), a 5–4 majority, per WHITE, J., held that where the police have probable cause to arrest a suspect, the exclusionary rule does not bar the use of a statement made by the suspect outside his home even though the statement is obtained after an in-house arrest in violation of *Payton v. New York,* 7th ed., p. 232. The police had probable cause to believe Harris had killed a woman. They went to his apartment to take him into custody, but did not first obtain an arrest warrant. After being advised of his *Miranda* rights and waiving them, Harris reportedly admitted that he had committed the homicide. He was then taken to the station house, where, after again being advised of his rights and again waiving them, he signed a written inculpatory statement. Since the state did not challenge the trial court's suppression of Harris' statement to the police while still inside his home, the sole issue was the admissibility of the statement he made at the station house. The New York Court of Appeals ruled that the station house statement was the inadmissible fruit of the *Payton* violation, but the Supreme Court reversed:

"Nothing in the reasoning of [*Payton*] suggests that an arrest in a home without a warrant but with probable cause somehow renders unlawful continued custody of the suspect once he is removed from the house. * * * Because the officers had probable cause to arrest Harris for a crime, Harris was not unlawfully in custody when he was removed to the station house, given *Miranda* warnings and allowed to talk. For Fourth Amendment purposes, the legal issue is the same as it would be had the police arrested Harris on his door step, illegally entered his home to search for evidence, and later interrogated Harris at the station house. Similarly, if the police had made a warrantless entry into Harris' home, not found him there, but arrested him on the street when he returned, a later statement made by him after proper warnings would no doubt be admissible.

"[In *Brown, Dunaway* and *Taylor*], evidence obtained from a criminal defendant following arrest was suppressed because the police lacked probable cause. The three cases stand for the familiar proposition that the indirect fruits of an illegal search or arrest should be suppressed when they bear a sufficiently close relationship to the underlying illegality. We have emphasized, however, that attenuation analysis is only appropriate where, as a threshold matter, courts determine that 'the challenged evidence is in some sense the product of illegal governmental activity.' *Crews.*

* * *

"Harris's statement taken at the police station was not the product of being in unlawful custody. Neither was it the fruit of having been arrested in the home rather than someplace else. The case is analogous to *Crews.* In that case, we refused to suppress a victim's in-court identification despite the defendant's illegal arrest. The Court found that the evidence was not 'come at by exploitation [of] the defendant's Fourth Amendment rights,' and that it was not necessary to inquire whether the 'taint' of the Fourth Amendment violation was sufficiently attenuated to permit the introduction of the evidence. Here, likewise, the police had a justification to question Harris prior to his arrest; therefore, his subsequent statement was not an exploitation of the illegal entry into Harris' home.

"We do not hold, as the dissent suggests, that a statement taken by the police while a suspect is in custody is always admissible as long as the suspect is in legal custody.

Statements taken during legal custody would of course be inadmissible for example, if, they were the product of coercion, if *Miranda* warnings were not given, or if there was a violation of the rule of *Edwards*. We do hold that the station-house statement in this case was admissible because Harris was in legal custody, as the dissent concedes, and because the statement, while the product of an arrest and being in custody, was not the fruit of the fact that the arrest was made in the house rather than someplace else.

"To put the matter another way, suppressing the statement taken outside the house would not serve the purpose of the rule that made Harris's in-house arrest illegal. The warrant requirement for an arrest in the home is imposed to protect the home, and anything incriminating the police gathered from arresting Harris in his home, rather than elsewhere, has been excluded, as it should have been; the purpose of the rule has thereby been vindicated. We are not required by the Constitution to go further and suppress statements later made by Harris in order to deter police from violating *Payton*. * * * Even though we decline to suppress statements made outside the home following a *Payton* violation, the principal incentive to obey *Payton* still obtains: the police know that a warrantless entry will lead to the suppression of any evidence found or statements taken inside the home. If we did suppress statements like Harris', moreover, the incremental deterrent value would be minimal. Given that the police have probable cause to arrest a suspect in Harris' position, they need not violate *Payton* in order to interrogate the suspect. It is doubtful therefore that the desire to secure a statement from a criminal suspect would motivate the police to violate *Payton*. As a result, suppressing a station-house statement obtained after a *Payton* violation will have little effect on the officers' actions, one way or another."

Dissenting JUSTICE MARSHALL, joined by Brennan, Blackmun and Stevens, JJ., deemed *Brown v. Illinois* controlling:

"An application of the *Brown* factors to this case compels the conclusion that Harris' statement at the station house must be suppressed. About an hour elapsed between the illegal arrest and Harris' confession, without any intervening factor other than the warnings required by *Miranda*. This Court has held, however, that '*Miranda* warnings, *alone* and *per se*, . . . cannot assure in every case that the Fourth Amendment violation has not been unduly exploited.' *Brown*. Indeed, in *Brown*, we held that a statement made almost *two* hours after an illegal arrest, and after *Miranda* warnings had been given, was not sufficiently removed from the violation so as to dissipate the taint.

"As to the flagrancy of the violation, petitioner does not dispute that the officers were aware that the Fourth Amendment prohibited them from arresting Harris in his home without a warrant. Notwithstanding the officers' knowledge that a warrant is required for a routine arrest in the home,

'the police * * * made no attempt to obtain a warrant although five days had elapsed between the killing and the arrest and they had developed evidence of probable cause early in their investigation. Indeed, one of the officers testified that it was departmental policy not to get warrants before making arrests in the home. From this statement a reasonable inference can be drawn [that] the department's policy was a device used to avoid restrictions on questioning a suspect until after the police had strengthened their case with a confession. Thus, the police illegality was knowing and intentional, in the language of *Brown*, it "had a quality of purposefulness," and the linkage between the illegality and the confession is clearly established.' [quoting from the court below.] [2]

"In short, the officers decided, apparently consistent with a 'departmental policy,' to violate Harris' Fourth Amendment rights so they could get evidence that they could not otherwise obtain. As the trial court held, 'No more clear violation of [*Payton*], in my view, could be established.' Where, as here, there is a particularly flagrant constitutional violation and little in the way of elapsed time or intervening circumstances, the statement in the police station must be suppressed.

"Had the Court analyzed this case as our precedents dictate that it should, I could end my discussion here—the dispute would reduce to an application of the *Brown* factors to the constitutional wrong and the inculpatory statement that followed. But the majority chooses no such unremarkable battleground. Instead, the Court redrafts our cases in the service of conclusions they straightforwardly and explicitly reject. Specifically, the Court finds suppression unwarranted on the authority of its newly-fashioned *per se* rule. In the majority's view, when police officers make a warrantless home arrest in violation of *Payton,* their physical exit from the suspect's home *necessarily* breaks the causal chain between the illegality and any subsequent statement by the suspect, such that the statement is admissible regardless of the *Brown* factors.

"[The] majority's *per se* rule in this case fails to take account of our repeated holdings that violations of privacy in the home are especially invasive. Rather, its rule is necessarily premised on the proposition

that the effect of a *Payton* violation magically vanishes once the suspect is dragged from his home. But the concerns that make a warrantless home arrest a violation of the Fourth Amendment are nothing so evanescent. A person who is forcibly separated from his family and home in the dark of night after uniformed officers have broken down his door, handcuffed him, and forced him at gunpoint to accompany them to a police station does not suddenly breathe a sigh of relief at the moment he is dragged across his doorstep. Rather, the suspect is likely to be so frightened and rattled that he will say something incriminating. These effects, of course, extend far beyond the moment the physical occupation of the home ends. The entire focus of the *Brown* factors is to fix the point at which those effects are sufficiently dissipated that deterrence is not meaningfully advanced by suppression. The majority's assertion, as though the proposition were axiomatic, that the effects of such an intrusion *must* end when the violation ends is both undefended and indefensible.

* * *

"Perhaps the most alarming aspect of the Court's ruling is its practical consequences for the deterrence of *Payton* violations. Imagine a police officer who has probable cause to arrest a suspect but lacks a warrant. The officer knows if he were to break into the home to make the arrest without first securing a warrant, he would violate the Fourth Amendment and any evidence he finds in the house would be suppressed. Of course, if he does not enter the house, he will not be able to use any evidence inside the house either, for the simple reason that he will never see it.

---

2. The "restrictions on questioning" to which the court refers are restrictions imposed by New York law. New York law provides that an arrest warrant may not issue until an "accusatory instrument" has been filed against the suspect. The New York courts have held that police officers may not question a suspect in the absence of an attorney once such an accusatory instrument has been filed. These two rules operate to prohibit police from questioning a suspect after arresting him in his home unless his lawyer is

present. If the police comply with *Payton,* the suspect's lawyer will likely tell him not to say anything, and the police will get nothing. On the other hand, if they violate *Payton* by refusing to obtain a warrant, the suspect's right to counsel will not have attached at the time of the arrest, and the police may be able to question him without interference by a lawyer. The lower court's inference that a departmental policy of violating the Fourth Amendment existed was thus fully justified.

The officer also knows, though, that waiting for the suspect to leave his house before arresting him could entail a lot of waiting, and the time he would spend getting a warrant would be better spent arresting criminals. The officer could leave the scene to obtain a warrant, thus avoiding some of the delay, but that would entail giving the suspect an opportunity to flee.

"More important, the officer knows that if he breaks into the house without a warrant and drags the suspect outside, the suspect, shaken by the enormous invasion of privacy he has just undergone, may say something incriminating. Before today's decision, the government would only be able to use that evidence if the Court found that the taint of the arrest had been attenuated; after the decision, the evidence will be admissible regardless of whether it was the product of the unconstitutional arrest.[5] Thus, the officer envisions the following best-case scenario if he chooses to violate the Constitution: he avoids a major expenditure of time and effort, ensures that the suspect will not escape, and procures the most damaging evidence of all, a confession. His worst-case scenario is that he will avoid a major expenditure of effort, ensure that the suspect will not escape, and will see evidence in the house (which would have remained unknown absent the constitutional violation) that cannot be used in the prosecution's case-in-chief. The Court thus creates powerful incentives for police officers to violate the Fourth Amendment. In the context of our constitutional rights and the sanctity of our homes, we cannot afford to presume that officers will be entirely impervious to those incentives."

---

5. Indeed, if the officer, as here, works in New York State, the Court's assertion that "[i]t is doubtful therefore that the desire to secure a statement from a criminal suspect would motivate the police to violate *Payton*" takes on a

SECTION 3. USE OF ILLEGALLY OBTAINED EVIDENCE FOR IMPEACHMENT PURPOSES

A. THE EXPANSION OF A ONCE-NARROW EXCEPTION

7th ed., p. 777; after Note 5, add:

6. In JAMES v. ILLINOIS, 493 U.S. 307, 110 S.Ct. 648, 107 L.Ed.2d 676 (1990), a 5–4 majority, per BRENNAN, J., refused to expand the "impeachment exception" to the exclusionary rule to permit the prosecution to impeach the testimony of *all* defense witnesses with illegally obtained evidence. According to the majority, expanding the impeachment exception to such an extent "would not further the truthseeking value with equal force but would appreciably undermine the deterrent effect of the exclusionary rule."

Facts

The case arose as follows: A day after a murder occurred, the police took James, a suspect, into custody. He was found at his mother's beauty salon sitting under a hair dryer; when he emerged, his hair was black and curly. When the police questioned James about his prior hair color, he told them it had been reddish-brown, long, and combed straight back. When questioned later at the police station, James stated that he had his hair dyed black and curled at the beauty parlor in order to change his appearance. Because the police lacked probable cause for James' arrest, both statements regarding his hair were suppressed.

At the trial, five eye witnesses testified that the person responsible for the murder had long, "reddish" hair, worn in a slicked-back style and that they had seen James several weeks earlier, at which time he had the aforementioned hair color and style. James did not testify in his own defense. He called as a witness Jewel Henderson, a family friend. She testified that on the

singularly ironic cast. The court below found as a matter of fact that the officers in this case had intentionally violated *Payton* for *precisely* the reason the Court identifies as "doubtful." See n. 2 and accompanying text.

day of the shooting James' hair had been black. The state then impeached Henderson's testimony by reporting James' prior admissions that he had reddish hair at the time of the shooting and had dyed and curled his hair the next day in order to change his appearance. James ultimately was convicted of murder.

The Illinois Supreme Court concluded, that, in order to deter "perjury by proxy," the impeachment exception ought to allow the state to impeach the testimony of defense witnesses other than the defendant himself. The U.S. Supreme Court reversed:

"[T]he Illinois Supreme Court held that our balancing approach in *Walder* and its progeny justifies expanding the scope of the impeachment exception to permit prosecutors to use illegally obtained evidence to impeach the credibility of defense witnesses. We disagree. Expanding the class of impeachable witnesses from the defendant alone to all defense witnesses would create different incentives affecting the behavior of both defendants and law enforcement officers. As a result, this expansion would not promote the truthseeking function to the same extent as did creation of the original exception, and yet it would significantly undermine the deterrent effect of the general exclusionary rule. Hence, we believe that this proposed expansion would frustrate rather than further the purposes underlying the exclusionary rule.

"The previously recognized exception penalizes defendants for committing perjury by allowing the prosecution to expose their perjury through impeachment using illegally obtained evidence. Thus defendants are discouraged in the first instance from 'affirmatively resort[ing] to perjurious testimony.' But the exception leaves defendants free to testify truthfully on

their own behalf; they can offer probative and exculpatory evidence to the jury without opening the door to impeachment by carefully avoiding any statements that directly contradict the suppressed evidence. The exception thus generally discourages perjured testimony without discouraging truthful testimony.

"In contrast, expanding the impeachment exception to encompass the testimony of all defense witnesses would not have the same beneficial effects. First, the mere threat of a subsequent criminal prosecution for perjury is far more likely to deter a witness from intentionally lying on a defendant's behalf than to deter a defendant, already facing conviction for the underlying offense, from lying on his own behalf. Hence the Illinois Supreme Court's underlying premise that a defendant frustrated by our previous impeachment exception can easily find a witness to engage in 'perjury by proxy' is suspect.[4]

"More significantly, expanding the impeachment exception to encompass the testimony of all defense witnesses likely would chill some defendants from presenting their best defense—and sometimes any defense at all—through the testimony of others. Whenever police obtained evidence illegally, defendants would have to assess prior to trial the likelihood that the evidence would be admitted to impeach the otherwise favorable testimony of any witness they call. Defendants might reasonably fear that one or more of their witnesses, in a position to offer truthful and favorable testimony, would also make some statement in sufficient tension with the tainted evidence to allow the prosecutor to introduce that evidence for impeachment. First, defendants sometimes need to call 'reluctant' or 'hostile' witnesses to provide reliable and probative exculpatory testimony, and such witnesses likely will

---

4. The dissent concedes, as it must, that "of course, false testimony can result from faulty recollection" as opposed to intentional lying. Even assuming that Henderson's testimony in this case (as opposed to the detective's contrary

testimony) was indeed false, nothing in the record suggests that Henderson intentionally committed perjury rather than honestly provided her best (even if erroneous) perception and recollection of events.

not share the defendants' concern for avoiding statements that invite impeachment through contradictory evidence. Moreover, defendants often cannot trust even 'friendly' witnesses to testify without subjecting themselves to impeachment, simply due to insufficient care or attentiveness. This concern is magnified in those occasional situations when defendants must call witnesses to testify despite having had only a limited opportunity to consult with or prepare them in advance. For these reasons, we have recognized in a variety of contexts that a party 'cannot be absolutely certain that his witnesses will testify as expected.' As a result, an expanded impeachment exception likely would chill some defendants from calling witnesses who would otherwise offer probative evidence.

"This realization alters the balance of values underlying the current impeachment exception governing defendants' testimony. Our prior cases make clear that defendants ought not be able to 'pervert' the exclusion of illegally obtained evidence into a shield for perjury, but it seems no more appropriate for the State to brandish such evidence as a sword with which to dissuade defendants from presenting a meaningful defense through other witnesses. Given the potential chill created by expanding the impeachment exception, the conceded gains to the truth-seeking process from discouraging or disclosing perjured testimony would be offset to some extent by the concomitant loss of probative witness testimony. Thus, the truthseeking rationale supporting the impeachment of defendants in *Walder* and its progeny does not apply to other witnesses with equal force.

"Moreover, the proposed expansion of the current impeachment exception would significantly weaken the exclusionary rule's deterrent effect on police misconduct. This Court has characterized as a mere 'speculative possibility,' *Harris v. New York,* the likelihood that permitting prosecutors to impeach defendants with illegally

obtained evidence would encourage police misconduct. Law enforcement officers will think it unlikely that the defendant will first decide to testify at trial and will also open the door inadvertently to admission of any illegally obtained evidence. Hence, the officers' incentive to acquire evidence through illegal means is quite weak.

"In contrast, expanding the impeachment exception to *all* defense witnesses would significantly enhance the expected value to the prosecution of illegally obtained evidence. First, this expansion would vastly increase the number of occasions on which such evidence could be used. Defense witnesses easily outnumber testifying defendants, both because many defendants do not testify themselves and because many if not most defendants call multiple witnesses on their behalf. Moreover, due to the chilling effect identified above, illegally obtained evidence holds even greater value to the prosecution for each individual witness than for each defendant. The prosecutor's access to impeachment evidence would not just deter perjury; it would also deter defendants from calling witnesses in the first place, thereby keeping from the jury much probative exculpatory evidence. For both of these reasons, police officers and their superiors would recognize that obtaining evidence through illegal means stacks the deck heavily in the prosecution's favor. It is thus far more than a 'speculative possibility' that police misconduct will be encouraged by permitting such use of illegally obtained evidence.

"The United States argues that this result is constitutionally acceptable because excluding illegally obtained evidence solely from the prosecution's case in chief would still provide a quantum of deterrence sufficient to protect the privacy interests underlying the exclusionary rule. We disagree. Of course, a police officer might in certain situations believe that obtaining particular evidence through illegal means, resulting in its suppression from the case in chief, would prevent the prosecution from establishing a prima facie case to take to a jury. In such situations, the officer likely would be deterred from obtaining the evidence illegally for fear of jeopardizing the entire case. But much if not most of the time, police officers confront opportunities to obtain evidence illegally after they have already legally obtained (or know that they have other means of legally obtaining) sufficient evidence to sustain a prima facie case. In these situations, a rule requiring exclusion of illegally obtained evidence from only the government's case in chief would leave officers with little to lose and much to gain by overstepping constitutional limits on evidence gathering.[8] Narrowing the exclusionary rule in this manner, therefore, would significantly undermine the rule's ability 'to compel respect for the constitutional guaranty in the only effectively available way—by removing the incentive to disregard it.' So long as we are committed to protecting the people from the disregard of their constitutional rights during the course of criminal investigations, inadmissibility of illegally obtained evidence must remain the rule, not the exception." [a]

Dissenting JUSTICE KENNEDY, joined by Rehnquist, C.J., and O'Connor and Scalia, JJ., maintained that the majority had given the exclusionary rule excessive protection but had afforded the truth-seeking function of the criminal trial inadequate weight:

"To deprive the prosecution of probative evidence acquired in violation of the law may be a tolerable and necessary cost of the exclusionary rule. Implementation of the rule requires us to draw certain lines to effect its purpose of deterring unlawful conduct. But the line drawn by today's

opinion grants the defense side in a criminal case broad immunity to introduce whatever false testimony it can produce from the mouth of a friendly witness. Unless petitioner's conviction is reversed, we are told, police would flout the Fourth Amendment, and as a result, the accused would be unable to offer any defense. This exaggerated view leads to a drastic remedy: The jury cannot learn that defense testimony is inconsistent with probative evidence of undoubted value. A more cautious course is available, one that retains Fourth Amendment protections and yet safeguards the truth-seeking function of the criminal trial. * * *

"I agree with the majority that the resolution of this case depends on a balance of values that informs our exclusionary rule jurisprudence. We weigh the 'likelihood [of] deterrence against the costs of withholding reliable information from the truth-seeking process.' The majority adopts a sweeping rule that the testimony of witnesses other than the defendant may never be rebutted with excludable evidence. I cannot draw the line where the majority does.

"The interest in protecting the truth-seeking function of the criminal trial is every bit as strong in this case as in our earlier cases that allowed rebuttal with evidence that was inadmissible as part of the prosecution's case in chief. Here a witness who knew the accused well took the stand to testify about the accused's personal appearance. The testimony could be expected to create real doubt in the mind of jurors concerning the eyewitness identifications by persons who did not know the accused. To deprive the jurors of knowledge that statements of the defendant himself revealed the witness' testimony to be false would result in a decision by triers of

---

8. Indeed, the detectives who unlawfully detained James and elicited his incriminating statements already knew that there were several eyewitnesses to the shooting. Because the detectives likely believed that the exclusion of any statement they obtained from James probably would not have precluded the prosecution from making

a prima facie case, an exclusionary rule applicable only to the prosecution's case in chief likely would have provided little deterrent effect in this case.

a. Stevens, J., who joined the opinion of the Court, also wrote a separate opinion.

fact who were not just kept in the dark as to excluded evidence, but positively misled. The potential for harm to the truth-seeking process resulting from the majority's new rule in fact will be greater than if the defendant himself had testified. It is natural for jurors to be skeptical of self-serving testimony by the defendant. Testimony by a witness said to be independent has the greater potential to deceive. And if a defense witness can present false testimony with impunity, the jurors may find the rest of the prosecution's case suspect, for ineffective and artificial cross-examination will be viewed as a real weakness in the State's case. Jurors will assume that if the prosecution had any proof the statement was false, it would make the proof known. The majority does more than deprive the prosecution of evidence. The State must also suffer the introduction of false testimony and appear to bolster the falsehood by its own silence.

"The majority's fear that allowing the jury to know the whole truth will chill defendants from putting on any defense seems to me far too speculative to justify the rule here announced. No restriction on the defense results if rebuttal of testimony by witnesses other than the defendant is confined to the introduction of excludable evidence that is in direct contradiction of the testimony. If mere 'tension with the tainted evidence' opened the door to introduction of *all* the evidence subject to suppression, then the majority's fears might be justified. But in this context rebuttal can and should be confined to situations where there is direct conflict, which is to say where, within reason, the witness' testimony and the excluded testimony cannot both be true.

"Also missing from the majority's analysis is the almost certain knowledge that the testimony immunized from rebuttal is false. The majority's apparent assumption that defense witnesses protected by today's rule have only truth-telling in mind strikes me as far too sanguine to support acceptance of a rule that controls the hard reality

of contested criminal trials. The majority expresses the common sense of the matter in saying that presentation of excluded evidence must sometimes be allowed because it 'penalizes defendants for committing perjury.'

"In some cases, of course, false testimony can result from faulty recollection. But the majority's ironclad rule is one that applies regardless of the witness' motives, and may be misused as a license to perjure. Even if the witness testifies in good faith, the defendant and his lawyer, who offer the testimony, know the facts. Indeed, it is difficult here to imagine the defense attorney's reason for asking Henderson about petitioner's hair color if he did not expect her to cast doubt on the eyewitness identification of petitioner by giving a description of petitioner's hair color contrary to that contained in his own (suppressed) statement.

"The suggestion that the threat of a perjury prosecution will provide sufficient deterrence to prevent false testimony is not realistic. A heightened proof requirement applies in Illinois and other States, making perjury convictions difficult to sustain. Where testimony presented on behalf of a friend or family member is involved, the threat that a future jury will convict the witness may be an idle one.

"The damage to the truth-seeking process caused by the majority's rule is certain to be great whether the testimony is perjured or merely false. In this case there can be little doubt of the falsity, since petitioner's description of his own hair was at issue. And as a general matter the alternative to rebuttal is endorsement of judicial proceedings conducted in reliance on information known to be untrue. Suppressed evidence is likely to consist of either voluntary statements by the defendant himself or physical evidence. Both have a high degree of reliability, and testimony in direct conflict to such evidence most often will represent an attempt to place falsehoods before the jury.

"The suggestion that all this is so far beyond the control of the defendant that he will put on no defense is not supported. As to sympathetic witnesses, such as the family friend here, it should not be too hard to assure the witness does not volunteer testimony in contradiction of the facts. The defendant knows the content of the suppressed evidence. Even in cases where the time for consultation is limited, the defense attorney can take care not to elicit contradicting testimony. And in the case of truly neutral witnesses, or witnesses hostile to the accused, it is hard to see the danger that they will present false testimony for the benefit of the defense.

"The majority's concerns may carry greater weight where contradicting testimony is elicited from a defense witness on cross-examination. In that situation there might be a concern that the prosecution would attempt to produce such testimony as the foundation to put excluded evidence before the jury. We have found that possibility insufficient to justify immunity for a defendant's own false testimony on cross-examination. *Havens.* As to cross-examination of other witnesses, perhaps a different rule could be justified. Rather than wait for an appropriate case to consider this or similar measures, however, the majority opts for a wooden rule immunizing all defense testimony from rebuttal, without regard to knowledge that the testimony introduced at the behest of the defendant is false or perjured.

"I also cannot agree that admission of excluded evidence on rebuttal would lead to the 'disregard [of] constitutional rights' by law enforcement officers that the majority fears. This argument has been raised in our previous cases in this area of the

law. To date we have rejected it. Now the spectre appears premised on an assumption that a single slip of the tongue by any defense witness will open the door to any suppressed evidence at the prosecutor's disposal. If this were so, the majority's concern that officers would be left with little to lose from conducting an illegal search would be understandable. And the argument might hold more force if, as the majority speculates, police confront the temptation to seize evidence illegally 'much if not most of the time' after gathering sufficient evidence to present proof of guilt beyond a reasonable doubt in the case in chief. Again, however, I disagree with the predictions.

"It is unrealistic to say that the decision to make an illegal search turns on a precise calculation of the possibilities of rebuttal at some future trial. There is no reason to believe a police officer, unschooled in the law, will assess whether evidence already in his possession would suffice to survive a motion for acquittal following the case in chief. The officer may or may not even know the identity of the ultimate defendant.[3] He certainly will not know anything about potential defense witnesses, much less what the content of their testimony might be. What he will know for certain is that evidence from an illegal search or arrest (which may well be crucial to securing a conviction) will be lost to the case in chief. Our earlier assessments of the marginal deterrent effect are applicable here. 'Assuming that the exclusionary rule has a deterrent effect on proscribed police conduct, sufficient deterrence flows when the evidence in question is made unavailable to the prosecution in its case in chief.' *Harris.*

3. In this case, contrary to the impression conveyed by the majority, n. 8, the arresting officers knew almost nothing of the state of a future prosecution case. The officers did know there were several eyewitnesses to the shooting. But these eyewitnesses had made no identification of any suspect. The officers did not know petitioner's real name or his true appearance, but had sought him out at the beauty parlor on an

anonymous tip. They could not know what physical evidence, such as the murder weapon, they might find on petitioner, or might lose, to the case in chief as a result of illegal conduct. The suggestion that the officers' calculated assessment of a future trial allowed them to ignore the exclusionary rule finds no support in the record and, in fact, is pure speculation.

"In this case, the defense witness, one Jewel Henderson, testified that petitioner's hair was black on the date of the offense. Her statement, perjured or not, should not have been offered to the jurors without giving them the opportunity to consider the unequivocal and contradicting description by the person whose own hair it was. I would allow the introduction of petitioner's statement that his hair was red on the day of the shootings. The result is consistent with our line of cases from *Walder* to *Havens*, and compelled by their reasoning.[b] * * *

"Where the jury is misled by false testimony, otherwise subject to flat contradiction by evidence illegally seized, the protection of the exclusionary rule is 'perverted into a license to use perjury by way of a defense, free from the risk of confrontation with prior inconsistent utterances.' *Havens*. The perversion is the same where the perjury is by proxy."

B. What Kinds of Constitutional or Other Violations are Encompassed Within the Impeachment Exception?

7th ed., p. 777; substitute Note 3 below for old Note 3:

3. *Use of statements obtained in violation of Sixth Amendment right to counsel.* In MICHIGAN v. HARVEY, 494 U.S. 344, 110 S.Ct. 1176, 108 L.Ed.2d 293 (1990), a 5–4 majority, per REHNQUIST, C.J., held that statements obtained in violation of the rule established in *Michigan v. Jackson*, 7th ed., pp. 522–23, may be used to impeach a defendant's false or inconsistent testimony:

"*Michigan v. Jackson* is based on the Sixth Amendment, but its roots lie in this Court's decisions in *Miranda* and suc-

ceeding cases. * * * *Edwards* [7th ed., p. 511] added a second layer of protection [to] *Miranda,* [establishing a] prophylactic rule designed to prevent police from badgering a defendant into waiving his previously asserted *Miranda* rights.

"*Jackson* simply superimposed the Fifth Amendment analysis of *Edwards* onto the Sixth Amendment. Reasoning that 'the Sixth Amendment right to counsel at a postarraignment interrogation requires at least as much protection as the Fifth Amendment right to counsel at any custodial interrogation,' [the *Jackson* Court] concluded that the *Edwards* protections should apply when a suspect charged with a crime requests counsel outside the context of interrogation. This rule, like *Edwards*, is based on the supposition that suspects who assert their right to counsel are unlikely to waive that right voluntarily in subsequent interrogations.

"We have already decided that although statements taken in violation of only the prophylactic *Miranda* rules may not be used in the prosecution's case-in-chief, they are admissible to impeach conflicting testimony by the defendant. *Harris v. New York; Oregon v. Hass.* * * * There is no reason for a different result in a *Jackson* case, where the prophylactic rule is designed to ensure voluntary, knowing, and intelligent waivers of the Sixth Amendment right to counsel rather than the Fifth Amendment privilege against self-incrimination or 'right to counsel.' We have mandated the exclusion of reliable and probative evidence for *all* purposes only when it is derived from involuntary statements. We have never prevented use by the prosecution of relevant voluntary statements by a defendant, particularly when the violations alleged by a defendant relate only to procedural safeguards that are 'not

---

b. The dissent noted that the prosecution had also used defendant's statement that he went to the beauty parlor to "change his appearance" to suggest that defendant had a guilty mind and an intention to evade capture by disguise. "This," observed the dissent, "goes beyond what was necessary to rebut Henderson's testimony and raises

many of the concerns expressed in the majority opinion." Nonetheless, added the dissent, because of the overwhelming evidence of guilt, it agreed with the court below that "any error as to the additional statements or the effect of the prosecutor's argument had no effect on [the] trial and may be considered harmless."

themselves rights protected by the Constitution,' but are instead measures designed to ensure that constitutional rights are protected. In such cases, we have decided that the 'search for truth in a criminal case' outweighs the 'speculative possibility' that exclusion of evidence might deter future violations of rules not compelled directly by the Constitution in the first place. *Hass.* [The *Hass* case] was decided 15 years ago, and no new information has come to our attention which should lead us to think otherwise now.

"* * * Both *Jackson* and *Edwards* establish prophylactic rules that render some otherwise valid waivers of constitutional rights invalid when they result from police-initiated interrogation, and in neither case should 'the shield provided by [the prophylactic rule] be perverted into a license to use perjury by way of a defense, free from the risk of confrontation with prior inconsistent utterances.' *Harris.*"

Dissenting JUSTICE STEVENS (author of the Court's opinion in *Jackson*), joined by Brennan, Marshall and Blackmun, JJ., maintained that the Court had made it clear that "the constitutional rule recognized in *Jackson* is based on the Sixth Amendment interest in preserving 'the integrity of an accused's choice to communicate with police only through counsel,' " and that "the Court should acknowledge as much and hold that the Sixth Amendment is violated when the fruits of the State's impermissible encounter with the represented defendant are used for impeachment just as it is when the fruits are used in the prosecutor's case in chief":

"[Unlike the situation when evidence is seized in violation of the Fourth Amendment or a statement is obtained in violation of *Miranda,* the] exclusion of statements made by a represented and indicted defendant outside the presence of counsel follows not as a remedy for a violation that has preceded trial but as a necessary incident of the constitutional right itself.[7] '[T]he Sixth Amendment right to counsel exists, and is needed, in order to protect the fundamental right to a fair trial.' It is not implicated, as a general matter, in the absence of some effect of the challenged conduct on the trial process itself. It is thus the use of the evidence for trial, not the method of its collection prior to trial, that is the gravamen of the Sixth Amendment claim. * * *

"[The] police misconduct in *Walder, Harris, Havens,* and *Hass* all occurred before the defendant had been formally charged, when the unsolved crime was still being investigated and the questioning of a suspect might be expected to produce evidence that is necessary to obtain an indictment. Knowledge that the improper conduct of an interrogation will destroy its use as substantive evidence provides a powerful incentive to follow the dictates of *Miranda* and its progeny with great care.

"Once a defendant is formally charged with an offense, however, the State is no longer merely engaged in the task of determining who committed an unsolved crime; rather, it is preparing to convict the defendant of the crime he allegedly committed. '[T]he government's role shifts from investigation to accusation.' The

---

7. As Professor Schulhofer has commented:

"[T]he *Massiah* 'exclusionary rule' is not merely a prophylactic device; it is not designed to reduce the *risk* of actual constitutional violations and is not intended to deter any pretrial behavior whatsoever. Rather, *Massiah* explicitly permits government efforts to obtain information from an indicted suspect, so long as that information is not used 'as evidence against *him* at his trial.' The failure to exclude evidence, therefore, cannot be considered *collateral* to some more fundamental violation. Instead, it is the admission at trial that in itself

denies the constitutional right." Schulhofer, *Confessions and the Court,* 79 Mich.L.Rev. 865, 889 (1981).

See also Loewy, *Police-Obtained Evidence and the Constitution: Distinguishing Unconstitutionally Obtained Evidence from Unconstitutionally Used Evidence,* 87 Mich.L.Rev. 907, 931 (1989) ("The justification for disallowing such evidence would not be the 'exclusionary rule,' but the sixth amendment's rules governing fair trials"); Wasserstrom & Mertens, *The Exclusionary Rule on the Scaffold: But Was it a Fair Trial?,* 22 Am.Crim.L.Rev. 85, 175 (1984).

State has obtained sufficient evidence to establish probable cause and the ethical prosecutor has sufficient admissible evidence to convict. In practice, the investigation is often virtually complete. Any subsequent investigation is a form of discovery. The cost of an illegal interrogation is therefore greatly reduced. The police would have everything to gain and nothing to lose by repeatedly visiting with the defendant and seeking to elicit as many comments as possible about the pending trial. Knowledge that such conversations could not be used affirmatively would not detract from the State's interest in obtaining them for their value as impeachment evidence."

Part Three

THE COMMENCEMENT OF FORMAL PROCEEDINGS

Chapter 12

PRETRIAL RELEASE

SECTION 1. THE RIGHT TO BAIL; PRETRIAL RELEASE PROCEDURES

7th ed., p. 797; end of fn. d, add:

In some localities, arrestees are subject to urinalysis drug tests, and the results are taken into account by the judge in determining the risks which would be involved in releasing the defendant. For description and evaluation of these practices, see Abell, *Pretrial Drug Testing: Expanding Rights and Protecting Public Safety,* 57 Geo.Wash.L.Rev. 943 (1989); Rosen & Goldkamp, *The Constitutionality of Drug Testing at the Bail Stage,* 80 J.Crim.L. & C. 114 (1989).

SECTION 2. PREVENTIVE DETENTION

7th ed., p. 809; in first column, line 30 after "juror" put fn. b:

b. The Act states that this detention hearing, except upon a grant of a continuance, "shall be held immediately upon the person's first appearance before the judicial officer." "Nothing in § 3142(f) indicates that compliance with the first appearance requirement is a precondition to holding the hearing or that failure to comply with the requirement renders such a hearing a nullity," and thus "a failure to comply with the first appearance requirement does not defeat the Government's authority to seek detention of the person charged." *United States v. Montalvo–Murillo,* 495 U.S. 711, 110 S.Ct. 2072, 109 L.Ed.2d 720 (1990).

SECTION 3. PREVENTING DETENTION; USE OF THE CITATION AND SUMMONS

7th ed., p. 823; end of Note 4, add:

In *State v. Greenslit,* 559 A.2d 672 (Vt.1989), where (unlike *Robinson*) the notice to appear was given for an offense—present use of marijuana—as to which there would likely be evidence on the person, the court ruled "it is the existence of probable cause for the arrest which brings the search within constitutional limits, not merely the act of taking an individual into custody."

Chapter 15

GRAND JURY REVIEW

SECTION 3. CHALLENGES TO THE EVIDENCE BEFORE THE GRAND JURY

7th ed., p. 933; add to the end of Note 7:

Consider also *United States v. Williams*, set forth below. Does *Williams* override even the first group of lower court rulings described by Professor Arenella?

SECTION 4. CHALLENGES TO GRAND JURY PROCEDURES

7th ed., p. 942; prior to The Notes on Misconduct Challenges, add:

UNITED STATES v. WILLIAMS

___ U.S. ___, 112 S.Ct. 1735, 118 L.Ed.2d 352 (1992).

JUSTICE SCALIA delivered the opinion of the Court.

The question presented in this case is whether a district court may dismiss an otherwise valid indictment because the Government failed to disclose to the grand jury "substantial exculpatory evidence" in its possession. * * *

On May 4, 1988, respondent John H. Williams, Jr., a Tulsa, Oklahoma, investor, was indicted by a federal grand jury on seven counts of "knowingly mak[ing] [a] false statement or report . . . for the purpose of influencing . . . the action [of a federally insured financial institution]," in violation of 18 U.S.C. § 1014 (1988 ed., Supp. II). According to the indictment, between September 1984 and November 1985 Williams supplied four Oklahoma banks with "materially false" statements that variously overstated the value of his current assets and interest income in order to influence the banks' actions on his loan requests.

Williams' misrepresentation was allegedly effected through two financial statements provided to the banks, a "Market Value Balance Sheet" and a "Statement of Projected Income and Expense." The former included as "current assets" approximately $6 million in notes receivable from three venture capital companies. Though it contained a disclaimer that these assets were carried at cost rather than at market value, the Government asserted that listing them as "current assets"—*i.e.*, assets quickly reducible to cash—was misleading, since Williams knew that none of the venture capital companies could afford to satisfy the notes in the short term. The second document— the Statement of Projected Income and Expense—allegedly misrepresented Williams' interest income, since it failed to reflect that the interest payments received on the notes of the venture capital companies were funded entirely by Williams' own loans to those companies. The Statement thus falsely implied, according to the Government, that Williams was deriving interest income from "an independent outside source." Brief for United States 3.

Shortly after arraignment, the District Court granted Williams' motion for disclosure of all exculpatory portions of the grand jury transcripts, see *Brady v. Maryland* [7th ed., p. 1180]. Upon reviewing this material, Williams demanded that the District Court dismiss the indictment, alleging that the Government had failed to fulfill its obligation under the Tenth Circuit's prior decision in *United States v. Page*, 808 F.2d 723, 728 (1987), to present "substantial exculpatory evidence" to the grand jury (emphasis omitted). His contention was that evidence which the Government had chosen not to present to the grand jury—in particular, Williams' general ledgers and tax returns, and Williams' testimony in his contemporaneous Chapter 11 bankruptcy proceeding—disclosed that, for tax purposes and otherwise, he had regularly accounted for the "notes receivable" (and the interest on them) in a manner consistent with the Balance Sheet and the Income Statement. This, he contended, belied an intent to mislead the banks, and thus directly negated an essential element of the charged offense.

The District Court initially denied Williams' motion, but upon reconsideration ordered the indictment dismissed without prejudice. It found, after a hearing, that the withheld evidence was "relevant to an essential element of the crime charged," created " 'a reasonable doubt about [respondent's] guilt,' " and thus "render[ed] the grand jury's decision to indict gravely suspect." Upon the Government's appeal, the Court of Appeals affirmed the District Court's order, following its earlier decision in *Page, supra.* It first sustained as not "clearly erroneous" the District Court's determination that the Government had withheld "substantial exculpatory evidence" from the grand jury. It then found that the Government's behavior " 'substantially influence[d]' " the grand jury's decision to indict, or at the very least raised a " 'grave doubt that the decision to indict was free from such substantial influence,' " (quoting *Bank of Nova Scotia v. United States*). Under these circumstances, the Tenth Circuit concluded, it was not an abuse of discretion for the District Court to require the Government to begin anew before the grand jury. We granted certiorari. * * *

Respondent does not contend that the Fifth Amendment itself obliges the prosecutor to disclose substantial exculpatory evidence in his possession to the grand jury. Instead, building on our statement that the federal courts "may, within limits, formulate procedural rules not specifically required by the Constitution or the Congress," *United States v. Hasting* [7th ed., p. 46], he argues that imposition of the Tenth Circuit's disclosure rule is supported by the courts' "supervisory power." We think not. *Hasting,* and the cases that rely upon the principle it expresses, deal strictly with the courts' power to control their *own* procedures. That power has been applied not only to improve the truth-finding process of the trial, but also to prevent parties from reaping benefit or incurring harm from violations of substantive or procedural rules (imposed by the Constitution or laws) governing matters apart from the trial itself, see, *e.g., Weeks v. United States* [7th ed., p. 118]. Thus, *Bank of Nova Scotia v. United States* makes clear that the supervisory power can be used to dismiss an indictment because of misconduct before the grand jury, at least where that misconduct amounts to a violation of one of those "few, clear rules which were carefully drafted and approved by this Court and by Congress to ensure the integrity of the grand jury's functions," *United States v. Mechanik* [7th ed., p. 948] (O'Connor, J., concurring in judgment).[6]

---

6. Rule 6 of the Federal Rules of Criminal Procedure contains a number of such rules, providing, for example, that "no person other than the jurors may be present while the grand jury is deliberating or voting," Rule 6(d), and placing strict controls on disclosure of "matters occurring before the grand jury," Rule 6(e). * * * Additional standards of behavior for prosecutors (and others) are set forth in the United States Code. See 18 U.S.C. §§ 6002, 6003 (setting forth procedures for granting a witness immunity from prosecution); § 1623 (criminalizing false declarations before grand jury); § 2515 (prohibiting grand jury use of unlawfully intercepted wire or oral communications); § 1622 (criminalizing subornation of perjury). That some of the misconduct alleged in *Bank of Nova Scotia v. United States,* was not specifically proscribed by Rule, statute, or the Constitution does not make the case stand for a judicially prescribable grand jury code * * *. All of the allegations of violation were dismissed by the Court—without considering their validity in law—for failure to meet *Nova Scotia's* dismissal standard. See *Bank of Nova Scotia.*

We did not hold in *Bank of Nova Scotia,* however, that the courts' supervisory power could be used, not merely as a means of enforcing or vindicating legally compelled standards of prosecutorial conduct before the grand jury, but as a means of *prescribing* those standards of prosecutorial conduct in the first instance—just as it may be used as a means of establishing standards of prosecutorial conduct before the courts themselves. It is this latter exercise that respondent demands. Because the grand jury is an institution separate from the courts, over whose functioning the courts do not preside, we think it clear that, as a general matter at least, no such "supervisory" judicial authority exists, and that the disclosure rule applied here exceeded the Tenth Circuit's authority. * * *

"[R]ooted in long centuries of Anglo-American history," the grand jury is mentioned in the Bill of Rights, but not in the body of the Constitution. It has not been textually assigned, therefore, to any of the branches described in the first three Articles. It " 'is a constitutional fixture in its own right.' " *United States v. Chanen,* 549 F.2d 1306 (9th Cir.1977). In fact the whole theory of its function is that it belongs to no branch of the institutional government, serving as a kind of buffer or referee between the Government and the people. See *Stirone v. United States* [7th ed., p. 976]. * * * Although the grand jury normally operates, of course, in the courthouse and under judicial auspices, its institutional relationship with the judicial branch has traditionally been, so to speak, at arm's length. Judges' direct involvement in the functioning of the grand jury has generally been confined to the constitutive one of calling the grand jurors together and administering their oaths of office. See *United States v. Calandra* [7th ed., pp. 662, 933]; Fed.Rule Crim.Proc. 6(a).

The grand jury's functional independence from the judicial branch is evident both in the scope of its power to investigate criminal wrongdoing, and in the manner in which that power is exercised. "Unlike [a] [c]ourt, whose jurisdiction is predicated upon a specific case or controversy, the grand jury 'can investigate merely on suspicion that the law is being violated, or even because it wants assurance that it is not.' " *United States v. R. Enterprises* [Supp. p. 68]. It need not identify the offender it suspects, or even "the precise nature of the offense" it is investigating. *Blair v. United States* [7th ed., p. 644]. The grand jury requires no authorization from its constituting court to initiate an investigation, nor does the prosecutor require leave of court to seek a grand jury indictment. And in its day-to-day functioning, the grand jury generally operates without the interference of a presiding judge. See *Calandra,* supra. It swears in its own witnesses, Fed.Rule Crim.Proc. 6(c), and deliberates in total secrecy.

True, the grand jury cannot compel the appearance of witnesses and the production of evidence, and must appeal to the court when such compulsion is required. See *Brown v. United States,* 359 U.S. 41, 49, 79 S.Ct. 539, 545, 3 L.Ed.2d 609 (1959). And the court will refuse to lend its assistance when the compulsion the grand jury seeks would override rights accorded by the Constitution, see, *e.g., Gravel v. United States,* 408 U.S. 606, 92 S.Ct. 2614, 33 L.Ed.2d 583 (1972) (grand jury subpoena effectively qualified by order limiting questioning so as to preserve Speech or Debate Clause immunity), or even testimonial privileges recognized by the common law, see *In re Grand Jury Investigation of Hugle,* 754 F.2d 863 (9th Cir.1985) (same with respect to privilege for confidential marital communications) (opinion of Kennedy, J.). Even in this setting, however, we have insisted that the grand jury remain "free to pursue its investigations unhindered by external influence or supervision so long as it does not trench upon the legitimate rights of any witness called before it." *United States v. Dionisio* [7th ed., p. 635]. Recognizing this tradition of independence, we have said that the Fifth Amendment's "constitutional guarantee *presupposes* an investigative body 'acting independently of either prosecuting attorney *or judge*'. . . ." *Dionisio.*

No doubt in view of the grand jury proceeding's status as other than a constituent element of a "criminal prosecutio[n]," U.S. Const., Amdt. VI, we have said that certain constitutional protections afforded defendants in criminal proceedings have no application before that body. The Double Jeopardy Clause of the Fifth Amendment does not bar a grand jury from returning an indictment when a prior grand jury has refused to do so. * * * We have twice suggested, though not held, that the Sixth Amendment right to counsel does not attach when an individual is summoned to appear before a grand jury, even if he is the subject of the investigation. See *United States v. Mandujano* [7th ed., p. 762]; *In re Groban* [7th ed., p. 675], see also Fed.Rule Crim.Proc. 6(d). And although "the grand jury may not force a witness to answer questions in violation of [the Fifth Amendment's] constitutional guarantee" against self-incrimination, *Calandra,* supra, our cases suggest that an indictment obtained through the use of evidence previously obtained in violation of the privilege against self-incrimination "is nevertheless valid." *Calandra,* supra.

Given the grand jury's operational separateness from its constituting court, it should come as no surprise that we have been reluctant to invoke the judicial supervisory power as a basis for prescribing modes of grand jury procedure. Over the years, we have received many requests to exercise supervision over the grand jury's evidence-taking process, but we have refused them all, including some more appealing than the one presented today. In *Calandra,* supra, a grand jury witness faced questions that were allegedly based upon physical evidence the Government had obtained through a violation of the Fourth Amendment; we rejected the proposal that the exclusionary rule be extended to grand jury proceedings, because of "the potential injury to the historic role and functions of the grand jury." In *Costello v. United States* [7th ed., p. 928], we declined to enforce the hearsay rule in grand jury proceedings, since that "would run counter to the whole history of the grand jury institution, in which laymen conduct their inquiries unfettered by technical rules."

These authorities suggest that any power federal courts may have to fashion, on their own initiative, rules of grand jury procedure is a very limited one, not remotely comparable to the power they maintain over their own proceedings. See *United States v. Chanen,* supra. It certainly would not permit judicial reshaping of the grand jury institution, substantially altering the traditional relationships between the prosecutor, the constituting court, and the grand jury itself. Cf., *e.g., United States v. Payner* [7th ed., p. 45] (supervisory power may not be applied to permit defendant to invoke third party's Fourth Amendment rights); see generally Beale, Reconsidering Supervisory Power in Criminal Cases [7th ed., Note 5, p. 646]. As we proceed to discuss, that would be the consequence of the proposed rule here. * * *

Respondent argues that the Court of Appeals' rule can be justified as a sort of Fifth Amendment "common law," a necessary means of assuring the constitutional right to the judgment "of an independent and informed grand jury," *Wood v. Georgia* [7th ed., p. 914]. Respondent makes a generalized appeal to functional notions: Judicial supervision of the quantity and quality of the evidence relied upon by the grand jury plainly facilitates, he says, the grand jury's performance of its twin historical responsibilities, *i.e.,* bringing to trial those who may be justly accused and shielding the innocent from unfounded accusation and prosecution. We do not agree. The rule would neither preserve nor enhance the traditional functioning of the institution that the Fifth Amendment demands. To the contrary, requiring the prosecutor to present exculpatory as well as inculpatory evidence would alter the grand jury's historical role, transforming it from an accusatory to an adjudicatory body.

It is axiomatic that the grand jury sits not to determine guilt or innocence, but to assess whether there is adequate basis for bringing a criminal charge. See *United States v. Calandra,* supra. That has always been so; and to make the assessment it has always been thought sufficient to hear only the prosecutor's side. As Blackstone described the prevailing practice in 18th-century England, the grand jury was "only to hear evidence on behalf of the prosecution[,] for the finding of an indictment is only in the nature of an enquiry or accusation, which is afterwards to be tried and determined." 4 W. Blackstone, Commentaries 300 (1769); see also 2 M. Hale, Pleas of the Crown 157 (1st Am. ed. 1847). So also in the United States. According to the description of an early American court, three years before the Fifth Amendment was ratified, it is the grand jury's function not "to enquire . . . upon what foundation [the charge may be] denied," or otherwise to try the suspect's defenses, but only to examine "upon what foundation [the charge] is made" by the prosecutor. *Respublica v. Shaffer,* 1 U.S. (1 Dall.) 236, 1 L.Ed. 116 (Philadelphia Oyer and Terminer 1788). See also F. Wharton, Criminal Pleading and Practice § 360, pp. 248–249 (8th ed. 1880). As a consequence, neither in this country nor in England has the suspect under investigation by the grand jury ever been thought to have a right to testify, or to have exculpatory evidence presented.

Imposing upon the prosecutor a legal obligation to present exculpatory evidence in his possession would be incompatible with this system. If a "balanced" assessment of the entire matter is the objective, surely the first thing to be done—rather than requiring the prosecutor to say what he knows in defense of the target of the investigation—is to entitle the target to tender his own defense. To require the former while denying (as we do) the latter would be quite absurd. It would also be quite pointless, since it would merely invite the target to circumnavigate the system by delivering his exculpatory evidence to the prosecutor, whereupon it would *have* to be passed on to the grand jury— unless the prosecutor is willing to take the chance that a court will not deem the evidence important enough to qualify for mandatory disclosure. * * *

Respondent acknowledges (as he must) that the "common law" of the grand jury is not violated if the *grand jury itself* chooses to hear no more evidence than that which suffices to convince it an indictment is proper. Thus, had the Government offered to familiarize the grand jury in this case with the five boxes of financial statements and deposition testimony alleged to contain exculpatory information, and had the grand jury rejected the offer as pointless, respondent would presumably agree that the resulting indictment would have been valid. Respondent insists, however, that courts must require the modern prosecutor to alert the grand jury to the nature and extent of the available exculpatory evidence, because otherwise the grand jury "merely functions as an arm of the prosecution." We reject the attempt to convert a nonexistent duty of the grand jury itself into an obligation of the prosecutor. The authority of the prosecutor to seek an indictment has long been understood to be "coterminous with the authority of the grand jury to entertain [the prosecutor's] charges." *United States v. Thompson,* 251 U.S. 407, 414, 40 S.Ct. 289, 292, 64 L.Ed. 333 (1920). If the grand jury has no obligation to consider all "substantial exculpatory" evidence, we do not understand how the prosecutor can be said to have a binding obligation to present it.

There is yet another respect in which respondent's proposal not only fails to comport with, but positively contradicts, the "common law" of the Fifth Amendment grand jury. Motions to quash indictments based upon the sufficiency of the evidence relied upon by the grand jury were unheard of at common law in England, see, *e.g., People v. Restenblatt,* 1 Abb. Prac. 268, 269 (Ct.Gen.Sess.N.Y.1855). And the traditional American practice was described by Justice Nelson, riding circuit in 1852, as follows:

> "No case has been cited, nor have we been able to find any, furnishing an authority for looking into and revising the judgment of the grand jury upon the evidence, for the purpose of determining whether or not the finding was founded upon sufficient proof, or whether there was a deficiency in respect to any part of the complaint. . . ." *United States v. Reed,* 27 Fed.Cas. 727, 738 (No. 16,134) (CCNDNY 1852).

We accepted Justice Nelson's description in *Costello v. United States,* supra, where we held that "it would run counter to the whole history of the grand jury institution" to permit an indictment to be challenged "on the ground that there was incompetent or inadequate evidence before the grand jury." And we reaffirmed this principle recently in *Bank of Nova Scotia,* where we held that "the mere fact that evidence itself is unreliable is not sufficient to require a dismissal of the indictment," and that "a challenge to the reliability or competence of the evidence presented to the grand jury" will not be heard. It would make little sense, we think, to abstain from reviewing the evidentiary support for the grand jury's judgment while scrutinizing the sufficiency of the prosecutor's presentation. A complaint about the quality or adequacy of the evidence can always be recast as a complaint that the prosecutor's presentation was "incomplete" or "misleading." [8] Our words in *Costello* bear repeating: Review of facially valid indictments on such grounds "would run counter to the whole history of the grand jury institution[,] [and] [n]either justice nor the concept of a fair trial requires [it]."

* * * Echoing the reasoning of the Tenth Circuit in *United States v. Page,* supra, respondent argues that a rule requiring the prosecutor to disclose exculpatory evidence to the grand jury would, by removing from the docket unjustified prosecutions, save valuable judicial time. That depends, we suppose, upon what the ratio would turn out to be between unjustified prosecutions eliminated and grand jury indictments challenged—for the latter as well as the former consume "valuable judicial time." We need not pursue the matter; if there is an advantage to the proposal, Congress is free to prescribe it. For the reasons set forth above, however, we conclude that courts have no authority to prescribe such a duty pursuant to their inherent supervisory authority over their own proceedings. The judgment of the Court of Appeals is accordingly reversed and the cause remanded for further proceedings consistent with this opinion.

JUSTICE STEVENS, with whom JUSTICE BLACKMUN and JUSTICE O'CONNOR join, and with whom JUSTICE THOMAS joins as to Parts II and III, dissenting. * * *[a]

Like the Hydra slain by Hercules, prosecutorial misconduct has many heads. * * * [It has not] been limited to judicial proceedings: the reported [lower

---

8. In *Costello,* for example, instead of complaining about the grand jury's *reliance* upon hearsay evidence the petitioner could have complained about the prosecutor's *introduction* of it. See, *e.g., United States v. Estepa,* 471 F.2d 1132, 1136–1137 (2d Cir.1972) (prosecutor should not introduce hearsay evidence before grand jury when direct evidence is available); see also

Arenella, Reforming the Federal Grand Jury [7th ed., Note 7, p. 933].

---

a. Part I of Justice Stevens, deleted here, argued that certiorari was improvidently granted. That portion of the majority's opinion responding to this argument also has been deleted.

court] cases indicate that it has sometimes infected grand jury proceedings as well. The cases contain examples of prosecutors presenting perjured testimony, questioning a witness outside the presence of the grand jury and then failing to inform the grand jury that the testimony was exculpatory, failing to inform the grand jury of its authority to subpoena witnesses, operating under a conflict of interest, misstating the law, and misstating the facts on cross-examination of a witness. * * *

[As] Justice Sutherland [explained in *Berger v. United States,* 7th ed., p. 1399, fn. f]: "The United States Attorney is the representative not of an ordinary party to a controversy, but of a sovereign whose obligation is to govern impartially is as compelling as its obligation to govern at all; and whose interest, therefore, in a criminal prosecution is not that it shall win a case, but that justice shall be done. * * * It is as much his duty to refrain from improper methods calculated to produce a wrongful conviction as it is to use every legitimate means to bring about a just one." It is equally clear that the prosecutor has the same duty to refrain from improper methods calculated to produce a wrongful indictment. Indeed, the prosecutor's duty to protect the fundamental fairness of judicial proceedings assumes special importance when he is presenting evidence to a grand jury. As the Court of Appeals for the Third Circuit recognized, "the costs of continued unchecked prosecutorial misconduct" before the grand jury are particularly substantial because there

"the prosecutor operates without the check of a judge or a trained legal adversary, and virtually immune from public scrutiny. The prosecutor's abuse of his special relationship to the grand jury poses an enormous risk to defendants as well. For while in theory a trial provides the defendant with a full opportunity to contest and disprove the charges against him, in practice, the handing up of an indictment will often have a devastating personal and professional impact

that a later dismissal or acquittal can never undo. Where the potential for abuse is so great, and the consequences of a mistaken indictment so serious, the ethical responsibilities of the prosecutor, and the obligation of the judiciary to protect against even the appearance of unfairness, are correspondingly heightened." *United States v. Serubo,* 604 F.2d 807, 817 (CA3 1979).

* * * The standard for judging the consequences of prosecutorial misconduct during grand jury proceedings is essentially the same as the standard applicable to trials. In *United States v. Mechanik* [7th ed., p. 948], we held that there was "no reason not to apply [the harmless error rule] to 'errors, defects, irregularities, or variances' occurring before a grand jury just as we have applied it to such error occurring in the criminal trial itself." We repeated that holding in *Bank of Nova Scotia v. United States,* when we rejected a defendant's argument that an indictment should be dismissed because of prosecutorial misconduct and irregularities in proceedings before the grand jury. Referring to the prosecutor's misconduct before the grand jury, we "concluded that our customary harmless-error inquiry is applicable where, as in the cases before us, a court is asked to dismiss an indictment prior to the conclusion of the trial." Moreover, in reviewing the instances of misconduct in that case, we applied precisely the same standard to the prosecutor's violations of Rule 6 of the Federal Rules of Criminal Procedure and to his violations of the general duty of fairness that applies to all judicial proceedings. This point is illustrated by the Court's comments on the prosecutor's abuse of a witness. [The dissent here quotes the last paragraph in the first column of p. 940 of the 7th edition.] Unquestionably, the plain implication of that discussion is that if the misconduct, even though not expressly forbidden by any written rule, had played a critical role in persuading the jury to return the indictment, dismissal would have been required.

In an opinion that I find difficult to comprehend, the Court today repudiates the assumptions underlying these cases and seems to suggest that the court has no authority to supervise the conduct of the prosecutor in grand jury proceedings so long as he follows the dictates of the Constitution, applicable statutes, and Rule 6 of the Federal Rules of Criminal Procedure. The Court purports to support this conclusion by invoking the doctrine of separation of powers and citing a string of cases in which we have declined to impose categorical restraints on the grand jury. Needless to say, the Court's reasoning is unpersuasive.

Although the grand jury has not been "textually assigned" to "any of the branches described in the first three Articles" of the Constitution, it is not an autonomous body completely beyond the reach of the other branches. Throughout its life, from the moment it is convened until it is discharged, the grand jury is subject to the control of the court. As Judge Learned Hand recognized over sixty years ago, "a grand jury is neither an officer nor an agent of the United States, but a part of the court." *Falter v. United States,* 23 F.2d 420, 425 (2d Cir.1928). This Court has similarly characterized the grand jury:

> "A grand jury is clothed with great independence in many areas, but it remains an appendage of the court, powerless to perform its investigative function without the court's aid, because powerless itself to compel the testimony of witnesses. It is the court's process which summons the witness to attend and give testimony, and it is the court which must compel a witness to testify if, after appearing, he refuses to do so." *Brown v. United States,* 359 U.S. 41, 49, 79 S.Ct. 539, 546, 3 L.Ed.2d 609 (1959).

10. Indeed, even the Court acknowledges that Congress has the power to regulate the grand jury, for it concedes that Congress "is free to

* * * This Court has, of course, long recognized that the grand jury has wide latitude to investigate violations of federal law as it deems appropriate and need not obtain permission from either the court or the prosecutor. Correspondingly, we have acknowledged that "its operation generally is unrestrained by the technical procedural and evidentiary rules governing the conduct of criminal trials." *United States v. Calandra* [7th ed., p. 662]. But this is because Congress and the Court have generally thought it best not to impose procedural restraints on the grand jury; it is not because they lack all power to do so.[10]

To the contrary, the Court has recognized that it has the authority to create and enforce limited rules applicable in grand jury proceedings. Thus, for example, the Court has said that the grand jury "may not itself violate a valid privilege, whether established by the Constitution, statutes, or the common law." *Calandra,* supra. And the Court may prevent a grand jury from violating such a privilege by quashing or modifying a subpoena, or issuing a protective order forbidding questions in violation of the privilege. *Gravel v. United States,* 408 U.S. 606, 92 S.Ct. 2614, 33 L.Ed.2d 583 (1972). Moreover, there are, as the Court notes, a series of cases in which we declined to impose categorical restraints on the grand jury. In none of those cases, however, did we question our power to reach a contrary result.

Although the Court recognizes that it may invoke its supervisory authority to fashion and enforce privilege rules applicable in grand jury proceedings, and suggests that it may also invoke its supervisory authority to fashion other limited rules of grand jury procedure, it concludes that it has no authority to *"prescrib[e]* standards of prosecutorial conduct before the grand jury," because that would alter the grand jury's historic role as an independent, inquisitorial institution. I disagree.

prescribe" a rule requiring the prosecutor to disclose substantial exculpatory evidence to the grand jury.

We do not protect the integrity and independence of the grand jury by closing our eyes to the countless forms of prosecutorial misconduct that may occur inside the secrecy of the grand jury room. After all, the grand jury is not merely an investigatory body; it also serves as a "protector of citizens against arbitrary and oppressive governmental action." *Calandra,* supra. * * * It blinks reality to say that the grand jury can adequately perform this important historic role if it is intentionally misled by the prosecutor—on whose knowledge of the law and facts of the underlying criminal investigation the jurors will, of necessity, rely.

Unlike the Court, I am unwilling to hold that countless forms of prosecutorial misconduct must be tolerated—no matter how prejudicial they may be, or how seriously they may distort the legitimate function of the grand jury—simply because they are not proscribed by Rule 6 of the Federal Rules of Criminal Procedure or a statute that is applicable in grand jury proceedings. Such a sharp break with the traditional role of the federal judiciary is unprecedented, unwarranted, and unwise. Unrestrained prosecutorial misconduct in grand jury proceedings is inconsistent with the administration of justice in the federal courts and should be redressed in appropriate cases by the dismissal of indictments obtained by improper methods.[12]

* * *

What, then, is the proper disposition of this case? I agree with the Government that the prosecutor is not required to place all exculpatory evidence before the grand jury. A grand jury proceeding is an *ex parte* investigatory proceeding to determine whether there is probable cause to believe a violation of the criminal laws has occurred,

not a trial. Requiring the prosecutor to ferret out and present all evidence that could be used at trial to create a reasonable doubt as to the defendant's guilt would be inconsistent with the purpose of the grand jury proceeding and would place significant burdens on the investigation. But that does not mean that the prosecutor may mislead the grand jury into believing that there is probable cause to indict by withholding clear evidence to the contrary. I thus agree with the Department of Justice that "when a prosecutor conducting a grand jury inquiry is personally aware of substantial evidence which directly negates the guilt of a subject of the investigation, the prosecutor must present or otherwise disclose such evidence to the grand jury before seeking an indictment against such a person." U.S. Dept. of Justice, United States Attorneys' Manual, Title 9, ch. 11, ¶ 9–11.233, 88 (1988).

Although I question whether the evidence withheld in this case directly negates respondent's guilt,[13] I need not resolve my doubts because the Solicitor General did not ask the Court to review the nature of the evidence withheld. Instead, he asked us to decide the legal question whether an indictment may be dismissed because the prosecutor failed to present exculpatory evidence. Unlike the Court and the Solicitor General, I believe the answer to that question is yes, if the withheld evidence would plainly preclude a finding of probable cause. I therefore cannot endorse the Court's opinion.

* * *

———

To what extent does *Williams* require reexamination, as to federal courts, of the material presented in the following Notes on Misconduct Challenges?

Franks v. Delaware [7th ed., p. 192] (discussing analogous considerations in holding that a search warrant affidavit may be challenged when supported by deliberately false police statements)." Brief for United States 22, n. 8.

---

12. Although the Court's opinion barely mentions the fact that the grand jury was intended to serve the invaluable function of standing between the accuser and the accused, I must assume that in a proper case it will acknowledge—as even the Solicitor General does—that unrestrained prosecutorial misconduct in grand jury proceedings "could so subvert the integrity of the grand jury process as to justify judicial intervention. Cf.

13. I am reluctant to rely on the lower courts' judgment in this regard, as they apparently applied a more lenient legal standard. * * *

Chapter 18

THE SCOPE OF THE PROSECUTION: JOINDER AND SEVERANCE OF OFFENSES AND DEFENDANTS

SECTION 2. FAILURE TO JOIN RELATED OFFENSES

7th ed., p. 998; in lieu of *Vitale* case and Note 1 following, add:

GRADY v. CORBIN

495 U.S. 508, 110 S.Ct. 2084, 109 L.Ed.2d 548 (1990).

JUSTICE BRENNAN delivered the opinion of the Court. * * *

For purposes of this proceeding, we take the following facts as true. At approximately 6:35 p.m. on October 3, 1987, respondent Thomas Corbin drove his automobile across the double yellow line of Route 55 in LaGrange, New York, striking two oncoming vehicles. Assistant District Attorney (ADA) Thomas Dolan was called to the scene, where he learned that both Brenda Dirago, who had been driving the second vehicle to be struck, and her husband Daniel had been seriously injured. Later that evening, ADA Dolan was informed that Brenda Dirago had died from injuries sustained in the accident. That same evening, while at the hospital being treated for his own injuries, respondent was served with two uniform traffic tickets directing him to appear at the LaGrange Town Justice Court on October 29, 1987. One ticket charged him with

the misdemeanor of driving while intoxicated; the other charged him with failing to keep right of the median. A blood test taken at the hospital that evening indicated a blood alcohol level of 0.19%, nearly twice the level at which it is *per se* illegal to operate a motor vehicle in New York.

Three days later, Assistant District Attorney Frank Chase began gathering evidence for a homicide prosecution in connection with the accident. "Despite his active involvement in building a homicide case against [Corbin], however, Chase did not attempt to ascertain the date [Corbin] was scheduled to appear in Town Justice Court on the traffic tickets, nor did he inform either the Town Justice Court or the Assistant District Attorney covering that court about his pending investigation." Thus, Assistant District Attorney Mark Glick never mentioned Brenda Dirago's death in the statement of readiness for trial and other pretrial pleadings he submitted to respondent and the LaGrange Town Justice Court on October 14, 1987.

Accordingly, when respondent pleaded guilty to the two traffic tickets on October 27, 1987, a date on which no member of the District Attorney's office was present in court,[3] the presiding judge was unaware

---

3. The record does not indicate why the return dates for the traffic tickets were changed from October 29 to October 27. In any event, the District Attorney was not deprived of a meaningful opportunity to participate in this prosecution. If the District Attorney had wanted to prevent

Corbin from pleading guilty to the traffic tickets so that the State could combine all charges into a single prosecution containing the later-charged felony counts, he could have availed himself of [statutory adjournment procedures].

of the fatality stemming from the accident. Corbin was never asked if any others had been injured on the night in question and did not voluntarily incriminate himself by providing such information.[4] The presiding judge accepted his guilty plea, but because the District Attorney's office had not submitted a sentencing recommendation, the judge postponed sentencing until November 17, 1987, when an Assistant District Attorney was scheduled to be present in court. The Assistant District Attorney present at sentencing on that date, Heidi Sauter, was unaware that there had been a fatality, was unable to locate the case file, and had not spoken to ADA Glick about the case. Nevertheless, she did not seek an adjournment so that she could ascertain the facts necessary to make an informed sentencing recommendation. Instead, she recommended a "minimum sentence," and the presiding judge sentenced Corbin to a $350 fine, a $10 surcharge, and a 6–month license revocation.

Two months later, on January 19, 1988, a grand jury investigating the October 3, 1987, accident indicted Corbin, charging him with reckless manslaughter, second-degree vehicular manslaughter, and criminally negligent homicide for causing the death of Brenda Dirago; third-degree reckless assault for causing physical injury to Daniel Dirago; and driving while intoxicated. The prosecution filed a bill of particulars that identified the three reckless or negligent acts on which it would rely to prove the homicide and assault charges: (1) operating a motor vehicle on a public

highway in an intoxicated condition, (2) failing to keep right of the median, and (3) driving approximately 45 to 50 miles per hour in heavy rain, "which was a speed too fast for the weather and road conditions then pending." Respondent moved to dismiss the indictment on statutory and constitutional double jeopardy grounds. After a hearing, the Dutchess County Court denied respondent's motion, ruling that the failure of Corbin or his counsel to inform the Town Justice Court at the time of the guilty plea that Corbin had been involved in a fatal accident constituted a "material misrepresentation of fact" that "was prejudicial to the administration of justice."[6]

Respondent then sought a writ of prohibition barring prosecution on all counts of the indictment. The Appellate Division denied the petition without opinion, but the New York Court of Appeals reversed. The court prohibited prosecution of the driving while intoxicated counts pursuant to New York's statutory double jeopardy provision. The court further ruled that prosecution of the two vehicular manslaughter counts would violate the Double Jeopardy Clause of the Fifth Amendment pursuant to the *Blockburger* test because, as a matter of state law, driving while intoxicated "is unquestionably a lesser included offense of second degree vehicular manslaughter." Finally, relying on the "pointed dictum" in this Court's opinion in *Vitale*, the court barred prosecution of the remaining counts because the bill of particulars expressed an intention to "rely on the prior traffic offenses as the acts neces-

---

Furthermore, the District Attorney's participation in this prosecution amounted to more than a failure to move for an adjournment. ADA Glick filed papers indicating a readiness to proceed to trial, and Assistant District Attorney Heidi Sauter appeared at Corbin's sentencing on behalf of the People of the State of New York.

4. The New York Court of Appeals held that, although an attorney may not misrepresent facts, "a practitioner representing a client at a traffic violation prosecution should not be expected to *volunteer* information that is likely to be highly damaging to his client's position." Because the

Court of Appeals refused to characterize as misconduct the behavior of either Corbin or his attorney, we need not decide whether our double jeopardy analysis would be any different if affirmative misrepresentations of fact by a defendant or his counsel were to mislead a court into accepting a guilty plea it would not otherwise accept.

6. The New York Court of Appeals found no misrepresentations and no misconduct during the guilty plea colloquy on October 27, 1987. We accept its characterization of the proceedings.

sary to prove the homicide and assault charges." Two judges dissented, arguing that respondent had deceived the Town Justice Court when pleading guilty to the traffic tickets. We granted certiorari, and now affirm.

The facts and contentions raised here mirror almost exactly those raised in this Court 10 years ago in *Illinois v. Vitale,* 447 U.S. 410, 100 S.Ct. 2260, 65 L.Ed.2d 228 (1980). Like Thomas Corbin, John Vitale allegedly caused a fatal car accident. A police officer at the scene issued Vitale a traffic citation charging him with failure to reduce speed to avoid an accident. Vitale was convicted of that offense and sentenced to pay a $15 fine. The day after his conviction, the State charged Vitale with two counts of involuntary manslaughter based on his reckless driving. Vitale argued that this subsequent prosecution was barred by the Double Jeopardy Clause.

This Court held that the second prosecution was not barred under the traditional *Blockburger* test because each offense "require[d] proof of a fact which the other [did] not." Although involuntary manslaughter required proof of a death, failure to reduce speed did not. Likewise, failure to slow was not a statutory element of involuntary manslaughter. Thus, the subsequent prosecution survived the *Blockburger* test.

But the Court did not stop at that point. Justice White, writing for the Court, added that, even though the two prosecutions did not violate the *Blockburger* test:

"[I]t may be that to sustain its manslaughter case the State may find it necessary to prove a failure to slow or to rely on conduct necessarily involving such failure; it may concede as much

prior to trial. In that case, because Vitale has already been convicted for conduct that is a necessary element of the more serious crime for which he has been charged, his claim of double jeopardy would be substantial under *Brown* [*v. Ohio,* 432 U.S. 161, 97 S.Ct. 2221, 53 L.Ed.2d 187 (1977)] and our later decision in *Harris v. Oklahoma,* 433 U.S. 682 [97 S.Ct. 2912, 53 L.Ed.2d 1054] (1977)."

We believe that this analysis is correct and governs this case.[7] To determine whether a subsequent prosecution is barred by the Double Jeopardy Clause, a court must first apply the traditional *Blockburger* test. If application of that test reveals that the offenses have identical statutory elements or that one is a lesser included offense of the other, then the inquiry must cease, and the subsequent prosecution is barred.

The State argues that this should be the last step in the inquiry and that the Double Jeopardy Clause permits successive prosecutions whenever the offenses charged satisfy the *Blockburger* test. We disagree. The Double Jeopardy Clause embodies three protections: "It protects against a second prosecution for the same offense after acquittal. It protects against a second prosecution for the same offense after conviction. And it protects against multiple punishments for the same offense." The *Blockburger* test was developed "in the context of multiple punishments imposed in a single prosecution." In that context, "the Double Jeopardy Clause does no more than prevent the sentencing court from prescribing greater punishment than the legislature intended." The *Blockburger* test is simply a "rule of statutory construction," a guide to determining whether the legislature intended multiple punishments.[8]

7. We recognized in *Brown v. Ohio* that when application of our traditional double jeopardy analysis would bar a subsequent prosecution, "[a]n exception may exist where the State is unable to proceed on the more serious charge at the outset because the additional facts necessary to sustain that charge have not occurred or have

not been discovered despite the exercise of due diligence." Because ADA Dolan was informed of Brenda Dirago's death on the night of the accident, such an exception is inapplicable here.

8. Justice Scalia's dissent contends that *Blockburger* is not just a guide to legislative in-

the prosecution's theory of proof is binding on the State until amended, and the State has not amended it to date. The bill of particulars states that the prosecution will prove the following:

"[T]he defendant [(1)] operated a motor vehicle on a public highway in an intoxicated condition having more than .10 percent of alcohol content in his blood, [(2)] failed to keep right and in fact crossed nine feet over the median of the highway [and (3) drove] at approximately forty-five to fifty miles an hour in heavy rain, which was a speed too fast for the weather and road conditions then pending. . . . By so operating his vehicle in the manner above described, the defendant was aware of and consciously disregarded a substantial and unjustifiable risk of the likelihood of the result which occurred. . . . By his failure to perceive this risk while operating a vehicle in a criminally negligent and reckless manner, he caused physical injury to Daniel Dirago and the death of his wife, Brenda Dirago."

By its own pleadings, the State has admitted that it will prove the entirety of the conduct for which Corbin was convicted—driving while intoxicated and failing to keep right of the median—to establish essential elements of the homicide and assault offenses. Therefore, the Double Jeopardy Clause bars this successive prosecution, and the New York Court of Appeals properly granted respondent's petition for a writ of prohibition. This holding would not bar a subsequent prosecution on the homicide and assault charges

requires more than a technical comparison of statutory elements when a defendant is confronting successive prosecutions, have adopted an essential procedural mechanism for assessing double jeopardy claims prior to a second trial. All nine federal Circuits which have addressed the issue have held that "when a defendant puts double jeopardy in issue with a non-frivolous showing that an indictment charges him with an offense for which he was formerly placed in jeopardy, the burden shifts to the government to establish that there were in fact two separate offenses." *United States v. Ragins*, 840 F.2d

if the bill of particulars revealed that the State would not rely on proving the conduct for which Corbin had already been convicted (*i.e.,* if the State relied solely on Corbin's driving too fast in heavy rain to establish recklessness or negligence).[15]

* * *

The judgment of the New York Court of Appeals is

Affirmed.

JUSTICE O'CONNOR, dissenting.

I agree with much of what Justice Scalia says in his dissenting opinion. I write separately, however, to note that my dissent is premised primarily on my view that the inconsistency between the Court's opinion today and *Dowling v. United States,* decided earlier this Term, indicates that the Court has strayed from a proper interpretation of the scope of the Double Jeopardy Clause. * * *

JUSTICE SCALIA, with whom CHIEF JUSTICE REHNQUIST and JUSTICE KENNEDY join, dissenting. * * *

Subject to the *Harris* and *Ashe* exceptions, I would adhere to the *Blockburger* rule that successive prosecutions under two different statutes do not constitute double jeopardy if each statutory crime contains an element that the other does not, regardless of the overlap between the proof required for each prosecution in the particular case. That rule best gives effect to the language of the Clause, which protects individuals from being twice put in jeopardy "for the same *offence,*" not for the same *conduct* or *actions.* "Offence" was commonly understood in 1791 to mean "trans-

1184, 1192 (CA4 1988) (collecting cases). This procedural mechanism will ensure that the test set forth today is in fact "implementable".

15. Adoption of a "same transaction" test would bar the homicide and assault prosecutions even if the State were able to establish the essential elements of those crimes without proving the conduct for which Corbin previously was convicted. The Court, however, has "steadfastly refused to adopt the 'single transaction' view of the Double Jeopardy Clause." *Garrett v. United States,* [7th ed., p. 1003].

gression," that is, "the Violation or Breaking of a Law." * * *

Another textual element also supports the *Blockburger* test. Since the Double Jeopardy Clause protects the defendant from being "twice put in jeopardy," *i.e.,* made to stand trial for the "same offence," it presupposes that sameness can be determined before the second trial. Otherwise, the Clause would have prohibited a second "conviction" or "sentence" for the same offense. A court can always determine, before trial, whether the second prosecution involves the "same offence" in the *Blockburger* sense, since the Constitution entitles the defendant "to be informed of the nature and cause of the accusation." But since the Constitution does not entitle the defendant to be informed of the *evidence* against him, the Court's "proof-of-same-conduct" test will be implementable before trial only if the indictment happens to show that the same evidence is at issue, or only if the jurisdiction's rules of criminal procedure happen to require the prosecution to submit a bill of particulars that cannot be exceeded. More often than not, in other words, the Court's test will not succeed in preventing the defendant from being tried twice.

Relying on text alone, therefore, one would conclude that the Double Jeopardy Clause meant what *Blockburger* said. But there is in addition a wealth of historical evidence to the same effect. The Clause was based on the English common-law pleas of *auterfoits acquit* and *auterfoits convict,* which pleas were valid only "upon a prosecution for the same identical act *and* crime." * * *

The English practice, as understood in 1791, did not recognize *auterfoits acquit* and *auterfoits convict* as good pleas against successive prosecutions for crimes whose elements were distinct, even though based on the same act.

The early American cases adhere to the same rule. * * *

Thus, the *Blockburger* definition of "same offence" was not invented in 1932 * * *.

[T]he argument that *Vitale* said to be "substantial" finds no support whatever in the two cases that *Vitale* thought gave it substance, *Brown v. Ohio* and *Harris v. Oklahoma.* The first, *Brown,* involved nothing more than a straightforward application of *Blockburger.* There a car thief was first convicted of "joyriding," an offense that consisted of "tak[ing], operat[ing], or keep[ing] any motor vehicle without the consent of its owner." He was then charged with auto theft, which required all the elements of joyriding plus an intent permanently to deprive the owner of his car. We held that *Blockburger* barred the second prosecution: because joyriding was simply a lesser included offense of auto theft, proof of the latter would "invariably" require proof of the former. We did not even hint that double jeopardy would also have barred the prosecution if the two statutes had *passed* the *Blockburger* test but the second prosecution could not be successful without proving the same facts. The second case, our brief *per curiam* disposition in *Harris,* involved a prosecution for armed robbery that followed a conviction for felony murder based on the same armed robbery. The felony murder statute by definition incorporated all of the elements of the underlying felony charged; thus the later prosecution (rather than, as in *Brown,* the earlier conviction) involved a lesser included offense. "When," we said, "conviction of a greater crime, murder, cannot be had without conviction of the lesser crime, robbery with firearms, the Double Jeopardy Clause bars prosecution for the lesser crime after conviction of the greater one." Again, we gave no indication that the second prosecution would have been barred if—not because of the statutory definition of the crimes but merely because of the circumstances of the particular case—guilt could not be established without proving the same conduct charged in the first prosecution. In short, to call the latter proposition "substantial" in *Vitale* took more than a little stretching of the cited cases.

I would have thought the result the Court reaches today foreclosed by our decision just a few months ago in *Dowling v. United States*. There the State, in a prosecution for robbery, introduced evidence of the defendant's perpetration of another robbery committed in similar fashion (both involved ski masks), of which he had previously been acquitted. Proof of the prior robbery tended to establish commission of the later one. The State, in other words, "to establish an essential element of an offense charged in [the second] prosecution, [had] prove[d] conduct that constitute[d] an offense for which the defendant ha[d] already been prosecuted." We held, however, that the Double Jeopardy Clause was not violated. The difference in our holding today cannot rationally be explained by the fact that in *Dowling,* unlike the present case, the two crimes were part of separate transactions; that in no way alters the central vice (according to today's holding) that the defendant was forced a second time to defend against proof that he had committed a robbery for which he had already been prosecuted. In *Dowling,* as here, conduct establishing a previously prosecuted offense was relied upon, not because that offense was a statutory element of the second offense, but only because the conduct would *prove the existence* of a statutory element. If that did not offend the Double Jeopardy Clause in *Dowling,* it should not do so here.

The principle the Court adopts today is not only radically out of line with our double jeopardy jurisprudence; its practical effect, whenever it applies, will come down to a requirement that where the charges arise from a " 'single criminal act, occurrence, episode, or transaction,' " they "must be tried in a single proceeding"—a requirement we have hitherto "steadfastly refused" to impose. Suppose, for example, that the State prosecutes a group of individuals for a substantive offense, and

then prosecutes them for conspiracy. In the conspiracy trial it *will prove* (if it can) that the defendants actually committed the substantive offense—even though there is evidence of other overt acts sufficient to sustain the conspiracy charge. For proof of the substantive offense, though not an *element* of the conspiracy charge, will assuredly be *persuasive* in establishing that a conspiracy existed. Or suppose an initial prosecution for burglary and a subsequent prosecution for murder that occurred in the course of the same burglary. In the second trial the State *will prove* (if it can) that the defendant was engaged in a burglary—not because that is itself an element of the murder charge, but because by providing a motive for intentional killing it will be *persuasive* that murder occurred. Under the analysis embraced by the Court today, I take it that the second prosecution in each of these cases would be barred, because the State, "to establish an essential element of an offense charged in that prosecution, will prove conduct that constitutes an offense for which the defendant has already been prosecuted." Just as, in today's case, proof of drunk driving or of crossing the median strip invalidates the second prosecution even though they are not elements of the homicide and assault offenses of which respondent is charged; so also, in the hypotheticals given, proof of the substantive offense will invalidate the conspiracy prosecution and proof of the burglary the murder prosecution.

The Court seeks to shrink the apparent application of its novel principle by saying that repetitive proof violates the Double Jeopardy Clause only if it is introduced "to establish an essential element of an offense charged in [the second] prosecution." That is a meaningless limitation, of course. *All* evidence pertaining to guilt seeks "to establish an essential element of [the] offense," and should be excluded if it does not have that tendency.

The other half of the Court's new test does seem to import some limitation, though I am not sure precisely what it means and cannot imagine what principle justifies it. I refer to the requirement that the evidence introduced in the second prosecution must "prove conduct that constitutes an offense for which the defendant has already been prosecuted." This means, presumably, that prosecutors who wish to use facts sufficient to prove one crime in order to establish guilt of another crime must bring both prosecutions simultaneously; but that those who wish to use only *some of* the facts establishing one crime—not enough facts to "prove conduct that constitutes an offense"—can bring successive prosecutions. But, one may reasonably ask, what justification is there *even in reason alone* (having abandoned text and precedent) for limiting the Court's new rule in this fashion? The Court defends the rule on the ground that a successive prosecution based on the same proof exposes the defendant to the burden and embarrassment of resisting proof of the same facts in multiple proceedings, and enables the State to "rehearse its presentation of proof, thus increasing the risk of an erroneous conviction for one or more of the offenses charged." But that vice does not exist only when the second prosecution seeks to prove *all* the facts necessary to support the first prosecution; it exists as well when the second prosecution seeks to prove some, rather than all of them—*i.e.,* whenever two prosecutions each require proof of facts (or even a single fact) common to both. If the Court were correct that the Double Jeopardy Clause protects individuals against the necessity of twice proving (or refuting) the same *evidence,* as opposed to the necessity of twice defending against the same *charge,* then the second prosecution should be equally bad whether it contains all or merely some of the proof necessary for the first.

Apart from the lack of rational basis for this latter limitation, I am greatly perplexed (as will be the unfortunate trial-court judges who must apply today's rootless decision) as to what precisely it means. It is not at all apparent how a court is to go about deciding whether the evidence that has been introduced (or that will be introduced) at the second trial "proves conduct" that constitutes an offense for which the defendant has already been prosecuted. Is the judge in the second trial supposed to pretend that he is the judge in the first one, and to let the second trial proceed *only if* the evidence would not be enough to go to the jury on the earlier charge? Or (as the language of the Court's test more readily suggests) is the judge in the second trial supposed to decide on his own whether the evidence before him really "proves" the earlier charge (perhaps beyond a reasonable doubt)? Consider application of the Court's new rule in the unusually simple circumstances of the present case: Suppose that, in the trial upon remand, the prosecution's evidence shows, among other things, that when the vehicles came to rest after the collision they were located on what was, for the defendant's vehicle, the wrong side of the road. The prosecution also produces a witness who testifies that prior to the collision the defendant's vehicle was "weaving back and forth"—*without* saying, however, that it was weaving back and forth over the center line. Is this enough to meet today's requirement of "proving" the offense of operating a vehicle on the wrong side of the road? If not, suppose in addition that defense counsel asks the witness on cross-examination, "When you said the defendant's vehicle was 'weaving back and forth,' did you mean weaving back and forth across the center line?"—to which the witness replies yes. Will this self-inflicted wound count for purposes of determining what the prosecution has "proved"? If so, can the prosecution then seek to impeach its own witness by showing that his recollection of the vehicle's crossing the center line was inaccurate? Or can it at least introduce another witness to establish that fact? There are many questions here, and the answers to all of them are ridiculous. Whatever line is selected as the criterion of "proving" the prior offense—enough evidence to go to the jury, more likely than not, or beyond a reasonable doubt—the prosecutor in the second trial will presumably seek to introduce as much evidence as he can without crossing that line; and the defense attorney will presumably seek to provoke the prosecutor into (or assist him in) proving the defendant guilty of the earlier crime. This delicious role-reversal, discovered to have been mandated by the Double Jeopardy Clause lo these 200 years, makes for high comedy but inferior justice. Often, the performance will even have an encore. If the judge initially decides that the previously prosecuted offense "will not be proved" (whatever that means) he will have to decide at the conclusion of the trial whether it "has been proved" (whatever that means). Indeed, he may presumably be asked to make the latter determination periodically during the course of the trial, since the Double Jeopardy Clause assuredly entitles the defendant to have the proceedings terminated as soon as its violation is evident. Even if we had no constitutional text and no prior case-law to rely upon, rejection of today's opinion is adequately supported by the modest desire to protect our criminal legal system from ridicule. * * * [P]rosecutors confronted with the inscrutability of today's opinion will be well advised to proceed on the assumption that the "same transaction" theory has already been adopted. It is hard to tell what else has. * * *

Notes and Questions

1. In UNITED STATES v. FELIX, ___ U.S. ___, 112 S.Ct. 1377, 118 L.Ed. 2d 25 (1992), Felix manufactured methamphetamine in Oklahoma during the summer until raided in July by federal agents. He then ordered precursor chemicals and equipment for such manufacture which he received in Missouri on August 31. Felix was charged in federal court for the Missouri attempt to manufacture an illegal drug, and when he defended by claiming lack of criminal intent the government countered with evidence of the Oklahoma manufacturing. After Felix was convicted, he was charged in federal court in Oklahoma in a multi-count indictment. One of the counts charged a conspiracy to manufacture between May 1 and August 31; two of the overt acts specified related to the order and receipt of the items for which he had already been prosecuted. Other counts related to the actual manufacture and possession. Felix was convicted on all counts, but the court of appeals reversed as to most of them on double jeopardy grounds. The Supreme Court, per REHNQUIST, C.J., disagreed.

The Court noted that one court of appeals ruling, that prosecution for the Oklahoma activity was barred because that conduct was introduced to show intent as to the Missouri attempt to manufacture, apparently rested "on an assumption that if the Government offers in evidence in one prosecution acts of misconduct that might ultimately be charged as criminal offenses in a second prosecution, the latter prosecution is barred." Such an assumption is not supported by *Grady,* the Court responded, for it "disclaimed any intention of adopting a ' "same evidence" ' test." Rather, applicable here is "the basic, yet important, principle that the introduction of relevant evidence of particular misconduct in a case is not the same thing as prosecution for that conduct." Because the government at the Missouri trial "did not in any way *prosecute* Felix for the Oklahoma methamphetamine transactions" but merely introduced them "as prior acts evidence," the government was free to prosecute for those offenses later.

As for the court of appeals' decision that the conspiracy count was barred, the Court acknowledged that "that court—with considerable justification—relied upon language from our *Grady* opinion to support its conclusion." But the Court held "that because of long established precedent in this area, which was not questioned in *Grady,* Felix' claim of double jeopardy fails." That precedent is "the rule that a substantive crime, and a conspiracy to commit that crime, are not the 'same offense' for double jeopardy purposes." In opting to adhere to that rule, the Court found support in *Garrett,* Note 2, cautioning against the "ready transposition" of lesser included offense principles of double jeopardy to "multilayered conduct, both as to time and to place," as illustrated by the conspiracy charge in the instant case. STEVENS, J., joined by BLACKMUN, J., concurring, would have instead upheld the conspiracy conviction on the ground that *Grady* only bars proof of an earlier-prosecuted offense to show "an essential element of an offense," not the case here "because there is no overt act requirement in the federal drug conspiracy statute and the overt acts did not establish an agreement between Felix and his coconspirators."

What result, then, if the Oklahoma offenses had been prosecuted *before* the Missouri crime?

7th ed., p. 1013, in lieu of last 7 lines in Note 3, add:

Dowling v. United States, 493 U.S. 342, 110 S.Ct. 668, 107 L.Ed.2d 708 (1990) (earlier acquittal, even if it established a reasonable doubt as to the existence of a matter to be proved as an evidentiary fact at a later trial, is no bar to proof of the evidentiary fact by a lesser standard).

SECTION 3. JOINDER AND SEVERANCE OF DEFENDANTS

7th ed., p. 1025; end of fn. b, add:

More recent contrary holdings rely on *Richardson.* See, e.g., *United States v. Vasquez,* 874 F.2d 1515 (11th Cir.1989) (upholding substitution of "individual" for defendant's name).

Chapter 19

THE RIGHT TO A "SPEEDY TRIAL"—AND TO "SPEEDY DISPOSITION" AT OTHER STEPS IN THE CRIMINAL PROCESS

SECTION 1. SPEEDY TRIAL

7th ed., p. 1034; before Notes and Questions, add:

DOGGETT v. UNITED STATES

—— U.S. ——, 112 S.Ct. ——, —— L.Ed.2d —— (1992).

JUSTICE SOUTER delivered the opinion of the Court. * * *

On February 22, 1980, petitioner Marc Doggett was indicted for conspiring with several others to import and distribute cocaine. Douglas Driver, the Drug Enforcement Administration's principal agent investigating the conspiracy, told the United States Marshal's Service that the DEA would oversee the apprehension of Doggett and his confederates. On March 18, 1980, two police officers set out under Driver's orders to arrest Doggett at his parents' house in Raleigh, North Carolina, only to find that he was not there. His mother told the officers that he had left for Colombia four days earlier.

To catch Doggett on his return to the United States, Driver sent word of his outstanding arrest warrant to all United States Customs stations and to a number of law enforcement organizations. He also placed Doggett's name in the Treasury Enforcement Communication System (TECS), a computer network that helps Customs agents screen people entering the country, and in the National Crime Information Center computer system, which serves similar ends. The TECS entry ex-

pired that September, however, and Doggett's name vanished from the system.

In September 1981, Driver found out that Doggett was under arrest on drug charges in Panama and, thinking that a formal extradition request would be futile, simply asked Panama to "expel" Doggett to the United States. Although the Panamanian authorities promised to comply when their own proceedings had run their course, they freed Doggett the following July and let him go to Colombia, where he stayed with an aunt for several months. On September 25, 1982, he passed unhindered through Customs in New York City and settled down in Virginia. Since his return to the United States, he has married, earned a college degree, found a steady job as a computer operations manager, lived openly under his own name, and stayed within the law.

Doggett's travels abroad had not wholly escaped the Government's notice, however. In 1982, the American Embassy in Panama told the State Department of his departure to Colombia, but that information, for whatever reason, eluded the DEA, and Agent Driver assumed for several years that his quarry was still serving time in a Panamanian prison. Driver never asked DEA officials in Panama to check into Doggett's status, and only after his own fortuitous assignment to that country in 1985 did he discover Doggett's departure for Colombia. Driver then simply assumed Doggett had settled there, and he made no effort to find out for sure or to track Doggett down, either abroad or in the United States. Thus Doggett remained lost to the American criminal justice system until September 1988, when the Marshal's Service ran a simple credit check on several thousand people subject to outstanding arrest warrants and, within minutes, found out where Doggett lived and worked. On September 5, 1988, nearly 6 years after his return to the United States and 8½ years after his indictment, Doggett was arrested.

He naturally moved to dismiss the indictment, arguing that the Government's failure to prosecute him earlier violated his Sixth Amendment right to a speedy trial. The Federal Magistrate hearing his motion * * * found, however, that Doggett had made no affirmative showing that the delay had impaired his ability to mount a successful defense or had otherwise prejudiced him. In his recommendation to the District Court, the Magistrate contended that this failure to demonstrate particular prejudice sufficed to defeat Doggett's speedy trial claim.

The District Court took the recommendation and denied Doggett's motion. * * *

A split panel of the Court of Appeals affirmed. * * *

The Sixth Amendment guarantees that, "[i]n all criminal prosecutions, the accused shall enjoy the right to a speedy . . . trial. . . ." On its face, the Speedy Trial Clause is written with such breadth that, taken literally, it would forbid the government to delay the trial of an "accused" for any reason at all. Our cases, however, have qualified the literal sweep of the provision by specifically recognizing the relevance of four separate enquiries: whether delay before trial was uncommonly long, whether the government or the criminal defendant is more to blame for that delay, whether, in due course, the defendant asserted his right to a speedy

trial, and whether he suffered prejudice as the delay's result.

The first of these is actually a double enquiry. Simply to trigger a speedy trial analysis, an accused must allege that the interval between accusation and trial has crossed the threshold dividing ordinary from "presumptively prejudicial" delay, since, by definition, he cannot complain that the government has denied him a "speedy" trial if it has, in fact, prosecuted his case with customary promptness. If the accused makes this showing, the court must then consider, as one factor among several, the extent to which the delay stretches beyond the bare minimum needed to trigger judicial examination of the claim. This latter enquiry is significant to the speedy trial analysis because, as we discuss below, the presumption that pretrial delay has prejudiced the accused intensifies over time. In this case, the extraordinary 8½ year lag between Doggett's indictment and arrest clearly suffices to trigger the speedy trial enquiry; its further significance within that enquiry will be dealt with later.

As for *Barker*'s second criterion, the Government claims to have sought Doggett with diligence. The findings of the courts below are to the contrary, however, and we review trial court determinations of negligence with considerable deference. The Government gives us nothing to gainsay the findings that have come up to us, and we see nothing fatal to them in the record. For six years, the Government's investigators made no serious effort to test their progressively more questionable assumption that Doggett was living abroad, and, had they done so, they could have found him within minutes. While the Government's lethargy may have reflected no more than Doggett's relative unimportance in the world of drug trafficking, it was still findable negligence, and the finding stands.

The Government goes against the record again in suggesting that Doggett knew of his indictment years before he was arrested. Were this true, *Barker's* third factor, concerning invocation of the right to a speedy trial, would be weighed heavily against him. But here again, the Government is trying to revisit the facts. At the hearing on Doggett's speedy trial motion, it introduced no evidence challenging the testimony of Doggett's wife, who said that she did not know of the charges until his arrest, and of his mother, who claimed not to have told him or anyone else that the police had come looking for him.

* * *

The Government is left, then, with its principal contention: that Doggett fails to make out a successful speedy trial claim because he has not shown precisely how he was prejudiced by the delay between his indictment and trial.

We have observed in prior cases that unreasonable delay between formal accusation and trial threatens to produce more than one sort of harm, including "oppressive pretrial incarceration," "anxiety and concern of the accused," and "the possibility that the [accused's] defense will be impaired" by dimming memories and loss of exculpatory evidence. Of these forms of prejudice, "the most serious is the last, because the inability of a defendant adequately to prepare his case skews the fairness of the entire system." Doggett claims this kind of prejudice, and there is probably no other kind that he can claim, since he was subjected neither to pretrial detention nor, he has successfully contended, to awareness of unresolved charges against him.

The Government answers Doggett's claim by citing language in three cases, *United States v. Marion,* [7th ed., p. 1040], *United States v. MacDonald,* [7th ed., p. 1044], and *United States v. Loud Hawk,* [7th ed., p. 1045], for the proposition that the Speedy Trial Clause does not significantly protect a criminal defendant's interest in fair adjudication. In so arguing, the Government asks us, in effect, to read part of *Barker* right out of the law, and that we will not do. In context, the cited passages support nothing beyond the principle, which we have independently based on textual and historical grounds, that the Sixth Amendment right of the accused to a speedy trial has no application beyond the confines of a formal criminal prosecution. Once triggered by arrest, indictment, or other official accusation, however, the speedy trial enquiry must weigh the effect of delay on the accused's defense just as it has to weigh any other form of prejudice that *Barker* recognized.

As an alternative to limiting *Barker,* the Government claims Doggett has failed to make any affirmative showing that the delay weakened his ability to raise specific defenses, elicit specific testimony, or produce specific items of evidence. Though Doggett did indeed come up short in this respect, the Government's argument takes it only so far: consideration of prejudice is not limited to the specifically demonstrable, and, as it concedes, affirmative proof of particularized prejudice is not essential to every speedy trial claim. *Barker* explicitly recognized that impairment of one's defense is the most difficult form of speedy trial prejudice to prove because time's erosion of exculpatory evidence and testimony "can rarely be shown." And though time can tilt the case against either side, one cannot generally be sure which of them it has prejudiced more severely. Thus, we generally have to recognize that excessive delay presumptively compromises the reliability of a trial in ways that neither party can prove or, for that matter, identify. While such presumptive prejudice cannot alone carry a Sixth Amendment claim without regard to the other *Barker* criteria, it is part of the mix of relevant facts, and its importance increases with the length of delay.

This brings us to an enquiry into the role that presumptive prejudice should play in the disposition of Doggett's speedy trial claim. We begin with hypothetical and somewhat easier cases and work our way to this one.

Our speedy trial standards recognize that pretrial delay is often both inevitable and wholly justifiable. The government may need time to collect witnesses against the accused, oppose his pretrial motions, or, if he goes into hiding, track him down. We attach great weight to such considerations when balancing them against the costs of going forward with a trial whose probative accuracy the passage of time has begun by degrees to throw into question. Thus, in this case, if the Government had pursued Doggett with reasonable diligence from his indictment to his arrest, his speedy trial claim would fail. Indeed, that conclusion would generally follow as a matter of course however great the delay, so long as Doggett could not show specific prejudice to his defense.

The Government concedes, on the other hand, that Doggett would prevail if he could show that the Government had intentionally held back in its prosecution of him to gain some impermissible advantage at trial. That we cannot doubt. *Barker* stressed that official bad faith in causing delay will be weighed heavily against the government, and a bad-faith delay the length of this negligent one would present an overwhelming case for dismissal.

Between diligent prosecution and bad-faith delay, official negligence in bringing an accused to trial occupies the middle ground. While not compelling relief in every case where bad-faith delay would make relief virtually automatic, neither is negligence automatically tolerable simply because the accused cannot demonstrate exactly how it has prejudiced him. It was on this point that the Court of Appeals erred, and on the facts before us, it was reversible error.

Barker made it clear that "different weights [are to be] assigned to different reasons" for delay. Although negligence is obviously to be weighed more lightly than a deliberate intent to harm the ac-

cused's defense, it still falls on the wrong side of the divide between acceptable and unacceptable reasons for delaying a criminal prosecution once it has begun. And such is the nature of the prejudice presumed that the weight we assign to official negligence compounds over time as the presumption of evidentiary prejudice grows. Thus, our toleration of such negligence varies inversely with its protractedness, and its consequent threat to the fairness of the accused's trial. Condoning prolonged and unjustifiable delays in prosecution would both penalize many defendants for the state's fault and simply encourage the government to gamble with the interests of criminal suspects assigned a low prosecutorial priority. The Government, indeed, can hardly complain too loudly, for persistent neglect in concluding a criminal prosecution indicates an uncommonly feeble interest in bringing an accused to justice; the more weight the Government attaches to securing a conviction, the harder it will try to get it.

To be sure, to warrant granting relief, negligence unaccompanied by particularized trial prejudice must have lasted longer than negligence demonstrably causing such prejudice. But even so, the Government's egregious persistence in failing to prosecute Doggett is clearly sufficient. The lag between Doggett's indictment and arrest was 8½ years, and he would have faced trial 6 years earlier than he did but for the Government's inexcusable oversights. The portion of the delay attributable to the Government's negligence far exceeds the threshold needed to state a speedy trial claim; indeed, we have called shorter delays "extraordinary." When the Government's negligence thus causes delay six times as long as that generally sufficient to trigger judicial review, and when the presumption of prejudice, albeit unspecified, is neither extenuated, as by the defendant's acquiescence, nor persuasively rebutted, the defendant is entitled to relief.

JUSTICE THOMAS, with whom THE CHIEF JUSTICE and JUSTICE SCALIA join, dissenting. * * * [a]

We have long identified the "major evils" against which the Speedy Trial Clause is directed as "undue and oppressive incarceration" and the "anxiety and concern accompanying public accusation."

* * *

Thus, this unusual case presents the question whether, independent of these core concerns, the Speedy Trial Clause protects an accused from two additional harms: (1) prejudice to his ability to defend himself caused by the passage of time; and (2) disruption of his life years after the alleged commission of his crime. The Court today proclaims that the first of these additional harms is indeed an independent concern of the Clause, and on that basis compels reversal of Doggett's conviction and outright dismissal of the indictment against him. As to the second of these harms, the Court remains mum—despite the fact that we requested supplemental briefing on this very point.

I disagree with the Court's analysis. In my view, the Sixth Amendment's speedy trial guarantee does not provide independent protection against either prejudice to an accused's defense or the disruption of his life. I shall consider each in turn.

* * *

We are * * * confronted with two conflicting lines of authority, the one declaring that "limit[ing] the possibility that the defense will be impaired" is an independent and fundamental objective of the Speedy Trial Clause, e.g., *Barker,* supra, and the other declaring that it is not, e.g., *Marion,* supra; *MacDonald,* supra; *Loud Hawk,* supra. The Court refuses to acknowledge this conflict. Instead, it simply reiterates the relevant language from *Barker* and asserts that *Marion, MacDonald,* and *Loud Hawk* "support nothing beyond the

principle . . . . that the Sixth Amendment right of the accused to a speedy trial has no application beyond the confines of a formal criminal prosecution." That attempt at reconciliation is eminently unpersuasive.

It is true, of course, that the Speedy Trial Clause by its terms applies only to an "accused"; the right does not attach before indictment or arrest. But that limitation on the Clause's protection only confirms that preventing prejudice to the defense is not one of its independent and fundamental objectives. For prejudice to the defense stems from the interval between crime and trial, which is quite distinct from the interval between accusation and trial. If the Clause were indeed aimed at safeguarding against prejudice to the defense, then it would presumably limit all prosecutions that occur long after the criminal events at issue. A defendant prosecuted 10 years after a crime is just as hampered in his ability to defend himself whether he was indicted the week after the crime or the week before the trial—but no one would suggest that the Clause protects him in the latter situation, where the delay did not substantially impair his liberty, either through oppressive incarceration or the anxiety of known criminal charges.

* * *

It is misleading, then, for the Court to accuse the Government of "ask[ing] us, in effect, to read part of *Barker* right out of the law," a course the Court resolutely rejects. For the issue here is not simply whether the relevant language from *Barker* should be read out of the law, but whether that language trumps the contrary logic of *Marion, MacDonald,* and *Loud Hawk.* The Court's protestations notwithstanding, the two lines of authority cannot be reconciled; to reaffirm the one is to undercut the other.

---

a. O'Connor, J., dissented separately on the ground that "a showing of actual prejudice to the defense" is required.

In my view, the choice presented is not a hard one. *Barker's* suggestion that preventing prejudice to the defense is a fundamental and independent objective of the Clause is plainly dictum. Never, until today, have we confronted a case where a defendant subjected to a lengthy delay after indictment nonetheless failed to suffer any substantial impairment of his liberty. I think it fair to say that *Barker* simply did not contemplate such an unusual situation. Moreover, to the extent that the *Barker* dictum purports to elevate considerations of prejudice to the defense to fundamental and independent status under the Clause, it cannot be deemed to have survived our subsequent decisions in *MacDonald* and *Loud Hawk*. * * *

Therefore, I see no basis for the Court's conclusion that Doggett is entitled to relief under the Speedy Trial Clause simply because the Government was negligent in prosecuting him and because the resulting delay may have prejudiced his defense.

It remains to be considered, however, whether Doggett is entitled to relief under the Speedy Trial Clause because of the disruption of his life years after the criminal events at issue. In other words, does the Clause protect a right to repose, free from secret or unknown indictments? In my view, it does not, for much the same reasons set forth above.

The common law recognized no right of criminals to repose. * * *

That is not to deny that our legal system has long recognized the value of repose, both to the individual and to society. But that recognition finds expression not in the sweeping commands of the Constitution, or in the common law, but in any number of specific statutes of limitations enacted by the federal and state legislatures. * * *

6. It is quite likely, in fact, that the delay benefitted Doggett. At the time of his arrest, he had been living an apparently normal, law-abiding life for some five years—a point not lost on the District Court Judge, who, instead of imposing a prison term, sentenced him to three years' probation and a $1000 fine. Thus, the delay gave

Doggett, however, asks us to hold that a defendant's interest in repose is a value independently protected by the Speedy Trial Clause. He emphasizes that at the time of his arrest he was "leading a normal, productive and law-abiding life," and that his "arrest and prosecution at this late date interrupted his life as a productive member of society and forced him to answer for actions taken in the distant past." However uplifting this tale of personal redemption, our task is to illuminate the protections of the Speedy Trial Clause, not to take the measure of one man's life.

There is no basis for concluding that the disruption of an accused's life years after the commission of his alleged crime is an evil independently protected by the Speedy Trial Clause. Such disruption occurs regardless of whether the individual is under indictment during the period of delay. Thus, had Doggett been indicted shortly before his 1988 arrest rather than shortly after his 1980 crime, his repose would have been equally shattered—but he would not have even a colorable speedy-trial claim. To recognize a constitutional right to repose is to recognize a right to be tried speedily after the offense. That would, of course, convert the Speedy Trial Clause into a constitutional statute of limitations—a result with no basis in the text or history of the Clause or in our precedents. * * *

Today's opinion, I fear, will transform the courts of the land into boards of law-enforcement supervision. For the Court compels dismissal of the charges against Doggett not because he was harmed in any way by the delay between his indictment and arrest,[6] but simply because the Government's efforts to catch him are found wanting. * * * Our Constitution neither contemplates nor tolerates such a role. I respectfully dissent.

Doggett the opportunity to prove what most defendants can only promise: that he no longer posed a threat to society. There can be little doubt that, had he been tried immediately after his cocaine-importation activities, he would have received a harsher sentence.

Part Four

THE ADVERSARY SYSTEM AND THE DETERMINATION OF GUILT OR INNOCENCE

Chapter 20

THE ASSISTANCE OF COUNSEL

SECTION 3. THE RIGHT TO "EFFECTIVE" ASSISTANCE OF COUNSEL

7th ed., p. 1075; at the end of fn. c, add:

Consider also the discussion in *Coleman v. Thompson*, Supp., p. 126.

Chapter 22

COERCED, INDUCED, AND NEGOTIATED GUILTY PLEAS; PROFESSIONAL RESPONSIBILITY

SECTION 2. REJECTED, KEPT AND BROKEN BARGAINS; UNREALIZED EXPECTATIONS

7th ed., p. 1225; end of first paragraph of Note 3, add:

What then of a plea conditioned upon the defendant not interviewing the victim? See *State v. Draper,* 784 P.2d 259 (Ariz.1989) (not per se improper, but requires close judicial scrutiny because it "may interfere with a defendant's due process rights to prepare a defense").

7th ed., p. 1228; end of Note 4, add:

Where, as in *Rosa,* there is no per se rule against judicial participation, the outcome of a later challenge to the plea will turn on the extent and character of the judge's involvement. Compare, e.g., *State v. Ditter,* 441 N.W.2d 622 (Neb.1989) (did not coerce plea, as defense initiated the discussion, judge talked only with defense counsel and defendant was not present, judge only indicated possible penalties depending on defendant's course of action, and judge made no comments on the weight of the evidence or that he thought defendant was guilty); with *State v. Svoboda*, 287 N.W.2d 41 (Neb.1980) (coerced the plea, as judge initiated discussion directly with defendant and told defendant the evidence was overwhelming and that defendant should not go to trial).

7th ed., p. 1230; end of Note 8, add:

Evans is a minority but constitutionally permissible alternative. As stated in *Carwile v. Smith*, 874 F.2d 382 (6th Cir.1989), the fact "that under federal law, as well as under the law of 40 out of 49 states, a criminal defendant who has pleaded guilty must be given an opportunity to withdraw his plea when an agreed sentencing recommendation is rejected by the sentencing court" does not mean it is a violation of due process for a state not to permit withdrawal absent a showing "that petitioner was 'misled' into thinking that the judge would be bound by the prosecutor's recommendation."

In a state which, unlike *Evans*, provides that a defendant must be allowed to withdraw his plea if the judge decides upon a sentence higher than contemplated in the plea agreement, should the prosecution have a corresponding right to withdraw if the judge opts for a sentence lower than the parties earlier agreed to? See *State v. Warren*, 558 A.2d 1312 (N.J.1989) (no, as though "notions of fairness apply to each side, * * * the defendant's constitutional rights and interests weigh more heavily in the scale").

7th ed., p. 1233; before Note 5, add:

4a. The new federal sentencing guidelines have given rise to other types of plea bargain terms regarding the sentence to be imposed. For example, one possibility is that the prosecutor will stipulate to some fact (e.g., that defendant was a minor participant in the crime) which, if true, would permit reduction of defendant's offense level for sentencing purposes. The federal sentencing guidelines expressly state that the court is not bound by such a stipulation, and consequently there is no broken

bargain if the court concludes the mitigating circumstance was not present and that therefore defendant should not receive the contemplated sentence reduction. *United States v. Howard*, 894 F.2d 1085 (9th Cir.1990). (The result would presumably be otherwise if, as is permitted under the federal guidelines, the defendant entered a guilty plea on the express condition that the judge find, e.g., that he was a minor participant.) Moreover, in the stipulation-only case, if the defendant then appeals from the trial judge's determination, the prosecution does not violate the plea bargain by arguing the lower court did not err. *United States v. Howard*, supra. In somewhat the reverse situation, where the plea bargain stipulation is that the sentence will not exceed a certain amount, and that amount would be appropriate if the court found an aggravating circumstance present which sufficed to take the case above the usual guideline range, the stipulation does not bar the defendant from questioning on appeal whether there was a sufficient finding of the necessary aggravating circumstance. *United States v. Newsome*, 894 F.2d 852 (6th Cir.1990).

7th ed., p. 1235; end of Note 8, add:

Consider *Staten v. Neal*, 880 F.2d 962 (7th Cir.1989) (though "United States Attorneys arguably speak for the entire federal government, the same cannot be said of state's attorneys in Illinois," and thus plea agreement term that defendant would not be prosecuted in another county not entitled to specific performance).

SECTION 3. PROFESSIONAL RESPONSIBILITY; THE ROLE OF PROSECUTOR AND DEFENSE COUNSEL

7th ed., p. 1249; end of Note 2, add:

Query, what level of noninvestigation, under what circumstances, will entitle the guilty plea defendant to relief on Sixth Amendment grounds? Recall that *Strickland*, 7th ed., p. 1077, also requires proof of prejudice for the defendant to prevail on an ineffective assistance claim while *Chronic,* 7th ed., p. 1090, says prejudice is presumed upon complete lack of representation, including when counsel "fails to subject the prosecutor's case to meaningful adversarial testing." Consider *Woodard v. Collins,* 898 F.2d 1027 (5th Cir.1990) ("a decision to investigate some issues and not others or even a decision to conduct virtually no investigation is governed by *Strickland*").

SECTION 4. RECEIVING THE DEFENDANT'S PLEA; PLEA WITHDRAWAL

7th ed., p. 1271; after Note 4, add:

5. What then of somewhat the reverse situation? That is, if a court finds that the factual basis only establishes a lesser-included offense, may the court direct entry of a guilty plea to such an offense? See *State v. Barboza,* 558 A.2d 1303 (N.J.1989) (no, as this would be "tantamount to permitting a court to direct a verdict against a defendant in a criminal case").

Chapter 23

TRIAL BY JURY

SECTION 2. JURY SELECTION

7th ed., p. 1303; end of Note 1, add:

The Court continues to be divided as to just how many "distinctive groups" there might be. In *Holland v. Illinois,* Supp. p. 128, Scalia, J., for the Court, said that if the cross-section requirement applied to juries (rather than the panels from which juries are chosen) then "many commonly exercised bases for peremptory challenges would be rendered unavailable," while Marshall, J., dissenting, objected to the "majority's exaggerated claim that 'postmen, or lawyers, or clergymen' are distinctive groups within the meaning of our fair cross-section cases."

7th ed., p. 1304; end of first paragraph of Note 4, add:

In *Powers v. Ohio,* Supp. p. 128, the Court held that a white defendant may raise an equal protection claim on behalf of excluded black prospective jurors.

7th ed., p. 1306; in Note 5 after *Zicarelli*, add:

Indeed, *Jones* was itself overruled in *Hernandez v. Municipal Court,* 781 P.2d 547 (Cal.1989), reasoning that in a state context "the boundaries of the vicinage are coterminous with the boundaries of the county" and that consequently it is sufficient that the jurors are selected from the county—they need not be from the particular judicial district therein where the crime occurred.

7th ed., p. 1313; before *Ross*, add:

5a. In MORGAN v. ILLINOIS, ___ U.S. ___, 112 S.Ct. 2222, ___ L.Ed.2d ___ (1992), the Court, per WHITE, J.,

rejected the state court's conclusion that a trial judge need not, on defendant's request, ask a "reverse-*Witherspoon*" question on voir dire so as to identify and exclude any prospective juror who would vote for the death penalty in every capital case. "A juror who will automatically vote for the death penalty in every case will fail in good faith to consider the evidence of aggravating and mitigating circumstances as the instructions require him to do. Indeed, because such a juror has already formed an opinion on the merits, the presence or absence of either aggravating or mitigating circumstances is entirely irrelevant to such a juror. Therefore, based on the requirement of impartiality embodied in the Due Process Clause of the Fourteenth Amendment, a capital defendant may challenge for cause any prospective juror who maintains such views. If even one such juror is empaneled and the death sentence is imposed, the State is disentitled to execute the sentence. * * *

"The only issue remaining is whether the questions propounded by the trial court were sufficient to satisfy petitioner's right to make inquiry. * * * Illinois suggests that general fairness and 'follow the law' questions, of the like employed by the trial court here, are enough to detect those in the venire who automatically would vote for the death penalty. The State's own request for questioning under *Witherspoon* and *Witt* of course belies this argument. *Witherspoon* and its succeeding cases would be in large measure superfluous were this Court convinced that such general inquiries could detect those jurors with views preventing or substantially impairing their duties in accordance with their instructions and oath. But such jurors—whether they be unalterably in favor of or opposed to the death penalty in every case—by definition are ones who cannot perform their duties in accordance with law, their protestations to the contrary notwithstanding."

Noting that the applicable Illinois statute directs the court to instruct the jury "to consider aggravating and any mitigating factors" and further states that the death penalty may be imposed only if the jury unanimously finds one or more statutory aggravating factors and also "that there are not mitigating factors sufficient to preclude the imposition of the death sentence," the *Morgan* majority concluded: "Any juror who states that he or she will automatically vote for the death penalty without regard to the mitigating evidence is announcing an intention not to follow the instructions to consider the mitigating evidence and to decide if it is sufficient to preclude imposition of the death penalty. Any contrary reading of this instruction, or more importantly, the controlling statute, renders the term 'sufficient' meaningless."

But SCALIA, J., for the three dissenters, construed the Illinois death penalty system somewhat differently and thus concluded the exclusions mandated by *Morgan* were unlike those permitted under *Witherspoon:* "By reason of Illinois' death-penalty unanimity requirement, the practical consequences of allowing the two types of jurors to serve are vastly different. A single death-penalty opponent can block that punishment, but 11 unwavering advocates cannot impose it. And more fundamentally, the asymmetry is not unfair because, under Illinois law as reflected in the statute and instructions in this case, the *Witherspoon*-disqualified juror is a lawless juror, whereas the juror to be disqualified under the Court's new rule is not. In the first stage of Illinois' two-part sentencing hearing, jurors must determine, on the facts,

specified aggravating factors, and at the second, weighing stage, they must impose the death penalty for murder with particular aggravators if they find 'no mitigating factors sufficient to preclude [its] imposition.' But whereas the finding of aggravation is mandatory, the finding of mitigation is optional; what constitutes mitigation is not defined, and is left up to the judgment of each juror. Given that there will always be aggravators to be considered at the weighing stage, the juror who says he will never vote for the death penalty, no matter what the facts, is saying that he will not apply the law (the classic case of partiality)—since the facts may show no mitigation. But the juror who says that he will always vote for the death penalty is not promising to be lawless, since there is no case in which he is by law compelled to find a mitigating fact 'sufficiently mitigating.' "

7th ed., p. 1317; end of Note 8, add:

Ristaino was relied upon in *Mu'Min v. Virginia,* Supp. p. 131, holding a trial judge need not question prospective jurors about the specific contents of news reports to which they have been exposed.

7th ed., p. 1329; in lieu of Note 4, add:

4. In GEORGIA v. McCOLLUM, ____ U.S. ____, 112 S.Ct. 2348, ____ L.Ed.2d ____ (1992), where white defendants were charged with assaulting black victims, the prosecutor claimed the *defendants* should be barred from striking prospective jurors merely because they were black. The Court, noting it had earlier held in *Edmonson v. Leesville Concrete Co.,* 500 U.S. ____, 111 S.Ct. 2077, 114 L.Ed.2d 660 (1991), that racial discrimination in a civil litigant's exercise of peremptory challenges violates the equal protection clause, ruled in *McCollum* that *Batson* likewise applies to the exercise of peremptories by a criminal defendant. BLACKMUN, J., for the Court, reached this conclusion by consideration of four issues. The first, "whether a criminal defendant's exercise of peremptory chal-

lenges in a racially discriminatory manner inflicts the harms addressed by *Batson*," was answered in the affirmative, as in these circumstances as well prospective jurors are denied the opportunity to participate in jury service on account of their race, and public confidence in the fairness of jury verdicts is consequently undermined.

As for the second issue, "whether the exercise of peremptory challenges by a criminal defendant constitutes state action," the Court again answered in the affirmative, stressing three points: (i) The defendant relied on government assistance to bring about the deprivation, as "the peremptory challenge system * * * 'simply could not exist' without the 'overt and significant participation of the government.'" (ii) The defendant in exercising peremptories "is performing a traditional governmental function," as "the selection of a jury in a criminal case fulfills a unique and constitutionally compelled governmental function." (iii) The "courtroom setting in which the peremptory challenge is exercised intensifies the harmful effects" of the discrimination, as "regardless of who precipitated the jurors' removal, the perception and the reality in a criminal trial will be that the court has excused jurors based on race, an outcome that will be attributed to the State."

On the third issue, "whether the State has standing to challenge a defendant's discriminatory use of peremptory challenges," the Court also responded in the affirmative. Such third-party standing, the Court explained, is proper where, as here, (i) the state also suffers injury "when the fairness and integrity of its own judicial process is undermined"; (ii) the state has a close relationship with the excluded jurors as "the representative of all its citizens"; and (iii) there are significant barri-

ers to the excluded jurors acting to vindicate their own rights.

As for the final question in *McCollum*, "whether the interests served by *Batson* must give way to the rights of a criminal defendant," the Court concluded that neither a defendant's right to a fair trial nor his Sixth Amendment rights to counsel and to an impartial jury "includes the right to discriminate against a group of citizens based upon their race."

REHNQUIST, C.J., concurred on the ground that *Edmonson* required such a result, as did THOMAS, J., who also noted *Batson* "has taken us down a slope of inquiry that has no clear stopping point. Today, we decide only that white defendants may not strike black veniremen on the basis of race. Eventually, we will have to decide whether black defendants may strike white veniremen.[2]" One of the two dissenters, O'CONNOR, J., cautioned:

"Considered in purely pragmatic terms, * * * the Court's holding may fail to advance nondiscriminatory criminal justice. It is by now clear that conscious and unconscious racism can affect the way white jurors perceive minority defendants and the facts presented at their trials, perhaps determining the verdict of guilt or innocence. Using peremptory challenges to secure minority representation on the jury may help to overcome such racial bias, for there is substantial reason to believe that the distorting influence of race is minimized on a racially mixed jury. As amicus NAACP Legal Defense and Education Fund explained in this case: 'the ability to use peremptory challenges to exclude majority race jurors may be crucial to empaneling a fair jury. In many cases an African American, or other minority defendant, may be faced with a jury array in which his racial group is underrepresented to some degree, but not sufficiently to

2. The NAACP has submitted a brief arguing, in all sincerity, that "whether white defendants can use peremptory challenges to purge minority jurors presents quite different issues from whether a minority defendant can strike majority

group jurors." Although I suppose that this issue technically remains open, it is difficult to see how the result could be different if the defendants here were black.

permit challenge under the Fourteenth Amendment. The only possible chance the defendant may have of having any minority jurors on the jury that actually tries him will be if he uses his peremptories to strike members of the majority race.' In a world where the outcome of a minority defendant's trial may turn on the misconceptions or biases of white jurors, there is cause to question the implications of this Court's good intentions."

7th ed., p. 1329; in lieu of Note 5, add:

5. A *Batson*-type challenge to the prosecutor's use of peremptories, grounded instead in the Sixth Amendment's cross-section requirement, was rejected 5–4 in HOLLAND v. ILLINOIS, 493 U.S. 474, 110 S.Ct. 803, 107 L.Ed.2d 905 (1990). SCALIA, J., for the majority, reasoned:

"The Sixth Amendment requirement of a fair cross section on the venire is a means of assuring, not a *representative* jury (which the Constitution does not demand), but an *impartial* one (which it does). Without that requirement, the State could draw up jury lists in such manner as to produce a pool of prospective jurors disproportionately ill disposed towards one or all classes of defendants, and thus more likely to yield petit juries with similar disposition. The State would have, in effect, unlimited peremptory challenges to compose the pool in its favor. The fair-cross-section venire requirement assures, in other words, that in the process of selecting the petit jury the prosecution and defense will compete on an equal basis.

"But to say that the Sixth Amendment deprives the State of the ability to 'stack the deck' in its favor is not to say that each side may not, once a fair hand is dealt, use peremptory challenges to eliminate prospective jurors belonging to groups it believes would unduly favor the other side. Any theory of the Sixth Amendment leading to that result is implausible. The tradition of peremptory challenges for both the prosecution and the accused was already venerable at the time of Blackstone,

was reflected in a federal statute enacted by the same Congress that proposed the Bill of Rights, was recognized in an opinion by Justice Story to be part of the common law of the United States, and has endured through two centuries in all the States. The constitutional phrase 'impartial jury' must surely take its content from this unbroken tradition. * * *

"The rule we announce today is not only the only plausible reading of the text of the Sixth Amendment, but we think it best furthers the Amendment's central purpose as well. Although the constitutional guarantee runs only to the individual and not to the State, the goal it expresses is jury impartiality with respect to both contestants: neither the defendant nor the State should be favored. This goal, it seems to us, would positively be obstructed by a petit jury cross section requirement which, as we have described, would cripple the device of peremptory challenge."

Marshall, J., dissenting, argued that "the purposes of the cross-section requirement [as stated in *Taylor*, 7th ed., p. 1300] cannot be served unless prosecutors are precluded from exercising racially motivated peremptory challenges of prospective jurors."

7th ed., p. 1330; in lieu of Note 7, add:

7. In POWERS v. OHIO, ___ U.S. ___, 111 S.Ct. 1364, 113 L.Ed.2d 411 (1991), the Court held, 7–2, that "a white defendant may object to the prosecution's peremptory challenges of black venirepersons." The majority, per KENNEDY, J., reasoned that such challenges, if based upon race, violate the venirepersons' right to equal protection under the Fourteenth Amendment, as to which "a criminal defendant has standing" to object because the three criteria for recognizing third-party standing are present: (1) The defendant has "suffered an 'injury-in-fact'" by such peremptory challenges adequate to give "him or her a 'sufficiently concrete interest' in the outcome of the issue in

dispute," for the "overt wrong, often apparent to the entire jury panel, casts doubt over the obligation of the parties, the jury, and indeed the court to adhere to the law throughout the trial of the cause." (2) The defendant has "a close relation to the third party" excluded venirepersons, as he or she "will be a motivated, effective advocate for the excluded venirepersons' rights" given "that discrimination in the jury selection process may lead to the reversal of a conviction." (3) There exists "some hindrance to the third party's ability to protect his or her own interests," for potential jurors "have no opportunity to be heard at the time of their exclusion," cannot "easily obtain declaratory or injunctive relief" later given the need to show a likely reoccurrence of their own exclusion based on race, and are unlikely to undertake an action for damages "because of the small financial stake involved and the economic burdens of litigation."

The Court indicated, however, that the case of a white defendant and of a black defendant might, as a practical matter, be somewhat different: "Racial identity between the defendant and the excused person might in some cases be the explanation for the prosecution's adoption of the forbidden stereotype, and if the alleged race bias takes this form, it may provide one of the easier cases to establish both a prima facie case and a conclusive showing that wrongful discrimination has occurred. But to say that the race of the defendant may be relevant to discerning bias in some cases does not mean that it will be a factor in others, for race prejudice stems from various causes and may manifest itself in different forms."

SCALIA, J., in dissent, objected: "The sum and substance of the Court's lengthy analysis is that, since a denial of equal protection to other people occurred at the defendant's trial, though it did not affect the fairness of that trial, the defendant must go free. Even if I agreed that the exercise of peremptory strikes constitutes unlawful discrimination (which I do not), I

would not understand why the release of a convicted murderer who has not been harmed by those strikes is an appropriate remedy."

7th ed., p. 1330; end of Note 8, add:

In *Hernandez v. New York*, Note 10(a) infra, the Court stated: "In holding that a race-neutral reason for a peremptory challenge means a reason other than race, we do not resolve the more difficult question of the breadth with which the concept of race should be defined for equal protection purposes. We would face a quite different case if the prosecutor had justified his peremptory challenges with the explanation that he did not want Spanish-speaking jurors. It may well be, for certain ethnic groups and in some communities, that proficiency in a particular language, like skin color, should be treated as a surrogate for race under an equal protection analysis."

7th ed., p. 1331; before Note 11, add:

10(a). In HERNANDEZ v. NEW YORK, ___ U.S. ___, 111 S.Ct. 1859, 114 L.Ed.2d 395 (1991), KENNEDY, J., for four members of the Court, concluded: "The prosecutor here offered a race-neutral basis for these peremptory strikes. As explained by the prosecutor, the challenges rested neither on the intention to exclude Latino or bilingual jurors, nor on stereotypical assumptions about Latinos or bilinguals. The prosecutor's articulated basis for those whose conduct during *voir dire* would persuade him they might have difficulty in accepting the translator's rendition of Spanish-language testimony and those potential jurors who gave no such reason for doubt. Each category would include both Latinos and non-Latinos. While the prosecutor's criterion might well result in the disproportionate removal of prospective Latino jurors, that disproportionate impact does not turn the prosecutor's actions into a *per se* violation of the Equal Protection Clause. [However, if] a prosecutor articulates a basis for a peremptory challenge that results in the disproportionate exclusion of members of a certain race, the trial judge may consider that fact as evidence that the prosecutor's stated reason constitutes a pretext for racial discrimination." The Court then concluded the state court's finding of no discriminatory intent should stand because not clearly erroneous.

O'CONNOR, J., for two concurring members of the Court, emphasized that if "the trial court believes the prosecutor's nonracial justification, and that finding is not clearly erroneous, that is the end of the matter," meaning disproportionate effect is then irrelevant. STEVENS, J., for the three dissenters, concluded the prosecutor's explanation "was insufficient for three reasons. First, the justification would inevitably result in a disproportionate disqualification of Spanish-speaking venirepersons. An explanation that is 'race-neutral' on its face is nonetheless unacceptable if it is merely a proxy for a discriminatory practice. Second, the prosecutor's concern could easily have been accommodated by less drastic means. As is the practice in many jurisdictions, the jury could have been instructed that the official translation alone is evidence; bilingual jurors could have been instructed to bring to the attention of the judge any disagreements they might have with the translation so that any disputes could be resolved by the court. Third, if the prosecutor's concern was valid and substantiated by the record, it would have supported a challenge for cause. The fact that the prosecutor did not make any such challenge should disqualify him from advancing the concern as a justification for a peremptory challenge."

Compare *Minniefield v. State*, 539 N.E.2d 464 (Ind.1989) (striking black veniremen because prosecution's evidence would of necessity reveal that victim enjoyed racist jokes not a neutral explanation, as "race-based use of peremptory challenges * * *, even if allegedly dictated by strategic considerations, is a *per se* violation of the equal protection clause").

Chapter 24

"TRIAL BY NEWSPAPER"—AND TELEVISION

SECTION 1. PRETRIAL PUBLICITY

7th ed., p. 1337; in connection with *A.B.A. Standard* 8–3.5(a), add the following:

In MU'MIN v. VIRGINIA, ___ U.S. ___, 111 S.Ct. 1899, 114 L.Ed.2d 493 (1991), a 5–4 majority held, despite petitioner's reliance on *A.B.A. Standard* 8–3.5(a), that a trial judge's refusal to question jurors specifically about the *content* of the news reports to which each had been exposed violated neither the defendant's Sixth Amandment right to an impartial jury nor her Fourteenth Amendment right to due process. Observed the Court, per REHNQUIST, C.J.:

"[The A.B.A. Standards] require interrogation of each juror individually with respect to 'what the prospective juror has read and heard about the case' 'if there is a substantial possibility that individual jurors will be ineligible to serve because of exposure to potentially prejudicial material.' These standards, of course, leave to the trial court the initial determination of whether there is such a substantial possibility. But, more importantly, the standards relating to *voir dire* are based on a substantive rule that renders a potential juror subject to challenge for cause, without regard to his state of mind, if he has been exposed to and remembers 'highly significant information' or 'other incriminating matters that may be inadmissible in evidence.' That is a stricter standard of juror eligibility than that which we have held the Constitution to require. Under the A.B.A. standard, answers to questions about content, without more, could disqualify the juror from sitting. Under the constitutional standard, on the other hand, '[t]he relevant question is not whether the community remembered the case, but whether the jurors [had] such fixed opinions that they could not judge impartially the guilt of the defendant.' *Patton v. Yount.* Under this constitutional standard, answers to questions about content alone, which reveal that a juror remembered facts about the case, would not be sufficient to disqualify a juror. 'It is not required [that] the jurors be totally ignorant of the facts and issues involved.' *Irvin.*

"The A.B.A. standards [have] not commended themselves to a majority of the courts that have considered the question. The fact that a particular rule may be thought to be the 'better' view does not mean that it is incorporated into the Fourteenth Amendment."

Concurring JUSTICE O'CONNOR whose vote was necessary for the Court's decision, emphasized that "the only question before us is whether the trial court erred by crediting the assurance of eight jurors that they could put aside what they had read or heard and render a fair verdict based on the evidence." She answered that question in the negative:

Although the trial judge did not know precisely what each juror had read about the case, "[h]e was undeniably aware [of] the full range of information that had been reported. This is because Mu'Min submitted to the court, in support of a motion for a change of venue, 47 newspaper articles relating to the murder. The trial judge was thus aware, long before *voir dire,* of all of the allegedly prejudicial information to which prospective jurors might have been exposed."

Because Justice O'Connor could not conclude that questioning prospective jurors about the specific content of the news reports to which they had been exposed is "so indispensable that it violates the Sixth Amendment for a trial court to evaluate a juror's credibility instead by reference to the full range of potentially prejudicial information that has been reported," she joined the Court's opinion.

Dissenting JUSTICE MARSHALL, joined by Blackmun and Stevens, JJ., emphasized that defendant's capital murder trial "was preceded by exceptionally prejudicial publicity, and at jury selection 8 of the 12 jurors who ultimately convicted [him] of murder and sentenced him to death admitted exposure to this publicity." When a prospective juror has been exposed to prejudicial pretrial publicity, argued the dissenters, "a trial court cannot realistically assess the juror's impartially without first establishing what the juror already has learned about the case." Justice Kennedy also dissented, maintaining that when a prospective juror admits exposure to pretrial publicity about a case, "findings of impartiality must be based on something more than the mere silence of the individual in response to questions asked en masse."

SECTION 2. CHANGE OF VENUE
7th ed., p. 1341; after Note 5, add:

6. *The Rodney King beating trial and its aftermath.* When a change of venue is granted, should the new location be chosen for its demographic similarity to the scene of the crime? Consider Margolick, *As Venues Are Changed, Many Ask How Important a Role Race Should Play,* N.Y. Times, May 23, 1992, p. 7:

"By law and tradition, judges have always selected alternate trial sites solely on the basis of cost and convenience.

[But] in times of saturation news coverage and racial turmoil, seemingly neutral decisions can prove as crucial as a smoking gun. Lawyers on both sides of the [Rodney King beating trial] concur that more than anything else, the [acquittal of the police officers] was attributable to relocating the case from polygot Los Angeles to largely white Simi Valley in Ventura County.

* * *

"Legislators in California and New Jersey are drafting bills that would require judges who change the venue of a case to select a site similar demographically to the original location. The NAACP Legal Defense and Education Fund is also examining how best to curb what is now unfettered judicial discretion.

" 'Because our society is so segregated, you're not going to have any trust in verdicts unless the justice system does a much better job of seeing that jurors are chosen from pools in which many parts of the community are adequately represented,' said George Kendell, a lawyer with the group. * * *

"[The] legislation proposed in California would specifically authorize judges who have decided to move cases to weigh 'race, age, income, or other appropriate characteristics' in selecting an alternate site. [The] measure under consideration in New Jersey would require judges changing venue to select a locale similar demographically to the original site."

See also Professor Timothy O'Neill, *Wrong Place, Wrong Jury,* N.Y. Times, May 9, 1992, p. 15:

"[V]icinage is about more than just a defendant's rights. It provides for a jury that will function as the conscience of the community. [A] lack of vicinage is the heart of the problem with the Rodney King trial. The Simi Valley jury had no stake in the verdict; it may as well have decided a hypothetical case. Conversely, Los Angeles County was deprived of a chance to render a legal and moral judgment. Ventura County was given all the power but none of the responsibility. The resulting frustration in Los Angeles was measured in lives and physical damage.

"The Supreme Court has never explicitly applied the Sixth Amendment's vicinage clause to state prosecutions. But this should not prevent states from upholding the concept. It is encouraging that, in the wake of the Los Angeles riots, the California Legislature is considering proposals that would insure that when the site of a trial is changed, the new venue must reflect the demographics of the community where the crime was committed."

But consider Professor Joseph Grano, *Change of Venue Rules Protect Rights of Accused,* Detroit News, May 10, 1992, p. 3B:

"Some critics of the King outcome argue that if venue is going to be changed, the new trial location should reflect, to the extent possible, the racial composition of the original. This is a flawed proposal, especially for cases with racial overtones.

"Consider the case of a black defendant accused of a widely publicized inter-racial crime in a virtually all-white community such as a black man charged with murdering a white police officer in Simi Valley. Such a defendant would seek to change venue to a less hostile community, and many of the venue change critics in the King case would vocally endorse such a change. * * *

"The possibility that race played a role in the King case cannot be denied. Defendants are presumed innocent, even when there are video tapes. Venue changes are intended to assure the defendant a jury that will acquit when it has a reasonable doubt, even if, on balance, it thinks him guilty. Moreover, we traditionally have thought that acquitting a guilty person is a lesser evil than convicting an innocent one.

"The cost of venue rules that err on the side of defendants is an occasional King case. The cost of reversing this prefer-

ence is one many black defendants, with reason, would be reluctant to bear."

SECTION 4. PREVENTING PREJUDICIAL PUBLICITY

A. RESTRICTING PUBLIC STATEMENTS

7th ed., p. 1347; in lieu of Note 3, add:

In GENTILE v. STATE BAR OF NEVADA, ___ U.S. ___, 111 S.Ct. 2720, 115 L.Ed.2d 888 (1991), a 5–4 majority, per REHNQUIST, C.J., upheld the constitutionality of Nevada Rule 177, a rule identical to Model Rule 3.6 (set forth at 7th ed., p. 1346) that prohibits a lawyer (in this case, a defense lawyer) from making extrajudicial statements to the press that he "knows or reasonably should know * * * will have a substantial likelihood of materially prejudicing an adjudicative proceeding." However, a different 5–4 majority, per KENNEDY, J., held that the "substantial likelihood of material prejudice" standard, as interpreted by the Nevada Supreme Court—taking into account the Nevada rule's "safe harbor" provision—was "void for vagueness" because it failed to furnish "fair notice to those to whom [it] is directed." The "safe harbor" provision, identical to Model Rule 3.6(c) (set forth at 7th ed., p. 1346), allows a lawyer, "notwithstanding" various prohibitions against making extrajudicial statements, to "state without elaboration [the] general nature of the claim or defense."

The "swing vote" belonged to Justice O'Connor. She agreed with the Rehnquist group (Rehnquist, C.J., joined by White, Scalia, and Souter, JJ.,) that, as officers of the court, lawyers "may legitimately be subject to ethical precepts that keep them from engaging in what otherwise might be constitutionally protected speech." But she agreed with the Kennedy group (Kennedy, J., joined by Marshall, Blackmun and Stevens, JJ.) that, considering its "safe harbor" provision, the Nevada rule was "void for vagueness."

The case arose as follows: When undercover officers with the Las Vegas Metropolitan Police Department reported large amounts of cocaine and travelers' checks missing from a safety deposit box at Western Vault Corporation (a company owned by petitioner Gentile's client, Sanders), suspicion initially focused on Detective Scholl and another police officer. Both officers had had free access to the deposit box. But then the news reports indicated that the attention of the investigators had shifted to Sanders, owner of Western Vault. The story took a sensational turn with news stories that Scholl and the other officer had been "cleared" after passing lie detector tests, but that Sanders had refused to take such a test.

The day after his client was indicted and the same day as the arraignment, Gentile held a press conference. At the time he met with the press, Gentile knew that a jury would not be empaneled for six months.

Gentile maintained that his primary motivation in holding the press conference was to counter prejudicial publicity already released by the police and prosecutors. The state disciplinary board found that he had attempted "to counter public opinion which he perceived as adverse to Mr. Sanders"; "to fight back against the perceived efforts of the prosecution to poison the prospective juror pool" and "to publicly present Sanders' side of the case."

At the press conference, Gentile stated, inter alia: (1) the case was similar to those in other cities where the authorities had been "honest enough to indict the people who did it"—"the police department, crooked cops"; (2) when the case is tried the evidence will prove "not only [that] Sanders is an innocent person," but that Detective Scholl "was in the most direct position to have stolen the drugs and money"; (3) there is "far more evidence [that] Detective Scholl took the drugs [and] travelers' checks than any other living human being"; (4) "I feel [that] Sanders is being used as a scapegoat to cover up for what has to be obvious to [law enforcement authorities]"; and (5) with respect to other charges contained in the indictment against Sanders, "the so-called victims" "are known drug dealers and convicted money launderers and drug dealers." In addition, in response to a question from a reporter, Gentile strongly implied that Detective Scholl could be observed in a videotape suffering from symptoms of cocaine use.

The two newspaper stories and the two TV news broadcasts that mentioned Gentile's press conferences also mentioned a prosecution response and a police press conference in response. The chief deputy district attorney was quoted as saying that this was a legitimate indictment and that prosecutors cannot bring an indictment unless they can prove the charges in it beyond a reasonable doubt. A deputy police chief stated that Detective Scholl and another officer who had access to the safety deposit box "had nothing to do with this theft or any other" and that the police department was satisfied that both officers were "above reproach."

Some six months later, Sanders' criminal case was tried by a jury and he was acquitted on all counts. A state disciplinary board then brought proceedings against Gentile and concluded that he had violated Rule 177. The board recommended a private reprimand. The state supreme court affirmed the decision.

In concluding that the "substantial likelihood of material prejudice" standard utilized by Nevada and most other states satisfies the First Amendment, the Court, per REHNQUIST, C.J., observed:

"The [disciplinary board] found that petitioner knew the detective he accused of perpetrating the crime and abusing drugs would be a witness for the prosecution. It also found that petitioner believed others whom he characterized as money launderers and drug dealers would be called as prosecution witnesses. Petitioner's admitted purpose for calling the press conference was to counter public opinion which he percieved as adverse to his client * * *. The Board found that in light of the statements, their timing, and petitioner's purpose, petitioner knew or should have known that there was a substantial likelihood that the statements would materially prejudice the Sanders trial.

"The Nevada Supreme Court affirmed the Board's decision, [noting] that the case was 'highly publicized'; that the press conference [was] 'timed to have maximum impact'; and that petitioner's comments 'related to the character, credibility, reputation or criminal record of the police detective and other potential witnesses.' The court concluded that the 'absence of actual prejudice does not establish that there was no substantial likelihood of material prejudice.'

" * * * Currently, 31 states in addition to Nevada have adopted—either verbatim or with insignificant variations—[Model Rule 3.6]. Eleven states have adopted Disciplinary Rule 7–107 of the ABA's Code of Professional Responsibility, which is less protective of lawyer speech than Model Rule 3.6, in that it applies a 'reasonable likelihood of prejudice' standard. Only one state, Virginia, has explicitly adopted a clear and present danger standard, while four states and the District of Columbia have adopted standards that arguably approximate 'clear and present danger.'

"Petitioner maintains, however, that the First Amendment * * * requires a state

[to] demonstrate a 'clear and present danger' of 'actual prejudice or an imminent threat' before any discipline may be imposed on a lawyer who initiates a press conference such as occurred here.[4] He relies on decision such as *Nebraska Press Ass'n v. Stuart* [7th ed., p. 1348] to support his position.

"[In] *Sheppard v. Maxwell*, [we] held that a new trial was a remedy for [extensive prejudicial pretrial] publicity, but [added:]

'[W]e must remember that reversals are but palliatives; the cure lies in those remedial measures that will prevent the prejudice at its inception. * * * Neither prosecutors, counsel for the defense, the accused, witnesses, court staff nor enforcement officers coming under the jurisdiction of the court should be permitted to frustrate its function. *Collaboration between counsel and the press as to information affecting the fairness of a criminal trial is not only subject to regulation, but is highly curable and worthy of disciplinary measures.'* (Emphasis added.)

"We expressly contemplated that the speech of *those participating before the court* could be limited.[5] This distinction between participants in the litigation and strangers to it is brought into sharp relief by our holding in *Seattle Times Co. v. Rhinehart*, 467 U.S. 20, 104 S.Ct. 2199, 81 L.Ed.2d 17 (1984). There we unanimously held that a newspaper, which was itself a defendant in a libel action, could be restrained from publishing material about the plaintiffs and their supporters to which it had gained access through court-ordered

---

4. We disagree with Justice Kennedy's statement that this case "does not call into question the constitutionality of other states' prohibitions upon attorney speech that will have a 'substantial likelihood of materially prejudicing the adjudicative proceeding,' but is limited to Nevada's interpretation of that standard." Petitioner challenged Rule 177 as being unconstitutional on its face in addition to as applied, contending that the "substantial likelihood of material prejudice" test was unconstitutional, and that lawyer speech should be punished only if it violates the standard for clear and present danger set forth in

Nebraska Press. The validity of the rules in the many states applying the "substantial likelihood of material prejudice" test has, therefore, been called into question in this case.

5. The Nevada Supreme Court has consistently read all parts of Rule 177 as applying only to lawyers in pending cases and not to other lawyers or nonlawyers. We express no opinion on the constitutionality of a rule regulating the statement of a lawyer who is not participating in the pending case about which statements are made.

* * *

Rule's terms are given any meaningful content. * * *

"Neither the disciplinary board nor the reviewing court explain any sense in which petitioner's statements had a substantial likelihood of causing material prejudice. The only evidence against Gentile was the videotape of his statement and his own testimony at the disciplinary hearing. The Bar's whole case rests on the fact of the statement, the time it was made, and petitioner's own justifications. Full deference to these factual findings does not justify abdication of our responsibility to determine whether petitioner's statements can be punished consistent with First Amendment standards. * * *

"Our decision earlier this Term in *Mu'Min v. Virginia* [Supp., p. 131], provides a pointed contrast to respondent's contention in this case. There, the community had been subjected to a barrage of publicity prior to Mu'Min's trial for capital murder. News stories appeared over a course of several months and included, in addition to details of the crime itself, numerous items of prejudicial information inadmissible at trial. Eight of the twelve individuals seated on Mu'Min's jury admitted some exposure to pretrial publicity. We held that the publicity did not rise even to a level requiring questioning of individual jurors about the content of publicity. In light of that holding, the Nevada court's conclusion that petitioner's abbreviated, general comments six months before trial created a 'substantial likelihood of materially prejudicing' the proceeding is, to say the least, most unconvincing.

" * * * As petitioner explained to the disciplinary board, his primary motivation was the concern that, unless some of the weaknesses in the state's case were made public, a potential jury venire would be poisoned by repetition in the press of information being released by the police and prosecutors, in particular the repeated press reports about polygraph tests and the fact that the two police officers were no longer suspects. Respondent distorts Rule 177 when it suggests that explanation admits a purpose to prejudice the venire and so proves a violation of the Rule. * * * Petitioner did not indicate he thought he could sway the pool of potential jurors to form an opinion in advance of the trial, nor did he seek to discuss evidence that would be inadmissible at trial. He sought only to counter publicity already deemed prejudicial. [The disciplinary board] so found.

"[An] attorney's duties do not begin inside the courtroom door. He or she cannot ignore the practical implications of a legal proceeding for the client. Just as an attorney may recommend a plea bargain or civil settlement to avoid adverse consequences of a possible loss after trial, so too an attorney may take reasonable steps to defend a client's reputation and reduce the adverse consequences of indictment, especially in the face of a prosecution deemed unjust or commenced with improper motives. A defense attorney may pursue lawful strategies to obtain dismissal of an indictment or reduction of charges, including an attempt to demonstrate in the court of public opinion that the client does not deserve to be tried.

"[On] the evening before the press conference, petitioner and two colleagues spent several hours researching the extent of an attorney's obligations under Rule 177. He decided, as we have held, see *Patton v. Yount* [7th ed., p. 1335], that the timing of a statement was crucial in the assessment of possible prejudice and the Rule's application.

"Upon return of the indictment, the court set a trial date [for] some six months in the future. Petitioner knew, at the time of his statement, that a jury would not be empaneled for six months at the earliest, if ever. He recalled reported cases finding no prejudice resulting from juror exposure to 'far worse' information two and four months before trial, and concluded that his proposed statement was not substantially likely to result in material prejudice.

"A statement which reaches the attention of the venire on the eve of *voir dire* might require a continuance or cause difficulties in securing an impartial jury, and at the very least could complicate the jury selection process. As turned out to be the case here, exposure to the same statement six months prior to trial would not result in prejudice, the content fading from memory long before the trial date.

"In 1988, Clark County, Nevada had a population in excess of 600,000 persons. Given the size of the community from which any potential jury venire would be drawn and the length of time before trial, only the most damaging of information could give rise to any likelihood of prejudice. The innocuous content of petitioner's statement reinforces my conclusion.

"[The news stories reporting Gentile's statements] mentioned not only Gentile's press conference but also a prosecution response and police press conference. [G]iven the repetitive publicity from the police investigation, it is difficult to come to any conclusion but that the balance remained in favor of the prosecution.

"Much of the information provided by petitioner had been published in one form or another, obviating any potential for prejudice. The remainder, and details petitioner refused to provide, were available to any journalist willing to do a little bit of investigative work.

"Petitioner's statement lacks any of the more obvious bases for a finding of prejudice. Unlike the police, he refused to comment on polygraph tests except to confirm earlier reports that Sanders had not submitted to the police polygraph; he mentioned no confessions, and no evidence from searches or test results; he refused to elaborate upon his charge that the other so-called victims were not credible, except to explain his general theory that they were pressured to testify in an attempt to avoid drug-related legal trouble, and that some of them may have asserted claims in an attempt to collect insurance money.

"[Petitioner's] judgment that no likelihood of material prejudice would result from his comments was vindicated by events at trial. While it is true that Rule 177's standard for controlling pretrial publicity must be judged at the time a statement is made, *ex post* evidence can have probative value in some cases. Here, where the Rule purports to demand, and the Constitution requires, consideration of the character of the harm and its heightened likelihood of occurrence, the record is altogether devoid of facts one would expect to follow upon any statement that created a real likelihood of material prejudice to a criminal jury trial.

"The trial took place on schedule [with] no request by either party for a venue change or continuance. The jury was empaneled with no apparent difficulty.

"[At] trial, all material information disseminated during petitioner's press conference was admitted in evidence before the jury, including information questioning the motives and credibility of supposed victims who testified against Sanders, and Detective Scholl's ingestion of drugs in the course of undercover operations (in order, he testified, to gain the confidence of suspects). [There] is no support for the conclusion that petitioner's statement created a likelihood of material prejudice, or indeed of any harm of sufficient magnitude or imminence to support a punishment for speech. ✳ ✳ ✳

"Only the occasional case presents a danger of prejudice from pretrial publicity. Empirical research suggests that in the few instances when jurors have been exposed to extensive and prejudicial publicity, they are able to disregard it and base their verdict upon the evidence presented in court. *Voir dire* can play an important role in reminding jurors to set aside out-of-court information, and to decide the case upon the evidence presented at trial. All of these factors weigh in favor of affording an attorney's speech about ongoing proceedings our traditional First Amendment protections. Our colleagues' historical survey notwithstanding, respondent has not demonstrated any sufficient state interest in restricting the speech of attorneys to justify a lower standard of First Amendment scrutiny.

"Still less justification exists for a lower standard of scrutiny here, as this speech involved not the prosecutor or police, but a criminal defense attorney. Respondent and its *amici* present not a single example where a defense attorney has managed by public statements to prejudice the prosecution of the state's case.

"[The] various bar association and advisory commission reports which resulted in promulgation of ABA Model Rule of Professional Conduct 3.6 (1981), and other regulations of attorney speech, and sources they cite, present no convincing case for restrictions upon the speech of defense attorneys. The police, the prosecution, other government officials, and the community at large hold innumerable avenues for the dissemination of information adverse to a criminal defendant, many of which are not within the scope of Rule 177 or any other regulation. By contrast, a defendant cannot speak without fear of incriminating himself and prejudicing his defense, and most criminal defendants have insufficient means to retain a public relations team apart from defense counsel for the sole purpose of countering prosecution statements. These factors underscore my conclusion that blanket rules restricting speech of defense attorneys should not be accepted without careful First Amendment scrutiny.

"Respondent uses the 'officer of the court' label to imply that attorney contact with the press somehow is inimical to the attorney's proper role. Rule 177 posits no such inconsistency between an attorney's role and discussions with the press. It permits all comment to the press absent 'a substantial likelihood of materially prejudicing an adjudicative proceeding.' Respondent does not articulate the principle that contact with the press cannot be reconciled with the attorney's role or explain how this might be so.

"Because attorneys participate in the criminal justice system and are trained in its complexities, they hold unique qualifications as a source of information about pending cases. [To] the extent the press and public rely upon attorneys for information because attorneys are well-informed, this may prove the value to the public of speech by members of the bar. If the dangers of their speech arise from its persuasiveness, from their ability to explain judicial proceedings, or from the likelihood the speech will be believed, these are not the sort of dangers that can validate restrictions. The First Amendment does not permit suppression of speech because of its power to command assent.

"[The] instant case is a poor vehicle for defining with precision the outer limits under the Constitution of a court's ability to regulate an attorney's statements about ongoing adjudicative proceedings. At the very least, however, we can say that the Rule which punished petitioner's statement represents a limitation of First Amendment freedoms greater than is necessary or essential to the protection of the particular governmental interest, and does not protect against a danger of the necessary gravity, imminence, or likelihood."

Although he dissented on the issue of the constitutionality of the "substantial likelihood of material prejudice" standard, as applied by Nevada, JUSTICE KENNEDY announced the judgment of the Court overturning Gentile's reprimand and the opinion of the Court holding that Rule 177 was "void for vagueness":

"As interpreted by the Nevada Supreme Court, [Rule 177] is void for vagueness [for] its safe harbor provision, Rule

177(3), misled petitioner into thinking that he could give his press conferences without fear of discipline. Rule 177(3)(a) provides that a lawyer 'may state without elaboration [the] general nature of [the] defense.' Statements under this provision are protected [n]otwithstanding [the general prohibition against extrajudicial statements in subsection 1 and the specific example of statements likely to prejudice a criminal trial in subsection 2]. By necessary operation of the word 'notwithstanding,' the Rule contemplates that a lawyer describing the 'general nature of [the] defense' 'without elaboration' need fear no discipline, even if he comments on '[t]he character, credibility, reputation or criminal record of [a] witness,' and even if he 'knows or reasonably should have known that [the statement] will have a substantial likelihood of materially prejudicing an adjudicative proceeding.'

"Given this grammatical structure, and absent any clarifying interpretation by the state court, the Rule fails to provide ' "fair notice to those to whom [it] is directed." ' The right to explain the 'general' nature of the defense without 'elaboration' provides insufficient guidance because 'general' and 'elaboration' are both classic terms of degree. In the context before us, these terms have no settled usage or tradition of interpretation in law. The lawyer has no principle for determining when his remarks pass from the safe harbor of the general to the forbidden sea of the elaborated."

On this issue, CHIEF JUSTICE REHNQUIST, joined by White, Scalia and Souter, JJ. dissented:

"Rule 177 was drafted with the intent to provide 'an illustrative compilation that gives fair notice of conduct ordinarily posing unacceptable dangers to the fair administration of justice.' Proposed Final Draft. The Rule provides sufficient notice of the nature of the prohibited conduct.

Under the circumstances of his case, petitioner cannot complain about lack of notice, as he has admitted that his primary objective in holding the press conference was the violation of Rule 177's core prohibition—to prejudice the upcoming trial by influencing potential jurors. Petitioner was clearly given notice that such conduct was forbidden, and the list of conduct likely to cause prejudice, while only advisory, certainly gave notice that the statements made would violate the rule if they had the intended effect.[a]

" * * * Section 3 allows an attorney to state 'the general nature of the claim or defense' notwithstanding the prohibition contained in § 1 and the examples contained in § 2. It is of course true [that] the word 'general' and the word 'elaboration' are both terms of degree. But combined as they are in the first sentence of § 3, they convey the very definite proposition that the authorized statements must not contain the sort of detailed allegations that petitioner made at his press conference. No sensible person could think that the following were 'general' statements of a claim or defense made 'without elaboration': 'the person that was in the most direct position to have stolen the drugs and the money [is] Detective Steve Scholl'; 'there is far more evidence that will establish that Detective Scholl took these drugs and took these American Express travelers' checks than any other living human being'; [and] 'the so-called other victims [are] known drug dealers and convicted money launderers.' § 3, as an exception to the provisions of §§ 1 and 2, must be read in the light of the prohibitions and examples contained in the first two sections. It was obviously not intended to negate the prohibitions or the examples wholesale, but simply intended to provide a 'safe harbor' where there might be doubt as to whether one of the examples covered proposed conduct. These provisions were not vague as to the conduct for

---

a. Rule 177(2), which is identical to Model Rule 3.6(b), set forth at 7th ed., p. 1346, contains

a list of statements "ordinarily * * * likely to prejudice a criminal trial."

which petitioner was disciplined; '[i]n determining the sufficiency of the notice a statute must of necessity be examined in the light of the conduct with which a defendant is charged.'

"Petitioner's strongest arguments are that the statement was made well in advance of trial, and that the statements did not in fact taint the jury panel. But the Supreme Court of Nevada pointed out that petitioner's statements were not only highly inflammatory [but] timed to have maximum impact, when public interest in the case was at its height immediately after Sanders was indicted. Reviewing inde-

pendently the entire record, we are convinced that petitioner's statements were 'substantially likely to cause material prejudice' to the proceedings. [We] find it persuasive that, by his own admission, petitioner called the press conference for the express purpose of influencing the venire. It is difficult to believe that he went to such trouble, and took such a risk, if there was no substantial likelihood that he would succeed. * * *[6]"

7th ed., pp. 1347–48; in lieu of Note 4, add:

See *Gentile v. State Bar of Nevada*, immediately above.

---

6. Justice Kennedy appears to contend that there can be no material prejudice when the lawyer's publicity is in response to publicity favorable to the other side. [He] would find that publicity designed to counter prejudicial publicity cannot be itself prejudicial, despite its likelihood of influencing potential jurors, unless it actually would go so far as to cause jurors to be affirmatively biased in favor of the lawyer's client. In the first place, such a test would be difficult, if not impossible, to apply. But more fundamental-

ly, it misconceives the constitutional test for an impartial juror—whether the "juror can lay aside his impression or opinion and render a verdict on the evidence presented in Court." *Murphy v. Florida*. A juror who may have been initially swayed from open-mindedness by publicity favorable to the prosecution is not rendered fit for service by being bombarded by publicity favorable to the defendant. The basic premise of our legal system is that law suits should be tried in court, not in the media.

Chapter 25

THE CRIMINAL TRIAL

SECTION 2. PRESENCE OF THE DEFENDANT

7th ed., p. 1371, end of fn. b, add:

In *Maryland v. Craig,* 497 U.S. 836, 110 S.Ct. 3157, 111 L.Ed.2d 666 (1990), the Court responded to the issue left open in *Coy,* and in an opinion by Justice O'Connor, adopted the position suggested by her *Coy* concurrence. The *Craig* majority upheld a statutory procedure that allows the use of one-way closed circuit television to provide the testimony of a child witness who is alleged to be the victim of child abuse (in *Craig,* the testimony of a six-year-old alleged to have been sexually abused by defendant while attending her pre-school center). Use of the televised testimony is conditioned on the trial court first determining, after a factfinding hearing, that requiring the child to give courtroom testimony would result, because of the presence of the defendant, in the child "suffering serious emotion distress, such that the child cannot reasonably communicate." The Court ruled that the state interest in protecting the child from trauma caused by defendant's physical presence, "at least where such trauma would impair the child's ability to communicate," as supported by a case-specific finding of necessity, justified dispensing with element of face-to-face confrontation. It stressed that all other elements of confrontation—oath, cross-examination by defense counsel present in the room in which the child testified (with defendant in electronic communication with counsel), and observation of demeanor by the judge and jury (who remained in the courtroom)—would be preserved. Justice Scalia, in a dissent joined by Justices Brennan, Marshall, and Stevens, characterized the Court's ruling as a "subordination of explicit constitutional text to currently favored public policy."

SECTION 7. DELIBERATIONS AND VERDICT

7th ed., p. 1403–1404; in lieu of Notes 2, 3 and 4, add:

2. In SCHAD v. ARIZONA, ___ U.S. ___, 111 S.Ct. 2491, 115 L.Ed.2d 555 (1991), the defendant was convicted of first degree murder, defined by state law

as murder that is "wilful, deliberate or premeditated * * * or which is committed * * * in the perpetration of, or attempt to perpetrate * * * robbery." The case was submitted to the jury under instructions that did not require unanimity on either of the available theories of premeditated murder and felony murder. In an opinion joined by three other members of the Court, SOUTER, J., declared that the due process clause places "limits on a State's capacity to define different courses of conduct, or states of mind, as merely alternative means of committing a single offense, thereby permitting a defendant's conviction without jury agreement as to which course or state actually occurred." In concluding those limits were not exceeded in the instant case, the plurality opinion deemed "history and widely shared practice as concrete indications of what fundamental fairness and rationality require." * * *

"Thus it is significant that Arizona's equation of the mental states of premeditated murder and felony murder as species of the blameworthy state of mind required to prove a single offense of first-degree murder finds substantial historical and contemporary echoes. At common law, murder was defined as the unlawful killing of another human being with 'malice aforethought.' The intent to kill and the intent to commit a felony were alternative aspects of the single concept of 'malice aforethought.' Although American jurisdictions have modified the common law by legislation classifying murder by degrees, the resulting statutes have in most cases retained premeditated murder and some form of felony murder (invariably including murder committed in perpetrating or attempting to penetrate a robbery) as alternative means of satisfying the mental state that first-degree murder presupposes.

* * *

"A series of state court decisions * * * have agreed that 'it was not necessary that all the jurors should agree in the determination that there was a deliberate and premeditated design to take the life of the deceased, or in the conclusion that the defendant was at the time engaged in the commission of a felony, or an attempt to commit one; it was sufficient that each juror was convinced beyond a reasonable doubt that the defendant had committed the crime of murder in the first degree as that offense is defined by the statute.' Although the state courts have not been unanimous in this respect, there is sufficiently widespread acceptance of the two mental states as alternative means of satisfying the *mens rea* element of the single crime of first-degree murder to persuade us that Arizona has not departed from the norm."

Cautioning that it cannot be said "that either history or current practice is dispositive," the plurality opinion next emphasized the lack of "moral disparity" in the two alternative mental states. "Whether or not everyone would agree that the mental state that precipitates death in the course of robbery is the moral equivalent of premeditation, it is clear that such equivalence could reasonably be found, which is enough to rule out the argument that this moral disparity bars treating them as alternative means to satisfy the mental element of a single offense." By contrast, SCALIA, J., concurring, relied solely upon the fact that the challenged practice was "as old as the common law and still in existence in the vast majority of States," and was critical of the plurality's "moral equivalence" test: "We would not permit, for example, an indictment charging that the defendant assaulted either X on Tues-

day or Y on Wednesday, despite the 'moral equivalence' of those two acts."

WHITE, J., for the four dissenters, relying upon the holding in *In re Winship*, 7th ed., p. 788, that due process mandates "proof beyond a reasonable doubt of every fact necessary to constitute the crime with which [the defendant] is charged," objected that "the plurality affirms this conviction without knowing that even a single element of either of the ways for proving first-degree murder, except the fact of a killing, has been found by a majority of the jury, let alone found unanimously by the jury as required by Arizona law. A defendant charged with first-degree murder is at least entitled to a verdict—something petitioner did not get in this case as long as the possibility exists that no more than six jurors voted for any one element of first-degree murder, except the fact of a killing.

"* * * The problem is that the Arizona statute, under a single heading, criminalizes several alternative patterns of conduct. While a State is free to construct a statute in this way, it violates due process for a State to invoke more than one statutory alternative, each with different specified elements, without requiring that the jury indicate on which of the alternatives it has based the defendant's guilt."

3. The leading pre-*Schad* case was *United States v. Gipson*, 553 F.2d 453 (5th Cir. 1977), involving a statute covering one who "receives, conceals, stores, barters, sells or disposes" of known stolen property moving in interstate or foreign commerce, where the jury instruction did not require unanimity as to which of the six statutory alternatives was proved. As the *Schad* plurality said of *Gipson*, that court "reversed, reasoning that the defendant's right to 'jury consensus as to [his] course of action' was violated by the joinder in a single count of 'two distinct conceptual groupings,' receiving, concealing, and storing forming the first grouping (referred to by the court as 'housing'), and bartering, sell-

ing, and disposing ('marketing') constituting the second. In that court's view, the acts within a conceptual grouping are sufficiently similar to obviate the need for jurors to agree about which of them was committed, whereas the acts in distinct conceptual groupings are so unrelated that the jury must decide separately as to each grouping. * * *

"We are not persuaded that the *Gipson* approach really answers the question, however. Although the classification of alternatives into 'distinct conceptual groupings' is a way to express a judgment about the limits of permissible alternatives, the notion is too indeterminate to provide concrete guidance to courts faced with verdict specificity questions. This is so because conceptual groupings may be identified at various levels of generality, and we have no *a priori* standard to determine what level of generality is appropriate. Indeed, as one judge has noted, even on the facts of *Gipson* itself, '[o]ther conceptual groupings of the six acts are possible. [One might] put all six acts into one conceptual group, namely trafficking in stolen vehicles.' "

Part Five

APPEALS, POST-CONVICTION REVIEW

Chapter 27

APPEALS

SECTION 4. THE SCOPE OF AP-PELLATE REVIEW

7th ed., p. 1514; end of Note 2, add:

In ARIZONA v. FULMINANTE, ___ U.S. ___, 111 S.Ct. 1246, 113 L.Ed.2d 302 (1991) (other aspects of which are discussed at Supp., p. 65), a divided Court held that the *Chapman* harmless error standard should be applied to the admission of involuntary confessions. Speaking for the Court on this issue, Chief Justice REHN-QUIST initially noted that the footnote 8 reference in *Chapman* to *Payne v. Arkansas* [see 7th ed., p. 1502] had been misplaced since the *Payne* Court had rejected a much more lenient harmless error rule than that subsequently adopted in *Chapman*. The Chief Justice then explained that, under the analysis of post-*Chapman* rulings, the admission of a coerced confession properly did not fall within the automatic reversal category:

"The admission of an involuntary confession—a classic 'trial error'—is markedly different from the other two constitutional violations referred to in the *Chapman* footnote as not being subject to harmless-error analysis. One of those cases, *Gideon v. Wainwright,* involved the total deprivation of the right to counsel at trial. The other, *Tumey v. Ohio,* involved a judge who was

not impartial. These are structural defects in the constitution of the trial mechanism, which defy analysis by 'harmless-error' standards. The entire conduct of the trial from beginning to end is obviously affected by the absence of counsel for a criminal defendant, just as it is by the presence on the bench of a judge who is not impartial. Since our decision in *Chapman,* other cases have added to the category of constitutional errors which are not subject to harmless error the following: [citing the *Vasquez, McKaskle,* and *Waller* rulings noted in *Rose* and in Note 1 supra]. Each of these constitutional deprivations is a similar structural defect affecting the framework within which the trial proceeds, rather than simply an error in the trial process itself. * * *

"It is evident from a comparison of the constitutional violations which we have held subject to harmless error, and those which we have held not, that involuntary statements or confessions belong in the former category. The admission of an involuntary confession is a 'trial error,' similar in both degree and kind to the erroneous admission of other types of evidence. The evidentiary impact of an involuntary confession, and its effect upon the composition of the record, is indistinguishable from that of a confession obtained in violation of the Sixth Amendment—of evidence seized in violation of the Fourth Amendment—or of a prosecutor's improper comment on a defendant's silence at trial in violation of the Fifth Amendment. When reviewing the erroneous admission of an involuntary confession, the appellate court, as it does with the admission of other forms of improperly admitted evidence, simply reviews the remainder of the evidence against the defendant to determine whether the admission of the confession was harmless beyond a reasonable doubt.

"Nor can it be said that the admission of an involuntary confession is the type of error which 'transcends the criminal process.' This Court has applied harmless-error analysis to the violation of other constitutional rights similar in magnitude and importance and involving the same level of police misconduct. For instance, we have previously held that the admission of a defendant's statements obtained in violation of the Sixth Amendment is subject to harmless-error analysis. * * * We have also held that the admission of an out-of-court statement by a nontestifying codefendant is subject to harmless-error analysis. * * * The inconsistent treatment of statements elicited in violation of the Sixth and Fourteenth Amendments, respectively, can be supported neither by evidentiary or deterrence concerns nor by a belief that there is something more 'fundamental' about involuntary confessions. * * * Of course an involuntary confession may have a more dramatic effect on the course of a trial than do other trial errors—in particular cases it may be devastating to a defendant—but this simply means that a reviewing court will conclude in such a case that its admission was not harmless error; it is not a reason for eschewing the harmless error test entirely."

Justice WHITE, speaking for himself and Justices Marshall, Blackmun, and Stevens, dissented on this issue:

"The four of us remain convinced * * *, that we should abide by our cases that have refused to apply the harmless error rule to coerced confessions, for a coerced confession is fundamentally different from other types of erroneously admitted evidence to which the rule has been applied. * * * *Chapman* specifically noted three constitutional errors that could not be categorized as harmless error: using a coerced confession against a defendant in a criminal trial, depriving a defendant of counsel, and trying a defendant before a biased judge. The majority attempts to distinguish the use of a coerced confession from the other two errors listed in *Chapman* first by distorting the decision in *Payne,* and then by drawing a meaningless dichotomy between 'trial errors' and 'structural defects' in the trial process. * * * It is clear, though, that in *Payne* the Court recognized that *regardless* of the amount of other evidence, 'the admission in evidence, over objection, of the coerced confession vitiates the judgment,' because 'where, as here, a coerced confession constitutes a part of the evidence before the jury and a general verdict is returned, no one can say what credit and weight the jury gave to the confession.' The inability to assess its effect on a conviction causes the admission at trial of a coerced confession to 'defy analysis by "harmless-error" standards,' just as certainly as do deprivation of counsel and trial before a biased judge.

"The majority also attempts to distinguish 'trial errors' which occur 'during the presentation of the case to the jury,' and which it deems susceptible to harmless error analysis, from 'structural defects in the constitution of the trial mechanism,' which the majority concedes cannot be so analyzed. This effort fails, for our jurisprudence on harmless error has not classified so neatly the errors at issue. For example, we have held susceptible to harmless error analysis the failure to instruct the jury on the presumption of innocence, while finding it impossible to analyze in terms of harmless error the failure to instruct a jury on the reasonable doubt standard. These cases cannot be reconciled by labeling the former 'trial error' and the latter not, for both concern the exact same stage in the trial proceedings. Rather, these cases can be reconciled only by considering the nature of the right at issue and the effect of an error upon the trial. A jury instruction on the presumption of innocence is not constitutionally required in every case to satisfy due process, because such an instruction merely offers an additional safeguard beyond that provided by the constitutionally required instruction on reasonable doubt. While it may be possible to analyze as harmless the omission of a presumption of innocence instruction when the required reasonable doubt instruction has been given, it is impossible to assess the effect on the jury of the omission of the more fundamental instruction on reasonable doubt. In addition, omission of a reasonable doubt instruction, though a 'trial error,' distorts the very structure of the trial because it creates the risk that the jury will convict the defendant even if the State has not met its required burden of proof.

"These same concerns counsel against applying harmless error analysis to the admission of a coerced confession. A defendant's confession is 'probably the most probative and damaging evidence that can be admitted against him,' so damaging that a jury should not be expected to ignore it even if told to do so, and because in any event it is impossible to know what credit and weight the jury gave to the confession. Concededly, this reason is insufficient to justify a *per se* bar to the use of any confession. Thus, *Milton v. Wainwright*, applied harmless-error analysis to a confession obtained and introduced in circumstances that violated the defendant's Sixth Amendment right to counsel. Similarly, the Court of Appeals have held that the introduction of incriminating statements taken from defendants in violation of *Miranda v. Arizona*, is subject to treatment as harmless

error. Nevertheless, in declaring that it is 'impossible to create a meaningful distinction between confessions elicited in violation of the Sixth Amendment and those in violation of the Fourteenth Amendment,' the majority overlooks the obvious. Neither *Milton v. Wainwright* nor any of the other cases upon which the majority relies involved a defendant's coerced confession, nor were there present in these cases the distinctive reasons underlying the exclusion of coerced incriminating statements of the defendant. First, some coerced confessions may be untrustworthy. Consequently, admission of coerced confessions may distort the truth-seeking function of the trial upon which the majority focuses. More importantly, however, the use of coerced confessions, 'whether true or false,' is forbidden 'because the methods used to extract them offend an underlying principle in the enforcement of our criminal law: that ours is an accusatorial and not an inquisitorial system—a system in which the State must establish guilt by evidence independently and freely secured and may not by coercion prove its charge against an accused out of his own mouth.' * * * Thus, permitting a coerced confession to be part of the evidence on which a jury is free to base its verdict of guilty is inconsistent with the thesis that ours is not an inquisitorial system of criminal justice.

"As the majority concedes, there are other constitutional errors that invalidate a conviction even though there may be no reasonable doubt that the defendant is guilty and would be convicted absent the trial error. * * * In *Vasquez v. Hillery,* a defendant was found guilty beyond reasonable doubt, but the conviction had been set aside because of the unlawful exclusion of members of the defendant's race from the grand jury that indicted him despite overwhelming evidence of his guilt. The error at the grand jury stage struck at fundamental values of our society, and 'undermine[d] the structural integrity of the criminal tribunal itself, and [was] not amenable to harmless-error review.' * * * The search for truth is indeed central to our system of justice, but 'certain constitutional rights are not, and should not be, subject to harmless-error analysis because those rights protect important values that are unrelated to the truth-seeking function of the trial.' *Rose v. Clark* (Stevens, J., concurring in judgment). The right of a defendant not to have his coerced confession used against him is among those rights, for using a coerced confession 'abort[s] the basic trial process' and 'render[s] a trial fundamentally unfair.'

"For the foregoing reasons the four of us would adhere to the consistent line of authority that has recognized as a basic tenet of our criminal justice system, before and after both *Miranda* and *Chapman,* the prohibition against using a defendant's coerced confession against him at his criminal trial. *Stare decisis* is 'of fundamental importance to the rule of law.' * * * [T]he majority offers no convincing reason for overturning our long line of decisions requiring the exclusion of coerced confessions."

Chapter 28

HABEAS CORPUS AND RELATED COLLATERAL REMEDIES

SECTION 1. ISSUES COGNIZABLE

7th ed., p. 1555; end of Note 1, add:

In *Saffle v. Parks,* 494 U.S. 484, 110 S.Ct. 1257, 108 L.Ed.2d 415 (1990), the four Justices in the plurality in *Teague* were joined by Justice White in applying *Teague* to reject consideration of a habeas claim deemed to require creation of a "new rule." The majority noted that, under *Teague,* it could "neither announce nor apply the new rule sought by [habeas petitioner] Parks unless it would fall into one of two narrow exceptions." The majority also looked to Justice O'Connor's plurality opinion in *Teague* in defining those exceptions and in determining that the habeas petitioner's claim would rest on a new rule.[a] Subsequent cases have looked to the *Teague* plurality opinion as setting forth the Court's settled position on retroactivity.

7th ed., p. 1556; end of Note 3, add:

In BUTLER v. McKELLAR, 494 U.S. 407, 110 S.Ct. 1212, 108 L.Ed.2d 347 (1990), a 5–4 Court held that the ruling in *Arizona v. Roberson* (7th ed., p. 512) was a new ruling under the *Teague* standard. The majority reasoned (per REHNQUIST, C.J.):

a. In *Collins v. Youngblood,* 494 U.S. 1015, 110 S.Ct. 1316, 108 L.Ed.2d 492 (1990), the Court noted: "Although the *Teague* rule is grounded on important considerations of federal-state relations, we think it is not 'jurisdictional' in the sense that this Court, despite a limited grant of certiorari *must* raise and decide the issue *sua*

"The 'new rule' principle * * * validates reasonable, good faith interpretations of existing precedents made by state courts even though they are shown to be contrary to later decisions. Cf. *United States v. Leon* [7th ed., p. 124]. * * * According to [petitioner's] counsel, the opinion in *Roberson* showed that the Court believed Roberson's case to be within the 'logical compass' of *Edwards.* But the fact that a court says that its decision is within the 'logical compass' of an earlier decision, or indeed that it is 'controlled' by a prior decision, is not conclusive for purposes of deciding whether the current decision is a 'new rule' under *Teague.* Courts frequently view their decisions as being 'controlled' or 'governed' by prior opinions even when aware of reasonable contrary conclusions reached by other courts. In *Roberson,* for instance, the Court found *Edwards* controlling but acknowledged a significant difference of opinion on the part of several lower courts that had considered the question previously. That the outcome in *Roberson* was susceptible to debate among reasonable minds is evidenced further by the differing positions taken by the judges of the Courts of Appeals for the Fourth and Seventh Circuits. * * * It would not have been an illogical or even a grudging application of *Edwards* to decide that it did

sponte." Where certiorari was granted to consider the merits of the defendant's claim, and the state failed to raise a *Teague* issue in its brief and expressly disclaimed reliance on *Teague* in oral argument, the Court decided the claim on the merits without deciding whether its adoption would constitute a "new rule."

not extend to the facts of *Roberson.* We hold, therefore, that *Roberson* announced a 'new rule.' "

Justice BRENNAN, speaking for the four dissenters in *Butler,* found "perplexing" the majority's reliance on the "fact that the court below and several state courts had incorrectly predicted the outcome of *Roberson.*" It would be an "odd criterion for 'reasonableness' "to "suggest that a particular result is reasonable so long as a certain number of courts reach the same result," yet the majority had not otherwise indicated why "the lower court decisions foreshadowing the dissent's position in *Roberson,* though ultimately erroneous, were nevertheless 'reasonable.' " The end result of the majority's position, Justice Brennan contended, was to "limit [the] federal courts' habeas corpus function to reviewing state courts' legal analysis under the equivalent of a 'clearly erroneous' standard of review." The Court thus was departing from a fundamental feature of the retroactivity jurisprudence of Justice Harlan that "undergirds *Teague*"—the recognition that the state courts' obligation of "adjudication according to prevailing law demands that a court exhibit 'conceptual faithfulness' to the principles underlying prior precedents, not just 'decisional obedience' to precise holdings based upon their unique factual patterns."

In STRINGER v. BLACK, ___ U.S. ___, 112 S.Ct. 1130, 116 L.Ed.2d 747 (1992), the Court held that the *Butler* analysis also governed where the habeas petitioner relies on a precedent that did not itself announce a new rule, "but granting the relief sought would create a new rule because the prior decision is applied in a novel setting, thereby extending the precedent." "The interests in finality, predictability and comity underlying our new rule jurisprudence," the Court noted, "may be undermined to an equal degree" both "by the invocation of a rule that was not dictated by precedent" and "the appli-

cation of an old rule in a manner that was not dictated by precedent."

The *Stringer* majority held that the Supreme Court precedent upon which petitioner relied did not establish a new rule, and a new ruling also would not be established by applying that precedent to Mississippi's capital punishment statute. Although the Supreme Court precedent had involved a Georgia capital punishment statute which did not have a weighing element (unlike the Mississippi statute), there was "no arguable basis" for distinguishing the applicability of the underlying constitutional prohibition to the two statutes. The Fifth Circuit had earlier held that the same constitutional principle did not apply to the Mississippi statute, but that ruling, though "relevant" to the Court's "new rule" inquiry under *Butler,* was "not dispositive." The Court majority noted: "The purpose of the new rule doctrine is to validate reasonable interpretations of existing precedents. Reasonableness in this, as in many other contexts, is an objective standard, and the ultimate decision * * * [must be] based on an objective reading of the relevant cases. The short answer to the state's argument is that the Fifth Circuit made a serious mistake [in its rulings]." Three dissenting Justices concluded otherwise, arguing that it could not be said that "no reasonable jurist could have believed in 1985" that the holding establishing the underlying constitutional principle would apply to the Mississippi statute.

7th ed., p. 1557, end of Note 4, add:

Consider also SAWYER v. SMITH, 497 U.S. 227, 110 S.Ct. 2822, 111 L.Ed.2d 193 (1990), holding that the ruling in *Caldwell v. Mississippi,* 472 U.S. 320, 105 S.Ct. 2633, 86 L.Ed.2d 231 (1985)— prohibiting imposition of a death sentence by a jury that had been led to the false belief that the responsibility for determining the appropriateness of the defendant's capital sentence rested with the appellate court—constituted a new rule under

Teague. Justice KENNEDY's opinion for the Court noted:

"The second *Teague* exception applies to new 'watershed rules of criminal procedure' that are necessary to the fundamental fairness of the criminal proceeding. Petitioner here challenges the Court of Appeals' conclusion that *Caldwell* does not come within this exception. Petitioner contends that the second *Teague* exception should be read to include new rules of capital sentencing that 'preserve the accuracy and fairness of capital sentencing judgments.' But this test looks only to half of our definition of the second exception. * * * [It is] not enough under *Teague* to say that a new rule is aimed at improving the accuracy of trial. More is required. A rule that qualifies under this exception must not only improve accuracy, but also 'alter our understanding of the *bedrock procedural elements*' essential to the fairness of a proceeding. * * *

"At the time of petitioner's trial and appeal, the rule of *Donnelly* [7th ed., p. 1393] was in place to protect any defendant who could show that a prosecutor's remarks had in fact made a proceeding fundamentally unfair. * * * Petitioner has not contested the Court of Appeals' finding that he has no claim for relief under the *Donnelly* standard. And as the Court of Appeals stated: '[T]he only defendants who need to rely on *Caldwell* rather than *Donnelly* are those who must concede that the prosecutorial argument in their case was not so harmful as to render their sentencing trial "fundamentally unfair." ' * * * Rather than focusing on the prejudice to the defendant that must be shown to establish a *Donnelly* violation, our concern in *Caldwell* was with the 'unacceptable risk' that misleading remarks could affect the reliability of the sentence. *Caldwell* must therefore be read as providing an additional measure of protection against error, beyond that afforded by *Donnelly,* in the special context of capital sentencing.

See *Darden v. Wainwright,* n. 15 [7th ed., p. 1393]. The *Caldwell* rule was designed as an enhancement of the accuracy of capital sentencing, a protection of systemic value for state and federal courts charged with reviewing capital proceedings. But given that it was added to an existing guarantee of due process protection against fundamental unfairness, we cannot say this systemic rule enhancing reliability is an 'absolute prerequisite to fundamental fairness,' of the type that may come within *Teague* 's second exception."

A dissent by MARSHALL, J. (joined in this part by Justices Brennan, Blackmun and Stevens) contended that: (i) "*Caldwell* did not create a new rule," and (ii) "even if *Caldwell* established a new rule, that rule nonetheless is available on federal habeas corpus because it is a rule 'without which the likelihood of an accurate [verdict] is seriously diminished, *Teague.*' " The dissent reasoned: "The majority's contrary conclusion rests on a misunderstanding of the relationship between *Caldwell* and *Donnelly.* * * * *Caldwell* is not, as the majority argues, 'an additional measure of protection against error, beyond that afforded by *Donnelly,* in the special text of capital sentencing.' This analysis erroneously presumes precisely what *Caldwell* denies, that 'focused, unambiguous, and strong,' prosecutorial arguments that mislead a jury about its sentencing role in the capital context can ever be deemed harmless. *Caldwell* rests on the view that *any* strong, uncorrected, and unequivocal prosecutorial argument minimizing the jury's sense of responsibility for its capital sentencing decision 'presents an intolerable danger that the jury will in fact choose to minimize the importance of its role.' *Caldwell* thus tells us that a capital trial in which the jury has been misled about its sentencing role is fundamentally unfair and therefore violates *Donnelly* as well."

7th ed., p. 1559; after Note 6, add:

WRIGHT v. WEST

__ U.S. __, 112 S.Ct. 2482, __ L.Ed.2d __
(1992).

THOMAS, J., announced the judgment of the Court and delivered an opinion, in which the CHIEF JUSTICE and JUSTICE SCALIA joined.

[The habeas petitioner West had challenged his burglary conviction on the ground that the evidence was insufficient to support a finding of guilt and therefore violated due process. See *Jackson v. Virginia* [7th ed., p. 1539]. After the state courts rejected that claim, West presented it before the federal courts on a habeas petition and was successful before the Fourth Circuit.]

After the Fourth Circuit denied rehearing en banc by an equally divided court, the warden and the State Attorney General sought review in this Court on, among other questions, whether the Court of Appeals had applied *Jackson* correctly in this case. We granted certiorari and requested additional briefing on the question whether a federal habeas court should afford deference to state-court determinations applying law to the specific facts of a case. We now reverse.

* * * Before 1953, * * * absent an alleged jurisdictional defect, "habeas corpus would not lie for a [state] prisoner . . . if he had been given an adequate opportunity to obtain full and fair consideration of his federal claim in the state courts." *Fay v. Noia* (Harlan, J., dissenting). * * * [However, in 1953], we rejected the principle of absolute deference in our landmark decision in *Brown v. Allen* [7th ed., p. 1519]. There, we held that a state-court judgment of conviction "is not res judicata" on federal habeas with respect to federal constitutional claims, even if the state court has rejected all such claims after a full and fair hearing. Instead, we held, a district court must determine whether the state-court adjudication "has resulted in a satisfactory con-

clusion." We had no occasion to explore in detail the question whether a "satisfactory" conclusion was one that the habeas court considered correct, as opposed to merely reasonable, because we concluded that the constitutional claims advanced in *Brown* itself would fail even if the state courts' rejection of them were reconsidered de novo. Nonetheless, we indicated that the federal courts enjoy at least the discretion to take into consideration the fact that a state court has previously rejected the federal claims asserted on habeas. * * * In an influential separate opinion endorsed by a majority of the Court, Justice Frankfurter also rejected the principle of absolute deference to fairly-litigated state-court judgments. He emphasized that a state-court determination of federal constitutional law is not "binding" on federal habeas, regardless of whether the determination involves a pure question of law or a "so-called mixed question" requiring the application of law to fact. Nonetheless, he stated quite explicitly that "a prior State determination may guide [the] discretion [of the district court] in deciding upon the appropriate course to be followed in disposing of the application." Discussing mixed questions specifically, he noted further that "there is no need for the federal judge, if he could, to shut his eyes to the State consideration."

In subsequent cases, we repeatedly reaffirmed *Brown's* teaching that mixed constitutional questions are "open to review on collateral attack," without ever explicitly considering whether that "review" should be de novo or deferential. In some of these cases, we would have denied habeas relief even under de novo review [citing, e.g., *Strickland v. Washington*, 7th ed., p. 1077]; in others, we would have awarded habeas relief even under deferential review [citing, e.g., *Brewer v. Williams*, 7th ed., p. 575]; and in yet others, we remanded for application of a proper legal rule without addressing that standard of review question [citing, e.g., *Cuyler v. Sullivan*, 7th ed., p. 1011]. Nonetheless, because these cases never qualified our early citation of *Brown* for the proposition that a federal habeas court must reexamine mixed constitutional questions "independently," we have gradually come to treat as settled the rule that mixed constitutional questions are "subject to plenary federal review" on habeas. *Miller v. Fenton* [7th ed., p. 1592]. *Jackson* itself contributed to this trend. There, we held that a conviction violates due process if supported only by evidence from which "no rational trier of fact could find guilt beyond a reasonable doubt." We stated explicitly that a state-court judgment applying the *Jackson* rule in a particular case "is of course entitled to deference" on federal habeas. See also Stevens, J., concurring in judgment. ("State judges are more familiar with the elements of state offenses than are federal judges and should be better able to evaluate sufficiency claims"). Notwithstanding these principles, however, we then indicated that the habeas court itself should apply the *Jackson* rule, rather than merely reviewing the state courts' application of it for reasonableness. Ultimately, though, we had no occasion to resolve our conflicting statements on the standard of review question, because we concluded that the habeas petitioner was not entitled to relief even under our own de novo application of *Jackson*. * * *

Despite our apparent adherence to a standard of de novo habeas review with respect to mixed constitutional questions,

we have implicitly questioned that standard, at least with respect to pure legal questions, in our recent retroactivity precedents. In *Penry v. Lynaugh* [7th ed., p. 1556], a majority of this Court endorsed the retroactivity analysis advanced by Justice O'Connor for a plurality in *Teague v. Lane.* Under *Teague,* a habeas petitioner generally cannot benefit from a new rule of criminal procedure announced after his conviction has become final on direct appeal. *Teague* defined a "new" rule as one that was "not dictated by precedent existing at the time the defendant's conviction became final." In *Butler v. McKellar* [Supp. p. 150], we explained that the definition includes all rules "susceptible to debate among reasonable minds." Thus, if a state court has reasonably rejected the legal claim asserted by a habeas petitioner under existing law, then the claim seeks the benefit of a "new" rule under *Butler,* and is therefore not cognizable on habeas under *Teague.* In other words, a federal habeas court "must defer to the state court's decision rejecting the claim unless that decision is patently unreasonable." *Butler.*[8]

Teague was premised on the view that retroactivity questions in habeas corpus proceedings must take account of the nature and function of the writ, which we described as "a collateral remedy . . . not designed as a substitute for direct review." Justice Stevens reasoned similarly in *Jackson,* where he stressed that habeas

---

8. Justice O'Connor suggests that *Teague* and its progeny "did not establish standard of review at all." Instead, she contends, these cases merely prohibit the retroactive application of new rules on habeas, and establish the criterion for distinguishing new rules from old ones. We have no difficulty with describing *Teague* as a case about retroactivity, rather than standards of review, although we do not dispute Justice O'Connor's suggestion that the difference, at least in practice, might well be only a matter of phrasing. We do disagree, however, with Justice O'Connor's definition of what constitutes a new rule for *Teague* purposes. A rule is new, she contends, if it can be meaningfully distinguished from that established by binding precedent at the time [the] state court conviction became final. This definition leads her to suggest that a habeas court

must determine whether the state courts have interpreted old precedents properly. Our precedents, however, require a different standard. We have held that a rule is "new" for *Teague* purposes whenever its validity under existing precedents is subject to debate among "reasonable minds," *Butler,* or among "reasonable jurists," *Sawyer v. Smith* [Supp. p. 151]. Indeed, each of our last four relevant precedents has indicated that *Teague* insulates on habeas review the state courts' "reasonable, good-faith interpretations of existing precedents." *Sawyer.* See also *Butler, Saffle v. Parks* [Supp. p. 150], and *Stringer v. Black* [Supp. p. 151]. Thus, *Teague* bars habeas relief whenever the state courts have interpreted old precedents reasonably, not only when they have done so properly.

corpus "is not intended as a substitute for appeal, nor as a device for reviewing the merits of guilt determinations at criminal trials," but only "to guard against extreme malfunctions in the state criminal justice systems." Indeed, the notion that different standards should apply on direct and collateral review runs throughout our recent habeas jurisprudence. We have said, for example, that new rules always have retroactive application to criminal cases pending on direct review, but that they generally do not have retroactive application to criminal cases pending on habeas, see *Teague*. We have held that the Constitution guarantees the right to counsel on a first direct appeal, but that it guarantees no right to counsel on habeas, see, e.g., *Pennsylvania v. Finley* [7th ed., p. 95]. On direct review, we have announced and enforced the rule that state courts must exclude evidence obtained in violation of the Fourth Amendment. See, e.g., *Mapp v. Ohio* [7th ed., p. 20]. We have also held, however, that claims under *Mapp* are not cognizable on habeas as long as the state courts have provided a full and fair opportunity to litigate them at trial or on direct review. See *Stone v. Powell* [7th ed., p. 1531].

These differences simply reflect the fact that habeas review "entails significant costs." *Engle v. Isaac* [7th ed., p. 1578]. Among other things, "it disturbs the State's significant interest in repose for concluded litigation, denies society the right to punish some admitted offenders, and intrudes on state sovereignty to a degree matched by few exercises of federal judicial authority." *Duckworth v. Eagan* [7th ed., p. 1541] (O'Connor, J., concurring). In various contexts, we have emphasized that these costs, as well as the countervailing benefits, must be taken into consideration in defining the scope of the writ. See, e.g., *Coleman v. Thompson* [Supp. p. 161] (procedural default); *McCleskey v. Zant* [Supp. p. 163] (abuse of the writ); *Teague* (retroactivity); *Kuhlmann v.*

Wilson (opinion of Powell, J.) (successive petitions); *Stone v. Powell* (cognizability of particular claims).

In light of these principles, petitioners ask that we reconsider our statement in *Miller v. Fenton* that mixed constitutional questions are "subject to plenary federal review" on habeas. By its terms, *Teague* itself is not directly controlling, because West sought federal habeas relief under *Jackson*, which was decided a year before his conviction became final on direct review. Nonetheless, petitioners contend, the logic of *Teague* makes our statement in *Miller* untenable. Petitioners argue that if deferential review for reasonableness strikes an appropriate balance with respect to purely legal claims, then it must strike an appropriate balance with respect to mixed questions as well. Moreover, they note that under the habeas statute itself, a state-court determination of a purely factual question must be "presumed correct," and can be overcome only by "convincing evidence," unless one of eight statutorily enumerated exceptions is present. 28 U.S.C. § 2254(d) [see Note 4, 7th ed., p. 1589]. It makes no sense, petitioners assert, for a habeas court generally to review factual determinations and legal determinations deferentially, but to review applications of law to fact de novo. Finally, petitioners find the prospect of deferential review for mixed questions at least implicit in our recent statement that *Teague* concerns are fully implicated "by the application of an old rule in a manner that was not dictated by precedent." *Stringer v. Black* [Supp. p. 151]. For these reasons, petitioners invite us to reaffirm that a habeas judge need not—and indeed may not—"shut his eyes" entirely to state-court applications of law to fact. *Brown v. Allen* (opinion of Frankfurter, J.). West develops two principal counterarguments: first, that Congress implicitly codified a de novo standard with respect to mixed constitutional questions when it amended the habeas statute in 1966; and second, that de novo federal review is necessary to vindicate federal constitutional rights.[9]

We need not decide such far-reaching issues in this case. As in both *Brown* and *Jackson*, the claim advanced by the habeas petitioner must fail even assuming that the state court's rejection of it should be reconsidered de novo. Whatever the appropriate standard of review, we conclude that there was more than enough evidence to support West's conviction.

The case against West was strong. Two to four weeks after the Dardova home had been burglarized, over 15 of the items stolen were recovered from West's home. On direct examination at trial, West said nothing more than that he frequently bought and sold items at different flea markets. * * * When pressed on cross-examination about the details of his purchases, West contradicted himself repeatedly about where he supposedly had bought the stolen goods, and he gave vague, seemingly evasive answers to various other questions. * * * As the trier of fact, the jury was entitled to disbelieve West's uncorroborated and confused testimony. In evaluating that testimony, moreover, the jury was entitled to discount West's credibility on account of his prior felony conviction, and to take into account West's demeanor when testifying, which neither the Court of Appeals nor we may review. * * * In *Jackson*, we emphasized repeatedly the deference owed to the trier of fact and, correspondingly, the sharply limited nature of constitutional sufficiency review. We said that "all of the evidence is to be considered in the light most favorable to the prosecution"; that the prosecution need not affirmatively "rule out every hypothesis except of

guilt"; and that a reviewing court "faced with a record of historical facts that supports conflicting inferences must presume—even if it does not affirmatively appear in the record—that the trier of fact resolved any such conflicts in favor of the prosecution, and must defer to that resolution." Under these standards, we think it clear that the trial record contained sufficient evidence to support West's conviction. * * *

JUSTICE WHITE, concurring in the judgment.

Jackson v. Virginia required the federal courts to deny the requested writ of habeas corpus if, under the *Jackson* standard, there was sufficient evidence to support West's conviction, which, as the Court amply demonstrates, there certainly was.

JUSTICE O'CONNOR, with whom JUSTICE BLACKMUN and JUSTICE STEVENS join, concurring in the judgment.

I agree that the evidence sufficiently supported respondent's conviction. I write separately only to express disagreement with certain statements in Justice Thomas' extended discussion of this Court's habeas corpus jurisprudence.

[Justice O'Connor initially contended that Justice Thomas' opinion "errs in describing the pre-1953 law of habeas corpus," which she characterized as dealing with the scope of the issues cognizable on habeas review, rather than any standard of "deferential review" on cognizable issues. Justice O'Connor also contended that "Justice Thomas understates the certainty with which *Brown v. Allen* rejected a deferential standard of review of issues of law." The two opinions in that case [see Note 1, 7th ed., p. 1588] did refer to

---

9. Justice O'Connor criticizes our failure to highlight in text the fact that Congress has considered, but failed to enact, several bills introduced during the last 25 years to prohibit de novo review explicitly. See also Brief for Senator Biden et al. as Amici Curiae 10–16 (discussing various proposals). Our task, however, is not to construe bills that Congress has failed to enact, but to construe statutes that Congress has en-

acted. The habeas corpus statute was last amended in 1966. We have grave doubts that post-1966 legislative history is of any value in construing its provisions, for we have often observed that "the views of a subsequent Congress form a hazardous basis for inferring the intent of an earlier one." *Consumer Product Safety Comm'n v. GTE Sylvania, Inc.,* 447 U.S. 102, 117 (1980).

giving "some weight to the state court determinations," but those statements, she argued, referred only to the resolution of question of fact. Justice O'Connor further argued that "Justice Thomas incorrectly states that we never considered the standard of review to apply to mixed questions of law and fact raised in federal habeas." A long line of cases, including those cited by Justice Thomas, "stated quite clearly that mixed questions or the application of constitutional principles to the facts as found leave the duty of adjudication with the federal judge." Indeed, the respondents in *Jackson* "proposed a deferential standard of review, very much like the one Justice Thomas discusses today," and the Court there "expressly rejected [that] proposal," adhering instead to "the general rule of de novo review."]

＊ ＊ ＊ Justice Thomas [also] mischaracterizes *Teague v. Lane* and *Penry v. Lynaugh,* as "questioning the standard [of de novo review] with respect to pure legal questions." *Teague* did not establish a "deferential" standard of review of state court determinations of federal law. It did not establish a standard of review at all. Instead, *Teague* simply requires that a state conviction on federal habeas be judged according to the law in existence when the conviction became final. ＊ ＊ ＊ To determine what counts as a new rule, *Teague* requires courts to ask whether the rule a habeas petitioner seeks can be meaningfully distinguished from that established by binding precedent at the time his state court conviction became final. ＊ ＊ ＊ Even though we have characterized the new rule inquiry as whether "reasonable jurists" could disagree as to whether a result is dictated by precedent, *Sawyer v. Smith,* the standard for determining when a case establishes a new rule is "objective," and the mere existence of conflicting authority does not necessarily mean a rule is new. *Stringer v. Black.* If a proffered factual distinction between the case under consideration and pre-existing precedent does not change the force with

which the precedent's underlying principle applies, the distinction is not meaningful, and any deviation from precedent is not reasonable.

So, while Justice Thomas says that we "defer" to state courts' determinations of federal law, the statement is misleading. Although in practice, it may seem only "a matter of phrasing" whether one calls the *Teague* inquiry a standard of review or not, "phrasing mirrors thought, [and] it is important that the phrasing not obscure the true issue before a federal court." *Brown v. Allen* (opinion of Frankfurter, J.). As Justice Kennedy convincingly demonstrates, the duty of the federal court in evaluating whether a rule is "new" is not the same as deference; federal courts must make an independent evaluation of the precedent existing at the time the state conviction became final in order to determine whether the case under consideration is meaningfully distinguishable. *Teague* does not direct federal courts to spend less time or effort scrutinizing the existing federal law, on the ground that they can assume the state courts interpreted it properly.

＊ ＊ ＊ [T]hough Justice Thomas suggests otherwise, de novo review is not incompatible with the maxim that federal courts should "give great weight to the considered conclusions of a coequal state judiciary," *Miller v. Fenton,* just as they do to persuasive, well-reasoned authority from district or circuit courts in other jurisdictions. A state court opinion concerning the legal implications of precisely the same set of facts is the closest one can get to a "case on point," and is especially valuable for that reason. But this does not mean that we have held in the past that federal courts must presume the correctness of a state court's legal conclusions on habeas, or that a state court's incorrect legal determination has ever been allowed to stand because it was reasonable. We have always held that federal courts, even on habeas, have an independent obligation to say what the law is.

Finally, in his one-sentence summary of respondent's arguments, Justice Thomas fails to mention that Congress has considered habeas corpus legislation during 27 of the past 37 years, and on 13 occasions has considered adopting a deferential standard of review along the lines suggested by Justice Thomas. Congress has rejected each proposal. In light of the case law and Congress' position, a move away from de novo review of mixed questions of law and fact would be a substantial change in our construction of the authority conferred by the habeas corpus statute. As Justice Thomas acknowledges, to change the standard of review would indeed be "far-reaching," and we need not decide whether to do so in order to resolve this case.

JUSTICE SOUTER, concurring in the judgment.

While I could not disagree with the majority that sufficient evidence supported West's conviction, I do not think the Court should reach that issue. We have often said that when the principles first developed in *Teague v. Lane,* a threshold question on federal habeas review, it is only after an answer favorable to the prisoner that a court should address the merits. See e.g., *Collins v. Youngblood* [Supp. p. 150]; *Penry v. Lynaugh.* * * * This habeas case begins with a *Teague* question, and its answer does not favor West. I would go no further.[1]

The crux of the analysis when *Teague* is invoked * * * is identification of the rule on which the claim for habeas relief depends. To survive *Teague,* it must be "old" enough to have predated the finality of the prisoner's conviction, and specific enough to dictate the rule on which the conviction may be held to be unlawful. A rule old enough for *Teague* may of course be too general, and while identifying the required age of the rule of relief is a simple matter of comparing dates, passing on its requisite specificity calls for analyti-

cal care. See *Butler v. McKellar; Sawyer v. Smith.* * * * [O]ur cases have recognized that "the interests in finality, predictability, and comity underlying our new rule jurisprudence may be undermined to an equal degree by the invocation of a rule that was not dictated by precedent as by the application of an old rule in a manner that was not dictated by precedent." *Stringer v. Black.* This does not mean, of course, that a habeas petitioner must be able to point to an old case decided on facts identical to the facts of his own. But it does mean that, in light of authority extant when his conviction became final, its unlawfulness must be apparent.

In this case, the Court of Appeals overruled the Commonwealth's *Teague* objection by saying that West merely claimed that the evidence had been insufficient to support his conviction, so that the result he sought was dictated by *Jackson v. Virginia,* a case announced before petitioner's conviction became final for *Teague* purposes in 1980. Having thus surmounted *Teague*'s time hurdle, the court went on to say that "the evidence here consisted entirely . . . of the . . . facts . . . that about one-third in value of goods stolen between December 13 and December 26, 1978, were found on January 10, 1979, in the exclusive possession of . . . West, coupled with [West's] own testimony explaining his possession as having come about by purchases in the interval." Applied in this context, the court held, the unadorned *Jackson* norm translated into the more specific rule announced in *Cosby v. Jones,* 682 F.2d 1373 (11th Cir.1982), which held that the evidence of unexplained or unconvincingly explained possession of recently stolen goods was not, without more, sufficient to prove theft, but must be weighed more exactly after asking five questions: (1) Was "the possession . . . recent, relative to the crime"? (2) Was a large majority of the stolen items found in the defendant's possession? (3) Did the de-

---

1. Because my analysis ends the case for me without reaching historical questions, I do not

take a position in the disagreement between Justice Thomas and Justice O'Connor.

fendant attempt to conceal the stolen items? (4) Was the defendant's explanation, "even if discredited by the jury, . . . so implausible or demonstrably false as to give rise to positive evidence in favor of the government"? and (5) Was there corroborating evidence supporting the conviction? Applying *Cosby* to the facts of this case, the Court of Appeals found that all five factors were either neutral or advantageous to West. * * *

It is clear that the Court of Appeals [thus] misapplied the commands of *Teague* by defining the rule from which West sought to benefit at an unduly elevated level of generality. There can of course be no doubt that, in reviewing West's conviction, the Supreme Court of Virginia was not entitled to disregard *Jackson,* which antedated the finality of West's conviction. But from *Jackson*'s rule, that sufficiency depends on whether a rational trier, viewing the evidence most favorably to the prosecution, could find all elements beyond a reasonable doubt, it does not follow that the insufficiency of the evidence to support West's conviction was apparent. Virginia courts have long recognized a rule that evidence of unexplained or falsely explained possession of recently stolen goods is sufficient to sustain a finding that the possessor took the goods. * * * In this case, we are concerned only with the Virginia rule's second prong. West took the stand and gave an explanation that the jury rejected, thereby implying a finding that the explanation was false. Thus, the portion of the state rule under attack here is that falsely explained recent possession suffices to identify the possessor as the thief. The rule has the virtue of much common sense. It is utterly reasonable to conclude that a possessor of recently stolen goods who lies about where he got them is the thief who took them, and it should come as no surprise that the rule had been accepted as good law against the backdrop of a general state sufficiency standard no less stringent than that of *Jackson.* It is simply insupportable, then, to say that rea-

sonable jurists could not have considered this rule compatible with the *Jackson* standard. There can be no doubt, therefore, that in the federal courts West sought the benefit of a "new rule," and that his claim was barred by *Teague.*

JUSTICE KENNEDY, concurring in the judgment.

I do not enter the debate about the reasons that took us to the point where mixed constitutional questions are subject to de novo review in federal habeas corpus proceedings. Whatever the answer to that difficult historical inquiry, all agree that, at least prior to the Court's adoption of the retroactivity analysis of *Teague v. Lane,* the matter was settled. It seems that the real issue dividing my colleagues is whether the retroactivity analysis of *Teague* casts doubt upon the rule of *Miller v. Fenton.* * * * If vindication of the principles underlying *Teague* did require that state court rulings on mixed questions must be given deference in a federal habeas proceeding, then indeed it might be said that the *Teague* line of cases is on a collision course with the *Miller v. Fenton* line. And in the proper case we would have to select one at the expense of the other. But in my view neither the purpose for which *Teague* was adopted nor the necessary means for implementing its holding creates any real conflict with the requirement of de novo review of mixed questions.

In my view, it would be a misreading of *Teague* to interpret it as resting on the necessity to defer to state court determinations. *Teague* did not establish a deferential standard of review of state court decisions of federal law. It established instead a principle of retroactivity. * * * To be sure, the fact that our standard for distinguishing old rules from new ones turns on the reasonableness of a state court's interpretation of then existing precedents suggests that federal courts do in one sense defer to state court determinations. But we should not lose sight of the purpose of the reasonableness inquiry where a *Teague* issue is raised: the purpose is to determine whether application of a new rule would upset a conviction that was obtained in accordance with the constitutional interpretations existing at the time of the prisoner's conviction. * * * The comity interest [underlying *Teague*] is not * * * in saying that since the question is close the state court decision ought to be deemed correct because we are in no better position to judge. That would be the real thrust of a principle based on deference. We see that principle at work in the statutory requirement that, except in limited circumstances, the federal habeas court must presume the correctness of state court factual findings. See 28 U.S.C. § 2254(d). * * * Deference of this kind may be termed a comity interest, but it is not the comity interest that underlies *Teague*. The comity interest served by *Teague* is in not subjecting the States to a regime in which finality is undermined by our changing a rule once thought correct but now understood to be deficient on its own terms. It is in recognition of this principle that we ask whether the decision in question was dictated by precedent. See, e.g., *Saffle v. Parks*.

Teague does bear on applications of law to fact which result in the announcement of a new rule. Whether the prisoner seeks the application of an old rule in a novel setting, see *Stringer*, depends in large part on the nature of the rule. If the rule in question is one which of necessity requires a case-by-case examination of the evidence, then we can tolerate a number of specific applications without saying that those applications themselves create a new rule. The rule of *Jackson v. Virginia* is an example. By its very terms it provides a general standard which calls for some examination of the facts. The standard is whether any rational trier of fact could have found guilt beyond a reasonable doubt after a review of all the evidence, so of course there will be variations from case to case. Where the beginning point is a rule of this general application, a rule designed for the

specific purpose of evaluating a myriad of factual contexts, it will be the infrequent case that yields a result so novel that it forges a new rule, one not dictated by precedent.

Although as a general matter "new rules will not be applied or announced" in habeas proceedings, *Penry,* there is no requirement that we engage in the threshold *Teague* inquiry in a case in which it is clear that the prisoner would not be entitled to the relief he seeks even if his case were pending on direct review. See *Collins v. Youngblood.* Therefore, it is not necessary to the resolution of this case to consider the oddity that reversing respondent's conviction because of the quite fact-specific determination that there was insufficient evidence would have the arguably effect of undercutting the well-established general principle in Virginia and elsewhere that the trier of fact may infer theft from unexplained or falsely denied possession of recently stolen goods. Whether a holding that there was insufficient evidence would constitute one of those unusual cases in which an application of *Jackson* would create a new rule need not be addressed.

On these premises, the existence of *Teague* provides added justification for retaining de novo review, not a reason to abandon it. *Teague* gives substantial assurance that habeas proceedings will not use a new rule to upset a state conviction that conformed to rules then existing. With this safeguard in place, recognizing the importance of finality, de novo review can be exercised within its proper sphere.

For the foregoing reasons, I would not interpret *Teague* as calling into question the settled principle that mixed questions are subject to plenary review on federal habeas corpus. And, for the reasons I have mentioned, I do not think it necessary to consider whether the respondent brings one of those unusual *Jackson* claims which is *Teague*-barred. * * * I agree that the evidence in this case was sufficient to convince a rational factfinder of guilt beyond a reasonable doubt; and I concur in the judgment of the Court.

SECTION 2. CLAIMS FORE-CLOSED BY PROCEDURAL DE-FAULTS

7th ed., p. 1576; at the end of Note 1, add:

In COLEMAN v. THOMPSON, —— U.S. ——, 111 S.Ct. 2546, 115 L.Ed.2d 640 (1991), petitioner's counsel in a state habeas proceeding had failed to file a notice of appeal within the time limit specified under state law (see Supp., pp. 123, 126), and the state attorney general had responded with a motion to dismiss the appeal as untimely. The state appellate court subsequently issued a summary order dismissing the appeal. That order did not discuss the grounds for the dismissal, except to note that the appellate court acted "upon consideration" of the motion and the various memoranda and briefs filed by the parties with respect to the motion and the petition for appeal. Rejecting the contention that this ruling was subject to the plain statement requirement of *Harris v. Reed,* the Court majority held that "a predicate to the application of the *Harris* presumption is that the decision of the last state court to which the petitioner presented his federal claims must fairly appear to rest primarily on federal law or to be interwoven with federal law." *Harris'*

conclusive presumption, "like all conclusive presumptions, [was] designed to avoid the costs of excessive inquiry where a per se rule will achieve the correct result in almost all cases." Absent the necessary factual predicate, that justification failed because it could not then be said that the "most reasonable explanation is that the state judgment rested on federal grounds." While it "may be argued that a broadly applicable presumption is not counterfactual after it is announced," to "expand the *Harris* presumption" by making it applicable to all state court rulings, without regard to the necessary predicate, would be both counterproductive and inappropriate. After examining the burdens and benefits of such an expanded rule, the Court concluded: "There is, in sum, little that the federal courts will gain by applying a presumption of federal review in those cases where the relevant state court decision does not fairly appear to rest primarily on federal law or to be interwoven with such law, and much that the States and state courts will lose." While the Court could appropriately "establish a per se rule that eases the burden of inquiry on the federal courts in those cases where there are few costs to doing so, [it had] * * * no power to tell the state courts how they must write their opinions * * * in every case in which a state prisoner presents a federal claim * * *."[a]

a. The Court concluded that the necessary factual predicate for applying the *Harris* presumption clearly was not presented in the case before it. The state appellate court dismissed the habeas appeal in response to the attorney general's motion, which "was based solely on Coleman's failure to meet the [state's] time requirements," and there was "no mention of federal law in [its] three sentence dismissal order." State law did not support petitioner's claim that the state appellate court did not automatically apply the 30–day requirement, but looked to it only after first considering the merits of the petitioner's claim and concluding that application of the timing requirement would not result in the failure to remedy a constitutional violation. Justice White, in a concurring opinion, noted that he was troubled by the fact that the state appellate court had received briefs on both the merits and the timeliness of the appeal, but found that the evi-

dence was "too scanty" to conclude that there was a state practice of waiving the timing requirements for constitutional claims thought to be significant.

Justice Blackmun's dissent (see also Note 6, Supp. p. 126) accused the majority of having "managed to transform the duty to protect federal rights into a self-fashioned abdication" by "requir[ing] a federal court to scrutinize the state court judgment with an eye to denying a litigant review of his federal claims." The dissent maintained that the *Harris* opinion had not demanded a "factual predicate" for application of its plain statement rule, that the majority had "abandon[ed] * * * the plain-statement rule for purposes of summary orders," and that the combination of this ruling and the Court's ruling in *Ylst* (discussed infra) "needlessly resume[d] the [pre-*Harris*] piecemeal approach * * * [that] invites

In *Ylst v. Nunnemaker,* ___ U.S. ___, 111 S.Ct. 2590, 115 L.Ed.2d 706 (1991), the Court further limited the application of *Harris'* plain statement rule by adopting the following presumption: "[W]here there has been one reasoned state judgment rejecting a federal claim, later unexplained orders upholding that judgment or rejecting the same claim rest upon the same ground. If an earlier opinion 'fairly appears to rest primarily upon federal law,' *Coleman,* we will presume that no procedural default has been invoked by a subsequent unexplained order that leaves the judgment or its consequences in place. Similarly where, as here, the last reasoned opinion on the claim explicitly imposes a procedural default, we will presume that a later decision rejecting the claim did not silently disregard that bar and consider the merits."

7th ed., p. 1581; In lieu of the last paragraph of Note 7, add:

As to procedural defaults that fit in categories (1) to (3), consider COLEMAN v. THOMPSON, ___ U.S. ___, 111 S.Ct. 2546, 115 L.Ed.2d 640 (1991). The petitioner there, assisted by counsel, had sought to appeal from a state habeas ruling rejecting various constitutional challenges to his conviction and death sentence. Counsel, however, filed the notice of appeal 33 days after entry of final judgment, violating a state rule requiring filing within 30 days, and the state's motion to dismiss the appeal as untimely was granted (see Supp. p. 122). The federal habeas court held that this procedural default barred review of the petitioner's constitutional claims and the Supreme Court, per O'CONNOR, J., agreed. The Court first considered whether the deliberate bypass standard survived as to this situation, where, as in *Fay* itself, the procedural default consisted of a failure to file an appeal. Justice O'Connor noted that while this is-

intrusive and unsatisfactory federal inquiry into unfamiliar state law." While it was true that "state courts may chose to draw their orders as they wish, the right of a state prisoner, particu-

sue had been left open in *Wainwright v. Sykes* (see fn. 12) and in *Murray v. Carrier,* "our cases after *Fay* that have considered the effect of state procedural default on federal habeas review have taken a markedly different view of the important interests served by state procedural rules." After discussing the reasoning of those post-*Fay* rulings, Justice O'Connor concluded that the Court there had "described in broad terms the application of the cause and prejudice standard hinting strongly that *Fay* had been superseded." She then turned that hint into a holding:

"We now make it explicit: In all cases in which a state prisoner has defaulted his federal claims in state court pursuant to an independent and adequate state procedural rule, federal habeas review of the claims is barred unless the prisoner can demonstrate cause for the default and actual prejudice as a result of the alleged violation of federal law, or demonstrate that failure to consider the claims will result in a fundamental miscarriage of justice. *Fay* was based on a conception of federal/state relations that undervalued the importance of state procedural rules. The several cases after *Fay* that applied the cause and prejudice standard to a variety of state procedural defaults represent a different view. We now recognize the important interest in finality served by state procedural rules, and the significant harm to the States that results from the failure of federal courts to respect them. * * * *Carrier* applied the cause and prejudice standard to the failure to raise a particular claim on appeal. There is no reason that the same standard should not apply to a failure to appeal at all. All of the State's interests—in channeling the resolution of claims to the most appropriate forum, in finality, and in having an opportunity to correct its own errors—are implicated whether a prisoner defaults one claim or all of them. A fed-

larly one sentenced to death, to have his federal claim heard by a federal habeas court is simply too fundamental to yield to the state's incidental interest in issuing ambiguous summary orders."

eral court generally should not interfere in either case. By applying the cause and prejudice standard uniformly to all independent and adequate state procedural defaults, we eliminate the irrational distinction between *Fay* and the rule of cases like *Francis, Sykes, Engle,* and *Carrier.*"

Although the petitioner in *Coleman* was represented by counsel, the factors stressed by the Court there in finally laying *Fay* to rest and in holding that there was an inadequate showing of cause (see Note 6, Supp. p. 126) arguably also would apply where the habeas petitioner who failed to file an appeal was proceeding *pro se. Hughes v. Idaho State Board of Corrections,* 800 F.2d 905 (9th Cir.1986), a pre-*Coleman* ruling that correctly anticipated *Coleman,* held that the *Sykes* standard governed in such a case. The *Hughes* Court acknowledges that the "cases that developed the cause and prejudice standard involved counsel's errors," but concluded that an exception for *pro se* petitioners would rest on the unacceptable premise that prisoners are not competent to make basic decisions in presenting their habeas petitions. The court noted that "many state prisoners initiate their own state post-conviction actions," and even if their failure to appeal was a product of "unexcusable neglect" rather than deliberate strategy, that still did not present "a compelling case [for overriding] the principle that a federal court should not intrude" where the state courts have not been given a fair opportunity to rule on the habeas petitioner's constitutional claims.

7th ed., p. 1581; at the end of Note 8, add:

In McCLESKEY v. ZANT, ___ U.S. ___, 111 S.Ct. 1454, 113 L.Ed.2d 517 (1991), Justice MARSHALL, in dissent, argued that § 2244(b) and Rule 9(b) had codified *Sanders* and thereby restricted the abuse-of-writ doctrine to cases in which there was a "form of bad faith," akin to a deliberate bypass, in the petitioner's failure to have raised the new ground in a previous habeas petition. The majority, per

KENNEDY, J., responded that § 2244(b) and Rule 9(b) did no more than "incorporat[e] the judge made principle governing the abuse-of-writ set forth in *Sanders.*" Congress had not sought to "state the limits on the district court's discretion to entertain abusive petitions," nor had it "defin[ed] the term 'abuse of writ.'" Turning to the content of "the doctrine of abuse of writ," Justice Kennedy noted that this doctrine, "refers to a complex and evolving body of equitable principles informed and controlled by historical usage, statutory developments, and judicial decisions." *Sanders* had mentioned "deliberate abandonment as but one example of conduct that disentitled a petitioner to relief." It had referred also to a general concept of "unexcusable neglect," which subsequent decisions had applied to preclude new claims that could have been raised in earlier petitions "regardless of whether [that] failure * * * stemmed from a deliberate choice." That concept, however, had never been given the "content necessary to guide district courts." To provide a guideline familiar to the lower federal courts, the "determination of inexcusable neglect in the abuse of writ context" would now be assessed by reference to the "same standard used to determine whether to excuse procedural defaults."

Justice Marshall argued in dissent that the setting presented by successive federal habeas petitions was dramatically different from that presented by a failure to adhere to state procedures and therefore should lead to the striking of a different "balance between finality and review," in defining an abuse of writ. The dissent noted, in particular, that the "strictness of the cause-and-prejudice test had been justified on the ground that the defendant's procedural default is akin to an independent and adequate state-law ground for the judgment of conviction," but here similar concerns of comity were not present. The majority disagreed. It noted that the "doctrines of procedural default and abuse of the writ implicate nearly identical concerns flowing from the significant costs of federal habeas review." Both doctrines operated to ensure an appropriate degree of "procedural regularity." The majority explained: "Both doctrines impose on petitioners a burden of reasonable compliance with procedures designed to discourage baseless claims and to keep the system open for valid ones; both recognize the law's interest in finality; and both invoke equitable principles to define the court's discretion to excuse pleading and procedural requirements for petitioners who could not comply with them in the exercise of reasonable care and diligence. It is true that a habeas court's concern to honor state procedural default rules rests in part on respect for the integrity of procedures 'employed by a coordinate jurisdiction within the federal system,' *Wainwright v. Sykes,* and that such respect is not implicated when a petitioner defaults a claim by failing to raise it in the first round of federal habeas review. Nonetheless, the doctrines of procedural default and abuse of the writ are both designed to lessen the injury to a State that results through reexamination of a state conviction on a ground that the State did not have the opportunity to address at a prior, appropriate time; and both doctrines seek to vindicate the State's interest in the finality of its criminal judgments."

Interpreting the abuse of writ doctrine in light of the procedural default cases, the majority conclude that an abuse of writ will be present unless the failure of the petitioner to have raised the new claim in an earlier petition was justified under the "cause and prejudice" standard. In addition, consistent with the "ends of justice" standard of *Sanders,* a new claim would be considered, notwithstanding the absence of excuse under the cause and prejudice standard, where necessary to "correct a miscarriage of justice." This would require a "colorable showing of factual innocence," as set forth in *Kuhlmann* (Note 6, 7th ed., p. 1558) and such state-default cases as *Murray v. Carrier* (Note 2, 7th ed., p. 1586), and thereby would provide " 'an additional safeguard against compelling an innocent man to suffer an unconstitutional loss of liberty.' "

The *McCleskey* Court also set forth procedure through which the "cause and prejudice analysis" should be applied to "an abuse of writ inquiry." The Court noted: "When a prisoner files a second or subsequent application, the government bears the burden of pleading abuse of the writ. The government satisfies this burden if, with clarity and particularity, it notes petitioner's prior writ history, identifies the claims that appear for the first time, and alleges that petitioner has abused the writ. The burden to disprove abuse then becomes petitioner's. To excuse his failure to raise the claim earlier, he must show cause for failing to raise it and prejudice therefrom as those concepts have been defined in our procedural default decisions. The petitioner's opportunity to meet the burden of cause and prejudice will not include an evidentiary hearing if the district court determines as a matter of law that petitioner cannot satisfy the standard. If petitioner cannot show cause, the failure to raise the claim in an earlier petition may nonetheless be excused if he or she can show that a fundamental miscarriage of justice would result from a failure to entertain the claim." [a]

a. The *McCleskey* Court also concluded that there had not been a sufficient showing of "cause" in that case. The petitioner had claimed that cause existed because the state had suppressed a 21 page recorded statement of the informant (Evans) who testified at trial as to incriminating conversations with defendant while they were jailmates. Petitioner argued that this recorded statement provided critical evidence supporting his contention that Evans had acted as a government agent and had elicited petitioner's incriminating statements in violation of his Sixth Amendment right to counsel. Finding that the late discovery of the statement did not constitute cause, the Court cited several factors, including the following: (1) petitioner's counsel had raised the Sixth Amendment claim (without having the recorded statement) in the state habeas proceeding, but had then abandoned it in the original federal habeas petition; (2) the habeas

7th ed., p. 1585; at the end of fn. c., add:

See also fn. a below to *McCleskey v. Zant.*

7th ed., p. 1586; after Note 5 add:

6. Consider also COLEMAN v. THOMPSON, ___ U.S. ___, 111 S.Ct. 2546, 115 L.Ed.2d 640 (1991), involving the failure of counsel to file a notice of appeal from a denial of a state habeas petition within the 30–day jurisdictional time limit imposed by state law (see Supp. p. 122). The Court majority (per O'CONNOR, J.), finding that *Murray v. Carrier* controlled, reasoned:

"Applying the *Carrier* rule * * *, this case is at an end. There is no constitutional right to an attorney in state post conviction proceedings. *Pennsylvania v. Finley* [7th ed., p. 95]; *Murray v. Giarratano* [7th ed., p. 96]. Consequently, a petitioner cannot claim constitutionally ineffective assistance of counsel in such proceedings. See *Wainwright v. Torna* [7th ed., p. 1075] (where there is no constitutional right to counsel there can be no deprivation of effective assistance). Coleman contends that it was his attorney's error that led to the late filing of his state habeas appeal. This error cannot be constitutionally ineffective, therefore Coleman must 'bear the

risk of attorney error that results in a procedural default.' * * * Coleman attempts to avoid this reasoning by arguing that *Carrier* does not stand for such a broad proposition. He contends that *Carrier* applies by its terms only in those situations where it is possible to state a claim for ineffective assistance of counsel. Where there is no constitutional right to counsel, Coleman argues, it is enough that a petitioner demonstrate that his attorney's conduct would meet the *Strickland* standard, even though no independent Sixth Amendment claim is possible.

"This argument is inconsistent not only with the language of *Carrier,* but the logic of that opinion as well. We explained clearly that 'cause' under the cause and prejudice test must be something external to the petitioner, something that cannot fairly be attributed to him: * * * Attorney ignorance or inadvertence is not 'cause' because the attorney is the petitioner's agent when acting, or failing to act, in furtherance of the litigation, and the petitioner must 'bear the risk of attorney error.' *Carrier.* * * * Attorney error that constitutes ineffective assistance of counsel is cause, however. This is not because, as Coleman contends, the error is

court's finding that the document established "an *ab initio* relationship between Evans and the authorities" rested "in its entirety" on conversations known to petitioner and which he now admitted (in conflict with his sworn testimony at trial); (3) a defense request for any such recorded statement was not made at the time of McCleskey's first habeas petition, but was first presented in connection with the second habeas petition, long after the written logs and records of the prison had been destroyed pursuant to normal retention schedules; and (4) the habeas court "found no misrepresentation or wrongful conduct by the State in failing to hand over the document" prior to its eventual delivery upon request. The Court concluded that the document was not "critical" to the substance of petitioner's claim, that there had not been intentional government concealment of evidence that would fall within cause analysis of *Amadeo v. Zant* (see fn. c, 7th ed., at p. 1585), and that petitioner had sufficient information to raise the claim in his first petition in any event. The Court described the question before it in this regard as "whether petitioner possessed, or by reasonable means could have obtained, a sufficient basis to allege a claim in

the first petition and pursue the matter through the habeas process, see 28 U.S.C. § 2254 Rule 6 (Discovery); Rule 7 (Expansion of Record); Rule 8 (Evidentiary Hearing)." It noted further that a petitioner's inability to obtain relevant evidence "fails to establish cause if other known or discoverable evidence could have supported the claim," and that the failure to assert the claim "will not be excused merely because evidence discovered later might also have supported or strengthened the claim." The dissent argued that the majority "overstates McCleskey's and his counsel's awareness of the statement's contents," that without the statement counsel had no reasonable expectation of success on his *Massiah* claim and therefore was "perfectly justified in focusing his attention elsewhere in the first habeas petition," that the prosecution had adopted a "disinformation strategy" that included "affirmatively misleading counsel" as to the "state's involvement" with the informant, and that the state "open records" statute that had resulted in the eventual production of the statement had not been held to encompass police-investigative files until six year's after McCleskey's first federal habeas proceeding.

so bad that 'the lawyer ceases to be an agent of the petitioner.' In a case such as this, where the alleged attorney error is inadvertence in failing to file a timely notice, such a rule would be contrary to well-settled principles of agency law. See, e.g., Restatement (Second) of Agency § 242 (1958). Rather, as *Carrier* explains, 'if the procedural default is the result of ineffective assistance of counsel, the Sixth Amendment itself requires that responsibility for the default be imputed to the State.' In other words, it is not the gravity of the attorney's error that matters, but that it constitutes a violation of petitioner's right to counsel, so that the error must be seen as an external factor, i.e., 'imputed to the State.' * * * Where a petitioner defaults a claim as a result of the denial of the right to effective assistance of counsel, the State, which is responsible for the denial as a constitutional matter, must bear the cost of any resulting default and the harm to state interests that federal habeas review entails. A different allocation of costs is appropriate in those circumstances where the State has no responsibility to ensure that the petitioner was represented by competent counsel. As between the State and the petitioner, it is the petitioner who must bear the burden of a failure to follow state procedural rules. In the absence of a constitutional violation, the petitioner bears the risk in federal habeas for all attorney errors made in the course of the representation, as *Carrier* says explicitly.

"Among the claims Coleman brought in state habeas, and then again in federal habeas, is ineffective assistance of counsel during trial, sentencing, and appeal. Coleman contends that, at least as to these claims, attorney error in state habeas must constitute cause. This is because, under Virginia law at the time of Coleman's trial and direct appeal, ineffective assistance of counsel claims related to counsel's conduct during trial or appeal could be brought only in state habeas. Coleman argues that attorney error in failing to file timely in the first forum in which a federal claim can

be raised is cause. * * * We reiterate that counsel's ineffectiveness will constitute cause only if it is an independent constitutional violation. *Finley* and *Giarratano* established that there is no right to counsel in state collateral proceedings. For Coleman to prevail, therefore, there must be an exception to the rule of *Finley* and *Giarratano* in those cases where state collateral review is the first place a prisoner can present a challenge to his conviction. We need not answer this question broadly, however, for one state court has addressed Coleman's claims: the state habeas trial court. The effectiveness of Coleman's counsel before that court is not at issue here. Coleman contends that it was the ineffectiveness of his counsel during the appeal from that determination that constitutes cause to excuse his default. We thus need to decide only whether Coleman had a constitutional right to counsel on appeal from the state habeas trial court judgment. We conclude that he did not.

"*Douglas v. California* [7th ed., p. 76] established that an indigent criminal defendant has a right to appointed counsel in his first appeal as of right in state court. *Evitts v. Lucey* [7th ed., p. 1073] held that this right encompasses a right to effective assistance of counsel for all criminal defendants in their first appeal as of right. * * * Coleman has had his 'one and only appeal,' if that is what a state collateral proceeding may be considered; the Buchanan County Circuit Court, after a two-day evidentiary hearing, addressed Coleman's claims of trial error, including his ineffective assistance of counsel claims. What Coleman requires here is a right to counsel on appeal from that determination. Our case law will not support it. In *Ross v. Moffitt* [7th ed., p. 79] and *Pennsylvania v. Finley* [7th ed., p. 96] we declined to extend the right to counsel beyond the first appeal of a criminal conviction. We held in *Ross* that neither the fundamental fairness required by the Due Process Clause nor the Fourteenth Amendment's equal protection guarantee necessitated that States provide counsel in state discretionary appeals where defendants already had one appeal as of right. * * * These cases dictate the answer here. Given that a criminal defendant has no right to counsel beyond his first appeal in pursuing state discretionary or collateral review, it would defy logic for us to hold that Coleman had a right to counsel to appeal a state collateral determination of his claims of trial error. * * * Because Coleman had no right to counsel to pursue his appeal in state habeas, any attorney error that led to the default of Coleman's claims in state court cannot constitute cause to excuse the default in federal habeas. As Coleman does not argue in this Court that federal review of his claims is necessary to prevent a fundamental miscarriage of justice, he is barred from bringing these claims in federal habeas."

Dissenting in *Coleman*, BLACKMUN, J., joined by Marshall and Stevens, J., reasoned: "In a sleight of logic that would be ironic if not for its tragic consequences, the majority concludes that a state prisoner pursuing state collateral relief must bear the risk of his attorney's grave errors— even if the result of those errors is that the prisoner will be executed without having presented his federal claims to a federal court—because this attribution of risk represents the appropriate 'allocation of costs.' Whether unprofessional attorney conduct in a state postconviction proceeding should bar federal habeas review of a state prisoner's conviction and sentence of death is not a question of costs to be allocated most efficiently. It is, rather, another circumstance where this Court must determine whether federal rights should yield to state interests. * * * [N]otwithstanding the majority's protestations to the contrary, the language of *Murray v. Carrier* strongly suggests that the Court's resolution of the issue would have been the same regardless of when the procedural default occurred. * * * Rejecting Carrier's argument that, with respect to the standard for cause,

procedural defaults on appeal should be treated differently from those that occur during the trial, the Court stated that 'the standard for cause should not vary depending on the timing of a procedural default or on the strength of an uncertain and difficult assessment of the relative magnitude of the benefits attributable to the state procedural rules that attach at each successive stage of the judicial process.' The rule foreshadowed by this language, which the majority today evades, most faithfully adheres to a principled view of the role of federal habeas jurisdiction. * * * [F]ederal courts forgo the exercise of their habeas jurisprudence over claims that are procedurally barred out of respect for the state interests served by those rules. * * * No rule, however, can deter gross incompetence. To permit a procedural default caused by attorney error egregious enough to constitute ineffective assistance of counsel to preclude federal habeas review of a state prisoner's federal claims in no way serves the State's interest in preserving the integrity of its rules and proceedings. The interest in finality, standing alone, cannot provide a sufficient reason for a federal habeas court to compromise its protection of constitutional rights. * * *

"As the majority acknowledges, under state law as it existed at the time of Coleman's trial and appeal, Coleman could raise his ineffective assistance of counsel claim with respect to counsel's conduct during trial and appeal only in state habeas. This Court has made clear that the Fourteenth Amendment obligates a State 'to assure the indigent defendant an adequate opportunity to present his claims fairly in the context of the State's appellate process,' *Pennsylvania v. Finley*, and 'requires that the state appellate system be free from unreasoned distinctions.' While the State may have wide latitude to structure its appellate process as it deems most effective, it cannot, consistent with the Fourteenth Amendment, structure it in such a way as to deny indigent defendants meaningful access. Accordingly, if a State desires to remove from the process of direct appellate review a claim or category of claims, the Fourteenth Amendment binds the State to ensure that the defendant has effective assistance of counsel for the entirety of the procedure where the removed claims may be raised. Similarly, fundamental fairness dictates that the State, having removed certain claims from the process of direct review, bear the burden of ineffective assistance of counsel in the proceedings to which the claim has been removed."

7th ed., p. 1588; after Note 2, add:

3. SAWYER v. WHITLEY, ___ U.S. ___, 112 U.S. 2514, ___ L.Ed.2d ___ (1992), spoke further to the content of the "miscarriage of justice" or "actual innocence" standard in the context of a challenge to a capital punishment proceeding. The Court there, per REHNQUIST, C.J., noted:

"The issue before the Court is the standard for determining whether a petitioner bringing a successive, abusive, or defaulted federal habeas claim has shown he is 'actually innocent' of the death penalty to which he has been sentenced so that the court may reach the merits of the claim. * * * [We] hold that to show 'actual innocence' one must show by clear and convincing evidence that but for a constitutional error, no reasonable juror would have found the petitioner eligible for the death penalty under the applicable state law. * * *

"A prototypical example of 'actual innocence' in a colloquial sense is the case where the State has convicted the wrong person of the crime. Such claims are of course regularly made on motions for new trial after conviction in both state and federal courts, and quite regularly denied because the evidence adduced in support of this fails to meet the rigorous standards for granting such motions. But in rare instances it may turn out later, for example, that another person has credibly confessed to the crime, and it is evident that the law has made a mistake. In the context of a noncapital case, the concept of 'actual innocence' is easy to grasp.

"It is more difficult to develop an analogous framework when dealing with a defendant who has been sentenced to death. The phrase 'innocent of death' is not a natural usage of those words, but we must strive to construct an analog to the simpler situation represented by the case of a noncapital defendant. In defining this analog, we bear in mind that the exception for 'actual innocence' is a very narrow exception, and that to make it workable it must be subject to determination by relatively objective standards. In the every day context of capital penalty proceedings, a federal district judge typically will be present with a successive or abusive habeas petition a few days before, or even on the day of, a scheduled execution, and will have only a limited time to determine whether a petitioner has shown that his case falls within the 'actual innocence' exception if such a claim is made.

"Since our decision in *Furman v. Georgia*, 408 U.S. 238 (1972), our Eighth Amendment jurisprudence has required those States imposing capital punishment to adopt procedural safeguards protecting against arbitrary and capricious impositions of the death sentence. In response, the States have adopted various narrowing factors which limit the class of offenders upon which the sentencer is authorized to impose the death penalty. For example, the Louisiana statute under which petitioner was convicted defines first-degree murder, a capital offense, as something more than intentional killing. In addition, after a defendant is found guilty in Louisiana of capital murder, the jury must also find at the sentencing phase beyond a reasonable doubt at least one of a list of statutory aggravating factors before it may recommend that the death penalty be imposed. * * * But once eligibility for the death penalty has been established to the satisfaction of the jury, its deliberations assume a different tenor. * * * [T]he defendant must be permitted to introduce a wide variety of mitigating evidence pertaining to his character and background. The emphasis shifts from narrowing the class of eligible defendants by objective factors to individualized consideration of a particular defendant. Consideration of aggravating factors together with mitigating factors, in various combinations and methods dependent upon state law, results in the jury's or judge's ultimate decision as to what penalty shall be imposed.

"Considering Louisiana law as an example, then there are three possible ways in which 'actual innocence' might be defined. The strictest definition would be to limit any showing to the elements of the crime which the State has made a capital offense. The showing would have to negate an essential element of that offense. The Solicitor General, filing as amicus curiae in support of respondent, urges the Court to adopt this standard. We reject this submission as too narrow, because it is contrary to the statement in *Smith v. Murray* that the concept of 'actual innocence' could be applied to mean 'innocent' of the death penalty. This statement suggested a more expansive meaning to the term of 'actual innocence' in a capital case than simply innocence of the capital offense itself.

"The most lenient of the three possibilities would be to allow the showing of 'actual innocence' to extend not only to the elements of the crime, but also to the existence of aggravating factors, and to mitigating evidence which bore, not on the defendant's eligibility to receive the death penalty, but only on the ultimate discretionary decision between the death penalty and life imprisonment. This, in effect is what petitioner urges upon us. * * * Insofar as petitioner's standard would include not merely the elements of the crime itself, but the existence of aggravating circumstances, it broadens the extent of the inquiry but not the type of inquiry. Both the elements of the crime and statutory aggravating circumstances in Louisiana are used to narrow the class of defendants eligible for the death penalty. And proof or disproof of aggravating circumstances, like proof of the elements of the crime, is confined by the statutory definitions to a relatively obvious class of relevant evidence. Sensible meaning is given to the term 'innocent of the death penalty' by allowing a showing in addition to innocence of the capital crime itself a showing that there was no aggravating circumstance or that some other condition of eligibility had not been met.

"But we reject petitioner's submission that the showing should extend beyond these elements of the capital sentence to the existence of additional mitigating evidence. In the first place, such an extension would mean that 'actual innocence' amounts to little more than what is already required to show 'prejudice,' a necessary showing for habeas relief for many constitutional errors. If federal habeas review of capital sentences is to be at all rational, petitioner must show something more in order for a court to reach the merits of his claims on a successive habeas petition than he would have had to show to obtain relief on his first habeas petition. * * * But, more importantly, petitioner's standard would so broaden the inquiry as to make it anything but a 'narrow' exception to the principle of finality which we have previously described it to be. A federal district judge confronted with a claim of actual innocence may with relative ease determine whether a submission, for example, that a killing was not intentional, consists of credible, noncumulative and admissible evidence negating the elements of intent. But it is a far more difficult task to assess how jurors would have reacted to additional showings of mitigating factors, particularly considering the breadth of those factors that a jury under our decisions must be allowed to consider.

"The Court of Appeals in this case took the middle ground among these three possibilities for defining 'actual innocence' of the death penalty, and adopted this test:

We must require the petitioner to show, based on the evidence proffered plus all record evidence, a fair probability that a rational trier of fact would have entertained a reasonable doubt as to the existence of those facts which are prerequisites under state or federal law for the imposition of the death penalty.

The Court of Appeals standard therefore hones in on the objective factors or conditions which must be shown to exist before a defendant is eligible to have the death penalty imposed. * * * We agree * * * that the 'actual innocence' requirement must focus on those elements which render a defendant eligible for the death penalty, and not on additional mitigating evidence which was prevented from being introduced as a result of a claimed constitutional error."

Concurring separately, Justice STEVENS joined by Justices Blackmun and O'Connor, criticized the standard adopted by the Court as "deviat[ing] from our established jurisprudence in two ways. First, the 'clear and convincing evidence' standard departs from a line of decisions defining the 'actual innocence' exception to the cause-and-prejudice requirement. Second, and more fundamentally, the Court's focus on eligibility for the death penalty conflicts with the very structure of the constitutional law of capital punishment." As to the first criticism, Justice Stevens argued that *Murray v. Carrier* and other cases discussing the "actual innocence" standard had "consistently required a defendant to show that the alleged constitutional error has *more likely than* not created a fundamental miscarriage of justice." As to the second, Justice Stevens argued that the Court's standard fell short both in limiting consideration to aggravating factors and in requiring a total refutation of eligibility for the death penalty. Death penalty jurisprudence had long established that the sentencer must be allowed to consider all mitigating evidence, and as to aggravating factors, there was no reason to require that the defendant "call

into question" every such factor that was presented to the jury (which would be necessary to "show himself ineligible for the death penalty"). The dissent concluded that the various interests at stake "are best met by a standard that provides that a defendant is 'innocent of the death sentence' only if his capital sentence is clearly erroneous."

SECTION 3. THE SPECIAL STATUS OF STATE FACTFINDING

7th ed., p. 1589; add after Note 3:

3(a) In KEENEY v. TAMAYO-REYES, ___ U.S. ___, 112 S.Ct. 1715, 118 L.Ed.2d 318 (1992), a divided (5–4) Supreme Court held that the standard of *Wainwright v. Sykes,* 7th ed., p. 1518, *Murray v. Carrier,* 7th ed., pp. 1584, 1586, *McCleskey v. Zant,* Supp. p. 163, and *Coleman v. Thompson,* Supp. p. 162, also governed as to the right to an evidentiary hearing where the habeas petitioner had failed in a state proceeding to fully develop the facts applicable to a cognizable constitutional claim. The habeas petitioner there had originally challenged his guilty plea on collateral attack in a state court proceeding. He alleged that the plea had not been knowing and intelligent because he did not understand English and his translator in the plea proceeding had not translated accurately and completely the mens rea element of the manslaughter charge to which he pled. After a hearing, the state court rejected that claim, finding that the translation had been complete and correct. On application for a federal writ of habeas corpus, the habeas petitioner contended that material facts concerning the translation had not been adequately developed at the state court hearing and asked for a federal evidentiary hearing. The federal district court concluded that the previous failure to develop critical facts was attributable to excusable neglect and therefore no evidentiary hearing was required. The Ninth Circuit disagreed. It held that an evidentiary hearing was required under *Townsend v. Sain,* as this case presented the fifth *Townsend* circumstance (the material facts were not adequately developed at the state court hearing) and *Townsend* had recognized an exception for that circumstance only where the failure to develop the material facts was a product of a deliberate bypass as defined in *Fay v. Noia*. The Supreme Court reversed, holding that *Townsend v. Sain* was overruled insofar as it held that "*Fay v. Noia's* deliberate bypass standard is applicable in a case like this."

JUSTICE WHITE's opinion for the Court initially noted that, in the years since *Townsend* was decided, the Court had rejected application of the deliberate bypass standard, and applied instead the cause-and-prejudice standard, in a variety of habeas settings, as illustrated by *Wainwright, Murray, McCleskey* and *Coleman*. The reasoning advanced in those cases, Justice White noted, was equally applicable here. Justice O'Connor's dissent advanced three arguments as to why the issue presented here should be treated differently, but none of those arguments, Justice White noted, were persuasive. First, the dissent argued that the issue here was different because it involved a constitutional claim that was properly raised in the state proceedings and therefore was appropriately before the habeas court (in contrast to the other cause-and-prejudice cases, which involved the question of whether the habeas court should consider the merits of a claim not properly raised), but the same concerns of "finality, comity, judicial economy, and channeling the resolution of claims into the most appropriate forum," were applicable to the failure to fully present facts on a cognizable claim. Second, the dissent argued that *Townsend*, unlike *Fay v. Noia*, had not "launched the Court in any new direction," but had relied on a long line of cases that allowed for flexibility in the holding of evidentiary hearings.

However, none of those cases, J... White responded supported *Townsend's* novative requirements for a hearing where the petitioner's own neglect was the cause for a failure to develop material facts. Third, the dissent argued that Congress, in enacting 28 U.S.C. § 2254(d) (see Note 4 at 7th ed., p. 1589), had presumed a hearing would be afforded when it recognized as an exception to the "presumption of correctness" for situations in which "material facts were not adequately developed at the state court hearing," but that legislation dealt with a separate issue, and "does not mention or recognize any exception for inexcusable neglect, let alone the specific standard of deliberate bypass." Indeed, "to the extent that it even considered the issue of default, Congress sensibly could have read *Townsend* as holding that the federal habeas corpus standard for cases of default under *Townsend's* fifth circumstance and cases of procedural default should be the same."

In light of the above analysis, the Court remanded the case to the district court with the following direction: "Tamyo–Reyes is entitled to an evidentiary hearing if he can show cause for his failure to develop the facts in state-court proceedings and actual prejudice resulting from that failure. We also adopt the narrow exception to the cause-and-prejudice requirement: A habeas petitioner's failure to develop a claim in state-court proceedings will be excused and a hearing mandated if he can show that a fundamental miscarriage of justice would result from failure to hold a federal evidentiary hearing."

7th ed., p. 1593; at the end of Note 7, add:

Consider also the discussions in *Wright v. West*, Supp. p. 153, as to the bearing of *Teague v. Lane* upon the habeas court's consideration of a claim of the type raised in *Miller v. Fenton*.

Appendix A

SELECTED PROVISIONS OF THE UNITED STATES CONSTITUTION

ARTICLE I

Section 9. ＊ ＊ ＊

[2] The privilege of the Writ of Habeas Corpus shall not be suspended, unless when in Cases of Rebellion or Invasion the public Safety may require it.

[3] No Bill of Attainder or ex post facto Law shall be passed.

ARTICLE III

Section 1. The judicial Power of the United States, shall be vested in one supreme Court, and in such inferior Courts as the Congress may from time to time ordain and establish. The Judges, both of the supreme and inferior Courts, shall hold their Offices during good Behaviour, and shall, at stated Times, receive for their Services a Compensation, which shall not be diminished during their Continuance in Office.

Section 2. [1] The judicial Power shall extend to all Cases, in Law and Equity, arising under this Constitution, the Laws of the United States, and Treaties made, or which shall be made, under their Authority;—to all Cases affecting Ambassadors, other public Ministers and Consuls;—to all Cases of admiralty and maritime Jurisdiction;—to Controversies to which the United States shall be a Party;—to Controversies between two or more States;—between a State and Citizens of another State;—between Citizens of different States;—between Citizens of the same State claiming Lands under the Grants of different States, and between a State, or the Citizens thereof, and foreign States, Citizens or Subjects.

[3] The trial of all Crimes, except in Cases of Impeachment, shall be by Jury; and such Trial shall be held in the State where the said Crimes shall have been committed; but when not committed within any State, the Trial shall be at such Place or Places as the Congress may by Law have directed.

Section 3. [1] Treason against the United States, shall consist only in levying War against them, or, in adhering to their Enemies, giving them Aid and Comfort. No Person shall be convicted of Treason unless on the Testimony of two Witnesses to the same overt Act, or on Confession in open Court.

[2] The Congress shall have Power to declare the Punishment of Treason, but no Attainder of Treason shall work Corruption of Blood, or Forfeiture except during the Life of the Person attainted.

ARTICLE IV

Section 2. [1] The Citizens of each State shall be entitled to all Privileges and Immunities of Citizens in the several States.

[2] A Person charged in any State with Treason, Felony, or other Crime, who shall flee from Justice, and be found in another State, shall on demand of the executive Authority of the State from which he fled, be delivered up, to be removed to the State having Jurisdiction of the Crime.

ARTICLE VI

[2] This Constitution, and the Laws of the United States which shall be made in Pursuance thereof; and all Treaties made, or which shall be made, under the Authority of the United States, shall be the supreme Law.

AMENDMENT I [1791]

Congress shall make no law respecting an establishment of religion, or prohibiting the free exercise thereof; or abridging the freedom of speech, or of the press; or the right of the people peaceably to assemble, and to petition the Government for a redress of grievances.

AMENDMENT II [1791]

A well regulated Militia, being necessary to the security of a free State, the right of the people to keep and bear Arms, shall not be infringed.

AMENDMENT III [1791]

No Soldier shall, in time of peace be quartered in any house, without the consent of the Owner, nor in time of war, but in a manner to be prescribed by law.

AMENDMENT IV [1791]

The right of the people to be secure in their persons, houses, papers, and effects, against unreasonable searches and seizures, shall not be violated, and no Warrants shall issue, but upon probable cause, supported by Oath or affirmation, and particularly describing the place to be searched, and the persons or things to be seized.

AMENDMENT V [1791]

No person shall be held to answer for a capital, or otherwise infamous crime, unless on a presentment or indictment of a Grand Jury, except in cases arising in the land or naval forces, or in the Militia, when in actual service in time of War or public danger; nor shall any person be subject for the same offence to be twice put in jeopardy of life or limb; nor shall be compelled in any criminal case to be a witness against himself, nor be deprived of life, liberty, or property, without due process of law; nor shall private property be taken for public use, without just compensation.

AMENDMENT VI [1791]

not a strict interpretation

In all criminal prosecutions, the accused shall enjoy the right to a speedy and public trial, by an impartial jury of the State and district wherein the crime shall have been committed, which district shall have been previously ascertained by law, and to be informed of the nature and cause of the accusation; to be confronted with the witnesses against him; to have compulsory process for obtaining witnesses in his favor, and to have the Assistance of Counsel for his defence.

AMENDMENT VII [1791]

In Suits at common law, where the value in controversy shall exceed twenty dollars, the right of trial by jury shall be preserved, and no fact tried by jury, shall be otherwise re-examined in any Court of the United States, than according to the rules of the common law.

AMENDMENT VIII [1791]

Excessive bail shall not be required, nor excessive fines imposed, nor cruel and unusual punishments inflicted.

AMENDMENT IX [1791]

The enumeration in the Constitution, of certain rights, shall not be construed to deny or disparage others retained by the people.

Amendment X [1791]

The powers not delegated to the United States by the Constitution, nor prohibited by it to the States, are reserved to the States respectively, or to the people.

Amendment XIII [1865]

Section 1. Neither slavery nor involuntary servitude, except as a punishment for crime whereof the party shall have been duly convicted, shall exist within the United States, or any place subject to their jurisdiction.

Section 2. Congress shall have power to enforce this article by appropriate legislation.

Amendment XIV [1868]

Section 1. All persons born or naturalized in the United States, and subject to the jurisdiction thereof, are citizens of the United States and of the State wherein they reside. No State shall make or enforce any law which shall abridge the privileges or immunities of citizens of the United States; nor shall any State deprive any person of life, liberty, or property, without due process of law; nor deny to any person within its jurisdiction the equal protection of the laws.

Section 5. The Congress shall have power to enforce, by appropriate legislation, the provisions of the article.

Amendment XV [1870]

Section 1. The right of citizens of the United States to vote shall not be denied or abridged by the United States or by any State on account of race, color, or previous condition of servitude.

Section 2. The Congress shall have power to enforce this article by appropriate legislation.

Appendix B

SELECTED FEDERAL STATUTORY PROVISIONS

Analysis

WIRE AND ELECTRONIC COMMUNICATIONS INTERCEPTION AND INTERCEPTION OF ORAL COMMUNICATIONS

(18 U.S.C. §§ 2510–2511, 2515–2518, 2520–2521).

§ 2510. Definitions

As used in this chapter—

(1) "wire communication" means any aural transfer made in whole or in part through the use of facilities for the transmission of communications by the aid of wire, cable, or other like connection between the point of origin and the point of reception (including the use of such connection in a switching station) furnished or operated by any person engaged in providing or operating such facilities for the transmission of interstate or foreign communications or communications affecting interstate or foreign commerce and such term includes any electronic storage of such communication, but such term does not include the radio portion of a cordless telephone communication that is transmitted between the cordless telephone handset and the base unit;

(2) "oral communication" means any oral communication uttered by a person exhibiting an expectation that such communication is not subject to interception under circumstances justifying such expectation, but such term does not include any electronic communication;

(3) "State" means any State of the United States, the District of Columbia, the Commonwealth of Puerto Rico, and any territory or possession of the United States;

175

(4) "intercept" means the aural or other acquisition of the contents of any wire, electronic, or oral communication through the use of any electronic, mechanical, or other device;

(5) "electronic, mechanical, or other device" means any device or apparatus which can be used to intercept a wire, oral, or electronic communication other than—

(a) any telephone or telegraph instrument, equipment or facility, or any component thereof, (i) furnished to the subscriber or user by a provider of wire or electronic communication service in the ordinary course of its business and being used by the subscriber or user in the ordinary course of its business or furnished by such subscriber or user for connection to the facilities of such service and used in the ordinary course of its business; or (ii) being used by a provider of wire or electronic communication service in the ordinary course of its business, or by an investigative or law enforcement officer in the ordinary course of his duties;

(b) a hearing aid or similar device being used to correct subnormal hearing to not better than normal;

(6) "person" means any employee, or agent of the United States or any State or political subdivision thereof, and any individual, partnership, association, joint stock company, trust, or corporation;

(7) "Investigative or law enforcement officer" means any officer of the United States or of a State or political subdivision thereof, who is empowered by law to conduct investigations of or to make arrests for offenses enumerated in this chapter, and any attorney authorized by law to prosecute or participate in the prosecution of such offenses;

(8) "contents", when used with respect to any wire, oral, or electronic communication, includes any information concerning the substance, purport, or meaning of that communication;

(9) "Judge of competent jurisdiction" means—

(a) a judge of a United States district court or a United States court of appeals; and

(b) a judge of any court of general criminal jurisdiction of a State who is authorized by a statute of that State to enter orders authorizing interceptions of wire, oral, or electronic communications;

(10) "communication common carrier" shall have the same meaning which is given the term "common carrier" by section 153(h) of title 47 of the United States Code;

(11) "aggrieved person" means a person who was a party to any intercepted wire, oral, or electronic communication or a person against whom the interception was directed;

(12) "electronic communication" means any transfer of signs, signals, writing, images, sounds, data, or intelligence of any nature transmitted in whole or in part by a wire, radio, electromagnetic, photoelectronic or photooptical system that affects interstate or foreign commerce, but does not include—

(A) the radio portion of a cordless telephone communication that is transmitted between the cordless telephone handset and the base unit;

(B) any wire or oral communication;

(C) any communication made through a tone-only paging device; or

(D) any communication from a tracking device (as defined in section 3117 of this title);

(13) "user" means any person or entity who—

(A) uses an electronic communication service; and

(B) is duly authorized by the provider of such service to engage in such use;

(14) "electronic communications system" means any wire, radio, electromagnetic, photooptical or photoelectronic facilities for the transmission of electronic communications, and any computer facilities or related electronic equipment for the electronic storage of such communications;

(15) "electronic communication service" means any service which provides to users thereof the ability to send or receive wire or electronic communications;

(16) "readily accessible to the general public" means, with respect to a radio communication, that such communication is not—

(A) scrambled or encrypted;

(B) transmitted using modulation techniques whose essential parameters have been withheld from the public with the intention of preserving the privacy of such communication;

(C) carried on a subcarrier or other signal subsidiary to a radio transmission;

(D) transmitted over a communication system provided by a common carrier, unless the communication is a tone only paging system communication; or

(E) transmitted on frequencies allocated under part 25, subpart D, E, or F of part 74, or part 94 of the Rules of the Federal Communications Commission, unless, in the case of a communication transmitted on a frequency allocated under part 74 that is not exclusively allocated to broadcast auxiliary services, the communication is a two-way voice communication by radio;

(17) "electronic storage" means—

(A) any temporary, intermediate storage of a wire or electronic communication incidental to the electronic transmission thereof; and

(B) any storage of such communication by an electronic communication service for purposes of backup protection of such communication; and

(18) "aural transfer" means a transfer containing the human voice at any point between and including the point of origin and the point of reception.

§ 2511. Interception and disclosure of wire, oral, or electronic communications prohibited

(1) Except as otherwise specifically provided in this chapter any person who—

(a) intentionally intercepts, endeavors to intercept, or procures any other person to intercept or endeavor to intercept, any wire, oral, or electronic communication;

(b) intentionally uses, endeavors to use, or procures any other person to use or endeavor to use any electronic, mechanical, or other device to intercept any oral communication when—

(i) such device is affixed to, or otherwise transmits a signal through, a wire, cable, or other like connection used in wire communication; or

(ii) such device transmits communications by radio, or interferes with the transmission of such communication; or

(iii) such person knows, or has reason to know, that such device or any component thereof has been sent through the mail or transported in interstate or foreign commerce; or

(iv) such use or endeavor to use (A) takes place on the premises of any business or other commercial establishment the operations of which affect interstate or foreign commerce; or (B) obtains or is for the purpose of obtaining information relating to the operations of any business or other commercial establishment the operations of which affect interstate or foreign commerce; or

(v) such person acts in the District of Columbia, the Commonwealth of Puerto Rico, or any territory or possession of the United States;

(c) intentionally discloses, or endeavors to disclose, to any other person the contents of any wire, oral, or electronic communication, knowing or having reason to know that the information was obtained through the interception of a wire, oral, or electronic communication in violation of this subsection; or

(d) intentionally uses, or endeavors to use, the contents of any wire, oral, or electronic communication, knowing or having reason to know that the information was obtained through the interception of a wire, oral, or electronic communication in violation of this subsection;

shall be punished as provided in subsection (4) or shall be subject to suit as provided in subsection (5).

(2)(a)(i) It shall not be unlawful under this chapter for an operator of a switchboard, or an officer, employee, or agent of a provider of wire or electronic communication service, whose facilities are used in the transmission of a wire communication, to intercept, disclose, or use that communication in the normal course of his employment while engaged in any activity which is a necessary incident to the rendition of his service or to the protection of the rights or property of the provider of that service, except that a provider of wire communication service to the public shall not utilize service observing or random monitoring except for mechanical or service quality control checks.

(ii) Notwithstanding any other law, providers of wire or electronic communication service, their officers, employees, and agents, landlords, custodians, or other persons, are authorized to provide information, facilities, or technical assistance to persons authorized by law to intercept wire, oral, or electronic communications or to conduct electronic surveillance, as defined in section 101 of the Foreign Intelligence Surveillance Act of 1978, if such provider, its officers, employees, or agents, landlord, custodian, or other specified person, has been provided with—

(A) a court order directing such assistance signed by the authorizing judge, or

(B) a certification in writing by a person specified in section 2518(7) of this title or the Attorney General of the United States that no warrant or court order is required by law, that all statutory requirements have been met, and that the specified assistance is required,

setting forth the period of time during which the provision of the information, facilities, or technical assistance is authorized and specifying the information, facilities, or technical assistance required. No provider of wire or electronic communication service, officer, employee, or agent thereof, or landlord, custodian, or other specified person shall disclose the existence of any interception or surveillance or the device used to accomplish the interception or surveillance with respect to which the person has been furnished a court order or certification under this chapter except as may otherwise be required by legal process and then only after prior notification to the Attorney General or to the principal prosecuting attorney of a State or any political subdivision of a State, as may be appropriate. Any such disclosure, shall render such person liable for the civil damages provided for in section 2520. No cause of action shall lie in any court against any provider of wire or electronic communication service, its officers, employees, or agents, landlord, custodian, or other specified person for providing information, facilities, or assistance in accordance with the terms of an order or certification under this subpar.

(b) It shall not be unlawful under this chapter for an officer, employee, or agent of the Federal Communications Commission, in the normal course of his employment and in discharge of the monitoring responsibilities exercised by the Commission in the enforcement of chapter 5 of title 47 of the United States Code, to intercept a wire or electronic communication, or oral communication transmitted by radio, or to disclose or use the information thereby obtained.

(c) It shall not be unlawful under this chapter for a person acting under color of law to intercept a wire, oral, or electronic communication, where such person is a party to the communication or one of the parties to the communication has given prior consent to such interception.

(d) It shall not be unlawful under this chapter for a person not acting under color of law to intercept a wire, oral, or electronic communication where such person is a party to the communication or where one of the parties to the communication has given prior consent to such interception unless such communication is intercepted for the purpose of committing any criminal or tortious act in violation of the Constitution or laws of the United States or of any State.

(e) Notwithstanding any other provision of this title or section 705 or 706 of the Communications Act of 1934, it shall not be unlawful for an officer, employee, or agent of the United States in the normal course of his official duty to conduct electronic surveillance, as defined in section 101 of the Foreign Intelligence Surveillance Act of 1978, as authorized by that Act.

(f) Nothing contained in this chapter or chapter 121, or section 705 of the Communications Act of 1934, shall be deemed to affect the acquisition by the United States Government of foreign intelligence information from international or foreign communications, or foreign intelligence activities conducted in accordance with otherwise applicable Federal law involving a foreign electronic communications system, utilizing a means other than electronic surveillance as defined in section 101 of the Foreign Intelligence Surveillance Act of 1978, and procedures in this chapter and the Foreign Intelligence Surveillance Act of 1978 shall be the exclusive means by which electronic surveillance, as defined in section 101 of such Act, and the interception of domestic wire and oral communications may be conducted.

(g) It shall not be unlawful under this chapter or chapter 121 of this title for any person—

(i) to intercept or access an electronic communication made through an electronic communication system that is configured so that such electronic communication is readily accessible to the general public;

(ii) to intercept any radio communication which is transmitted—

(I) by any station for the use of the general public, or that relates to ships, aircraft, vehicles, or persons in distress;

(II) by any governmental, law enforcement, civil defense, private land mobile, or public safety communications system, including police and fire, readily accessible to the general public;

(III) by a station operating on an authorized frequency within the bands allocated to the amateur, citizens band, or general mobile radio services; or

(IV) by any marine or aeronautical communications system;

(iii) to engage in any conduct which—

(I) is prohibited by section 633 of the Communications Act of 1934; or

(II) is excepted from the application of section 705(a) of the Communications Act of 1934 by section 705(b) of that Act;

(iv) to intercept any wire or electronic communication the transmission of which is causing harmful interference to any lawfully operating station or consumer electronic equipment, to the extent necessary to identify the source of such interference; or

(v) for other users of the same frequency to intercept any radio communication made through a system that utilizes frequencies monitored by individuals engaged in the provision or the use of such system, if such communication is not scrambled or encrypted.

(h) It shall not be unlawful under this chapter—

(i) to use a pen register or a trap and trace device (as those terms are defined for the purposes of chapter 206 (relating to pen registers and trap and trace devices) of this title); or

(ii) for a provider of electronic communication service to record the fact that a wire or electronic communication was initiated or completed in order to protect such provider, another provider furnishing service toward the completion of the wire or electronic communication, or a user of that service, from fraudulent, unlawful or abusive use of such service.

(3)(a) Except as provided in paragraph (b) of this subsection, a person or entity providing an electronic communication service to the public shall not intentionally divulge the contents of any communication (other than one to such person or entity, or an agent thereof) while in transmission on that service to any person or entity other than an addressee or intended recipient of such communication or an agent of such addressee or intended recipient.

(b) A person or entity providing electronic communication service to the public may divulge the contents of any such communication—

(i) as otherwise authorized in section 2511(2)(a) or 2517 of this title;

(ii) with the lawful consent of the originator or any addressee or intended recipient of such communication;

(iii) to a person employed or authorized, or whose facilities are used, to forward such communication to its destination; or

(iv) which were inadvertently obtained by the service provider and which appear to pertain to the commission of a crime, if such divulgence is made to a law enforcement agency.

(4)(a) Except as provided in paragraph (b) of this subsection or in subsection (5), whoever violates subsection (1) of this section shall be fined under this title or imprisoned not more than five years, or both.

(b) If the offense is a first offense under paragraph (a) of this subsection and is not for a tortious or illegal purpose or for purposes of direct or indirect commercial advantage or private commercial gain, and the wire or electronic communication with respect to which the offense under paragraph (a) is a radio communication that is not scrambled or encrypted, then—

(i) if the communication is not the radio portion of a cellular telephone communication, a public land mobile radio service communication or a paging service communication, and the conduct is not that described in subsection (5), the offender shall be fined under this title or imprisoned not more than one year or both; and

(ii) if the communication is the radio portion of a cellular telephone communication, a public land mobile radio service communication or a paging service communication, the offender shall be fined not more than $500.

(c) Conduct otherwise an offense under this subsection that consists of or relates to the interception of a satellite transmission that is not encrypted or scrambled and that is transmitted—

(i) to a broadcasting station for purposes of retransmission to the general public; or

(ii) as an audio subcarrier intended for redistribution to facilities open to the public, but not including data transmissions or telephone calls,

is not an offense under this subsection unless the conduct is for the purposes of direct or indirect commercial advantage or private financial gain.

(5)(a)(i) If the communication is—

(A) a private satellite video communication that is not scrambled or encrypted and the conduct in violation of this chapter is the private viewing of that communication and is not for a tortious or illegal purpose or for purposes of direct or indirect commercial advantage or private commercial gain; or

(B) a radio communication that is transmitted on frequencies allocated under subpart D of part 74 of the rules of the Federal Communications Commission that is not scrambled or encrypted and the conduct in violation of this chapter is not for a tortious or illegal purpose or for purposes of direct or indirect commercial advantage or private commercial gain,

then the person who engages in such conduct shall be subject to suit by the Federal Government in a court of competent jurisdiction.

(ii) In an action under this subsection—

(A) if the violation of this chapter is a first offense for the person under paragraph (a) of subsection (4) and such person has not been found liable in a civil action under section 2520 of this title, the Federal Government shall be entitled to appropriate injunctive relief; and

(B) if the violation of this chapter is a second or subsequent offense under paragraph (a) of subsection (4) or such person has been found liable in any prior civil action under section 2520, the person shall be subject to a mandatory $500 civil fine.

(b) The court may use any means within its authority to enforce an injunction issued under paragraph (ii)(A), and shall impose a civil fine of not less than $500 for each violation of such an injunction.

§ 2515. Prohibition of use as evidence of intercepted wire or oral communications

Whenever any wire or oral communication has been intercepted, no part of the contents of such communication and no evidence derived therefrom may be received in evidence in any trial, hearing, or other proceeding in or before any court, grand jury, department, officer, agency, regulatory body, legislative committee, or other authority of the United States, a State, or a political subdivision thereof if the disclosure of that information would be in violation of this chapter.

§ 2516. Authorization for interception of wire, oral, or electronic communications

(1) The Attorney General, Deputy Attorney General, Associate Attorney General, any Assistant Attorney General, any acting Assistant Attorney General, or any Deputy Assistant Attorney General in the Criminal Division specially designated by the Attorney General, may authorize an application to a Federal judge of competent jurisdiction for, and such judge may grant in conformity with section 2518 of this chapter an order authorizing or approving the interception of wire or oral communications by the Federal Bureau of Investigation, or a Federal agency having responsibility for the investigation of the offense as to which the application is made, when such interception may provide or has provided evidence of—

(a) any offense punishable by death or by imprisonment for more than one year under sections 2274 through 2277 of title 42 of the United States Code (relating to the enforcement of the Atomic Energy Act of 1954), section 2284 of title 42 of the

United States Code (relating to sabotage of nuclear facilities or fuel), or under the following chapters of this title: chapter 37 (relating to espionage), chapter 105 (relating to sabotage), chapter 115 (relating to treason), chapter 102 (relating to riots); chapter 65 (relating to malicious mischief), chapter 111 (relating to destruction of vessels), or chapter 81 (relating to piracy);

(b) a violation of section 186 or section 501(c) of title 29, United States Code (dealing with restrictions on payments and loans to labor organizations), or any offense which involves murder, kidnapping, robbery, or extortion, and which is punishable under this title;

(c) any offense which is punishable under the following sections of this title: section 201 (bribery of public officials and witnesses), section 224 (bribery in sporting contests), subsection (d), (e), (f), (g), (h), or (i) of section 844 (unlawful use of explosives), section 1084 (transmission of wagering information), section 751 (relating to escape), sections 1503, 1512, and 1513 (influencing or injuring an officer, juror, or witness generally), section 1510 (obstruction of criminal investigations), section 1511 (obstruction of State or local law enforcement), section 1751 (Presidential and Presidential staff assassination, kidnaping, and assault), section 1951 (interference with commerce by threats or violence), section 1952 (interstate and foreign travel or transportation in aid of racketeering enterprises), section 1952A (relating to use of interstate commerce facilities in the commission of murder for hire), section 1952B (relating to violent crimes in aid of racketeering activity), section 1954 (offer, acceptance, or solicitation to influence operations of employee benefit plan), section 1955 (prohibition of business enterprises of gambling), section 1956 (laundering of monetary instruments), section 1957 (relating to engaging in monetary transactions in property derived from specified unlawful activity), section 659 (theft from interstate shipment), section 664 (embezzlement from pension and welfare funds), section 1343 (fraud by wire, radio, or television), sections 2251 and 2252 (sexual exploitation of children), sections 2312, 2313, 2314, and 2315 (interstate transportation of stolen property), the second section 2320 (relating to trafficking in certain motor vehicles or motor vehicle parts), section 1203 (relating to hostage taking), section 1029 (relating to fraud and related activity in connection with access devices), section 3146 (relating to penalty for failure to appear), section 3521(b)(3) (relating to witness relocation and assistance), section 32 (relating to destruction of aircraft or aircraft facilities), section 1963 (violations with respect to racketeer influenced and corrupt organizations), section 115 (relating to threatening or retaliating against a Federal official), the section in chapter 65 (relating to destruction of an energy facility), and section 1341 (relating to mail fraud), section 351 (violations with respect to congressional, Cabinet, or Supreme Court assassinations, kidnaping, and assault), section 831 (relating to prohibited transactions involving nuclear materials), section 33 (relating to destruction of motor vehicles or motor vehicle facilities), section 175 (relating to biological weapons), or section 1992 (relating to wrecking trains);

(d) any offense involving counterfeiting punishable under section 471, 472, or 473 of this title;

(e) any offense involving fraud connected with a case under title 11 or the manufacture, importation, receiving, concealment, buying, selling, or otherwise dealing in narcotic drugs, marihuana, or other dangerous drugs, punishable under any law of the United States;

(f) any offense including extortionate credit transactions under sections 892, 893, or 894 of this title;

(g) a violation of section 5322 of title 31, United States Code (dealing with the reporting of currency transactions);

(h) any felony violation of sections 2511 and 2512 (relating to interception and disclosure of certain communications and to certain intercepting devices) of this title;

(i) any felony violation of chapter 71 (relating to obscenity) of this title;

(j) any violation of section 1679a(c)(2) (relating to destruction of a natural gas pipeline) or subsection (i) or (n) of section 1472 (relating to aircraft piracy) of title 49, of the United States Code;

(k) any criminal violation of section 2778 of title 22 (relating to the Arms Export Control Act);

(l) the location of any fugitive from justice from an offense described in this section; or

(m) any conspiracy to commit any of the foregoing offenses.

(m) [1] any felony violation of sections 922 and 924 of title 18, United States Code (relating to firearms); and

(n) any violation of section 5861 of the Internal Revenue Code of 1986 (relating to firearms).

(2) The principal prosecuting attorney of any State, or the principal prosecuting attorney of any political subdivision thereof, if such attorney is authorized by a statute of that State to make application to a State court judge of competent jurisdiction for an order authorizing or approving the interception of wire, oral, or electronic communications, may apply to such judge for, and such judge may grant in conformity with section 2518 of this chapter and with the applicable State statute an order authorizing, or approving the interception of wire, oral, or electronic communications by investigative or law enforcement officers having responsibility for the investigation of the offense as to which the application is made, when such interception may provide or has provided evidence of the commission of the offense of murder, kidnapping, gambling, robbery, bribery, extortion, or dealing in narcotic drugs, marihuana or other dangerous drugs, or other crime dangerous to life, limb, or property, and punishable by imprisonment for more than one year, designated in any applicable State statute authorizing such interception, or any conspiracy to commit any of the foregoing offenses.

(3) Any attorney for the Government (as such term is defined for the purposes of the Federal Rules of Criminal Procedure) may authorize an application to a Federal judge of competent jurisdiction for, and such judge may grant, in conformity with section 2518 of this title, an order authorizing or approving the interception of electronic communications by an investigative or law enforcement officer having responsibility for the investigation of the offense as to which the application is made, when such interception may provide or has provided evidence of any Federal felony.

§ 2517. Authorization for disclosure and use of intercepted wire, oral, or electronic communications

(1) Any investigative or law enforcement officer who, by any means authorized by this chapter, has obtained knowledge of the contents of any wire, oral, or electronic communication, or evidence derived therefrom, may disclose such contents to another investigative or law enforcement officer to the extent that such disclosure is appropriate to the proper performance of the official duties of the officer making or receiving the disclosure.

(2) Any investigative or law enforcement officer who, by any means authorized by this chapter, has obtained knowledge of the contents of any wire, oral, or electronic

---

[1] So in original.

communication or evidence derived therefrom may use such contents to the extent such use is appropriate to the proper performance of his official duties.

(3) Any person who has received, by any means authorized by this chapter, any information concerning a wire, oral, or electronic communication, or evidence derived therefrom intercepted in accordance with the provisions of this chapter may disclose the contents of that communication or such derivative evidence while giving testimony under oath or affirmation in any proceeding held under the authority of the United States or of any State or political subdivision thereof.

(4) No otherwise privileged wire, oral, or electronic communication intercepted in accordance with, or in violation of, the provisions of this chapter shall lose its privileged character.

(5) When an investigative or law enforcement officer, while engaged in intercepting wire, oral, or electronic communications in the manner authorized herein, intercepts wire, oral, or electronic communications relating to offenses other than those specified in the order of authorization or approval, the contents thereof, and evidence derived therefrom, may be disclosed or used as provided in subsections (1) and (2) of this section. Such contents and any evidence derived therefrom may be used under subsection (3) of this section when authorized or approved by a judge of competent jurisdiction where such judge finds on subsequent application that the contents were otherwise intercepted in accordance with the provisions of this chapter. Such application shall be made as soon as practicable.

§ 2518. Procedure for interception of wire, oral, or electronic communications

(1) Each application for an order authorizing or approving the interception of a wire, oral, or electronic communication under this chapter shall be made in writing upon oath or affirmation to a judge of competent jurisdiction and shall state the applicant's authority to make such application. Each application shall include the following information:

(a) the identity of the investigative or law enforcement officer making the application, and the officer authorizing the application;

(b) a full and complete statement of the facts and circumstances relied upon by the applicant, to justify his belief that an order should be issued, including (i) details as to the particular offense that has been, is being, is about to be committed, (ii) except as provided in subsection (11), a particular description of the nature and location of the facilities from which or the place where the communication is to be intercepted, (iii) a particular description of the type of communications sought to be intercepted, (iv) the identity of the person, if known, committing the offense and whose communications are to be intercepted;

(c) a full and complete statement as to whether or not other investigative procedures have been tried and failed or why they reasonably appear to be unlikely to succeed if tried or to be too dangerous;

(d) a statement of the period of time for which the interception is required to be maintained. If the nature of the investigation is such that the authorization for interception should not automatically terminate when the described type of communication has been first obtained, a particular description of facts establishing probable cause to believe that additional communications of the same type will occur thereafter;

(e) a full and complete statement of the facts concerning all previous applications known to the individual authorizing and making the application, made to any judge for authorization to intercept, or for approval of interceptions of, wire, oral, or electronic communications involving any of the same persons, facilities or places specified in the application, and the action taken by the judge on each such application; and

(f) where the application is for the extension of an order, a statement setting forth the results thus far obtained from the interception, or a reasonable explanation of the failure to obtain such results.

(2) The judge may require the applicant to furnish additional testimony or documentary evidence in support of the application.

(3) Upon such application the judge may enter an ex parte order, as requested or as modified, authorizing or approving interception of wire, oral, or electronic communications within the territorial jurisdiction of the court in which the judge is sitting (and outside that jurisdiction but within the United States in the case of a mobile interception device authorized by a Federal court within such jurisdiction), if the judge determines on the basis of the facts submitted by the applicant that—

(a) there is probable cause for belief that an individual is committing, has committed, or is about to commit a particular offense enumerated in section 2516 of this chapter;

(b) there is probable cause for belief that particular communications concerning that offense will be obtained through such interception;

(c) normal investigative procedures have been tried and have failed or reasonably appear to be unlikely to succeed if tried or to be too dangerous;

(d) except as provided in subsection (11), there is probable cause for belief that the facilities from which, or the place where, the wire, oral, or electronic communications are to be intercepted are being used, or are about to be used, in connection with the commission of such offense, or are leased to, listed in the name of, or commonly used by such person.

(4) Each order authorizing or approving the interception of any wire, oral, or electronic communication under this chapter shall specify—

(a) the identity of the person, if known, whose communications are to be intercepted;

(b) the nature and location of the communications facilities as to which, or the place where, authority to intercept is granted;

(c) a particular description of the type of communication sought to be intercepted, and a statement of the particular offense to which it relates;

(d) the identity of the agency authorized to intercept the communications, and of the person authorizing the application; and

(e) the period of time during which such interception is authorized, including a statement as to whether or not the interception shall automatically terminate when the described communication has been first obtained.

An order authorizing the interception of a wire, oral, or electronic communication under this chapter shall, upon request of the applicant, direct that a provider of wire or electronic communication service, landlord, custodian or other person shall furnish the applicant forthwith all information, facilities, and technical assistance necessary to accomplish the interception unobtrusively and with a minimum of interference with the services that such service provider, landlord, custodian, or person is according the person whose communications are to be intercepted. Any provider of wire or electronic communication service, landlord, custodian or other person furnishing such facilities or technical assistance shall be compensated therefor by the applicant for reasonable expenses incurred in providing such facilities or assistance.

(5) No order entered under this section may authorize or approve the interception of any wire, oral, or electronic communication for any period longer than is necessary to achieve the objective of the authorization, nor in any event longer than thirty

days. Such thirty-day period begins on the earlier of the day on which the investigative or law enforcement officer first begins to conduct an interception under the order or ten days after the order is entered. Extensions of an order may be granted, but only upon application for an extension made in accordance with subsection (1) of this section and the court making the findings required by subsection (3) of this section. The period of extension shall be no longer than the authorizing judge deems necessary to achieve the purposes for which it was granted and in no event for longer than thirty days. Every order and extension thereof shall contain a provision that the authorization to intercept shall be executed as soon as practicable, shall be conducted in such a way as to minimize the interception of communications not otherwise subject to interception under this chapter, and must terminate upon attainment of the authorized objective, or in any event in thirty days. In the event the intercepted communication is in a code or foreign language, and an expert in that foreign language or code is not reasonably available during the interception period, minimization may be accomplished as soon as practicable after such interception. An interception under this chapter may be conducted in whole or in part by Government personnel, or by an individual operating under a contract with the Government, acting under the supervision of an investigative or law enforcement officer authorized to conduct the interception.

(6) Whenever an order authorizing interception is entered pursuant to this chapter, the order may require reports to be made to the judge who issued the order showing what progress has been made toward achievement of the authorized objective and the need for continued interception. Such reports shall be made at such intervals as the judge may require.

(7) Notwithstanding any other provision of this chapter, any investigative or law enforcement officer, specially designated by the Attorney General, the Deputy Attorney General, the Associate Attorney General or by the principal prosecuting attorney of any State or subdivision thereof acting pursuant to a statute of that State, who reasonably determines that—

(a) an emergency situation exists that involves—

(i) immediate danger of death or serious physical injury to any person,

(ii) conspiratorial activities threatening the national security interest, or

(iii) conspiratorial activities characteristic of organized crime,

that requires a wire, oral, or electronic communication to be intercepted before an order authorizing such interception can, with due diligence, be obtained, and

(b) there are grounds upon which an order could be entered under this chapter to authorize such interception,

may intercept such wire, oral, or electronic communication if an application for an order approving the interception is made in accordance with this section within forty-eight hours after the interception has occurred, or begins to occur. In the absence of an order, such interception shall immediately terminate when the communication sought is obtained or when the application for the order is denied, whichever is earlier. In the event such application for approval is denied, or in any other case where the interception is terminated without an order having been issued, the contents of any wire, oral, or electronic communication intercepted shall be treated as having been obtained in violation of this chapter, and an inventory shall be served as provided for in subsection (d) of this section on the person named in the application.

(8)(a) The contents of any wire, oral, or electronic communication intercepted by any means authorized by this chapter shall, if possible, be recorded on tape or wire or other comparable device. The recording of the contents of any wire, oral or electronic communication under this subsection shall be done in such way as will protect the recording from editing or other alterations. Immediately upon the expiration of the period of the order, or extensions thereof, such recordings shall be made available to the judge issuing such order and sealed under his directions. Custody of the recordings shall be wherever the judge orders. They shall not be destroyed except upon an order of the issuing or denying judge and in any event shall be kept for ten years. Duplicate recordings may be made for use or disclosure pursuant to the provisions of subsections (1) and (2) of section 2517 of this chapter for investigations. The presence of the seal provided for by this subsection, or a satisfactory explanation for the absence thereof, shall be a prerequisite for the use or disclosure of the contents of any wire, oral, or electronic communication or evidence derived therefrom under subsection (3) of section 2517.

(b) Applications made and orders granted under this chapter shall be sealed by the judge. Custody of the applications and orders shall be wherever the judge directs. Such applications and orders shall be disclosed only upon a showing of good cause before a judge of competent jurisdiction and shall not be destroyed except on order of the issuing or denying judge, and in any event shall be kept for ten years.

(c) Any violation of the provisions of this subsection may be punished as contempt of the issuing or denying judge.

(d) Within a reasonable time but not later than ninety days after the filing of an application for an order of approval under section 2518(7)(b) which is denied or the termination of the period of an order or extensions thereof, the issuing or denying judge shall cause to be served, on the persons named in the order or the application, and such other parties to intercepted communications as the judge may determine in his discretion that is in the interest of justice, an inventory which shall include notice of—

(1) the fact of the entry of the order or the application;

(2) the date of the entry and the period of authorized, approved or disapproved interception, or the denial of the application; and

(3) the fact that during the period wire, oral or electronic communications were or were not intercepted.

The judge, upon the filing of a motion, may in his discretion make available to such person or his counsel for inspection such portions of the intercepted communications, applications and orders as the judge determines to be in the interest of justice. On an ex parte showing of good cause to a judge of competent jurisdiction the serving of the inventory required by this subsection may be postponed.

(9) The contents of any wire, oral, or electronic communication intercepted pursuant to this chapter or evidence derived therefrom shall not be received in evidence or otherwise disclosed in any trial, hearing, or other proceeding in a Federal or State court unless each party, not less than ten days before the trial, hearing, or proceeding, has been furnished with a copy of the court order, and accompanying application, under which the interception was authorized or approved. This ten-day period may be waived by the judge if he finds that it was not possible to furnish the party with the above information ten days before the trial, hearing, or proceeding and that the party will not be prejudiced by the delay in receiving such information.

(10)(a) Any aggrieved person in any trial, hearing, or proceeding in or before any court, department, officer, agency, regulatory body, or other authority of the United States, a State, or a political subdivision thereof, may move to suppress the contents of any wire or oral communication intercepted pursuant to this chapter, or evidence derived therefrom, on the grounds that—

(i) the communication was unlawfully intercepted;

(ii) the order of authorization or approval under which it was intercepted is insufficient on its face; or

(iii) the interception was not made in conformity with the order of authorization or approval.

Such motion shall be made before the trial, hearing, or proceeding unless there was no opportunity to make such motion or the person was not aware of the grounds of the motion. If the motion is granted, the contents of the intercepted wire or oral communication, or evidence derived therefrom, shall be treated as having been obtained in violation of this chapter. The judge, upon the filing of such motion by the aggrieved person, may in his discretion make available to the aggrieved person or his counsel for inspection such portions of the intercepted communication or evidence derived therefrom as the judge determines to be in the interests of justice.

(b) In addition to any other right to appeal, the United States shall have the right to appeal from an order granting a motion to suppress made under paragraph (a) of this subsection, or the denial of an application for an order of approval, if the United States attorney shall certify to the judge or other official granting such motion or denying such application that the appeal is not taken for purposes of delay. Such appeal shall be taken within thirty days after the date the order was entered and shall be diligently prosecuted.

(c) The remedies and sanctions described in this chapter with respect to the interception of electronic communications are the only judicial remedies and sanctions for nonconstitutional violations of this chapter involving such communications.

(11) The requirements of subsections (1)(b)(ii) and (3)(d) of this section relating to the specification of the facilities from which, or the place where, the communication is to be intercepted do not apply if—

(a) in the case of an application with respect to the interception of an oral communication—

(i) the application is by a Federal investigative or law enforcement officer and is approved by the Attorney General, the Deputy Attorney General, the Associate Attorney General, an Assistant Attorney General, or an acting Assistant Attorney General;

(ii) the application contains a full and complete statement as to why such specification is not practical and identifies the person committing the offense and whose communications are to be intercepted; and

(iii) the judge finds that such specification is not practical; and

(b) in the case of an application with respect to a wire or electronic communication—

(i) the application is by a Federal investigative or law enforcement officer and is approved by the Attorney General, the Deputy Attorney General, the Associate Attorney General, an Assistant Attorney General, or an acting Assistant Attorney General;

(ii) the application identifies the person believed to be committing the offense and whose communications are to be intercepted and the applicant makes a showing of a purpose, on the part of that person, to thwart interception by changing facilities; and

(iii) the judge finds that such purpose has been adequately shown.

(12) An interception of a communication under an order with respect to which the requirements of subsections (1)(b)(ii) and (3)(d) of this section do not apply by reason of subsection (11) shall not begin until the facilities from which, or the place where, the communication is to be intercepted is ascertained by the person implementing the interception order. A provider of wire or electronic communications service that has received an order as provided for in subsection (11)(b) may move the court to modify or quash the order on the ground that its assistance with respect to the

interception cannot be performed in a timely or reasonable fashion. The court, upon notice to the government, shall decide such a motion expeditiously.

§ 2520. Recovery of civil damages authorized

(a) **In general.**—Except as provided in section 2511(2)(a)(ii), any person whose wire, oral, or electronic communication is intercepted, disclosed, or intentionally used in violation of this chapter may in a civil action recover from the person or entity which engaged in that violation such relief as may be appropriate.

(b) **Relief.**—In an action under this section, appropriate relief includes—

(1) such preliminary and other equitable or declaratory relief as may be appropriate;

(2) damages under subsection (c) and punitive damages in appropriate cases; and

(3) a reasonable attorney's fee and other litigation costs reasonably incurred.

(c) **Computation of damages.**—(1) In an action under this section, if the conduct in violation of this chapter is the private viewing of a private satellite video communication that is not scrambled or encrypted or if the communication is a radio communication that is transmitted on frequencies allocated under subpart D of part 74 of the rules of the Federal Communications Commission that is not scrambled or encrypted and the conduct is not for a tortious or illegal purpose or for purposes of direct or indirect commercial advantage or private commercial gain, then the court shall assess damages as follows:

(A) If the person who engaged in that conduct has not previously been enjoined under section 2511(5) and has not been found liable in a prior civil action under this section, the court shall assess the greater of the sum of actual damages suffered by the plaintiff, or statutory damages of not less than $50 and not more than $500.

(B) If, on one prior occasion, the person who engaged in that conduct has been enjoined under section 2511(5) or has been found liable in a civil action under this section, the court shall assess the greater of the sum of actual damages suffered by the plaintiff, or statutory damages of not less than $100 and not more than $1000.

(2) In any other action under this section, the court may assess as damages whichever is the greater of—

(A) the sum of the actual damages suffered by the plaintiff and any profits made by the violator as a result of the violation; or

(B) statutory damages of whichever is the greater of $100 a day for each day of violation or $10,000.

(d) **Defense.**—A good faith reliance on—

(1) a court warrant or order, a grand jury subpoena, a legislative authorization, or a statutory authorization;

(2) a request of an investigative or law enforcement officer under section 2518(7) of this title; or

(3) a good faith determination that section 2511(3) of this title permitted the conduct complained of;

is a complete defense against any civil or criminal action brought under this chapter or any other law.

(e) **Limitation.**—A civil action under this section may not be commenced later than two years after the date upon which the claimant first has a reasonable opportunity to discover the violation.

§ 2521. Injunction against illegal interception

Whenever it shall appear that any person is engaged or is about to engage in any act which constitutes or will constitute a felony violation of this chapter, the Attorney General may initiate a civil action in a district court of the United States to enjoin such violation. The court shall proceed as soon as practicable to the hearing and determination of such an action, and may, at any time before final determination, enter such a restraining order or prohibition, or take such other action, as is warranted to prevent a continuing and substantial injury to the United States or to any person or class of persons for whose protection the action is brought. A proceeding under this section is governed by the Federal Rules of Civil Procedure, except that, if an indictment has been returned against the respondent, discovery is governed by the Federal Rules of Criminal Procedure.

CRIMINAL JUSTICE ACT

(18 U.S.C. § 3006A).

§ 3006A. Adequate representation of defendants

(a) **Choice of plan.**—Each United States district court, with the approval of the judicial council of the circuit, shall place in operation throughout the district a plan for furnishing representation for any person financially unable to obtain adequate representation in accordance with this section. Representation under each plan shall include counsel and investigative, expert, and other services necessary for adequate representation. Each plan shall provide the following:

(1) Representation shall be provided for any financially eligible person who—

(A) is charged with a felony or a Class A misdemeanor;

(B) is a juvenile alleged to have committed an act of juvenile delinquency as defined in section 5031 of this title;

(C) is charged with a violation of probation;

(D) is under arrest, when such representation is required by law;

(E) is charged with a violation of supervised release or faces modification, reduction, or enlargement of a condition, or extension or revocation of a term of supervised release;

(F) is subject to a mental condition hearing under chapter 313 of this title;

(G) is in custody as a material witness;

(H) is entitled to appointment of counsel under the sixth amendment to the Constitution; or

(I) faces loss of liberty in a case, and Federal law requires the appointment of counsel; or

(J) is entitled to the appointment of counsel under section 4019 of this title.

(2) Whenever the United States magistrate or the court determines that the interests of justice so require, representation may be provided for any financially eligible person who—

(A) is charged with a Class B or C misdemeanor, or an infraction for which a sentence to confinement is authorized; or

(B) is seeking relief under section 2241, 2254, or 2255 of title 28.

(3) Private attorneys shall be appointed in a substantial proportion of the cases. Each plan may include, in addition to the provisions for private attorneys, either of the following or both:

(A) Attorneys furnished by a bar association or a legal aid agency.

(B) Attorneys furnished by a defender organization established in accordance with the provisions of subsection (g).

Prior to approving the plan for a district, the judicial council of the circuit shall supplement the plan with provisions for representation on appeal. The district court may modify the plan at any time with the approval of the judicial council of the circuit. It shall modify the plan when directed by the judicial council of the circuit. The district court shall notify the Administrative Office of the United States Courts of any modification of its plan.

(b) Appointment of counsel.—Counsel furnishing representation under the plan shall be selected from a panel of attorneys designated or approved by the court, or from a bar association, legal aid agency, or defender organization furnishing representation pursuant to the plan. In every case in which a person entitled to representation under a plan approved under subsection (a) appears without counsel, the United States magistrate or the court shall advise the person that he has the right to be represented by counsel and that counsel will be appointed to represent him if he is financially unable to obtain counsel. Unless the person waives representation by counsel, the United States magistrate or the court, if satisfied after appropriate inquiry that the person is financially unable to obtain counsel, shall appoint counsel to represent him. Such appointment may be made retroactive to include any representation furnished pursuant to the plan prior to appointment. The United States magistrate or the court shall appoint separate counsel for persons having interests that cannot properly be represented by the same counsel, or when other good cause is shown.

(c) Duration and substitution of appointments.—A person for whom counsel is appointed shall be represented at every stage of the proceedings from his initial appearance before the United States magistrate or the court through appeal, including ancillary matters appropriate to the proceedings. If at any time after the appointment of counsel the United States magistrate or the court finds that the person is financially able to obtain counsel or to make partial payment for the representation, it may terminate the appointment of counsel or authorize payment as provided in subsection (f), as the interests of justice may dictate. If at any stage of the proceedings, including an appeal, the United States magistrate or the court finds that the person is financially unable to pay counsel whom he had retained, it may appoint counsel as provided in subsection (b) and authorize payment as provided in subsection (d), as the interests of justice may dictate. The United States magistrate or the court may, in the interests of justice, substitute one appointed counsel for another at any stage of the proceedings.

(d) Payment for representation.—

(1) Hourly rate.—Any attorney appointed pursuant to this section or a bar association or legal aid agency or community defender organization which has provided the appointed attorney shall, at the conclusion of the representation or any segment thereof, be compensated at a rate not exceeding $60 per hour for time expended in court or before a United States magistrate and $40 per hour for time reasonably expended out of court, unless the Judicial Conference determines that a higher rate of not in excess of $75 per hour is justified for a circuit or for particular districts within a circuit, for time expended in court or before a United States magistrate and for time expended out of court. The Judicial Conference shall develop guidelines for determining the maximum hourly rates for each circuit in accordance with the preceding sentence, with variations by district, where appropriate, taking into account such factors as the minimum range of the prevailing hourly rates for qualified attorneys in the district in which the representation is provided and the recommendations of the judicial councils of the circuits. Not less than 3 years after the effective date of the Criminal Justice Act Revision of 1986, the

Judicial Conference is authorized to raise the maximum hourly rates specified in this paragraph up to the aggregate of the overall average percentages of the adjustments in the rates of pay under the General Schedule made pursuant to section 5305 of title 5 on or after such effective date. After the rates are raised under the preceding sentence, such maximum hourly rates may be raised at intervals of not less than 1 year each, up to the aggregate of the overall average percentages of such adjustments made since the last raise was made under this paragraph. Attorneys shall be reimbursed for expenses reasonably incurred, including the costs of transcripts authorized by the United States magistrate or the court.

(2) **Maximum amounts.**—For representation of a defendant before the United States magistrate or the district court, or both, the compensation to be paid to an attorney or to a bar association or legal aid agency or community defender organization shall not exceed $3,500 for each attorney in a case in which one or more felonies are charged, and $1,000 for each attorney in a case in which only misdemeanors are charged. For representation of a defendant in an appellate court, the compensation to be paid to an attorney or to a bar association or legal aid agency or community defender organization shall not exceed $2,500 for each attorney in each court. For representation of an offender before the United States Parole Commission in a proceeding under section 4106A of this title, the compensation shall not exceed $750 for each attorney in each proceeding; for representation of an offender in an appeal from a determination of such Commission under such section, the compensation shall not exceed 2,500 for each attorney in each court. For any other representation required or authorized by this section, the compensation shall not exceed $750 for each attorney in each proceeding.

(3) **Waiving maximum amounts.**—Payment in excess of any maximum amount provided in paragraph (2) of this subsection may be made for extended or complex representation whenever the court in which the representation was rendered, or the United States magistrate if the representation was furnished exclusively before him, certifies that the amount of the excess payment is necessary to provide fair compensation and the payment is approved by the chief judge of the circuit. The chief judge of the circuit may delegate such approval authority to an active circuit judge.

(4) **Filing claims.**—A separate claim for compensation and reimbursement shall be made to the district court for representation before the United States magistrate and the court, and to each appellate court before which the attorney provided representation to the person involved. Each claim shall be supported by a sworn written statement specifying the time expended, services rendered, and expenses incurred while the case was pending before the United States magistrate and the court, and the compensation and reimbursement applied for or received in the same case from any other source. The court shall fix the compensation and reimbursement to be paid to the attorney or to the bar association or legal aid agency or community defender organization which provided the appointed attorney. In cases where representation is furnished exclusively before a United States magistrate, the claim shall be submitted to him and he shall fix the compensation and reimbursement to be paid. In cases where representation is furnished other than before the United States magistrate, the district court, or an appellate court, claims shall be submitted to the district court which shall fix the compensation and reimbursement to be paid.

(5) **New trials.**—For purposes of compensation and other payments authorized by this section, an order by a court granting a new trial shall be deemed to initiate a new case.

(6) **Proceedings before appellate courts.**—If a person for whom counsel is appointed under this section appeals to an appellate court or petitions for a writ of

certiorari, he may do so without prepayment of fees and costs or security therefor and without filing the affidavit required by section 1915(a) of title 28.

(e) Services other than counsel.—

(1) Upon request.—Counsel for a person who is financially unable to obtain investigative, expert, or other services necessary for an adequate representation may request them in an ex parte application. Upon finding, after appropriate inquiry in an ex parte proceeding, that the services are necessary and that the person is financially unable to obtain them, the court, or the United States magistrate if the services are required in connection with a matter over which he has jurisdiction, shall authorize counsel to obtain the services.

(2) Without prior request.—(A) Counsel appointed under this section may obtain, subject to later review, investigative, expert, and other services without prior authorization if necessary for adequate representation. Except as provided in subparagraph (B) of this paragraph, the total cost of services obtained without prior authorization may not exceed $300 and expenses reasonably incurred.

(B) The court, or the United States magistrate (if the services were rendered in a case disposed of entirely before the United States magistrate), may, in the interest of justice, and upon the finding that timely procurement of necessary services could not await prior authorization, approve payment for such services after they have been obtained, even if the cost of such services exceeds $300.

(3) Maximum amounts.—Compensation to be paid to a person for services rendered by him to a person under this subsection, or to be paid to an organization for services rendered by an employee thereof, shall not exceed $1,000, exclusive of reimbursement for expenses reasonably incurred, unless payment in excess of that limit is certified by the court, or by the United States magistrate if the services were rendered in connection with a case disposed of entirely before him, as necessary to provide fair compensation for services of an unusual character or duration, and the amount of the excess payment is approved by the chief judge of the circuit. The chief judge of the circuit may delegate such approval authority to an active circuit judge.

(f) Receipt of other payments.—Whenever the United States magistrate or the court finds that funds are available for payment from or on behalf of a person furnished representation, it may authorize or direct that such funds be paid to the appointed attorney, to the bar association or legal aid agency or community defender organization which provided the appointed attorney, to any person or organization authorized pursuant to subsection (e) to render investigative, expert, or other services, or to the court for deposit in the Treasury as a reimbursement to the appropriation, current at the time of payment, to carry out the provisions of this section. Except as so authorized or directed, no such person or organization may request or accept any payment or promise of payment for representing a defendant.

(g) Defender organization.—

(1) Qualifications.—A district or a part of a district in which at least two hundred persons annually require the appointment of counsel may establish a defender organization as provided for either under subparagraphs (A) or (B) of paragraph (2) of this subsection or both. Two adjacent districts or parts of districts may aggregate the number of persons required to be represented to establish eligibility for a defender organization to serve both areas. In the event that adjacent districts or parts of districts are located in different circuits, the plan for furnishing representation shall be approved by the judicial council of each circuit.

(2) Types of defender organizations.—

(A) Federal Public Defender Organization.—A Federal Public Defender Organization shall consist of one or more full-time salaried attorneys. An organization for a district or part of a district or two adjacent districts or parts of districts shall be supervised by a Federal Public Defender appointed by the court of appeals of the circuit, without regard to the provisions of title 5 governing appointments in the competitive service, after considering recommendations from the district court or courts to be served. Nothing contained herein shall be deemed to authorize more than one Federal Public Defender within a single judicial district. The Federal Public Defender shall be appointed for a term of four years, unless sooner removed by the court of appeals of the circuit for incompetency, misconduct in office, or neglect of duty. Upon the expiration of his term, a Federal Public Defender may, by a majority vote of the judges of the court of appeals, continue to perform the duties of his office until his successor is appointed, or until one year after the expiration of such Defender's term, whichever is earlier. The compensation of the Federal Public Defender shall be fixed by the court of appeals of the circuit at a rate not to exceed the compensation received by the United States attorney for the district where representation is furnished or, if two districts or parts of districts are involved, the compensation of the higher paid United States attorney of the districts. The Federal Public Defender may appoint, without regard to the provisions of title 5 governing appointments in the competitive service, full-time attorneys in such number as may be approved by the court of appeals of the circuit and other personnel in such number as may be approved by the Director of the Administrative Office of the United States Courts. Compensation paid to such attorneys and other personnel of the organization shall be fixed by the Federal Public Defender at a rate not to exceed that paid to attorneys and other personnel of similar qualifications and experience in the Office of the United States attorney in the district where representation is furnished or, if two districts or parts of districts are involved, the higher compensation paid to persons of similar qualifications and experience in the districts. Neither the Federal Public Defender nor any attorney so appointed by him may engage in the private practice of law. Each organization shall submit to the Director of the Administrative Office of the United States Courts, at the time and in the form prescribed by him, reports of its activities and financial position and its proposed budget. The Director of the Administrative Office shall submit, in accordance with section 605 of title 28, a budget for each organization for each fiscal year and shall out of the appropriations therefor make payments to and on behalf of each organization. Payments under this subparagraph to an organization shall be in lieu of payments under subsection (d) or (e).

(B) Community Defender Organization.—A Community Defender Organization shall be a nonprofit defense counsel service established and administered by any group authorized by the plan to provide representation. The organization shall be eligible to furnish attorneys and receive payments under this section if its bylaws are set forth in the plan of the district or districts in which it will serve. Each organization shall submit to the Judicial Conference of the United States an annual report setting forth its activities and financial position and the anticipated caseload and expenses for the next fiscal year. Upon application an organization may, to the extent approved by the Judicial Conference of the United States:

(i) receive an initial grant for expenses necessary to establish the organization; and

(ii) in lieu of payments under subsection (d) or (e), receive periodic sustaining grants to provide representation and other expenses pursuant to this section.

* * *

BAIL REFORM ACT OF 1984

(18 U.S.C. §§ 3141–3150).

§ 3141. Release and detention authority generally

(a) **Pending Trial.**—A judicial officer authorized to order the arrest of a person under section 3041 of this title before whom an arrested person is brought shall order that such person be released or detained, pending judicial proceedings, under this chapter.

(b) **Pending sentence or appeal.**—A judicial officer of a court of original jurisdiction over an offense, or a judicial officer of a Federal appellate court, shall order that, pending imposition or execution of sentence, or pending appeal of conviction or sentence, a person be released or detained under this chapter.

§ 3142. Release or detention of a defendant pending trial

(a) **In general.**—Upon the appearance before a judicial officer of a person charged with an offense, the judicial officer shall issue an order that, pending trial, the person be—

(1) released on his personal recognizance or upon execution of an unsecured appearance bond, under subsection (b) of this section;

(2) released on a condition or combination of conditions under subsection (c) of this section;

(3) temporarily detained to permit revocation of conditional release, deportation, or exclusion under subsection (d) of this section; or

(4) detained under subsection (e) of this section.

(b) **Release on personal recognizance or unsecured appearance bond.**—The judicial officer shall order the pretrial release of the person on personal recognizance, or upon execution of an unsecured appearance bond in an amount specified by the court, subject to the condition that the person not commit a Federal, State, or local crime during the period of release, unless the judicial officer determines that such release will not reasonably assure the appearance of the person as required or will endanger the safety of any other person or the community.

(c) **Release on conditions.**—(1) If the judicial officer determines that the release described in subsection (b) of this section will not reasonably assure the appearance of the person as required or will endanger the safety of any other person or the community, such judicial officer shall order the pretrial release of the person—

(A) subject to the condition that the person not commit a Federal, State, or local crime during the period of release; and

(B) subject to the least restrictive further condition, or combination of conditions, that such judicial officer determines will reasonably assure the appearance of the person as required and the safety of any other person and the community, which may include the condition that the person—

(i) remain in the custody of a designated person, who agrees to assume supervision and to report any violation of a release condition to the court, if the designated person is able reasonably to assure the judicial officer that the person will appear as required and will not pose a danger to the safety of any other person or the community;

(ii) maintain employment, or, if unemployed, actively seek employment;

(iii) maintain or commence an educational program;

(iv) abide by specified restrictions on personal associations, place of abode, or travel;

(v) avoid all contact with an alleged victim of the crime and with a potential witness who may testify concerning the offense;

(vi) report on a regular basis to a designated law enforcement agency, pretrial services agency, or other agency;

(vii) comply with a specified curfew;

(viii) refrain from possessing a firearm, destructive device, or other dangerous weapon;

(ix) refrain from excessive use of alcohol, or any use of a narcotic drug or other controlled substance, as defined in section 102 of the Controlled Substances Act (21 U.S.C. 802), without a prescription by a licensed medical practitioner;

(x) undergo available medical or psychiatric treatment, including treatment for drug or alcohol dependency, and remain in a specified institution if required for that purpose;

(xi) execute an agreement to forfeit upon failing to appear as required, such designated property, including money, as is reasonably necessary to assure the appearance of the person as required, and post with the court such indicia of ownership of the property or such percentage of the money as the judicial officer may specify;

(xii) execute a bail bond with solvent sureties in such amount as is reasonably necessary to assure the appearance of the person as required;

(xiii) return to custody for specified hours following release for employment, schooling, or other limited purposes; and

(xiv) satisfy any other condition that is reasonably necessary to assure the appearance of the person as required and to assure the safety of any other person and the community.

(2) The judicial officer may not impose a financial condition that results in the pretrial detention of the person.

(3) The judicial officer may at any time amend the order to impose additional or different conditions of release.

(d) Temporary detention to permit revocation of conditional release, deportation, or exclusion.—If the judicial officer determines that—

(1) the person—

(A) is, and was at the time the offense was committed, on—

(i) release pending trial for a felony under Federal, State, or local law;

(ii) release pending imposition or execution of sentence, appeal of sentence or conviction, or completion of sentence, for any offense under Federal, State, or local law; or

(iii) probation or parole for any offense under Federal, State, or local law; or

(B) is not a citizen of the United States or lawfully admitted for permanent residence, as defined in section 101(a)(20) of the Immigration and Nationality Act (8 U.S.C. 1101(a)(20)); and

(2) the person may flee or pose a danger to any other person or the community;

such judicial officer shall order the detention of the person, for a period of not more than ten days, excluding Saturdays, Sundays, and holidays, and direct the attorney for the Government to notify the appropriate court, probation or parole official, or State or local law enforcement official, or the appropriate official of the Immigration and Naturalization Service. If the official fails or declines to take the person into custody during that period, the person shall be treated in accordance with the other provisions of this section, notwithstanding the applicability of other provisions of law governing release pending trial or deportation or exclusion proceedings. If temporary detention is sought under paragraph (1)(B) of this subsection, the person has the burden of proving to the court such person's United States citizenship or lawful admission for permanent residence.

(e) Detention.—If, after a hearing pursuant to the provisions of subsection (f) of this section, the judicial officer finds that no condition or combination of conditions will reasonably assure the appearance of the person as required and the safety of any other person and the community, such judicial officer shall order the detention of the person before trial. In a case described in (f)(1) of this section, a rebuttable presumption arises that no condition or combination of conditions will reasonably assure the safety of any other person and the community if such judicial officer finds that—

    (1) the person has been convicted of a Federal offense that is described in subsection (f)(1) of this section, or of a State or local offense that would have been an offense described in subsection (f)(1) of this section if a circumstance giving rise to Federal jurisdiction had existed;

    (2) the offense described in paragraph (1) of this subsection was committed while the person was on release pending trial for a Federal, State, or local offense; and

    (3) a period of not more than five years has elapsed since the date of conviction, or the release of the person from imprisonment, for the offense described in paragraph (1) of this subsection, whichever is later.

Subject to rebuttal by the person, it shall be presumed that no condition or combination of conditions will reasonably assure the appearance of the person as required and the safety of the community if the judicial officer finds that there is probable cause to believe that the person committed an offense for which a maximum term of imprisonment of ten years or more is prescribed in the Controlled Substances Act (21 U.S.C. 801 et seq.), the Controlled Substances Import and Export Act (21 U.S.C. 951 et seq.), section 1 of the Act of September 15, 1980 (21 U.S.C. 955a), or an offense under section 924(c) of title 18 of the United States Code.

(f) Detention hearing.—The judicial officer shall hold a hearing to determine whether any condition or combination of conditions set forth in subsection (c) of this section will reasonably assure the appearance of the person as required and the safety of any other person and the community in a case—

    (1) upon motion of the attorney for the Government, that involves—

        (A) a crime of violence;*

        (B) an offense for which the maximum sentence is life imprisonment or death;

        (C) an offense for which a maximum term of imprisonment of ten years or more is prescribed in the Controlled Substances Act (21 U.S.C. 801 et seq.), the Controlled Substances Import and Export Act (21 U.S.C. 951 et seq.), or section 1 of the Act of September 15, 1980 (21 U.S.C. 955a); or

        (D) any felony if the person had been convicted of two or more prior offenses described in subparagraphs (A) through (C) of this paragraph, or two or more State or local offenses that would have been offenses described in subparagraphs (A) through (C) of this paragraph if a circumstance giving rise to Federal jurisdiction had existed or a combination of such offenses; or

---

* The phrase "crime of violence" is defined in 18 U.S.C. § 3156(a)(4) as meaning: "(A) an offense that has an element of the offense the use, attempted use, or threatened use of physical force against the person or property of another, or (B) any other offense that is a felony and that, by its nature, involves a substantial risk that physical force against the person or property of another may be used in the course of committing the offense."

(2) upon motion of the attorney for the Government or upon the judicial officer's own motion in a case, that involves—

(A) a serious risk that such person will flee;

(B) a serious risk that the person will obstruct or attempt to obstruct justice, or threaten, injure, or intimidate, or attempt to threaten, injure, or intimidate, a prospective witness or juror.

The hearing shall be held immediately upon the person's first appearance before the judicial officer unless that person, or the attorney for the Government, seeks a continuance. Except for good cause, a continuance on motion of the person may not exceed five days, and a continuance on motion of the attorney for the Government may not exceed three days. During a continuance, the person shall be detained, and the judicial officer, on motion of the attorney for the Government or sua sponte, may order that, while in custody, a person who appears to be a narcotics addict receive a medical examination to determine whether such person is an addict. At the hearing, the person has the right to be represented by counsel, and, if financially unable to obtain adequate representation, to have counsel appointed. The person shall be afforded an opportunity to testify, to present witnesses, to cross-examine witnesses who appear at the hearing, and to present information by proffer or otherwise. The rules concerning admissibility of evidence in criminal trials do not apply to the presentation and consideration of information at the hearing. The facts the judicial officer uses to support a finding pursuant to subsection (e) that no condition or combination of conditions will reasonably assure the safety of any other person and the community shall be supported by clear and convincing evidence. The person may be detained pending completion of the hearing. The hearing may be reopened before or after a determination by the judicial officer, at any time before trial if the judicial officer finds that information exists that was not known to the movant at the time of the hearing and that has a material bearing on the issue of whether there are conditions of release that will reasonably assure the appearance of the person as required and the safety of any other person and the community.

(g) **Factors to be considered.**—The judicial officer shall, in determining whether there are conditions of release that will reasonably assure the appearance of the person as required and the safety of any other person and the community, take into account the available information concerning—

(1) the nature and circumstances of the offense charged, including whether the offense is a crime of violence or involves a narcotic drug;

(2) the weight of the evidence against the person;

(3) the history and characteristics of the person, including—

(A) the person's character, physical and mental condition, family ties, employment, financial resources, length of residence in the community, community ties, past conduct, history relating to drug or alcohol abuse, criminal history, and record concerning appearance at court proceedings; and

(B) whether, at the time of the current offense or arrest, the person was on probation, on parole, or on other release pending trial, sentencing, appeal, or completion of sentence for an offense under Federal, State, or local law; and

(4) the nature and seriousness of the danger to any person or the community that would be posed by the person's release. In considering the conditions of release described in subsection (c)(2)(K) or (c)(2)(L) [eds. note: intended references are to what is now subsection (c)(1)(B)(xi) or (c)(1)(B)(xii)], the judicial officer may upon his own motion, or shall upon the motion of the Government, conduct an inquiry into the source of the property to be designated for potential forfeiture or offered as collateral to secure a bond, and shall decline to accept the designation, or

the use as collateral, of property that, because of its source, will not reasonably assure the appearance of the person as required.

(h) Contents of release order.—In a release order issued under subsection (b) or (c) of this section, the judicial officer shall—

(1) include a written statement that sets forth all the conditions to which the release is subject, in a manner sufficiently clear and specific to serve as a guide for the person's conduct; and

(2) advise the person of—

(A) the penalties for violating a condition of release, including the penalties for committing an offense while on pretrial release;

(B) the consequences of violating a condition of release, including the immediate issuance of a warrant for the person's arrest; and

(C) the provisions of sections 1503 of this title (relating to intimidation of witnesses, jurors, and officers of the court), 1510 (relating to obstruction of criminal investigations), 1512 (tampering with a witness, victim, or an informant), and 1513 (retaliating against a witness, victim, or an informant).

(i) Contents of detention order.—In a detention order issued under subsection (e) of this section, the judicial officer shall—

(1) include written findings of fact and a written statement of the reasons for the detention;

(2) direct that the person be committed to the custody of the Attorney General for confinement in a corrections facility separate, to the extent practicable, from persons awaiting or serving sentences or being held in custody pending appeal;

(3) direct that the person be afforded reasonable opportunity for private consultation with counsel; and

(4) direct that, on order of a court of the United States or on request of an attorney for the Government, the person in charge of the corrections facility in which the person is confined deliver the person to a United States marshal for the purpose of an appearance in connection with a court proceeding.

The judicial officer may, by subsequent order, permit the temporary release of the person, in the custody of a United States marshal or another appropriate person, to the extent that the judicial officer determines such release to be necessary for preparation of the person's defense or for another compelling reason.

(j) Presumption of innocence.—Nothing in this section shall be construed as modifying or limiting the presumption of innocence.

§ 3143. Release or detention of a defendant pending sentence or appeal

(a) Release or detention pending sentence.—The judicial officer shall order that a person who has been found guilty of an offense and who is waiting imposition or execution of sentence, be detained, unless the judicial officer finds by clear and convincing evidence that the person is not likely to flee or pose a danger to the safety of any other person or the community if release pursuant to section 3142(b) or (c). If the judicial officer makes such a finding, such judicial officer shall order the release of the person in accordance with the provisions of section 3142(b) or (c).

(b) Release of detention pending appeal by the defendant.—The judicial officer shall order that a person who has been found guilty of an offense and sentenced to a term of imprisonment, and who has filed an appeal or a petition for a writ of certiorari, be detained, unless the judicial officer finds—

(1) by clear and convincing evidence that the person is not likely to flee or pose a danger to the safety of any other person or the community if released under section 3142(b) or (c) of this title; and

(2) that the appeal is not for the purpose of delay and raises a substantial question of law or fact likely to result in—

(A) reversal,

(B) an order for a new trial,

(C) a sentence that does not include a term of imprisonment, or

(D) a reduced sentence to a term of imprisonment less than the total of the time already served plus the expected duration of the appeal process.

If the judicial officer makes such findings, such judicial officer shall order the release of the person in accordance with the provisions of section 3142(b) or (c) of this title, except that in the circumstance described in paragraph (b)(2)(D), the judicial officer shall order the detention terminated at the expiration of the likely reduced sentence.

(c) **Release or detention pending appeal by the government.**—The judicial officer shall treat a defendant in a case in which an appeal has been taken by the United States under section 3731 of this title, in accordance with the provisions of section 3142 of this title, unless the defendant is otherwise subject to a release or detention order.

§ 3144. Release or detention of a material witness

If it appears from an affidavit filed by a party that the testimony of a person is material in a criminal proceeding, and if it is shown that it may become impracticable to secure the presence of the person by subpena, a judicial officer may order the arrest of the person and treat the person in accordance with the provisions of section 3142 of this title. No material witness may be detained because of inability to comply with any condition of release if the testimony of such witness can adequately be secured by deposition, and if further detention is not necessary to prevent a failure of justice. Release of a material witness may be delayed for a reasonable period of time until the deposition of the witness can be taken pursuant to the Federal Rules of Criminal Procedure.

§ 3145. Review and appeal of a release or detention order

(a) **Review of a release order.**—If a person is ordered released by a magistrate, or by a person other than a judge of a court having original jurisdiction over the offense and other than a Federal appellate court—

(1) the attorney for the Government may file, with the court having original jurisdiction over the offense, a motion for revocation of the order or amendment of the conditions of release; and

(2) the person may file, with the court having original jurisdiction over the offense, a motion for amendment of the conditions of release.

The motion shall be determined promptly.

(b) **Review of a detention order.**—If a person is ordered detained by a magistrate, or by a person other than a judge of a court having original jurisdiction over the offense and other than a Federal appellate court, the person may file, with the court having original jurisdiction over the offense, a motion for revocation or amendment of the order. The motion shall be determined promptly.

(c) **Appeal from a release or detention order.**—An appeal from a release or detention order, or from a decision denying revocation or amendment of such an order, is governed by the provisions of section 1291 of title 28 and section 3731 of this title. The appeal shall be determined promptly. A person subject to detention pursuant to section 3143(a)(2) or (b)(2), and who meets the conditions of release set forth in section 3143(a)(1) or (b)(1), may be ordered released, under appropriate conditions, by the judicial officer, if it is clearly shown that there are exceptional reasons why such person's detention would not be appropriate.

§ 3146. Penalty for failure to appear

(a) **Offense.**—Whoever, having been released under this chapter knowingly—

(1) fails to appear before a court as required by the conditions of his release; or

(2) fails to surrender for service of sentence pursuant to a court order; shall be punished as provided in subsection (b) of this section.

(b) **Punishment.**—(1) The punishment for an offense under this section is—

(A) if the person was released in connection with a charge of, or while awaiting sentence, surrender for service of sentence, or appeal or certiorari after conviction, for—

(i) an offense punishable by death, life imprisonment, or imprisonment for a term of 15 years or more, a fine under this title or imprisonment for not more than ten years, or both;

(ii) an offense punishable by imprisonment for a term of five years or more, a fine under this title or imprisonment for not more than five years, or both;

(iii) any other felony, a fine under this title or imprisonment for not more than two years, or both; or

(iv) a misdemeanor, a fine under this chapter or imprisonment for not more than one year, or both; and

(B) if the person was released for appearance as a material witness, a fine under this chapter or imprisonment for not more than one year, or both.

(2) A term of imprisonment imposed under this section shall be consecutive to the sentence of imprisonment for any other offense.

(c) **Affirmative defense.**—It is an affirmative defense to a prosecution under this section that uncontrollable circumstances prevented the person from appearing or surrendering, and that the person did not contribute to the creation of such circumstances in reckless disregard of the requirement that he appear or surrender, and that the person appeared or surrendered as soon as such circumstances ceased to exist.

(d) **Declaration of forfeiture.**—If a person fails to appear before a court as required, and the person executed an appearance bond pursuant to section 3142(b) of this title or is subject to the release condition set forth in clause (xi) or (xii) of section 3142(c)(1)(B) of this title, the judicial officer may, regardless of whether the person has been charged with an offense under this section, declare any property designated pursuant to that section to be forfeited to the United States.

§ 3147. Penalty for an offense committed while on release

A person convicted of an offense committed while released under this chapter shall be sentenced, in addition to the sentence prescribed for the offense to—

(1) a term of imprisonment of not less than two years and not more than ten years if the offense is a felony; or

(2) a term of imprisonment of not less than ninety days and not more than one year if the offense is a misdemeanor.

A term of imprisonment imposed under this section shall be consecutive to any other sentence of imprisonment.

§ 3148. Sanctions for violation of a release condition

(a) Available sanctions.—A person who has been released under section 3142 of this title, and who has violated a condition of his release, is subject to a revocation of release, an order of detention, and a prosecution for contempt of court.

(b) Revocation of release.—The attorney for the Government may initiate a proceeding for revocation of an order of release by filing a motion with the district court. A judicial officer may issue a warrant for the arrest of a person charged with violating a condition of release, and the person shall be brought before a judicial officer in the district in which such person's arrest was ordered for a proceeding in accordance with this section. To the extent practicable, a person charged with violating the condition of release that such person not commit a Federal, State, or local crime during the period of release shall be brought before the judicial officer who ordered the release and whose order is alleged to have been violated. The judicial officer shall enter an order of revocation and detention if, after a hearing, the judicial officer—

(1) finds that there is—

(A) probable cause to believe that the person has committed a Federal, State, or local crime while on release; or

(B) clear and convincing evidence that the person has violated any other condition of his release; and

(2) finds that—

(A) based on the factors set forth in section 3142(g) of this title, there is no condition or combination of conditions of release that will assure that the person will not flee or pose a danger to the safety of any other person or the community; or

(B) the person is unlikely to abide by any condition or combination of conditions of release.

If there is probable cause to believe that, while on release, the person committed a Federal, State, or local felony, a rebuttable presumption arises that no condition or combination of conditions will assure that the person will not pose a danger to the safety of any other person or the community. If the judicial officer finds that there are conditions of release that will assure that the person will not flee or pose a danger to the safety of any other person or the community, and that the person will abide by such conditions, the judicial officer shall treat the person in accordance with the provisions of section 3142 of this title and may amend the conditions of release accordingly.

(c) Prosecution for contempt.—The judge may commence a prosecution for contempt, pursuant to the provisions of section 401 of this title, if the person has violated a condition of release.

§ 3149. Surrender of an offender by a surety

A person charged with an offense, who is released upon the execution of an appearance bond with a surety, may be arrested by the surety, and if so arrested, shall be delivered promptly to a United States marshal and brought before a judicial officer. The judicial officer shall determine in accordance with the provisions of section 3148(b) whether to revoke the release of the person, and may absolve the surety of responsibility to pay all or part of the bond in accordance with the provisions of Rule 46 of the Federal Rules of Criminal Procedure. The person so committed shall be held in official detention until released pursuant to this chapter or another provision of law.

§ 3150. Applicability to a case removed from a State court

The provisions of this chapter apply to a criminal case removed to a Federal court from a State court.

SPEEDY TRIAL ACT OF 1974 (AS AMENDED)

(18 U.S.C. §§ 3161–3162, 3164).

§ 3161. Time limits and exclusions

(a) In any case involving a defendant charged with an offense, the appropriate judicial officer, at the earliest practicable time, shall, after consultation with the counsel for the defendant and the attorney for the Government, set the case for trial on a day certain, or list it for trial on a weekly or other short-term trial calendar at a place within the judicial district, so as to assure a speedy trial.

(b) Any information or indictment charging an individual with the commission of an offense shall be filed within thirty days from the date on which such individual was arrested or served with a summons in connection with such charges. If an individual has been charged with a felony in a district in which no grand jury has been in session during such thirty-day period, the period of time for filing of the indictment shall be extended an additional thirty days.

(c) (1) In any case in which a plea of not guilty is entered, the trial of a defendant charged in an information or indictment with the commission of an offense shall commence within seventy days from the filing date (and making public) of the information or indictment, or from the date the defendant has appeared before a judicial officer of the court in which such charge is pending, whichever date last occurs. If a defendant consents in writing to be tried before a magistrate on a complaint, the trial shall commence within seventy days from the date of such consent.

(2) Unless the defendant consents in writing to the contrary, the trial shall not commence less than thirty days from the date on which the defendant first appears through counsel or expressly waives counsel and elects to proceed pro se.

(d) (1) If any indictment or information is dismissed upon motion of the defendant, or any charge contained in a complaint filed against an individual is dismissed or otherwise dropped, and thereafter a complaint is filed against such defendant or individual charging him with the same offense or an offense based on the same conduct or arising from the same criminal episode, or an information or indictment is filed charging such defendant with the same offense or an offense based on the same conduct or arising from the same criminal episode, the provisions of subsections (b) and (c) of this section shall be applicable with respect to such subsequent complaint, indictment, or information, as the case may be.

(2) If the defendant is to be tried upon an indictment or information dismissed by a trial court and reinstated following an appeal, the trial shall commence within seventy days from the date the action occasioning the trial becomes final, except that the court retrying the case may extend the period for trial not to exceed one hundred and eighty days from the date the action occasioning the trial becomes final if the unavailability of witnesses or other factors resulting from the passage of time shall make trial within seventy days impractical. The periods of delay enumerated in section 3161(h) are excluded in computing the time limitations specified in this section. The sanctions of section 3162 apply to this subsection.

(e) If the defendant is to be tried again following a declaration by the trial judge of a mistrial or following an order of such judge for a new trial, the trial shall commence within seventy days from the date the action occasioning the retrial becomes final. If the defendant is to be tried again following an appeal or a collateral attack, the trial shall commence within seventy days from the date the action occasioning the retrial becomes final, except that the court retrying the case may extend the period for retrial not to exceed one hundred and eighty days from the date the action occasioning the retrial becomes final if unavailability of witnesses or other factors resulting from passage of time shall make trial within seventy days impractical. The periods of delay enumerated in section 3161(h) are excluded in computing the time limitations specified in this section. The sanctions of section 3162 apply to this subsection. ∗ ∗ ∗

(h) The following periods of delay shall be excluded in computing the time within which an information or an indictment must be filed, or in computing the time within which the trial of any such offense must commence:

(1) Any period of delay resulting from other proceedings concerning the defendant, including but not limited to—

(A) delay resulting from any proceeding, including any examinations, to determine the mental competency or physical capacity of the defendant;

(B) delay resulting from any proceeding, including any examination of the defendant, pursuant to section 2902 of title 28, United States Code;

(C) delay resulting from deferral of prosecution pursuant to section 2902 of title 28, United States Code;

(D) delay resulting from trial with respect to other charges against the defendant;

(E) delay resulting from any interlocutory appeal;

(F) delay resulting from any pretrial motion, from the filing of the motion through the conclusion of the hearing on, or other prompt disposition of, such motion;

(G) delay resulting from any proceeding relating to the transfer of a case or the removal of any defendant from another district under the Federal Rules of Criminal Procedure;

(H) delay resulting from transportation of any defendant from another district, or to and from places of examination or hospitalization, except that any time consumed in excess of ten days from the date an order of removal or an order directing such transportation, and the defendant's arrival at the destination shall be presumed to be unreasonable;

(I) delay resulting from consideration by the court of a proposed plea agreement to be entered into by the defendant and the attorney for the Government; and

(J) delay reasonably attributable to any period, not to exceed thirty days, during which any proceeding concerning the defendant is actually under advisement by the court.

(2) Any period of delay during which prosecution is deferred by the attorney for the Government pursuant to written agreement with the defendant, with the approval of the court, for the purpose of allowing the defendant to demonstrate his good conduct.

(3) (A) Any period of delay resulting from the absence or unavailability of the defendant or an essential witness.

(B) For purposes of subparagraph (A) of this paragraph, a defendant or an essential witness shall be considered absent when his whereabouts are unknown and, in addition, he is attempting to avoid apprehension or prosecution or his whereabouts cannot be determined by due diligence. For purposes of such subparagraph, a defendant or an essential witness shall be considered unavailable whenever his whereabouts are known but his presence for trial cannot be obtained by due diligence or he resists appearing at or being returned for trial.

(4) Any period of delay resulting from the fact that the defendant is mentally incompetent or physically unable to stand trial.

(5) Any period of delay resulting from the treatment of the defendant pursuant to section 2902 of title 28, United States Code.

(6) If the information or indictment is dismissed upon motion of the attorney for the Government and thereafter a charge is filed against the defendant for the same offense, or any offense required to be joined with that offense, any period of delay from the date the charge was dismissed to the date the time limitation would commence to run as to the subsequent charge had there been no previous charge.

(7) A reasonable period of delay when the defendant is joined for trial with a codefendant as to whom the time for trial has not run and no motion for severance has been granted.

(8) (A) Any period of delay resulting from a continuance granted by any judge on his own motion or at the request of the defendant or his counsel or at the request of the attorney for the Government, if the judge granted such continuance on the basis of his findings that the ends of justice served by taking such action outweigh the best interest of the public and the defendant in a speedy trial. No such period of delay resulting from a continuance granted by the court in accordance with this paragraph shall be excludable under this subsection unless the court sets forth, in the record of the case, either orally or in writing, its reasons for finding that the ends of justice served by the granting of such continuance outweigh the best interests of the public and the defendant in a speedy trial.

(B) The factors, among others, which a judge shall consider in determining whether to grant a continuance under subparagraph (A) of this paragraph in any case are as follows:

(i) Whether the failure to grant such a continuance in the proceeding would be likely to make a continuation of such proceeding impossible, or result in a miscarriage of justice.

(ii) Whether the case is so unusual or so complex, due to the number of defendants, the nature of the prosecution, or the existence of novel questions of fact or law, that it is unreasonable to expect adequate preparation for pretrial proceedings or for the trial itself within the time limits established by this section.

(iii) Whether, in a case in which arrest precedes indictment, delay in the filing of the indictment is caused because the arrest occurs at a time such that it is unreasonable to expect return and filing of the indictment within the period specified in section 3161(b), or because the facts upon which the grand jury must base its determination are unusual or complex.

(iv) Whether the failure to grant such a continuance in a case which, taken as a whole, is not so unusual or so complex as to fall within clause (ii), would deny the defendant reasonable time to obtain counsel, would unreasonably deny the defendant or the Government continuity of counsel, or would deny counsel for the defendant or the attorney for the Government the reasonable time necessary for effective preparation, taking into account the exercise of due diligence.

(C) No continuance under subparagraph (A) of this paragraph shall be granted because of general congestion of the court's calendar, or lack of diligent preparation or failure to obtain available witnesses on the part of the attorney for the Government.

(9) Any period of delay, not to exceed one year, ordered by a district court upon an application of a party and a finding by a preponderance of the evidence that an official request, as defined in section 3292 of this title, has been made for evidence of any such offense and that it reasonably appears, or reasonably appeared at the time the request was made, that such evidence is, or was, in such foreign country.

(i) If trial did not commence within the time limitation specified in section 3161 because the defendant had entered a plea of guilty or nolo contendere subsequently withdrawn to any or all charges in an indictment or information, the defendant shall be deemed indicted with respect to all charges therein contained within the meaning of section 3161, on the day the order permitting withdrawal of the plea becomes final.

(j) (1) If the attorney for the Government knows that a person charged with an offense is serving a term of imprisonment in any penal institution, he shall promptly—

(A) undertake to obtain the presence of the prisoner for trial; or

(B) cause a detainer to be filed with the person having custody of the prisoner and request him to so advise the prisoner and to advise the prisoner of his right to demand trial.

(2) If the person having custody of such prisoner receives a detainer, he shall promptly advise the prisoner of the charge and of the prisoner's right to demand trial. If at any time thereafter the prisoner informs the person having custody that he does demand trial, such person shall cause notice to that effect to be sent promptly to the attorney for the Government who caused the detainer to be filed.

(3) Upon receipt of such notice, the attorney for the Government shall promptly seek to obtain the presence of the prisoner for trial.

(4) When the person having custody of the prisoner receives from the attorney for the Government a properly supported request for temporary custody of such prisoner for trial, the prisoner shall be made available to that attorney for the Government (subject, in cases of interjurisdictional transfer, to any right of the prisoner to contest the legality of his delivery).

(k) (1) If the defendant is absent (as defined by subsection (h)(3)) on the day set for trial, and the defendant's subsequent appearance before the court on a bench warrant or other process or surrender to the court occurs more than 21 days after the day set for trial, the defendant shall be deemed to have first appeared before a judicial officer of the court in which the information or indictment is pending within the meaning of subsection (c) on the date of the defendant's subsequent appearance before the court.

(2) If the defendant is absent (as defined by subsection (h)(3)) on the day set for trial, and the defendant's subsequent appearance before the court on a bench warrant or other process or surrender to the court occurs not more than 21 days after the day set for trial, the time limit required by subsection (c), as extended by subsection (h), shall be further extended by 21 days.

§ 3162. Sanctions

(a) (1) If, in the case of any individual against whom a complaint is filed charging such individual with an offense, no indictment or information is filed within the time limit required by section 3161(b) as extended by section 3161(h) of this chapter, such charge against that individual contained in such complaint shall be dismissed or otherwise dropped. In determining whether to dismiss the case with or without prejudice, the court shall consider, among others, each of the following factors: the seriousness of the offense; the facts and circumstances of the case which led to the dismissal; and the impact of a reprosecution on the administration of this chapter and on the administration of justice.

(2) If a defendant is not brought to trial within the time limit required by section 3161(c) as extended by section 3161(h), the information or indictment shall be dismissed on motion of the defendant. The defendant shall have the burden of proof of supporting such motion but the Government shall have the burden of going forward with the evidence in connection with any exclusion of time under subparagraph 3161(h)(3). In determining whether to dismiss the case with or without prejudice, the court shall consider, among others, each of the following factors: the seriousness of the offense; the facts and circumstances of the case which led to the dismissal; and the impact of a reprosecution on the administration of this chapter and on the administration of justice. Failure of the defendant to move for dismissal prior to trial or entry of a plea of guilty or nolo contendere shall constitute a waiver of the right to dismissal under this section.

(b) In any case in which counsel for the defendant or the attorney for the Government (1) knowingly allows the case to be set for trial without disclosing the fact that a necessary witness would be unavailable for trial; (2) files a motion solely for the purpose of delay which he knows is totally frivolous and without merit; (3) makes a statement for the purpose of obtaining a continuance which he knows to be false and which is material to the granting of a continuance; or (4) otherwise willfully fails to proceed to trial without justification consistent with section 3161 of this chapter, the court may punish any such counsel or attorney, as follows:

(A) in the case of an appointed defense counsel, by reducing the amount of compensation that otherwise would have been paid to such counsel pursuant to section 3006A of this title in an amount not to exceed 25 per centum thereof;

(B) in the case of a counsel retained in connection with the defense of a defendant, by imposing on such counsel a fine of not to exceed 25 per centum of the compensation to which he is entitled in connection with his defense of such defendant;

(C) by imposing on any attorney for the Government a fine of not to exceed $250;

(D) by denying any such counsel or attorney for the Government the right to practice before the court considering such case for a period of not to exceed ninety days; or

(E) by filing a report with an appropriate disciplinary committee.

The authority to punish provided for by this subsection shall be in addition to any other authority or power available to such court.

(c) The court shall follow procedures established in the Federal Rules of Criminal Procedure in punishing any counsel or attorney for the Government pursuant to this section.

§ 3164. Persons detained or designated as being of high risk

(a) The trial or other disposition of cases involving—

(1) a detained person who is being held in detention solely because he is awaiting trial, and

(2) a released person who is awaiting trial and has been designated by the attorney for the Government as being of high risk,

shall be accorded priority.

(b) The trial of any person described in subsection (a)(1) or (a)(2) of this section shall commence not later than ninety days following the beginning of such continuous detention or designation of high risk by the attorney for the Government. The periods of delay enumerated in section 3161(h) are excluded in computing the time limitation specified in this section.

(c) Failure to commence trial of a detainee as specified in subsection (b), through no fault of the accused or his counsel, or failure to commence trial of a designated releasee as specified in subsection (b), through no fault of the attorney for the Government, shall result in the automatic review by the court of the conditions of release. No detainee, as defined in subsection (a), shall be held in custody pending trial after the expiration of such ninety-day period required for the commencement of his trial. A designated releasee, as defined in subsection (a), who is found by the court to have intentionally delayed the trial of his case shall be subject to an order of the court modifying his nonfinancial conditions of release under this title to insure that he shall appear at trial as required.

LITIGATION CONCERNING SOURCES OF EVIDENCE

(18 U.S.C. § 3504).

§ 3504. Litigation concerning sources of evidence

(a) In any trial, hearing, or other proceeding in or before any court, grand jury, department, officer, agency, regulatory body, or other authority of the United States—

(1) upon a claim by a party aggrieved that evidence is inadmissible because it is the primary product of an unlawful act or because it was obtained by the exploitation of an unlawful act, the opponent of the claim shall affirm or deny the occurrence of the alleged unlawful act;

(2) disclosure of information for a determination if evidence is inadmissible because it is the primary product of an unlawful act occurring prior to June 19, 1968, or because it was obtained by the exploitation of an unlawful act occurring prior to June 19, 1968, shall not be required unless such information may be relevant to a pending claim of such inadmissibility; and

(3) no claim shall be considered that evidence of an event is inadmissible on the ground that such evidence was obtained by the exploitation of an unlawful act occurring prior to June 19, 1968, if such event occurred more than five years after such allegedly unlawful act.

(b) As used in this section "unlawful act" means any act the use of any electronic, mechanical, or other device (as defined in section 2510(5) of this title) in violation of the Constitution or laws of the United States or any regulation or standard promulgated pursuant thereto.

CRIMINAL APPEALS ACT OF 1970 (AS AMENDED)

(18 U.S.C. § 3731).

§ 3731. Appeal by United States

In a criminal case an appeal by the United States shall lie to a court of appeals from a decision, judgment, or order of a district court dismissing an indictment or information or granting a new trial after verdict or judgment, as to any one or more counts, except that no appeal shall lie where the double jeopardy clause of the United States Constitution prohibits further prosecution.

An appeal by the United States shall lie to a court of appeals from a decision or order of a district court suppressing or excluding evidence or requiring the return of seized property in a criminal proceeding, not made after the defendant has been put in jeopardy and before the verdict or finding on an indictment or information, if the

United States attorney certifies to the district court that the appeal is not taken for purpose of delay and that the evidence is a substantial proof of a fact material in the proceeding.

An appeal by the United States shall lie to a court of appeals from a decision or order, entered by a district court of the United States, granting the release of a person charged with or convicted of an offense, or denying a motion for revocation of, or modification of the conditions of, a decision or order granting release.

The appeal in all such cases shall be taken within thirty days after the decision, judgment or order has been rendered and shall be diligently prosecuted.

The provisions of this section shall be liberally construed to effectuate its purposes.

JURY SELECTION AND SERVICE ACT OF 1968
(AS AMENDED)

(28 U.S.C. §§ 1861–1863, 1865–1867).

§ 1861. Declaration of policy

It is the policy of the United States that all litigants in Federal courts entitled to trial by jury shall have the right to grand and petit juries selected at random from a fair cross section of the community in the district or division wherein the court convenes. It is further the policy of the United States that all citizens shall have the opportunity to be considered for service on grand and petit juries in the district courts of the United States, and shall have an obligation to serve as jurors when summoned for that purpose.

§ 1862. Discrimination prohibited

No citizen shall be excluded from service as a grand or petit juror in the district courts of the United States or in the Court of International Trade on account of race, color, religion, sex, national origin, or economic status.

§ 1863. Plan for random jury selection

(a) Each United States district court shall devise and place into operation a written plan for random selection of grand and petit jurors that shall be designed to achieve the objectives of sections 1861 and 1862 of this title, and that shall otherwise comply with the provisions of this title. The plan shall be placed into operation after approval by a reviewing panel consisting of the members of the judicial council of the circuit and either the chief judge of the district whose plan is being reviewed or such other active district judge of that district as the chief judge of the district may designate. The panel shall examine the plan to ascertain that it complies with the provisions of this title. * * * The district court may modify a plan at any time and it shall modify the plan when so directed by the reviewing panel. * * *

(b) Among other things, such plan shall—

(1) either establish a jury commission, or authorize the clerk of the court, to manage the jury selection process. If the plan establishes a jury commission, the district court shall appoint one citizen to serve with the clerk of the court as the jury commission. * * * The citizen jury commissioner shall not belong to the same political party as the clerk serving with him. The clerk or the jury commission, as the case may be, shall act under the supervision and control of the chief judge of the district court or such other judge of the district court as the plan may provide. * * *

(2) specify whether the names of prospective jurors shall be selected from the voter registration lists or the lists of actual voters of the political subdivisions

within the district or division. The plan shall prescribe some other source or sources of names in addition to voter lists where necessary to foster the policy and protect the rights secured by sections 1861 and 1862 of this title. • • •

(3) specify detailed procedures to be followed by the jury commission or clerk in selecting names from the sources specified in paragraph (2) of this subsection. These procedures shall be designed to ensure the random selection of a fair cross section of the persons residing in the community in the district or division wherein the court convenes. They shall ensure that names of persons residing in each of the counties, parishes, or similar political subdivisions within the judicial district or division are placed in a master jury wheel; and shall ensure that each county, parish, or similar political subdivision within the district or division is substantially proportionally represented in the master jury wheel for that judicial district, division, or combination of divisions. For the purposes of determining proportional representation in the master jury wheel, either the number of actual voters at the last general election in each county, parish, or similar political subdivision, or the number of registered voters if registration of voters is uniformly required throughout the district or division, may be used.

(4) provide for a master jury wheel (or a device similar in purpose and function) into which the names of those randomly selected shall be placed. The plan shall fix a minimum number of names to be placed initially in the master jury wheel, which shall be at least one-half of 1 per centum of the total number of persons on the lists used as a source of names for the district or division; but if this number of names is believed to be cumbersome and unnecessary, the plan may fix a smaller number of names to be placed in the master wheel, but in no event less than one thousand. The chief judge of the district court, or such other district court judge as the plan may provide, may order additional names to be placed in the master jury wheel from time to time as necessary. The plan shall provide for periodic emptying and refilling of the master jury wheel at specified times, the interval for which shall not exceed four years.

(5) (A) except as provided in subparagraph (B), specify those groups of persons or occupational classes whose members shall, on individual request therefor, be excused from jury service. Such groups or classes shall be excused only if the district court finds, and the plan states, that jury service by such class or group would entail undue hardship or extreme inconvenience to the members thereof, and excuse of members thereof would not be inconsistent with sections 1861 and 1862 of this title.

(B) specify that volunteer safety personnel, upon individual request, shall be excused from jury service. For purposes of this subparagraph, the term "volunteer safety personnel" means individuals serving a public agency (as defined in section 1203(6) of title I of the Omnibus Crime Control and Safe Streets Act of 1968) in an official capacity, without compensation, as firefighters or members of a rescue squad or ambulance crew.

(6) specify that the following persons are barred from jury service on the ground that they are exempt: (A) members in active service in the Armed Forces of the United States; (B) members of the fire or police departments of any State, the District of Columbia, any territory or possession of the United States, or any subdivision of a State, the District of Columbia, or such territory or possession; (C) public officers in the executive, legislative, or judicial branches of the Government of the United States, or of any State, the District of Columbia, any territory or possession of the United States, or any subdivision of a State, the District of Columbia, or such territory or possession, who are actively engaged in the performance of official duties.

(7) fix the time when the names drawn from the qualified jury wheel shall be disclosed to parties and to the public. If the plan permits these names to be made public, it may nevertheless permit the chief judge of the district court, or such other district court judge as the plan may provide, to keep these names confidential in any case where the interests of justice so require.

(8) specify the procedures to be followed by the clerk or jury commission in assigning persons whose names have been drawn from the qualified jury wheel to grand and petit jury panels. * * *

§ 1865. Qualifications for jury service

(a) The chief judge of the district court, or such other district court judge as the plan may provide, on his initiative or upon recommendation of the clerk or jury commission, shall determine solely on the basis of information provided on the juror qualification form and other competent evidence whether a person is unqualified for, or exempt, or to be excused from jury service. The clerk shall enter such determination in the space provided on the juror qualification form and the alphabetical list of names drawn from the master jury wheel. If a person did not appear in response to a summons, such fact shall be noted on said list.

(b) In making such determination the chief judge of the district court, or such other district court judge as the plan may provide, shall deem any person qualified to serve on grand and petit juries in the district court unless he—

(1) is not a citizen of the United States eighteen years old who has resided for a period of one year within the judicial district;

(2) is unable to read, write, and understand the English language with a degree of proficiency sufficient to fill out satisfactorily the juror qualification form;

(3) is unable to speak the English language;

(4) is incapable, by reason of mental or physical infirmity, to render satisfactory jury service; or

(5) has a charge pending against him for the commission of, or has been convicted in a State or Federal court of record of, a crime punishable by imprisonment for more than one year and his civil rights have not been restored.

§ 1866. Selection and summoning of jury panels
* * *

(c) Except as provided in section 1865 of this title or in any jury selection plan provision adopted pursuant to paragraph (5) or (6) of section 1863(b) of this title, no person or class of persons shall be disqualified, excluded, excused, or exempt from service as jurors: *Provided*, That any person summoned for jury service may be (1) excused by the court, or by the clerk under supervision of the court if the court's jury selection plan so authorizes, upon a showing of undue hardship or extreme inconvenience, for such period as the court deems necessary, at the conclusion of which such person either shall be summoned again for jury service under subsections (b) and (c) of this section or, if the court's jury selection plan so provides, the name of such person shall be reinserted into the qualified jury wheel for selection pursuant to subsection (a) of this section, or (2) excluded by the court on the ground that such person may be unable to render impartial jury service or that his service as a juror would be likely to disrupt the proceedings, or (3) excluded upon peremptory challenge as provided by law, or (4) excluded pursuant to the procedure specified by law upon a challenge by any party for good cause shown, or (5) excluded upon determination by the court that his service as a juror would be likely to threaten the secrecy of the proceedings, or otherwise adversely affect the integrity of jury deliberations. No person shall be excluded under clause (5) of this subsection unless the judge, in open court, determines that such is warranted and that exclusion of the person will not be inconsistent with sections 1861 and 1862 of this title. The number of persons excluded under clause (5) of this subsection shall not exceed one per centum of the number of persons who return executed jury qualification forms during the period, specified in the plan, between two consecutive fillings of the master jury wheel. The names of persons excluded under clause (5) of this subsection, together with detailed explanations for the exclusions, shall be forwarded immediately to the judicial council of the circuit, which shall have the power to make any appropriate order, prospective or retroactive, to redress any misapplication of clause (5) of this subsection, but otherwise exclusions effectuated under such clause shall not be subject to challenge under the provisions of this title. Any person excluded from a particular jury under clause (2), (3), or (4) of this subsection shall be eligible to sit on another jury if the basis for his initial exclusion would not be relevant to his ability to serve on such other jury. * * *

§ 1867. Challenging compliance with selection procedures

(a) In criminal cases, before the voir dire examination begins, or within seven days after the defendant discovered or could have discovered, by the exercise of diligence, the grounds therefor, whichever is earlier, the defendant may move to dismiss the indictment or stay the proceedings against him on the ground of substantial failure to comply with the provisions of this title in selecting the grand or petit jury.

(b) In criminal cases, before the voir dire examination begins, or within seven days after the Attorney General of the United States discovered or could have discovered, by the exercise of diligence, the grounds therefor, whichever is earlier, the Attorney General may move to dismiss the indictment or stay the proceedings on the ground of substantial failure to comply with the provisions of this title in selecting the grand or petit jury. * * *

(d) Upon motion filed under subsection (a), (b), or (c) of this section, containing a sworn statement of facts which, if true, would constitute a substantial failure to comply with the provisions of this title, the moving party shall be entitled to present in support of such motion the testimony of the jury commission or clerk, if available, any relevant records and papers not public or otherwise available used by the jury commissioner or clerk, and any other relevant evidence. If the court determines that there has been a substantial failure to comply with the provisions of this title in selecting a grand jury, the court shall stay the proceedings pending the selection of a grand jury in conformity with this title or dismiss the indictment, whichever is appropriate. If the court determines that there has been a substantial failure to comply with the provisions of this title in selecting the petit jury, the court shall stay the proceedings pending the selection of a petit jury in conformity with this title.

(e) The procedures prescribed by this section shall be the exclusive means by which a person accused of a Federal crime, the Attorney General of the United States or a party in a civil case may challenge any jury on the ground that such jury was not selected in conformity with the provisions of this title. Nothing in this section shall preclude any person or the United States from pursuing any other remedy, civil or criminal, which may be available for the vindication or enforcement of any law prohibiting discrimination on account of race, color, religion, sex, national origin or economic status in the selection of persons for service on grand or petit juries. * * *

HABEAS CORPUS

(28 U.S.C. §§ 2241–2244, 2254–2255).

§ 2241. Power to grant writ

(a) Writs of habeas corpus may be granted by the Supreme Court, any justice thereof, the district courts and any circuit judge within their respective jurisdictions. The order of a circuit judge shall be entered in the records of the district court of the district wherein the restraint complained of is had.

(b) The Supreme Court, any justice thereof, and any circuit judge may decline to entertain an application for a writ of habeas corpus and may transfer the application for hearing and determination to the district court having jurisdiction to entertain it.

(c) The writ of habeas corpus shall not extend to a prisoner unless—

(1) He is in custody under or by color of the authority of the United States or is committed for trial before some court there of; or

(2) He is in custody for an act done or omitted in pursuance of an Act of Congress, or an order, process, judgment or decree of a court or judge of the United States; or

(3) He is in custody in violation of the Constitution or laws or treaties of the United States; or

(4) He, being a citizen of a foreign state and domiciled therein is in custody for an act done or omitted under any alleged right, title, authority, privilege, protection, or exemption claimed under the commission, order or sanction of any foreign state, or under color thereof, the validity and effect of which depend upon the law of nations; or

(5) It is necessary to bring him into court to testify or for trial.

(d) Where an application for a writ of habeas corpus is made by a person in custody under the judgment and sentence of a State court of a State which contains two or more Federal judicial districts, the application may be filed in the district court for the district wherein such person is in custody or in the district court for the district within which the State court was held which convicted and sentenced him and each of such district courts shall have concurrent jurisdiction to entertain the application. The district court for the district wherein such an application is filed in the exercise of its discretion and in furtherance of justice may transfer the application to the other district court for hearing and determination.

§ 2242. Application

Application for a writ of habeas corpus shall be in writing signed and verified by the person for whose relief it is intended or by someone acting in his behalf.

It shall allege the facts concerning the applicant's commitment or detention, the name of the person who has custody over him and by virtue of what claim or authority, if known.

It may be amended or supplemented as provided in the rules of procedure applicable to civil actions.

If addressed to the Supreme Court, a justice thereof or a circuit judge it shall state the reasons for not making application to the district court of the district in which the applicant is held.

§ 2243. Issuance of writ; return; hearing; decision

A court, justice or judge entertaining an application for a writ of habeas corpus shall forthwith award the writ or issue an order directing the respondent to show cause why the writ should not be granted, unless it appears from the application that the applicant or person detained is not entitled thereto.

The writ, or order to show cause shall be directed to the person having custody of the person detained. It shall be returned within three days unless for good cause additional time, not exceeding twenty days, is allowed.

The person to whom the writ or order is directed shall make a return certifying the true cause of the detention.

When the writ or order is returned a day shall be set for hearing, not more than five days after the return unless for good cause additional time is allowed.

Unless the application for the writ and the return present only issues of law the person to whom the writ is directed shall be required to produce at the hearing the body of the person detained.

The applicant or the person detained may, under oath, deny any of the facts set forth in the return or allege any other material facts.

The return and all suggestions made against it may be amended, by leave of court, before or after being filed.

The court shall summarily hear and determine the facts, and dispose of the matter as law and justice require.

§ 2244. Finality of determination

(a) No circuit or district judge shall be required to entertain an application for a writ of habeas corpus to inquire into the detention of a person pursuant to a judgment of a court of the United States if it appears that the legality of such detention has been determined by a judge or court of the United States on a prior application for a writ of habeas corpus and the petition presents no new ground not theretofore presented and determined, and the judge of court is satisfied that the ends of justice will not be served by such inquiry.

(b) When after an evidentiary hearing on the merits of a material factual issue, or after a hearing on the merits of an issue of law, a person in custody pursuant to the judgment of a State court has been denied by a court of the United States or a justice or judge of the United States release from custody or other remedy on an application for a writ of habeas corpus, a subsequent application for a writ of habeas corpus in behalf of such person need not be entertained by a court of the United States or a justice or judge of the United States unless the application alleges and is predicated on a factual or other ground not adjudicated on the hearing of the earlier application for the writ, and unless the court, justice, or judge is satisfied that the applicant has not on the earlier application deliberately withheld the newly asserted ground or otherwise abused the writ.

(c) In a habeas corpus proceeding brought in behalf of a person in custody pursuant to the judgment of a State court, a prior judgment of the Supreme Court of the United States on an appeal or review by a writ of certiorari at the instance of the prisoner of the decision of such State court, shall be conclusive as to all issues of fact or law with respect to an asserted denial of a Federal right which constitutes ground for discharge in a habeas corpus proceeding, actually adjudicated by the Supreme Court therein, unless the applicant for the writ of habeas corpus shall plead and the court shall find the existence of a material and controlling fact which did not appear in the record of the proceeding in the Supreme Court and the court shall further find that the applicant for the writ of habeas corpus could not have caused such fact to appear in such record by the exercise of reasonable diligence.

§ 2254. State custody; remedies in State courts

(a) The Supreme Court, a Justice thereof, a circuit judge, or a district court shall entertain an application for a writ of habeas corpus in behalf of a person in custody pursuant to the judgment of a State court only on the ground that he is in custody in violation of the Constitution or laws or treaties of the United States.

(b) An application for a writ of habeas corpus in behalf of a person in custody pursuant to the judgment of a State court shall not be granted unless it appears that the applicant has exhausted the remedies available in the courts of the State, or that there is either an absence of available State corrective process or the existence of circumstances rendering such process ineffective to protect the rights of the prisoner.

(c) An applicant shall not be deemed to have exhausted the remedies available in the courts of the State, within the meaning of this section, if he has the right under the law of the State to raise, by any available procedure, the question presented.

(d) In any proceeding instituted in a Federal court by an application for a writ of habeas corpus by a person in custody pursuant to the judgment of a State court, a determination after a hearing on the merits of a factual issue, made by a State court of competent jurisdiction in a proceeding to which the applicant for the writ and the State or an officer or agent thereof were parties, evidenced by a written finding, written opinion, or other reliable and adequate written indicia, shall be presumed to be correct, unless the applicant shall establish or it shall otherwise appear, or the respondent shall admit—

(1) that the merits of the factual dispute were not resolved in the State court hearing;

(2) that the factfinding procedure employed by the State court was not adequate to afford a full and fair hearing;

(3) that the material facts were not adequately developed at the State court hearing;

(4) that the State court lacked jurisdiction of the subject matter or over the person of the applicant in the State court proceeding;

(5) that the applicant was an indigent and the State court, in deprivation of his constitutional right, failed to appoint counsel to represent him in the State court proceeding;

(6) that the applicant did not receive a full, fair, and adequate hearing in the State court proceeding; or

(7) that the applicant was otherwise denied due process of law in the State court proceeding;

(8) or unless that part of the record of the State court proceeding in which the determination of such factual issue was made, pertinent to a determination of the sufficiency of the evidence to support such factual determination, is produced as provided for hereinafter, and the Federal court on a consideration of such part of the record as a whole concludes that such factual determination is not fairly supported by the record:

And in an evidentiary hearing in the proceeding in the Federal court, when due proof of such factual determination has been made, unless the existence of one or more of the circumstances respectively set forth in paragraphs numbered (1) to (7), inclusive, is shown by the applicant, otherwise appears, or is admitted by the respondent, or unless the court concludes pursuant to the provisions of paragraph numbered (8) that the record in the State court proceeding, considered as a whole, does not fairly support such factual determination, the burden shall rest upon the applicant to establish by convincing evidence that the factual determination by the State court was erroneous.

(e) If the applicant challenges the sufficiency of the evidence adduced in such State court proceeding to support the State court's determination of a factual issue made therein, the applicant, if able, shall produce that part of the record pertinent to a determination of the sufficiency of the evidence to support such determination. If the applicant, because of indigency or other reason is unable to produce such part of the record, then the State shall produce such part of the record and the Federal court shall direct the State to do so by order directed to an appropriate State official. If the State cannot provide such pertinent part of the record, then the court shall determine under the existing facts and circumstances what weight shall be given to the State court's factual determination.

(f) A copy of the official records of the State court, duly certified by the clerk of such court to be a true and correct copy of a finding, judicial opinion, or other reliable written indicia showing such a factual determination by the State court shall be admissible in the Federal court proceeding.

§ 2255. Federal custody; remedies on motion attacking sentence

A prisoner in custody under sentence of a court established by Act of Congress claiming the right to be released upon the ground that the sentence was imposed in violation of the Constitution or laws of the United States, or that the court was without jurisdiction to impose such sentence, or that the sentence was in excess of the maximum authorized by law, or is otherwise subject to collateral attack, may move the court which imposed the sentence to vacate, set aside or correct the sentence.

A motion for such relief may be made at any time.

Unless the motion and the files and records of the case conclusively show that the prisoner is entitled to no relief, the court shall cause notice thereof to be served upon the United States attorney, grant a prompt hearing thereon, determine the issues and make findings of fact and conclusions of law with respect thereto. If the court finds that the judgment was rendered without jurisdiction, or that the sentence imposed was not authorized by law or otherwise open to collateral attack, or that there has been such a denial or infringement of the constitutional rights of the prisoner as to render the judgment vulnerable to collateral attack, the court shall vacate and set the judgment aside and shall discharge the prisoner or resentence him or grant a new trial or correct the sentence as may appear appropriate.

A court may entertain and determine such motion without requiring the production of the prisoner at the hearing.

The sentencing court shall not be required to entertain a second or successive motion for similar relief on behalf of the same prisoner.

An appeal may be taken to the court of appeals from the order entered on the motion as from a final judgment on application for a writ of habeas corpus.

An application for a writ of habeas corpus in behalf of a prisoner who is authorized to apply for relief by motion pursuant to this section, shall not be entertained if it appears that the applicant has failed to apply for relief, by motion, to the court which sentenced him, or that such court has denied him relief, unless it also appears that the remedy by motion is inadequate or ineffective to test the legality of his detention.

PRIVACY PROTECTION ACT OF 1980

(42 U.S.C. §§ 2000aa–2000aa–12).

§ 2000aa. Searches and seizures by government officers and employees in connection with investigation or prosecution of criminal offenses

(a) Notwithstanding any other law, it shall be unlawful for a government officer or employee, in connection with the investigation or prosecution of a criminal offense, to search for or seize any work product materials possessed by a person reasonably believed to have a purpose to disseminate to the public a newspaper, book, broadcast, or other similar form of public communication, in or affecting interstate or foreign commerce; but this provision shall not impair or affect the ability of any government officer or employee, pursuant to otherwise applicable law, to search for or seize such materials, if—

(1) there is probable cause to believe that the person possessing such materials has committed or is committing the criminal offense to which the materials relate: *Provided, however,* That a government officer or employee may not search for or seize such materials under the provisions of this paragraph if the offense to which the materials relate consists of the receipt, possession, communication, or withholding of such materials or the information contained therein (but such a search or seizure may be conducted under the provisions of this paragraph if the offense consists of the receipt, possession, or communication of information relating to the national defense, classified information, or restricted data under the provisions of section 793, 794, 797, or 798 of Title 18, or section 2274, 2275 or 2277 of this title, or section 783 of Title 50); or

(2) there is reason to believe that the immediate seizure of such materials is necessary to prevent the death of, or serious bodily injury to, a human being.

(b) Notwithstanding any other law, it shall be unlawful for a government officer or employee, in connection with the investigation or prosecution of a criminal offense, to search for or seize documentary materials, other than work product materials, possessed by a person in connection with a purpose to disseminate to the public a newspaper, book, broadcast, or other similar form of public communication, in or affecting interstate or foreign commerce; but this provision shall not impair or affect the ability of any government officer or employee, pursuant to otherwise applicable law, to search for or seize such materials, if—

(1) there is probable cause to believe that the person possessing such materials has committed or is committing the criminal offense to which the materials relate: *Provided, however,* That a government officer or employee may not search for or seize such materials under the provisions of this paragraph if the offense to which the materials relate consists of the receipt, possession, communication, or withholding of such materials or the information contained therein (but such a search or seizure may be conducted under the provisions of this paragraph if the offense consists of the receipt, possession, or communication of information relating to the national defense, classified information, or restricted data under the provisions of section 793, 794, 797, or 798 of Title 18, or section 2274, 2275 or 2277 of this title, or section 783 of Title 50);

(2) there is reason to believe that the immediate seizure of such materials is necessary to prevent the death of, or serious bodily injury to, a human being;

(3) there is reason to believe that the giving of notice pursuant to a subpena duces tecum would result in the destruction, alteration, or concealment of such materials; or

(4) such materials have not been produced in response to a court order directing compliance with a subpena duces tecum, and—

(A) all appellate remedies have been exhausted; or

(B) there is reason to believe that the delay in an investigation or trial occasioned by further proceedings relating to the subpena would threaten the interests of justice.

(c) In the event a search warrant is sought pursuant to paragraph (4)(B) of subsection (b) of this section, the person possessing the materials shall be afforded adequate opportunity to submit an affidavit setting forth the basis for any contention that the materials sought are not subject to seizure.

§ 2000aa-5. Border and customs searches

This chapter shall not impair or affect the ability of a government officer or employee, pursuant to otherwise applicable law, to conduct searches and seizures at the borders of, or at international points of, entry into the United States in order to enforce the customs laws of the United States.

§ 2000aa-6. Civil actions by aggrieved persons

(a) A person aggrieved by a search for or seizure of materials in violation of this chapter shall have a civil cause of action for damages for such search or seizure—

(1) against the United States, against a State which has waived its sovereign immunity under the Constitution to a claim for damages resulting from a violation of this chapter, or against any other governmental unit, all of which shall be liable for violations of this chapter by their officers or employees while acting within the scope or under color of their office or employment; and

(2) against an officer or employee of a State who has violated this chapter while acting within the scope or under color of his office or employment, if such State has not waived its sovereign immunity as provided in paragraph (1).

(b) It shall be a complete defense to a civil action brought under paragraph (2) of subsection (a) of this section that the officer or employee had a reasonable good faith belief in the lawfulness of his conduct.

(c) The United States, a State, or any other governmental unit liable for violations of this chapter under subsection (a)(1) of this section, may not assert as a defense to a claim arising under this chapter the immunity of the officer or employee whose violation is complained of or his reasonable good faith belief in the lawfulness of his conduct, except that such a defense may be asserted if the violation complained of is that of a judicial officer.

(d) The remedy provided by subsection (a)(1) of this section against the United States, a State, or any other governmental unit is exclusive of any other civil action or proceeding for conduct constituting a violation of this chapter, against the officer or employee whose violation gave rise to the claim, or against the estate of such officer or employee.

(e) Evidence otherwise admissible in a proceeding shall not be excluded on the basis of a violation of this chapter.

(f) A person having a cause of action under this section shall be entitled to recover actual damages but not less than liquidated damages of $1,000, and such reasonable attorneys' fees and other litigation costs reasonably incurred as the court, in its discretion, may award: *Provided, however,* That the United States, a State, or any other governmental unit shall not be liable for interest prior to judgment.

(g) The Attorney General may settle a claim for damages brought against the United States under this section, and shall promulgate regulations to provide for the commencement of an administrative inquiry following a determination of a violation of this chapter by an officer or employee of the United States and for the imposition of administrative sanctions against such officer or employee, if warranted.

(h) The district courts shall have original jurisdiction of all civil actions arising under this section.

§ 2000aa–7. Definitions

(a) "Documentary materials", as used in this chapter, means materials upon which information is recorded, and includes, but is not limited to, written or printed materials, photographs, motion picture films, negatives, video tapes, audio tapes, and other mechanically, magnetically or electronically recorded cards, tapes, or discs, but does not include contraband or the fruits of a crime or things otherwise criminally possessed, or property designed or intended for use, or which is or has been used as, the means of committing a criminal offense.

(b) "Work product materials", as used in this chapter, means materials, other than contraband or the fruits of a crime or things otherwise criminally possessed, or property designed or intended for use, or which is or has been used, as the means of committing a criminal offense, and—

(1) in anticipation of communicating such materials to the public, are prepared, produced, authored, or created, whether by the person in possession of the materials or by any other person;

(2) are possessed for the purposes of communicating such materials to the public; and

(3) include mental impressions, conclusions, opinions, or theories of the person who prepared, produced, authored, or created such material.

(c) "Any other governmental unit", as used in this chapter, includes the District of Columbia, the Commonwealth of Puerto Rico, any territory or possession of the United States, and any local government, unit of local government, or any unit of State government.

§ 2000aa–11. Guidelines for federal officers and employees

(a) The Attorney General shall * * * issue guidelines for the procedures to be employed by any Federal officer or employee, in connection with the investigation or prosecution of an offense, to obtain documentary materials in the private possession of a person when the person is not reasonably believed to be a suspect in such offense or related by blood or marriage to such a suspect, and when the materials sought are not contraband or the fruits or instrumentalities of an offense. * * *

§ 2000aa–12. Binding nature of guidelines; disciplinary actions for violations; legal proceedings for non-compliance prohibited

Guidelines issued by the Attorney General under this subchapter shall have the full force and effect of Department of Justice regulations and any violation of these guidelines shall make the employee or officer involved subject to appropriate administrative disciplinary action. However, an issue relating to the compliance, or the failure to comply, with guidelines issued pursuant to this subchapter may not be litigated, and a court may not entertain such an issue as the basis for the suppression or exclusion of evidence.

[EDITOR'S NOTE: These guidelines appear in 28 C.F.R. Pt. 59. The procedural provisions are set out below.]

§ 59.4 Procedures

(a) *Provisions governing the use of search warrants generally.*

(1) A search warrant should not be used to obtain documentary materials believed to be in the private possession of a disinterested third party unless it appears that the use of a subpoena, summons, request, or other less intrusive alternative means of obtaining the materials would substantially jeopardize the availability or usefulness of the materials sought, and the application for the warrant has been authorized as provided in paragraph (a)(2) of this section.

(2) No federal officer or employee shall apply for a warrant to search for and seize documentary materials believed to be in the private possession of a disinterested third party unless the application for the warrant has been authorized by an attorney for the government. Provided, however, that in an emergency situation in which the immediacy of the need to seize the materials does not permit an opportunity to secure the authorization of an attorney for the government, the application may be authorized by a supervisory law enforcement officer in the applicant's department or agency, if the appropriate United States Attorney (or where the case is not being handled by a United States Attorney's Office, the appropriate supervisory official of the Department of Justice) is notified of the authorization and the basis for justifying such authorization under this part within 24 hours of the authorization.

(b) *Provisions governing the use of search warrants which may intrude upon professional, confidential relationships.*

(1) A search warrant should not be used to obtain documentary materials believed to be in the private possession of a disinterested third party physician, lawyer, or clergyman, under circumstances in which the materials sought, or other materials likely to be reviewed during the execution of the warrant, contain confidential information on patients, clients, or parishioners which was furnished or developed for the purposes of professional counseling or treatment, unless—

(i) It appears that the use of a subpoena, summons, request or other less intrusive alternative means of obtaining the materials would substantially jeopardize the availability or usefulness of the materials sought;

(ii) Access to the documentary materials appears to be of substantial importance to the investigation or prosecution for which they are sought; and

(iii) The application for the warrant has been approved as provided in paragraph (b)(2) of this section.

(2) No federal officer or employee shall apply for a warrant to search for and seize documentary materials believed to be in the private possession of a disinterested third party physician, lawyer, or clergyman under the circumstances described in paragraph (b)(1) of this section, unless, upon the recommendation of the United States Attorney (or where a case is not being handled by a United States Attorney's Office, upon the recommendation of the appropriate supervisory official of the Department of Justice), an appropriate Deputy Assistant Attorney General has authorized the application for the warrant. Provided, however, that in an emergency situation in which the immediacy of the need to seize the materials does not permit an opportunity to secure the authorization of a Deputy Assistant Attorney General, the application may be authorized by the United States Attorney (or where the case is not being handled by a United States Attorney's Office, by the appropriate supervisory official of the Department of Justice) if an appropriate Deputy Assistant Attorney General is notified of the authorization and the basis for justifying such authorization under this part within 72 hours of the authorization.

(3) Whenever possible, a request for authorization by an appropriate Deputy Assistant Attorney General of a search warrant application pursuant to paragraph (b)(2) of this section shall be made in writing and shall include:

(i) The application for the warrant; and

(ii) A brief description of the facts and circumstances advanced as the basis for recommending authorization of the application under this part.

If a request for authorization of the application is made orally or if, in an emergency situation, the application is authorized by the United States Attorney or a supervisory official of the Department of Justice as provided in paragraph (b)(2) of this section, a written record of the request including the materials specified in paragraphs (b)(3) (i) and (ii) of this section shall be transmitted to an appropriate Deputy Assistant Attorney General within 7 days. The Deputy Assistant Attorneys General shall keep a record of the disposition of all requests for authorizations of search warrant applications made under paragraph (b) of this section.

(4) A search warrant authorized under paragraph (b)(2) of this section shall be executed in such a manner as to minimize, to the greatest extent practicable, scrutiny of confidential materials.

(5) Although it is impossible to define the full range of additional doctor-like therapeutic relationships which involve the furnishing or development of private information, the United States Attorney (or where a case is not being handled by a United States Attorney's Office, the appropriate supervisory official of the Department of Justice) should determine whether a search for documentary materials held by other disinterested third party professionals involved in such relationships (e.g. psychologists or psychiatric social workers or nurses) would implicate the special privacy concerns which are addressed in paragraph (b) of this section. If the United States Attorney (or other supervisory official of the Department of Justice) determines that such a search would require review of extremely confidential information furnished or developed for the purposes of professional counseling or treatment, the provisions of this subsection should be applied. Otherwise, at a minimum, the requirements of paragraph (a) of this section must be met.

(c) *Considerations bearing on choice of methods.*

In determining whether, as an alternative to the use of a search warrant, the use of a subpoena or other less intrusive means of obtaining documentary materials would substantially jeopardize the availability or usefulness of the materials sought, the following factors, among others, should be considered:

(1) Whether it appears that the use of a subpoena or other alternative which gives advance notice of the government's interest in obtaining the materials would be likely to result in the destruction, alteration, concealment, or transfer of the materials sought; considerations, among others, bearing on this issue may include:

(i) Whether a suspect has access to the materials sought;

(ii) Whether there is a close relationship of friendship, loyalty, or sympathy between the possessor of the materials and a suspect;

(iii) Whether the possessor of the materials is under the domination or control of a suspect;

(iv) Whether the possessor of the materials has an interest in preventing the disclosure of the materials to the government;

(v) Whether the possessor's willingness to comply with a subpoena or request by the government would be likely to subject him to intimidation or threats of reprisal;

(vi) Whether the possessor of the materials has previously acted to obstruct a criminal investigation or judicial proceeding or refused to comply with or acted in defiance of court orders; or

(vii) Whether the possessor has expressed an intent to destroy, conceal, alter, or transfer the materials;

(2) The immediacy of the government's need to obtain the materials; considerations, among others, bearing on this issue may include:

(i) Whether the immediate seizure of the materials is necessary to prevent injury to persons or property;

(ii) Whether the prompt seizure of the materials is necessary to preserve their evidentiary value;

(iii) Whether delay in obtaining the materials would significantly jeopardize an ongoing investigation or prosecution; or

(iv) Whether a legally enforceable form of process, other than a search warrant, is reasonably available as a means of obtaining the materials.

The fact that the disinterested third party possessing the materials may have grounds to challenge a subpoena or other legal process is not in itself a legitimate basis for the use of a search warrant.

Appendix C

FEDERAL RULES OF CRIMINAL PROCEDURE FOR THE UNITED STATES DISTRICT COURTS

I. SCOPE, PURPOSE, AND CONSTRUCTION

Rule 1. Scope

These rules govern the procedure in all criminal proceedings in the courts of the United States, as provided in Rule 54(a); and, whenever specifically provided in one of the rules, to preliminary, supplementary, and special proceedings before United States magistrates and at proceedings before state and local judicial officers.

Rule 2. Purpose and Construction

These rules are intended to provide for the just determination of every criminal proceeding. They shall be construed to secure simplicity in procedure, fairness in administration and the elimination of unjustifiable expense and delay.

II. PRELIMINARY PROCEEDINGS

Rule 3. The Complaint

The complaint is a written statement of the essential facts constituting the offense charged. It shall be made upon oath before a magistrate.

Rule 4. Arrest Warrant or Summons upon Complaint

(a) **Issuance.** If it appears from the complaint, or from an affidavit or affidavits filed with the complaint, that there is probable cause to believe that an offense has been committed and that the defendant has committed it, a warrant for the arrest of the defendant shall issue to any officer authorized by law to execute it. Upon the request of the attorney for the government a summons instead of a warrant shall issue. More than one warrant or summons may issue on the same complaint. If a defendant fails to appear in response to the summons, a warrant shall issue.

(b) **Probable Cause.** The finding of probable cause may be based upon hearsay evidence in whole or in part.

(c) **Form.**

  (1) **Warrant.** The warrant shall be signed by the magistrate and shall contain the name of the defendant or, if the defendant's name is unknown, any name or description by which the defendant can be identified with reasonable certainty. It shall describe the offense charged in the complaint. It shall command that the defendant be arrested and brought before the nearest available magistrate.

  (2) **Summons.** The summons shall be in the same form as the warrant except that it shall summon the defendant to appear before a magistrate at a stated time and place.

(d) Execution or Service; and Return.

(1) By Whom. The warrant shall be executed by a marshal or by some other officer authorized by law. The summons may be served by any person authorized to serve a summons in a civil action.

(2) Territorial Limits. The warrant may be executed or the summons may be served at any place within the jurisdiction of the United States.

(3) Manner. The warrant shall be executed by the arrest of the defendant. The officer need not have the warrant at the time of the arrest but upon request shall show the warrant to the defendant as soon as possible. If the officer does not have the warrant at the time of the arrest, the officer shall then inform the defendant of the offense charged and of the fact that a warrant has been issued. The summons shall be served upon a defendant by delivering a copy to the defendant personally, or by leaving it at the defendant's dwelling house or usual place of abode with some person of suitable age and discretion then residing therein and by mailing a copy of the summons to the defendant's last known address.

(4) Return. The officer executing a warrant shall make return thereof to the magistrate or other officer before whom the defendant is brought pursuant to Rule 5. At the request of the attorney for the government any unexecuted warrant shall be returned to and canceled by the magistrate by whom it was issued. On or before the return day the person to whom a summons was delivered for service shall make return thereof to the magistrate before whom the summons is returnable. At the request of the attorney for the government made at any time while the complaint is pending, a warrant returned unexecuted and not canceled or a summons returned unserved or a duplicate thereof may be delivered by the magistrate to the marshal or other authorized person for execution or service.

Rule 5. Initial Appearance Before the Magistrate

(a) In General. An officer making an arrest under a warrant issued upon a complaint or any person making an arrest without a warrant shall take the arrested person without unnecessary delay before the nearest available federal magistrate or, in the event that a federal magistrate is not reasonably available, before a state or local judicial officer authorized by 18 U.S.C. § 3041. If a person arrested without a warrant is brought before a magistrate, a complaint shall be filed forthwith which shall comply with the requirements of Rule 4(a) with respect to the showing of probable cause. When a person, arrested with or without a warrant or given a summons, appears initially before the magistrate, the magistrate shall proceed in accordance with the applicable subdivisions of this rule.

(b) Misdemeanors and Other Petty Offenses. If the charge against the defendant is a misdemeanor or other petty offense triable by a United States magistrate under 18 U.S.C. § 3401, the United States magistrate shall proceed in accordance with Rule 58.

(c) Offenses Not Triable by the United States Magistrate. If the charge against the defendant is not triable by the United States magistrate, the defendant shall not be called upon to plead. The magistrate shall inform the defendant of the complaint against the defendant and of any affidavit filed therewith, of the defendant's right to retain counsel or to request the assignment of counsel if the defendant is unable to obtain counsel, and of the general circumstances under which the defendant may secure pretrial release. The magistrate shall inform the defendant that the defendant is not required to make a statement and that any statement made by the defendant may be used against the defendant. The magistrate shall also inform the defendant of the right to a preliminary examination. The magistrate shall allow the defendant reasonable time and opportunity to consult counsel and shall detain or conditionally release the defendant as provided by statute or in these rules.

A defendant is entitled to a preliminary examination, unless waived, when charged with any offense, other than a petty offense, which is to be tried by a judge of the district court. If the defendant waives preliminary examination, the magistrate shall forthwith hold the defendant to answer in the district court. If the defendant does not waive the preliminary examination, the magistrate shall schedule a preliminary examination. Such examination shall be held within a reasonable time but in any event not later than 10 days following the initial appearance if the defendant is in custody and no later than 20 days if the defendant is not in custody, provided, however, that the preliminary examination shall not be held if the defendant is indicted or if an information against the defendant is filed in district court before the date set for the preliminary examination. With the consent of the defendant and upon a showing of good cause, taking into account the public interest in the prompt disposition of criminal cases, time limits specified in this subdivision may be extended one or more times by a federal magistrate. In the absence of such consent by the defendant, time limits may be extended by a judge of the United States only upon a showing that extraordinary circumstances exist and that delay is indispensable to the interests of justice.

Rule 5.1. Preliminary Examination

(a) Probable Cause Finding. If from the evidence it appears that there is probable cause to believe that an offense has been committed and that the defendant committed it, the federal magistrate shall forthwith hold the defendant to answer in district court. The finding of probable cause may be based upon hearsay evidence in whole or in part. The defendant may cross-examine adverse witnesses and may introduce evidence. Objections to evidence on the ground that it was acquired by unlawful means are not properly made at the preliminary examination. Motions to suppress must be made to the trial court as provided in Rule 12.

(b) Discharge of Defendant. If from the evidence it appears that there is no probable cause to believe that an offense has been committed or that the defendant committed it, the federal magistrate shall dismiss the complaint and discharge the defendant. The discharge of the defendant shall not preclude the government from instituting a subsequent prosecution for the same offense.

(c) Records. After concluding the proceeding the federal magistrate shall transmit forthwith to the clerk of the district court all papers in the proceeding. The magistrate shall promptly make or cause to be made a record or summary of such proceeding.

(1) On timely application to a federal magistrate, the attorney for a defendant in a criminal case may be given the opportunity to have the recording of the hearing on preliminary examination made available to that attorney in connection with any further hearing or preparation for trial. The court may, by local rule, appoint the place for and define the conditions under which such opportunity may be afforded counsel.

(2) On application of a defendant addressed to the court or any judge thereof, an order may issue that the federal magistrate make available a copy of the transcript, or of a portion thereof, to defense counsel. Such order shall provide for prepayment of costs of such transcript by the defendant unless the defendant makes a sufficient affidavit that the defendant is unable to pay or to give security therefor, in which case the expense shall be paid by the Director of the Administrative Office of the United States Courts from available appropriated funds. Counsel for the government may move also that a copy of the transcript, in whole or in part, be made available to it, for good cause shown, and an order may be entered

granting such motion in whole or in part, on appropriate terms, except that the government need not prepay costs nor furnish security therefor.

III. INDICTMENT AND INFORMATION

Rule 6. The Grand Jury

(a) Summoning Grand Juries.

(1) **Generally.** The court shall order one or more grand juries to be summoned at such time as the public interest requires. The grand jury shall consist of not less than 16 nor more than 23 members. The court shall direct that a sufficient number of legally qualified persons be summoned to meet this requirement.

(2) **Alternate Jurors.** The court may direct that alternate jurors may be designated at the time a grand jury is selected. Alternate jurors in the order in which they were designated may thereafter be impanelled as provided in subdivision (g) of this rule. Alternate jurors shall be drawn in the same manner and shall have the same qualifications as the regular jurors, and if impanelled shall be subject to the same challenges, shall take the same oath and shall have the same functions, powers, facilities and privileges as the regular jurors.

(b) Objections to Grand Jury and to Grand Jurors.

(1) **Challenges.** The attorney for the government or a defendant who has been held to answer in the district court may challenge the array of jurors on the ground that the grand jury was not selected, drawn or summoned in accordance with law, and may challenge an individual juror on the ground that the juror is not legally qualified. Challenges shall be made before the administration of the oath to the jurors and shall be tried by the court.

(2) **Motion to Dismiss.** A motion to dismiss the indictment may be based on objections to the array or on the lack of legal qualification of an individual juror, if not previously determined upon challenge. It shall be made in the manner prescribed in 28 U.S.C. § 1867(e) and shall be granted under the conditions prescribed in that statute. An indictment shall not be dismissed on the ground that one or more members of the grand jury were not legally qualified if it appears from the record kept pursuant to subdivision (c) of this rule that 12 or more jurors, after deducting the number not legally qualified, concurred in finding the indictment.

(c) Foreperson and Deputy Foreperson. The court shall appoint one of the jurors to be foreperson and another to be deputy foreperson. The foreperson shall have power to administer oaths and affirmations and shall sign all indictments. The foreperson or another juror designated by the foreperson shall keep record of the number of jurors concurring in the finding of every indictment and shall file the record with the clerk of the court, but the record shall not be made public except on order of the court. During the absence of the foreperson, the deputy foreperson shall act as foreperson.

(d) Who May Be Present. Attorneys for the government, the witness under examination, interpreters when needed and, for the purpose of taking the evidence, a stenographer or operator of a recording device may be present while the grand jury is in session, but no person other than the jurors may be present while the grand jury is deliberating or voting.

(e) Recording and Disclosure of Proceedings.

(1) **Recording of Proceedings.** All proceedings, except when the grand jury is deliberating or voting, shall be recorded stenographically or by an electronic recording device. An unintentional failure of any recording to reproduce all or any portion of a proceeding shall not affect the validity of the prosecution. The

recording or reporter's notes or any transcript prepared therefrom shall remain in the custody or control of the attorney for the government unless otherwise ordered by the court in a particular case.

(2) General Rule of Secrecy. A grand juror, an interpreter, a stenographer, an operator of a recording device, a typist who transcribes recorded testimony, an attorney for the government, or any person to whom disclosure is made under paragraph (3)(A)(ii) of this subdivision shall not disclose matters occurring before the grand jury, except as otherwise provided for in these rules. No obligation of secrecy may be imposed on any person except in accordance with this rule. A knowing violation of Rule 6 may be punished as a contempt of court.

(3) Exceptions.

(A) Disclosure otherwise prohibited by this rule of matters occurring before the grand jury, other than its deliberations and the vote of any grand juror, may be made to—

(i) an attorney for the government for use in the performance of such attorney's duty; and

(ii) such government personnel (including personnel of a state or subdivision of a state) as are deemed necessary by an attorney for the government to assist an attorney for the government in the performance of such attorney's duty to enforce federal criminal law.

(B) Any person to whom matters are disclosed under subparagraph (A)(ii) of this paragraph shall not utilize that grand jury material for any purpose other than assisting the attorney for the government in the performance of such attorney's duty to enforce federal criminal law. An attorney for the government shall promptly provide the district court, before which was impaneled the grand jury whose material has been so disclosed, with the names of the persons to whom such disclosure has been made, and shall certify that the attorney has advised such persons of their obligation of secrecy under this rule.

(C) Disclosure otherwise prohibited by this rule of matters occurring before the grand jury may also be made—

(i) when so directed by a court preliminarily to or in connection with a judicial proceeding;

(ii) when permitted by a court at the request of the defendant, upon a showing that grounds may exist for a motion to dismiss the indictment because of matters occurring before the grand jury;

(iii) when the disclosure is made by an attorney for the government to another federal grand jury; or

(iv) when permitted by a court at the request of an attorney for the government, upon a showing that such matters may disclose a violation of state criminal law, to an appropriate official of a state or subdivision of a state for the purpose of enforcing such law.

If the court orders disclosure of matters occurring before the grand jury, the disclosure shall be made in such manner, at such time, and under such conditions as the court may direct.

(D) A petition for disclosure pursuant to subdivision (e)(3)(C)(i) shall be filed in the district where the grand jury convened. Unless the hearing is ex parte, which it may be when the petitioner is the government, the petitioner shall serve written notice of the petition upon (i) the attorney for the government, (ii) the parties to the judicial proceeding if disclosure is sought in connection with such a proceeding, and (iii) such other persons as the court may direct. The court shall afford those persons a reasonable opportunity to appear and be heard.

(E) If the judicial proceeding giving rise to the petition is in a federal district court in another district, the court shall transfer the matter to that court unless it can reasonably obtain sufficient knowledge of the proceeding to determine whether disclosure is proper. The court shall order transmitted to the court to which the matter is transferred the material sought to be disclosed, if feasible, and a written evaluation of the need for continued grand jury secrecy. The court to which the matter is transferred shall afford the aforementioned persons a reasonable opportunity to appear and be heard.

(4) Sealed Indictments. The federal magistrate to whom an indictment is returned may direct that the indictment be kept secret until the defendant is in custody or has been released pending trial. Thereupon the clerk shall seal the indictment and no person shall disclose the return of the indictment except when necessary for the issuance and execution of a warrant or summons.

(5) Closed Hearing. Subject to any right to an open hearing in contempt proceedings, the court shall order a hearing on matters affecting a grand jury proceeding to be closed to the extent necessary to prevent disclosure of matters occurring before a grand jury.

(6) Sealed Records. Records, orders and subpoenas relating to grand jury proceedings shall be kept under seal to the extent and for such time as is necessary to prevent disclosure of matters occurring before a grand jury.

(f) Finding and Return of Indictment. An indictment may be found only upon the concurrence of 12 or more jurors. The indictment shall be returned by the grand jury to a federal magistrate in open court. If a complaint or information is pending against the defendant and 12 jurors do not concur in finding an indictment, the foreperson shall so report to a federal magistrate in writing forthwith.

(g) Discharge and Excuse. A grand jury shall serve until discharged by the court, but no grand jury may serve more than 18 months unless the court extends the service of the grand jury for a period of six months or less upon a determination that such extension is in the public interest. At any time for cause shown the court may excuse a juror either temporarily or permanently, and in the latter event the court may impanel another person in place of the juror excused.

Rule 7. The Indictment and the Information

(a) Use of Indictment or Information. An offense which may be punished by death shall be prosecuted by indictment. An offense which may be punished by imprisonment for a term exceeding one year or at hard labor shall be prosecuted by indictment or, if indictment is waived, it may be prosecuted by information. Any other offense may be prosecuted by indictment or by information. An information may be filed without leave of court.

(b) Waiver of Indictment. An offense which may be punished by imprisonment for a term exceeding one year or at hard labor may be prosecuted by information if the defendant, after having been advised of the nature of the charge and of the rights of the defendant, waives in open court prosecution by indictment.

(c) Nature and Contents.

(1) In General. The indictment or the information shall be a plain, concise and definite written statement of the essential facts constituting the offense charged. It shall be signed by the attorney for the government. It need not contain a formal commencement, a formal conclusion or any other matter not necessary to such statement. Allegations made in one count may be incorporated by reference in another count. It may be alleged in a single count that the means by which the defendant committed the offense are unknown or that the defendant committed it by one or more specified means. The indictment or information shall state for each count the official or customary citation of the statute, rule, regulation or other provision of law which the defendant is alleged therein to have violated.

(2) Criminal Forfeiture. No judgment of forfeiture may be entered in a criminal proceeding unless the indictment or the information shall allege the extent of the interest or property subject to forfeiture.

(3) Harmless Error. Error in the citation or its omission shall not be ground for dismissal of the indictment or information or for reversal of a conviction if the error or omission did not mislead the defendant to the defendant's prejudice.

(d) Surplusage. The court on motion of the defendant may strike surplusage from the indictment or information.

(e) Amendment of Information. The court may permit an information to be amended at any time before verdict or finding if no additional or different offense is charged and if substantial rights of the defendant are not prejudiced.

(f) Bill of Particulars. The court may direct the filing of a bill of particulars. A motion for a bill of particulars may be made before arraignment or within ten days after arraignment or at such later time as the court may permit. A bill of particulars may be amended at any time subject to such conditions as justice requires.

Rule 8. Joinder of Offenses and of Defendants

(a) Joinder of Offenses. Two or more offenses may be charged in the same indictment or information in a separate count for each offense if the offenses charged, whether felonies or misdemeanors or both, are of the same or similar character or are based on the same act or transaction or on two or more acts or transactions connected together or constituting parts of a common scheme or plan.

(b) Joinder of Defendants. Two or more defendants may be charged in the same indictment or information if they are alleged to have participated in the same act or transaction or in the same series of acts or transactions constituting an offense or offenses. Such defendants may be charged in one or more counts together or separately and all of the defendants need not be charged in each count.

Rule 9. Warrant or Summons Upon Indictment or Information

(a) Issuance. Upon the request of the attorney for the government the court shall issue a warrant for each defendant named in an information supported by a showing of probable cause under oath as is required by Rule 4(a), or in an indictment. Upon the request of the attorney for the government a summons instead of a warrant shall issue. If no request is made, the court may issue either a warrant or a summons in its discretion. More than one warrant or summons may issue for the same defendant. The clerk shall deliver the warrant or summons to the marshal or other person authorized by law to execute or serve it. If a defendant fails to appear in response to the summons, a warrant shall issue. When a defendant arrested with a warrant or given a summons appears initially before a magistrate, the magistrate shall proceed in accordance with the applicable subdivisions of Rule 5.

(b) Form.

(1) Warrant. The form of the warrant shall be as provided in Rule 4(c)(1) except that it shall be signed by the clerk, it shall describe the offense charged in the indictment or information and it shall command that the defendant be arrested and brought before the nearest available magistrate. The amount of bail may be fixed by the court and endorsed on the warrant.

(2) Summons. The summons shall be in the same form as the warrant except that it shall summon the defendant to appear before a magistrate at a stated time and place.

(c) Execution or Service; and Return.

(1) Execution or Service. The warrant shall be executed or the summons served as provided in Rule 4(d)(1), (2) and (3). A summons to a corporation shall be served by delivering a copy to an officer or to a managing or general agent or to any other agent authorized by appointment or by law to receive service of process and, if the agent is one authorized by statute to receive service and the statute so requires, by also mailing a copy to the corporation's last known address within the district or at its principal place of business elsewhere in the United States. The officer executing the warrant shall bring the arrested person without unnecessary delay before the nearest available federal magistrate or, in the event that a federal magistrate is not reasonably available, before a state or local judicial officer authorized by 18 U.S.C. § 3041.

(2) Return. The officer executing a warrant shall make return thereof to the magistrate or other officer before whom the defendant is brought. At the request of the attorney for the government any unexecuted warrant shall be returned and cancelled. On or before the return day the person to whom a summons was delivered for service shall make return thereof. At the request of the attorney for the government made at any time while the indictment or information is pending, a warrant returned unexecuted and not cancelled or a summons returned unserved or a duplicate thereof may be delivered by the clerk to the marshal or other authorized person for execution or service.

[(d) Remand to United States Magistrate for Trial of Minor Offenses] (Abrogated Apr. 28, 1982, eff. Aug. 1, 1982).

IV. ARRAIGNMENT AND PREPARATION FOR TRIAL

Rule 10. Arraignment

Arraignment shall be conducted in open court and shall consist of reading the indictment or information to the defendant or stating to the defendant the substance of the charge and calling on the defendant to plead thereto. The defendant shall be given a copy of the indictment or information before being called upon to plead.

Rule 11. Pleas

(a) Alternatives.

(1) In General. A defendant may plead not guilty, guilty, or nolo contendere. If a defendant refuses to plead or if a defendant corporation fails to appear, the court shall enter a plea of not guilty.

(2) Conditional Pleas. With the approval of the court and the consent of the government, a defendant may enter a conditional plea of guilty or nolo contendere, reserving in writing the right, on appeal from the judgment, to review of the adverse determination of any specified pretrial motion. A defendant who prevails on appeal shall be allowed to withdraw the plea.

(b) Nolo Contendere. A defendant may plead nolo contendere only with the consent of the court. Such a plea shall be accepted by the court only after due consideration of the views of the parties and the interest of the public in the effective administration of justice.

(c) Advice to Defendant. Before accepting a plea of guilty or nolo contendere, the court must address the defendant personally in open court and inform the defendant of, and determine that the defendant understands, the following:

(1) the nature of the charge to which the plea is offered, the mandatory minimum penalty provided by law, if any, and the maximum possible penalty provided by law, including the effect of any special parole or supervised release term, the fact that the court is required to consider any applicable sentencing guidelines but many depart from those guidelines under some circumstances, and, when applicable, that the court may also order the defendant to make restitution to any victim of the offense; and

(2) if the defendant is not represented by an attorney, that the defendant has the right to be represented by an attorney at every stage of the proceeding and, if necessary, one will be appointed to represent the defendant; and

(3) that the defendant has the right to plead not guilty or to persist in that plea if it has already been made, the right to be tried by a jury and at that trial the right to the assistance of counsel, the right to confront and cross-examine adverse witnesses, and the right against compelled self-incrimination; and

(4) that if a plea of guilty or nolo contendere is accepted by the court there will not be a further trial of any kind, so that by pleading guilty or nolo contendere the defendant waives the right to a trial; and

(5) if the court intends to question the defendant under oath, on the record, and in the presence of counsel about the offense to which the defendant has pleaded, that the defendant's answers may later be used against the defendant in a prosecution for perjury or false statement.

(d) Insuring That the Plea is Voluntary. The court shall not accept a plea of guilty or nolo contendere without first, by addressing the defendant personally in open court, determining that the plea is voluntary and not the result of force or threats or of promises apart from a plea agreement. The court shall also inquire as to whether the defendant's willingness to plead guilty or nolo contendere results from prior discussions between the attorney for the government and the defendant or the defendant's attorney.

(e) Plea Agreement Procedure.

(1) In General. The attorney for the government and the attorney for the defendant or the defendant when acting pro se may engage in discussions with a view toward reaching an agreement that, upon the entering of a plea of guilty or nolo contendere to a charged offense or to a lesser or related offense, the attorney for the government will do any of the following:

(A) move for dismissal of other charges; or

(B) make a recommendation, or agree not to oppose the defendant's request, for a particular sentence, with the understanding that such recommendation or request shall not be binding upon the court; or

(C) agree that a specific sentence is the appropriate disposition of the case.

The court shall not participate in any such discussions.

(2) Notice of Such Agreement. If a plea agreement has been reached by the parties, the court shall, on the record, require the disclosure of the agreement in open court or, on a showing of good cause, in camera, at the time the plea is offered. If the agreement is of the type specified in subdivision (e)(1)(A) or (C), the court may accept or reject the agreement, or may defer its decision as to the acceptance or rejection until there has been an opportunity to consider the presentence report. If the agreement is of the type specified in subdivision (e)(1) (B), the court shall advise the defendant that if the court does not accept the recommendation or request the defendant nevertheless has no right to withdraw the plea.

(3) **Acceptance of a Plea Agreement.** If the court accepts the plea agreement, the court shall inform the defendant that it will embody in the judgment and sentence the disposition provided for in the plea agreement.

(4) **Rejection of a Plea Agreement.** If the court rejects the plea agreement, the court shall, on the record, inform the parties of this fact, advise the defendant personally in open court or, on a showing of good cause, in camera, that the court is not bound by the plea agreement, afford the defendant the opportunity to then withdraw the plea, and advise the defendant that if the defendant persists in a guilty plea or plea of nolo contendere the disposition of the case may be less favorable to the defendant than that contemplated by the plea agreement.

(5) **Time of Plea Agreement Procedure.** Except for good cause shown, notification to the court of the existence of a plea agreement shall be given at the arraignment or at such other time, prior to trial, as may be fixed by the court.

(6) **Inadmissibility of Pleas, Plea Discussions, and Related Statements.** Except as otherwise provided in this paragraph, evidence of the following is not, in any civil or criminal proceeding, admissible against the defendant who made the plea or was a participant in the plea discussions:

(A) a plea of guilty which was later withdrawn;

(B) a plea of nolo contendere;

(C) any statement made in the course of any proceedings under this rule regarding either of the foregoing pleas; or

(D) any statement made in the course of plea discussions with an attorney for the government which do not result in a plea of guilty or which result in a plea of guilty later withdrawn.

However, such a statement is admissible (i) in any proceeding wherein another statement made in the course of the same plea or plea discussions has been introduced and the statement ought in fairness be considered contemporaneously with it, or (ii) in a criminal proceeding for perjury or false statement if the statement was made by the defendant under oath, on the record, and in the presence of counsel.

(f) Determining Accuracy of Plea. Notwithstanding the acceptance of a plea of guilty, the court should not enter a judgment upon such plea without making such inquiry as shall satisfy it that there is a factual basis for the plea.

(g) Record of Proceedings. A verbatim record of the proceedings at which the defendant enters a plea shall be made and, if there is a plea of guilty or nolo contendere, the record shall include, without limitation, the court's advice to the defendant, the inquiry into the voluntariness of the plea including any plea agreement, and the inquiry into the accuracy of a guilty plea.

(h) Harmless Error. Any variance from the procedures required by this rule which does not affect substantial rights shall be disregarded.

Rule 12. Pleadings and Motions Before Trial; Defenses and Objections

(a) Pleadings and Motions. Pleadings in criminal proceedings shall be the indictment and the information, and the pleas of not guilty, guilty and nolo contendere. All other pleas, and demurrers and motions to quash are abolished, and defenses and objections raised before trial which heretofore could have been raised by one or more of them shall be raised only by motion to dismiss or to grant appropriate relief, as provided in these rules.

(b) Pretrial Motions. Any defense, objection, or request which is capable of determination without the trial of the general issue may be raised before trial by motion. Motions may be written or oral at the discretion of the judge. The following must be raised prior to trial:

(1) Defenses and objections based on defects in the institution of the prosecution; or

(2) Defenses and objections based on defects in the indictment or information (other than that it fails to show jurisdiction in the court or to charge an offense which objections shall be noticed by the court at any time during the pendency of the proceedings); or

(3) Motions to suppress evidence; or

(4) Requests for discovery under Rule 16; or

(5) Requests for a severance of charges or defendants under Rule 14.

(c) Motion Date. Unless otherwise provided by local rule, the court may, at the time of the arraignment or as soon thereafter as practicable, set a time for the making of pretrial motions or requests and, if required, a later date of hearing.

(d) Notice by the Government of the Intention to Use Evidence.

(1) At the Discretion of the Government. At the arraignment or as soon thereafter as is practicable, the government may give notice to the defendant of its intention to use specified evidence at trial in order to afford the defendant an opportunity to raise objections to such evidence prior to trial under subdivision (b)(3) of this rule.

(2) At the Request of the Defendant. At the arraignment or as soon thereafter as is practicable the defendant may, in order to afford an opportunity to move to suppress evidence under subdivision (b)(3) of this rule, request notice of the government's intention to use (in its evidence in chief at trial) any evidence which the defendant may be entitled to discover under Rule 16 subject to any relevant limitations prescribed in Rule 16.

(e) Ruling on Motion. A motion made before trial shall be determined before trial unless the court, for good cause, orders that it be deferred for determination at the trial of the general issue or until after verdict, but no such determination shall be deferred if a party's right to appeal is adversely affected. Where factual issues are involved in determining a motion, the court shall state its essential findings on the record.

(f) Effect of Failure To Raise Defenses or Objections. Failure by a party to raise defenses or objections or to make requests which must be made prior to trial, at the time set by the court pursuant to subdivision (c), or prior to any extension thereof made by the court, shall constitute waiver thereof, but the court for cause shown may grant relief from the waiver.

(g) Records. A verbatim record shall be made of all proceedings at the hearing, including such findings of fact and conclusions of law as are made orally.

(h) Effect of Determination. If the court grants a motion based on a defect in the institution of the prosecution or in the indictment or information, it may also order that the defendant be continued in custody or that bail be continued for a specified time pending the filing of a new indictment or information. Nothing in this rule shall be deemed to affect the provisions of any Act of Congress relating to periods of limitations.

(i) Production of Statements at Suppression Hearing. Except as herein provided, rule 26.2 shall apply at a hearing on a motion to suppress evidence under subdivision (b)(3) of this rule. For purposes of this subdivision, a law enforcement officer shall be deemed a witness called by the government, and upon a claim of privilege the court shall excise the portions of the statement containing privileged matter.

Rule 12.1. Notice of Alibi

(a) Notice by Defendant. Upon written demand of the attorney for the government stating the time, date, and place at which the alleged offense was committed, the defendant shall serve within ten days, or at such different time as the court may direct, upon the attorney for the government a written notice of the defendant's intention to offer a defense of alibi. Such notice by the defendant shall state the specific place or places at which the defendant claims to have been at the time of the alleged offense and the names and addresses of the witnesses upon whom the defendant intends to rely to establish such alibi.

(b) Disclosure of Information and Witness. Within ten days thereafter, but in no event less than ten days before trial, unless the court otherwise directs, the attorney for the government shall serve upon the defendant or the defendant's attorney a written notice stating the names and addresses of the witnesses upon whom the government intends to rely to establish the defendant's presence at the scene of the alleged offense and any other witnesses to be relied on to rebut testimony of any of the defendant's alibi witnesses.

(c) Continuing Duty to Disclose. If prior to or during trial, a party learns of an additional witness whose identity, if known, should have been included in the information furnished under subdivision (a) or (b), the party shall promptly notify the other party or the other party's attorney of the existence and identity of such additional witness.

(d) Failure to Comply. Upon the failure of either party to comply with the requirements of this rule, the court may exclude the testimony of any undisclosed witness offered by such party as to the defendant's absence from or presence at, the scene of the alleged offense. This rule shall not limit the right of the defendant to testify.

(e) Exceptions. For good cause shown, the court may grant an exception to any of the requirements of subdivisions (a) through (d) of this rule.

(f) Inadmissibility of Withdrawn Alibi. Evidence of an intention to rely upon an alibi defense, later withdrawn, or of statements made in connection with such intention, is not, in any civil or criminal proceeding, admissible against the person who gave notice of the intention.

Rule 12.2. Notice of Insanity Defense or Expert Testimony of Defendant's Mental Condition

(a) Defense of Insanity. If a defendant intends to rely upon the defense of insanity at the time of the alleged offense, the defendant shall, within the time provided for the filing of pretrial motions or at such later time as the court may direct, notify the attorney for the government in writing of such intention and file a copy of such notice with the clerk. If there is a failure to comply with the requirements of this subdivision, insanity may not be raised as a defense. The court may for cause shown allow late filing of the notice or grant additional time to the parties to prepare for trial or make such other order as may be appropriate.

(b) Expert Testimony of Defendant's Mental Condition. If a defendant intends to introduce expert testimony relating to a mental disease or defect or any other mental condition of the defendant bearing upon the issue of guilt, the defendant shall, within the time provided for the filing of pretrial motions or at such later time as the court may direct, notify the attorney for the government in writing of such intention and file a copy of such notice with the clerk. The court may for cause shown allow late filing of the notice or grant additional time to the parties to prepare for trial or make such other order as may be appropriate.

(c) Mental Examination of Defendant. In an appropriate case the court may, upon motion of the attorney for the government, order the defendant to submit to an examination pursuant to 18 U.S.C. 4241 or 4242. No statement made by the defendant in the course of any examination provided for by this rule, whether the examination be with or without the consent of the defendant, no testimony by the expert based upon such statement, and no other fruits of the statement shall be admitted in evidence against the defendant in any criminal proceeding except on an issue respecting mental condition on which the defendant has introduced testimony.

(d) Failure To Comply. If there is a failure to give notice when required by subdivision (b) of this rule or to submit to an examination when ordered under subdivision (c) of this rule, the court may exclude the testimony of any expert witness offered by the defendant on the issue of the defendant's guilt.

(e) Inadmissibility of Withdrawn Intention. Evidence of an intention as to which notice was given under subdivision (a) or (b), later withdrawn, is not, in any civil or criminal proceeding, admissible against the person who gave notice of the intention.

Rule 12.3. Notice of Defense Based Upon Public Authority

(a) Notice by Defendant; Government Response; Disclosure of Witnesses.

(1) Defendant's Notice and Government's Response. A defendant intending to claim a defense of actual or believed exercise of public authority on behalf of a law enforcement or Federal intelligence agency at the time of the alleged offense shall, within the time provided for the filing of pretrial motions or at such later time as the court may direct, serve upon the attorney for the Government a written notice of such intention and file a copy of such notice with the clerk. Such notice shall identify the law enforcement or Federal intelligence agency and any member of such agency on behalf of which and the period of time in which the defendant claims the actual or believed exercise of public authority occurred. If the notice identifies a Federal intelligence agency, the copy filed with the clerk shall be under seal. Within ten days after receiving the defendant's notice, but in no event less than twenty days before the trial, the attorney for the Government shall serve upon the defendant or the defendant's attorney a written response which shall admit or deny that the defendant exercised the public authority identified in the defendant's notice.

(2) Disclosure of Witnesses. At the time that the Government serves its response to the notice or thereafter, but in no event less than twenty days before the trial, the attorney for the Government may serve upon the defendant or the defendant's attorney a written demand for the names and addresses of the witnesses, if any, upon whom the defendant intends to rely in establishing the defense identified in the notice. Within seven days after receiving the Government's demand, the defendant shall serve upon the attorney for the Government a written statement of the names and addresses of any such witnesses. Within seven days after receiving the defendant's written statement, the attorney for the Government shall serve upon the defendant or the defendant's attorney a written statement of the names and addresses of the witnesses, if any, upon whom the Government intends to rely in opposing the defense identified in the notice.

(3) Additional Time. If good cause is shown, the court may allow a party additional time to comply with any obligation imposed by this rule.

(b) Continuing Duty to Disclose. If, prior to or during trial, a party learns of any additional witness whose identity, if known, should have been included in the written statement furnished under subdivision (a)(2) of this rule, that party shall promptly notify in writing the other party or the other party's attorney of the name and address of any such witness.

(c) Failure to Comply. If a party fails to comply with the requirements of this rule, the court may exclude the testimony of any undisclosed witness offered in support of or in opposition to the defense, or enter such other order as it deems just under the circumstances. This rule shall not limit the right of the defendant to testify.

(d) Protective Procedures Unaffected. This rule shall be in addition to and shall not supersede the authority of the court to issue appropriate protective orders, or the authority of the court to order that any pleading be filed under seal.

(e) Inadmissibility of Withdrawn Defense Based Upon Public Authority. Evidence of an intention as to which notice was given under subdivision (a), later withdrawn, is not, in any civil or criminal proceeding, admissible against the person who gave notice of the intention.

Rule 13. Trial Together of Indictments or Informations

The court may order two or more indictments or informations or both to be tried together if the offenses, and the defendants if there is more than one, could have been joined in a single indictment or information. The procedure shall be the same as if the prosecution were under such single indictment or information.

Rule 14. Relief from Prejudicial Joinder

If it appears that a defendant or the government is prejudiced by a joinder of offenses or of defendants in an indictment or information or by such joinder for trial together, the court may order an election or separate trials of counts, grant a severance of defendants or provide whatever other relief justice requires. In ruling on a motion by a defendant for severance the court may order the attorney for the government to deliver to the court for inspection *in camera* any statements or confessions made by the defendants which the government intends to introduce in evidence at the trial.

Rule 15. Depositions

(a) When Taken. Whenever due to exceptional circumstances of the case it is in the interest of justice that the testimony of a prospective witness of a party be taken and preserved for use at trial, the court may upon motion of such party and notice to the parties order that testimony of such witness be taken by deposition and that any designated book, paper, document, record, recording, or other material not privileged, be produced at the same time and place. If a witness is detained pursuant to section 3144 of title 18, United States Code, the court on written motion of the witness and upon notice to the parties may direct that the witness' deposition be taken. After the deposition has been subscribed the court may discharge the witness.

(b) Notice of Taking. The party at whose instance a deposition is to be taken shall give to every party reasonable written notice of the time and place for taking the deposition. The notice shall state the name and address of each person to be examined. On motion of a party upon whom the notice is served, the court for cause shown may extend or shorten the time or change the place for taking the deposition. The officer having custody of a defendant shall be notified of the time and place set for the examination and shall, unless the defendant waives in writing the right to be present, produce the defendant at the examination and keep the defendant in the presence of the witness during the examination, unless, after being warned by the court that disruptive conduct will cause the defendant's removal from the place of the taking of the deposition, the defendant persists in conduct which is such as to justify exclusion from that place. A defendant not in custody shall have the right to be present at the examination upon request subject to such terms as may be fixed by the court, but a failure, absent good cause shown, to appear after notice and tender of expenses in accordance with subdivision (c) of this rule shall constitute a waiver of that right and of any objection to the taking and use of the deposition based upon that right.

(c) **Payment of Expenses.** Whenever a deposition is taken at the instance of the government, or whenever a deposition is taken at the instance of a defendant who is unable to bear the expenses of the taking of the deposition, the court may direct that the expense of travel and subsistence of the defendant and the defendant's attorney for attendance at the examination and the cost of the transcript of the deposition shall be paid by the government.

(d) **How Taken.** Subject to such additional conditions as the court shall provide, a deposition shall be taken and filed in the manner provided in civil actions except as otherwise provided in these rules, provided that (1) in no event shall a deposition be taken of a party defendant without that defendant's consent, and (2) the scope and manner of examination and cross-examination shall be such as would be allowed in the trial itself. The government shall make available to the defendant or the defendant's counsel for examination and use at the taking of the deposition any statement of the witness being deposed which is in the possession of the government and to which the defendant would be entitled at the trial.

(e) **Use.** At the trial or upon any hearing, a part or all of a deposition, so far as otherwise admissible under the rules of evidence, may be used as substantive evidence if the witness is unavailable, as unavailability is defined in Rule 804(a) of the Federal Rules of Evidence, or the witness gives testimony at the trial or hearing inconsistent with that witness' deposition. Any deposition may also be used by any party for the purpose of contradicting or impeaching the testimony of the deponent as a witness. If only a part of a deposition is offered in evidence by a party, an adverse party may require the offering of all of it which is relevant to the part offered and any party may offer other parts.

(f) **Objections to Deposition Testimony.** Objections to deposition testimony or evidence or parts thereof and the grounds for the objection shall be stated at the time of the taking of the deposition.

(g) **Deposition by Agreement Not Precluded.** Nothing in this rule shall preclude the taking of a deposition, orally or upon written questions, or the use of a deposition, by agreement of the parties with the consent of the court.

Rule 16. Discovery and Inspection

(a) **Disclosure of Evidence by the Government.**

(1) **Information Subject to Disclosure.**

(A) **Statement of Defendant.** Upon request of a defendant the government shall disclose to the defendant and make available for inspection, copying, or photographing: any relevant written or recorded statements made by the defendant, or copies thereof, within the possession, custody or control of the government, the existence of which is known, or by the exercise of due diligence may become known, to the attorney for the government; that portion of any written record containing the substance of any relevant oral statement made by the defendant whether before or after arrest in response to interrogation by any person then known to the defendant to be a government agent; and recorded testimony of the defendant before a grand jury which relates to the offense charged. The government shall also disclose to the defendant the substance of any other relevant oral statement made by the defendant whether before or after arrest in response to interrogation by any person then known by the defendant to be a government agent if the government intends to use that statement at trial. Where the defendant is a corporation, partnership, association or labor union, the court may grant the defendant, upon its motion, discovery of relevant recorded testimony of any witness before a grand jury who (1) was, at the time of that testimony, so situated as an officer or employee as to have been able legally to bind the defendant in respect to conduct constituting the offense, or (2) was, at the time of the offense, personally involved in the alleged conduct constituting the offense and so situated as an officer or employee as to have been able legally to bind the defendant in respect to that alleged conduct in which the witness was involved.

(B) Defendant's Prior Record. Upon request of the defendant, the government shall furnish to the defendant such copy of the defendant's prior criminal record, if any, as is within the possession, custody, or control of the government, the existence of which is known, or by the exercise of due diligence may become known, to the attorney for the government.

(C) Documents and Tangible Objects. Upon request of the defendant the government shall permit the defendant to inspect and copy or photograph books, papers, documents, photographs, tangible objects, buildings or places, or copies or portions thereof, which are within the possession, custody or control of the government, and which are material to the preparation of the defendant's defense or are intended for use by the government as evidence in chief at the trial, or were obtained from or belong to the defendant.

(D) Reports of Examinations and Tests. Upon request of a defendant the government shall permit the defendant to inspect and copy or photograph any results or reports of physical or mental examinations, and of scientific tests or experiments, or copies thereof, which are within the possession, custody, or control of the government, the existence of which is known, or by the exercise of due diligence may become known, to the attorney for the government, and which are material to the preparation of the defense or are intended for use by the government as evidence in chief at the trial.

(2) Information Not Subject to Disclosure. Except as provided in paragraphs (A), (B), and (D) of subdivision (a)(1), this rule does not authorize the discovery or inspection of reports, memoranda, or other internal government documents made by the attorney for the government or other government agents in connection with the investigation or prosecution of the case, or of statements made by government witnesses or prospective government witnesses except as provided in 18 U.S.C. § 3500.

(3) Grand Jury Transcripts. Except as provided in Rules 6, 12(i) and 26.2, and subdivision (a)(1)(A) of this rule, these rules do not relate to discovery or inspection of recorded proceedings of a grand jury.

[**(4) Failure to Call Witness.**] (Deleted Dec. 12, 1975)

(b) Disclosure of Evidence by the Defendant.

(1) Information Subject to Disclosure.

(A) Documents and Tangible Objects. If the defendant requests disclosure under subdivision (a)(1)(C) or (D) of this rule, upon compliance with such request by the government, the defendant, on request of the government, shall permit the government to inspect and copy or photograph books, papers, documents, photographs, tangible objects, or copies or portions thereof, which are within the possession, custody, or control of the defendant and which the defendant intends to introduce as evidence in chief at the trial.

(B) Reports of Examinations and Tests. If the defendant requests disclosure under subdivision (a)(1)(C) or (D) of this rule, upon compliance with such request by the government, the defendant, on request of the government, shall permit the government to inspect and copy or photograph any results or reports of physical or mental examinations and of scientific tests or experiments made in connection with the particular case, or copies thereof, within the possession or control of the defendant, which the defendant intends to introduce as evidence in chief at the trial or which were prepared by a witness whom the defendant intends to call at the trial when the results or reports relate to that witness' testimony.

(2) Information Not Subject To Disclosure. Except as to scientific or medical reports, this subdivision does not authorize the discovery or inspection of reports, memoranda, or other internal defense documents made by the defendant, or the defendant's attorneys or agents in connection with the investigation or defense of the case, or of statements made by the defendant, or by government or defense witnesses, or by prospective government or defense witnesses, to the defendant, the defendant's agents or attorneys.

[(3) Failure to Call Witness.]   (Deleted Dec. 12, 1975)

(c) Continuing Duty to Disclose.   If, prior to or during trial, a party discovers additional evidence or material previously requested or ordered, which is subject to discovery or inspection under this rule, such party shall promptly notify the other party or that other party's attorney or the court of the existence of the additional evidence or material.

(d) Regulation of Discovery.

(1) Protective and Modifying Orders.   Upon a sufficient showing the court may at any time order that the discovery or inspection be denied, restricted, or deferred, or make such other order as is appropriate.   Upon motion by a party, the court may permit the party to make such showing, in whole or in part, in the form of a written statement to be inspected by the judge alone.   If the court enters an order granting relief following such an ex parte showing, the entire text of the party's statement shall be sealed and preserved in the records of the court to be made available to the appellate court in the event of an appeal.

(2) Failure To Comply With a Request.   If at any time during the course of the proceedings it is brought to the attention of the court that a party has failed to comply with this rule, the court may order such party to permit the discovery or inspection, grant a continuance, or prohibit the party from introducing evidence not disclosed, or it may enter such other order as it deems just under the circumstances.   The court may specify the time, place and manner of making the discovery and inspection and may prescribe such terms and conditions as are just.

(e) Alibi Witnesses.   Discovery of alibi witnesses is governed by Rule 12.1.

Rule 17. Subpoena

(a) For Attendance of Witnesses; Form; Issuance. A subpoena shall be issued by the clerk under the seal of the court. It shall state the name of the court and the title, if any, of the proceeding, and shall command each person to whom it is directed to attend and give testimony at the time and place specified therein. The clerk shall issue a subpoena, signed and sealed but otherwise in blank to a party requesting it, who shall fill in the blanks before it is served. A subpoena shall be issued by a United States magistrate in a proceeding before that magistrate, but it need not be under the seal of the court.

(b) Defendants Unable to Pay. The court shall order at any time that a subpoena be issued for service on a named witness upon an *ex parte* application of a defendant upon a satisfactory showing that the defendant is financially unable to pay the fees of the witness and that the presence of the witness is necessary to an adequate defense. If the court orders the subpoena to be issued the costs incurred by the process and the fees of the witness so subpoenaed shall be paid in the same manner in which similar costs and fees are paid in case of a witness subpoenaed in behalf of the government.

(c) **For Production of Documentary Evidence and of Objects.** A subpoena may also command the person to whom it is directed to produce the books, papers, documents or other objects designated therein. The court on motion made promptly may quash or modify the subpoena if compliance would be unreasonable or oppressive. The court may direct that books, papers, documents or objects designated in the subpoena be produced before the court at a time prior to the trial or prior to the time when they are to be offered in evidence and may upon their production permit the books, papers, documents or objects or portions thereof to be inspected by the parties and their attorneys.

(d) **Service.** A subpoena may be served by the marshal, by a deputy marshal or by any other person who is not a party and who is not less than 18 years of age. Service of a subpoena shall be made by delivering a copy thereof to the person named and by tendering to that person the fee for 1 day's attendance and the mileage allowed by law. Fees and mileage need not be tendered to the witness upon service of a subpoena issued in behalf of the United States or an officer or agency thereof.

(e) **Place of Service.**

(1) **In United States.** A subpoena requiring the attendance of a witness at a hearing or trial may be served at any place within the United States.

(2) **Abroad.** A subpoena directed to a witness in a foreign country shall issue under the circumstances and in the manner and be served as provided in Title 28, U.S.C., § 1783.

(f) **For Taking Deposition; Place of Examination.**

(1) **Issuance.** An order to take a deposition authorizes the issuance by the clerk of the court for the district in which the deposition is to be taken of subpoenas for the persons named or described therein.

(2) **Place.** The witness whose deposition is to be taken may be required by subpoena to attend at any place designated by the trial court, taking into account the convenience of the witness and the parties.

(g) **Contempt.** Failure by any person without adequate excuse to obey a subpoena served upon that person may be deemed a contempt of the court from which the subpoena issued or of the court for the district in which it issued if it was issued by a United States magistrate.

(h) **Information Not Subject to Subpoena.** Statements made by witnesses or prospective witnesses may not be subpoenaed from the government or the defendant under this rule, but shall be subject to production only in accordance with the provisions of Rule 26.2.

Rule 17.1. Pretrial Conference

At any time after the filing of the indictment or information the court upon motion of any party or upon its own motion may order one or more conferences to consider such matters as will promote a fair and expeditious trial. At the conclusion of a conference the court shall prepare and file a memorandum of the matters agreed upon. No admissions made by the defendant or the defendant's attorney at the conference shall be used against the defendant unless the admissions are reduced to writing and signed by the defendant and the defendant's attorney. This rule shall not be invoked in the case of a defendant who is not represented by counsel.

V. VENUE

Rule 18. Place of Prosecution and Trial

Except as otherwise permitted by statute or by these rules, the prosecution shall be had in a district in which the offense was committed. The court shall fix the place of trial within the district with due regard to the convenience of the defendant and the witnesses and the prompt administration of justice.

Rule 19. Rescinded Feb. 28, 1966, eff. July 1, 1966

Rule 20. Transfer From the District for Plea and Sentence

(a) Indictment or Information Pending. A defendant arrested, held, or present in a district other than that in which an indictment or information is pending against that defendant may state in writing a wish to plead guilty or nolo contendere, to waive trial in the district in which the indictment or information is pending, and to consent to disposition of the case in the district in which that defendant was arrested, held, or present, subject to the approval of the United States attorney for each district. Upon receipt of the defendant's statement and of the written approval of the United States attorneys, the clerk of the court in which the indictment or information is pending shall transmit the papers in the proceeding or certified copies thereof to the clerk of the court for the district in which the defendant is arrested, held, or present, and the prosecution shall continue in that district.

(b) Indictment or Information Not Pending. A defendant arrested, held, or present, in a district other than the district in which a complaint is pending against that defendant may state in writing a wish to plead guilty or nolo contendere, to waive venue and trial in the district in which the warrant was issued, and to consent to disposition of the case in the district in which that defendant was arrested, held, or present, subject to the approval of the United States attorney for each district. Upon filing the written waiver of venue in the district in which the defendant is present, the prosecution may proceed as if venue were in such district.

(c) Effect of Not Guilty Plea. If after the proceeding has been transferred pursuant to subdivision (a) or (b) of this rule the defendant pleads not guilty, the clerk shall return the papers to the court in which the prosecution was commenced, and the proceeding shall be restored to the docket of that court. The defendant's statement that the defendant wishes to plead guilty or nolo contendere shall not be used against that defendant.

(d) Juveniles. A juvenile (as defined in 18 U.S.C. § 5031) who is arrested, held, or present in a district other than that in which the juvenile is alleged to have committed an act in violation of a law of the United States not punishable by death or life imprisonment may, after having been advised by counsel and with the approval of the court and the United States attorney for each district, consent to be proceeded against as a juvenile delinquent in the district in which the juvenile is arrested, held, or present. The consent shall be given in writing before the court but only after the court has apprised the juvenile of the juvenile's rights, including the right to be returned to the district in which the juvenile is alleged to have committed the act, and of the consequences of such consent.

Rule 21. Transfer From the District for Trial

(a) For Prejudice in the District. The court upon motion of the defendant shall transfer the proceeding as to that defendant to another district whether or not such district is specified in the defendant's motion if the court is satisfied that there exists in the district where the prosecution is pending so great a prejudice against the defendant that the defendant cannot obtain a fair and impartial trial at any place fixed by law for holding court in that district.

(b) Transfer in Other Cases. For the convenience of parties and witnesses, and in the interest of justice, the court upon motion of the defendant may transfer the proceeding as to that defendant or any one or more of the counts thereof to another district.

(c) Proceedings on Transfer. When a transfer is ordered the clerk shall transmit to the clerk of the court to which the proceeding is transferred all papers in the proceeding or duplicates thereof and any bail taken, and the prosecution shall continue in that district.

Rule 22. Time of Motion to Transfer

A motion to transfer under these rules may be made at or before arraignment or at such other time as the court or these rules may prescribe.

VI. TRIAL

Rule 23. Trial by Jury or by the Court

(a) Trial by Jury. Cases required to be tried by jury shall be so tried unless the defendant waives a jury trial in writing with the approval of the court and the consent of the government.

(b) Jury of Less Than Twelve. Juries shall be of 12 but at any time before verdict the parties may stipulate in writing with the approval of the court that the jury shall consist of any number less than 12 or that a valid verdict may be returned by a jury of less than 12 should the court find it necessary to excuse one or more jurors for any just cause after trial commences. Even absent such stipulation, if the court finds it necessary to excuse a juror for just cause after the jury has retired to consider its verdict, in the discretion of the court a valid verdict may be returned by the remaining 11 jurors.

(c) Trial Without a Jury. In a case tried without a jury the court shall make a general finding and shall in addition, on request made before the general finding, find the facts specially. Such findings may be oral. If an opinion or memorandum of decision is filed, it will be sufficient if the findings of fact appear therein.

Rule 24. Trial Jurors

(a) Examination. The court may permit the defendant or the defendant's attorney and the attorney for the government to conduct the examination of prospective jurors or may itself conduct the examination. In the latter event the court shall permit the defendant or the defendant's attorney and the attorney for the government to supplement the examination by such further inquiry as it deems proper or shall itself submit to the prospective jurors such additional questions by the parties or their attorneys as it deems proper.

(b) Peremptory Challenges. If the offense charged is punishable by death, each side is entitled to 20 peremptory challenges. If the offense charged is punishable by imprisonment for more than one year, the government is entitled to 6 peremptory challenges and the defendant or defendants jointly to 10 peremptory challenges. If the offense charged is punishable by imprisonment for not more than one year or by fine or both, each side is entitled to 3 peremptory challenges. If there is more than one defendant, the court may allow the defendants additional peremptory challenges and permit them to be exercised separately or jointly.

(c) **Alternate Jurors.** The court may direct that not more than 6 jurors in addition to the regular jury be called and impanelled to sit as alternate jurors. Alternate jurors in the order in which they are called shall replace jurors who, prior to the time the jury retires to consider its verdict, become or are found to be unable or disqualified to perform their duties. Alternate jurors shall be drawn in the same manner, shall have the same qualifications, shall be subject to the same examination and challenges, shall take the same oath and shall have the same functions, powers, facilities and privileges as the regular jurors. An alternate juror who does not replace a regular juror shall be discharged after the jury retires to consider its verdict. Each side is entitled to 1 peremptory challenge in addition to those otherwise allowed by law if 1 or 2 alternate jurors are to be impanelled, 2 peremptory challenges if 3 or 4 alternate jurors are to be impanelled, and 3 peremptory challenges if 5 or 6 alternate jurors are to be impanelled. The additional peremptory challenges may be used against an alternate juror only, and the other peremptory challenges allowed by these rules may not be used against an alternate juror.

Rule 25. Judge; Disability

(a) **During Trial.** If by reason of death, sickness or other disability the judge before whom a jury trial has commenced is unable to proceed with the trial, any other judge regularly sitting in or assigned to the court, upon certifying familiarity with the record of the trial, may proceed with and finish the trial.

(b) **After Verdict or Finding of Guilt.** If by reason of absence, death, sickness or other disability the judge before whom the defendant has been tried is unable to perform the duties to be performed by the court after a verdict or finding of guilt, any other judge regularly sitting in or assigned to the court may perform those duties; but if that judge is satisfied that a judge who did not preside at the trial cannot perform those duties or that it is appropriate for any other reason, that judge may grant a new trial.

Rule 26. Taking of Testimony

In all trials the testimony of witnesses shall be taken orally in open court, unless otherwise provided by an Act of Congress or by these rules, the Federal Rules of Evidence, or other rules adopted by the Supreme Court.

Rule 26.1. Determination of Foreign Law

A party who intends to raise an issue concerning the law of a foreign country shall give reasonable written notice. The court, in determining foreign law, may consider any relevant material or source, including testimony, whether or not submitted by a party or admissible under the Federal Rules of Evidence. The court's determination shall be treated as a ruling on a question of law.

Rule 26.2. Production of Statements of Witnesses

(a) **Motion for Production.** After a witness other than the defendant has testified on direct examination, the court, on motion of a party who did not call the witness, shall order the attorney for the government or the defendant and the defendant's attorney, as the case may be, to produce, for the examination and use of the moving party, any statement of the witness that is in their possession and that relates to the subject matter concerning which the witness has testified.

(b) **Production of Entire Statement.** If the entire contents of the statement relate to the subject matter concerning which the witness has testified, the court shall order that the statement be delivered to the moving party.

(c) Production of Excised Statement. If the other party claims that the statement contains matter that does not relate to the subject matter concerning which the witness has testified, the court shall order that it be delivered to the court in camera. Upon inspection, the court shall excise the portions of the statement that do not relate to the subject matter concerning which the witness has testified, and shall order that the statement, with such material excised, be delivered to the moving party. Any portion of the statement that is withheld from the defendant over the defendant's objection shall be preserved by the attorney for the government, and, in the event of a conviction and an appeal by the defendant, shall be made available to the appellate court for the purpose of determining the correctness of the decision to excise the portion of the statement.

(d) Recess for Examination of Statement. Upon delivery of the statement to the moving party, the court, upon application of that party, may recess proceedings in the trial for the examination of such statement and for preparation for its use in the trial.

(e) Sanction for Failure to Produce Statement. If the other party elects not to comply with an order to deliver a statement to the moving party, the court shall order that the testimony of the witness be stricken from the record and that the trial proceed, or, if it is the attorney for the government who elects not to comply, shall declare a mistrial if required by the interest of justice.

(f) Definition. As used in this rule, a "statement" of a witness means:

(1) a written statement made by the witness that is signed or otherwise adopted or approved by the witness;

(2) a substantially verbatim recital of an oral statement made by the witness that is recorded contemporaneously with the making of the oral statement and that is contained in a stenographic, mechanical, electrical, or other recording or a transcription thereof; or

(3) a statement, however taken or recorded, or a transcription thereof, made by the witness to a grand jury.

Rule 27. Proof of Official Record

An official record or an entry therein or the lack of such a record or entry may be proved in the same manner as in civil actions.

Rule 28. Interpreters

The court may appoint an interpreter of its own selection and may fix the reasonable compensation of such interpreter. Such compensation shall be paid out of funds provided by law or by the government, as the court may direct.

Rule 29. Motion for Judgment of Acquittal

(a) Motion Before Submission to Jury. Motions for directed verdict are abolished and motions for judgment of acquittal shall be used in their place. The court on motion of a defendant or of its own motion shall order the entry of judgment of acquittal of one or more offenses charged in the indictment or information after the evidence on either side is closed if the evidence is insufficient to sustain a conviction of such offense or offenses. If a defendant's motion for judgment of acquittal at the close of the evidence offered by the government is not granted, the defendant may offer evidence without having reserved the right.

(b) Reservation of Decision on Motion. If a motion for judgment of acquittal is made at the close of all the evidence, the court may reserve decision on the motion, submit the case to the jury and decide the motion either before the jury returns a verdict or after it returns a verdict of guilty or is discharged without having returned a verdict.

(c) Motion After Discharge of Jury. If the jury returns a verdict of guilty or is discharged without having returned a verdict, a motion for judgment of acquittal may be made or renewed within 7 days after the jury is discharged or within such further time as the court may fix during the 7–day period. If a verdict of guilty is returned the court may on such motion set aside the verdict and enter judgment of acquittal. If no verdict is returned the court may enter judgment of acquittal. It shall not be necessary to the making of such a motion that a similar motion has been made prior to the submission of the case to the jury.

(d) Same: Conditional Ruling on Grant of Motion. If a motion for judgment of acquittal after verdict of guilty under this Rule is granted, the court shall also determine whether any motion for a new trial should be granted if the judgment of acquittal is thereafter vacated or reversed, specifying the grounds for such determination. If the motion for a new trial is granted conditionally, the order thereon does not affect the finality of the judgment. If the motion for a new trial has been granted conditionally and the judgment is reversed on appeal, the new trial shall proceed unless the appellate court has otherwise ordered. If such motion has been denied conditionally, the appellee on appeal may assert error in that denial, and if the judgment is reversed on appeal, subsequent proceedings shall be in accordance with the order of the appellate court.

Rule 29.1. Closing Argument

After the closing of evidence the prosecution shall open the argument. The defense shall be permitted to reply. The prosecution shall then be permitted to reply in rebuttal.

Rule 30. Instructions

At the close of the evidence or at such earlier time during the trial as the court reasonably directs, any party may file written requests that the court instruct the jury on the law as set forth in the requests. At the same time copies of such requests shall be furnished to all parties. The court shall inform counsel of its proposed action upon the requests prior to their arguments to the jury. The court may instruct the jury before or after the arguments are completed or at both times. No party may assign as error any portion of the charge or omission therefrom unless that party objects thereto before the jury retires to consider its verdict, stating distinctly the matter to which that party objects and the grounds of the objection. Opportunity shall be given to make the objection out of the hearing of the jury and, on request of any party, out of the presence of the jury.

Rule 31. Verdict

(a) Return. The verdict shall be unanimous. It shall be returned by the jury to the judge in open court.

(b) Several Defendants. If there are two or more defendants, the jury at any time during its deliberations may return a verdict or verdicts with respect to a defendant or defendants as to whom it has agreed; if the jury cannot agree with respect to all, the defendant or defendants as to whom it does not agree may be tried again.

(c) Conviction of Less Offense. The defendant may be found guilty of an offense necessarily included in the offense charged or of an attempt to commit either the offense charged or an offense necessarily included therein if the attempt is an offense.

(d) Poll of Jury. When a verdict is returned and before it is recorded the jury shall be polled at the request of any party or upon the court's own motion. If upon the poll there is not unanimous concurrence, the jury may be directed to retire for further deliberations or may be discharged.

(e) Criminal Forfeiture. If the indictment or the information alleges that an interest or property is subject to criminal forfeiture, a special verdict shall be returned as to the extent of the interest or property subject to forfeiture, if any.

VII.   JUDGMENT

Rule 32.   Sentence and Judgment

(a) Sentence.

(1) Imposition of Sentence. Sentence shall be imposed without unnecessary delay, but the court may, when there is a factor important to the sentencing determination that is not then capable of being resolved, postpone the imposition of sentence for a reasonable time until the factor is capable of being resolved. Prior to the sentencing hearing, the court shall provide the counsel for the defendant and the attorney for the Government with notice of the probation officer's determination, pursuant to the provisions of subdivision (c)(2)(B), of the sentencing classifications and sentencing guideline range believed to be applicable to the case. At the sentencing hearing, the court shall afford the counsel for the defendant and the attorney for the Government an opportunity to comment upon the probation officer's determination and on other matters relating to the appropriate sentence. Before imposing sentence, the court shall also—

(A) determine that the defendant and defendant's counsel have had the opportunity to read and discuss the presentence investigation report made available pursuant to subdivision (c)(3)(A) or summary thereof made available pursuant to subdivision (c)(3)(B);

(B) afford counsel for the defendant an opportunity to speak on behalf of the defendant; and

(C) address the defendant personally and determine if the defendant wishes to make a statement and to present any information in mitigation of the sentence.

The attorney for the Government shall have an equivalent opportunity to speak to the court. Upon a motion that is jointly filed by the defendant and by the attorney for the Government, the court may hear in camera such a statement by the defendant, counsel for the defendant, or the attorney for the Government.

(2) Notification of Right to Appeal. After imposing sentence in a case which has gone to trial on a plea of not guilty, the court shall advise the defendant of the defendant's right to appeal, including any right to appeal the sentence, and of the right of a person who is unable to pay the cost of an appeal to apply for leave to appeal in forma pauperis. There shall be no duty on the court to advise the defendant of any right of appeal after sentence is imposed following a plea of guilty or nolo contendere, except that the court shall advise the defendant of any right to appeal his sentence. If the defendant so requests, the clerk of the court shall prepare and file forthwith a notice of appeal on behalf of the defendant.

(b) Judgment.

(1) In General. A judgment of conviction shall set forth the plea, the verdict or findings, and the adjudication and sentence. If the defendant is found not guilty or for any other reason is entitled to be discharged, judgment shall be entered accordingly. The judgment shall be signed by the judge and entered by the clerk.

(2) Criminal Forfeiture. When a verdict contains a finding of property subject to a criminal forfeiture, the judgment of criminal forfeiture shall authorize the

Attorney General to seize the interest or property subject to forfeiture, fixing such terms and conditions as the court shall deem proper.

(c) Presentence Investigation.

(1) When Made. A probation officer shall make a presentence investigation and report to the court before the imposition of sentence unless the court finds that there is in the record information sufficient to enable the meaningful exercise of sentencing authority pursuant to 18 U.S.C. 3553, and the court explains this finding on the record.

Except with the written consent of the defendant, the report shall not be submitted to the court or its contents disclosed to anyone unless the defendant has pleaded guilty or nolo contendere or has been found guilty.

(2) Report. The report of the presentence investigation shall contain—

(A) information about the history and characteristics of the defendant, including prior criminal record, if any, financial condition, and any circumstances affecting the defendant's behavior that may be helpful in imposing sentence or in the correctional treatment of the defendant;

(B) the classification of the offense and of the defendant under the categories established by the Sentencing Commission pursuant to section 994(a) of title 28, that the probation officer believes to be applicable to the defendant's case; the kinds of sentence and the sentencing range suggested for such a category of offense committed by such a category of defendant as set forth in the guidelines issued by the Sentencing Commission pursuant to 28 U.S.C. 994(a)(1); and an explanation by the probation officer of any factors that may indicate that a sentence of a different kind or of a different length from one within the applicable guideline would be more appropriate under all the circumstances;

(C) any pertinent policy statement issued by the Sentencing Commission pursuant to 28 U.S.C. 994(a)(2);

(D) verified information stated in a nonargumentative style containing an assessment of the financial, social, psychological, and medical impact upon, and cost to, any individual against whom the offense has been committed;

(E) unless the court orders otherwise, information concerning the nature and extent of nonprison programs and resources available for the defendant; and

(F) such other information as may be required by the court.

(3) Disclosure.

(A) At least 10 days before imposing sentence, unless this minimum period is waived by the defendant the court shall provide the defendant and the defendant's counsel with a copy of the report of the presentence investigation, including the information required by subdivision (c)(2) but not including any final recommendation as to sentence, and not to the extent that in the opinion of the court the report contains diagnostic opinions which, if disclosed, might seriously disrupt a program of rehabilitation; or sources of information obtained upon a promise of confidentiality; or any other information which, if disclosed, might result in harm, physical or otherwise, to the defendant or other persons. The court shall afford the defendant and the defendant's counsel an opportunity to comment on the report and, in the discretion of the court, to introduce testimony or other information relating to any alleged factual inaccuracy contained in it.

(B) If the court is of the view that there is information in the presentence report which should not be disclosed under subdivision (c)(3)(A) of this rule, the court in lieu of making the report or part thereof available shall state orally or in writing a summary of the factual information contained therein to be relied on in determining sentence, and shall give the defendant and the defendant's counsel an opportunity to comment thereon. The statement may be made to the parties in camera.

(C) Any material which may be disclosed to the defendant and the defendant's counsel shall be disclosed to the attorney for the government.

(D) If the comments of the defendant and the defendant's counsel or testimony or other information introduced by them allege any factual inaccuracy in the presentence investigation report or the summary of the report or part thereof, the court shall, as to each matter controverted, make (i) a finding as to the allegation, or (ii) a determination that no such finding is necessary because the matter controverted will not be taken into account in sentencing. A written record of such findings and determinations shall be appended to and accompany any copy of the presentence investigation report thereafter made available to the Bureau of Prisons.

(E) The reports of studies and recommendations contained therein made by the Director of the Bureau of Prisons pursuant to 18 U.S.C. § 3552(b) shall be considered a presentence investigation within the meaning of subdivision (c)(3) of this rule.

(d) Plea Withdrawal. If a motion for withdrawal of a plea of guilty or nolo contendere is made before sentence is imposed, the court may permit withdrawal of the plea upon a showing by the defendant of any fair and just reason. At any later time, a plea may be set aside only on direct appeal or by motion under 28 U.S.C. § 2255.

(e) Probation. After conviction of an offense not punishable by death or by life imprisonment, the defendant may be placed on probation if permitted by law.

(f) [Revocation of Probation.] (Abrogated Apr. 30, 1979, eff. Dec. 1, 1980)

Rule 32.1. Revocation or Modification of Probation or Supervised Release

(a) Revocation of Probation or Supervised Release.

(1) Preliminary Hearing. Whenever a person is held in custody on the ground that the person has violated a condition of probation or supervised release, the person shall be afforded a prompt hearing before any judge, or a United States magistrate who has been given authority pursuant to 28 U.S.C. § 636 to conduct such hearings, in order to determine whether there is probable cause to hold the person for a revocation hearing. The person shall be given

(A) notice of the preliminary hearing and its purpose and of the alleged violation;

(B) an opportunity to appear at the hearing and present evidence in the person's own behalf;

(C) upon request, the opportunity to question witnesses against the person unless, for good cause, the federal magistrate decides that justice does not require the appearance of the witness; and

(D) notice of the person's right to be represented by counsel.

The proceedings shall be recorded stenographically or by an electronic recording device. If probable cause is found to exist, the person shall be held for a revocation hearing. The person may be released pursuant to Rule 46(c) pending the revocation hearing. If probable cause is not found to exist, the proceeding shall be dismissed.

(2) **Revocation Hearing.** The revocation hearing, unless waived by the person, shall be held within a reasonable time in the district of jurisdiction. The person shall be given

(A) written notice of the alleged violation;

(B) disclosure of the evidence against the person;

(C) an opportunity to appear and to present evidence in the person's own behalf;

(D) the opportunity to question adverse witnesses; and

(E) notice of the person's right to be represented by counsel.

(b) **Modification of Probation or Supervised Release.** A hearing and assistance of counsel are required before the terms or conditions of probation or supervised release can be modified, unless the relief to be granted to the person on probation or supervised release upon the person's request or the court's own motion is favorable to the person, and the attorney for the government, after having been given notice of the proposed relief and a reasonable opportunity to object, has not objected. An extension of the term of probation or supervised release is not favorable to the person for the purposes of this rule.

Rule 33. New Trial

The court on motion of a defendant may grant a new trial to that defendant if required in the interest of justice. If trial was by the court without a jury the court on motion of a defendant for a new trial may vacate the judgment if entered, take additional testimony and direct the entry of a new judgment. A motion for a new trial based on the ground of newly discovered evidence may be made only before or within two years after final judgment, but if an appeal is pending the court may grant the motion only on remand of the case. A motion for a new trial based on any other grounds shall be made within 7 days after verdict or finding of guilty or within such further time as the court may fix during the 7–day period.

Rule 34. Arrest of Judgment

The court on motion of a defendant shall arrest judgment if the indictment or information does not charge an offense or if the court was without jurisdiction of the offense charged. The motion in arrest of judgment shall be made within 7 days after verdict or finding of guilty, or after plea of guilty or *nolo contendere,* or within such further time as the court may fix during the 7–day period.

Rule 35. Correction of Sentence

(a) **Correction of a Sentence on Remand.** The court shall correct a sentence that is determined on appeal under 18 U.S.C. 3742 to have been imposed in violation of law, to have been imposed as a result of an incorrect application of the sentencing guidelines, or to be unreasonable, upon remand of the case to the court—

(1) for imposition of a sentence in accord with the findings of the court of appeals; or

(2) for further sentencing proceedings if, after such proceedings, the court determines that the original sentence was incorrect.

(b) **Reduction of Sentence for Changed Circumstances.** The court, on motion of the Government made within one year after the imposition of the sentence, may reduce a sentence to reflect a defendant's subsequent, substantial assistance in the investigation or prosecution of another person who has committed an offense, in accordance with the guidelines and policy statements issued by the Sentencing Commission pursuant to section 994 of title 28, United States Code.

The court may consider a government motion to reduce a sentence made one year or more after imposition of the sentence where the defendant's substantial assistance involves information or evidence not known by the defendant until one year or more after imposition of sentence. The court's authority to reduce a sentence under this subsection includes the authority to reduce such sentence to a level below that established by statute as a minimum sentence.

(c) **Correction of Sentence by Sentencing Court.** The Court, acting within 7 days after the imposition of sentence, may correct a sentence that was imposed as a result of arithmetical, technical, or other clear error.

Rule 36. Clerical Mistakes

Clerical mistakes in judgments, orders or other parts of the record and errors in the record arising from oversight or omission may be corrected by the court at any time and after such notice, if any, as the court orders.

[VIII. APPEAL] (Abrogated Dec. 4, 1967, eff. July 1, 1968)

[Rule 37. Taking Appeal; and Petition for Writ of Certiorari.] (Abrogated Dec. 4, 1967, Eff. July 1, 1968)

Rule 38. Stay of Execution

(a) **Death.** A sentence of death shall be stayed if an appeal is taken from the conviction or sentence.

(b) **Imprisonment.** A sentence of imprisonment shall be stayed if an appeal is taken from the conviction or sentence and the defendant is released pending disposition of appeal pursuant to Rule 9(b) of the Federal Rules of Appellate Procedure. If not stayed, the court may recommend to the Attorney General that the defendant be retained at, or transferred to, a place of confinement near the place of trial or the place where an appeal is to be heard, for a period reasonably necessary to permit the defendant to assist in the preparation of an appeal to the court of appeals.

(c) **Fine.** A sentence to pay a fine or a fine and costs, if an appeal is taken, may be stayed by the district court or by the court of appeals upon such terms as the court deems proper. The court may require the defendant pending appeal to deposit the whole or any part of the fine and costs in the registry of the district court, or to give bond for the payment thereof, or to submit to an examination of assets, and it may make any appropriate order to restrain the defendant from dissipating such defendant's assets.

(d) **Probation.** A sentence of probation may be stayed if an appeal from the conviction or sentence is taken. If the sentence is stayed, the court shall fix the terms of the stay.

(e) **Criminal Forfeiture, Notice to Victims, and Restitution.** A sanction imposed as part of the sentence pursuant to 18 U.S.C. 3554, 3555, or 3556 may, if an appeal of the conviction or sentence is taken, be stayed by the district court or by the court of appeals upon such terms as the court finds appropriate. The court may issue such orders as may be reasonably necessary to ensure compliance with the sanction upon disposition of the appeal, including the entering of a restraining order or an injunction or requiring a deposit in whole or in part of the monetary amount involved into the registry of the district court or execution of a performance bond.

(f) **Disabilities.** A civil or employment disability arising under a Federal statute by reason of the defendant's conviction or sentence, may, if an appeal is taken, be stayed by the district court or by the court of appeals upon such terms as the court finds appropriate. The court may enter a restraining order or an injunction, or take any other action that may be reasonably necessary to protect the interest represented by the disability pending disposition of the appeal.

[Rule 39. Supervision of Appeal.] (Abrogated Dec. 4, 1967, Eff. July 1, 1968)

IX. SUPPLEMENTARY AND SPECIAL PROCEEDINGS

Rule 40. Commitment to Another District

(a) **Appearance Before Federal Magistrate.** If a person is arrested in a district other than that in which the offense is alleged to have been committed, that person shall be taken without unnecessary delay before the nearest available federal magistrate. Preliminary proceedings concerning the defendant shall be conducted in accordance with Rules 5 and 5.1, except that if no preliminary examination is held because an indictment has been returned or an information filed or because the defendant elects to have the preliminary examination conducted in the district in which the prosecution is pending, the person shall be held to answer upon a finding that such person is the person named in the indictment, information or warrant. If held to answer, the defendant shall be held to answer in the district court in which the prosecution is pending, provided that a warrant is issued in that district if the arrest was made without a warrant, upon production of the warrant or a certified copy thereof.

(b) **Statement by Federal Magistrate.** In addition to the statements required by Rule 5, the federal magistrate shall inform the defendant of the provisions of Rule 20.

(c) **Papers.** If a defendant is held or discharged, the papers in the proceeding and any bail taken shall be transmitted to the clerk of the district court in which the prosecution is pending.

(d) **Arrest of Probationer or Supervised Releasee.** If a person is arrested for a violation of probation or supervised release in a district other than the district having jurisdiction, such person shall be taken without unnecessary delay before the nearest available federal magistrate. The federal magistrate shall:

(1) Proceed under Rule 32.1 if jurisdiction over the person is transferred to that district;

(2) Hold a prompt preliminary hearing if the alleged violation occurred in that district, and either (i) hold the person to answer in the district court of the district having jurisdiction or (ii) dismiss the proceedings and so notify that court; or

(3) otherwise order the person held to answer in the district court of the district having jurisdiction upon production of certified copies of the judgment, the warrant, and the application for the warrant, and upon a finding that the person before the magistrate is the person named in the warrant.

(e) **Arrest for Failure to Appear.** If a person is arrested on a warrant in a district other than that in which the warrant was issued, and the warrant was issued because of the failure of the person named therein to appear as required pursuant to a subpoena or the terms of that person's release, the person arrested shall be taken without unnecessary delay before the nearest available federal magistrate. Upon production of the warrant or a certified copy thereof and upon a finding that the person before the magistrate is the person named in the warrant, the federal magistrate shall hold the person to answer in the district in which the warrant was issued.

(f) **Release or Detention.** If a person was previously detained or conditionally released, pursuant to chapter 207 of title 18, United States Code, in another district where a warrant, information, or indictment issued, the federal magistrate shall take into account the decision previously made and the reasons set forth therefor, if any, but will not be bound by that decision. If the federal magistrate amends the release or detention decision or alters the conditions of release, the magistrate shall set forth the reasons therefore [1] in writing.

Rule 41. Search and Seizure

(a) **Authority to Issue Warrant.** Upon the request of a federal law enforcement officer or an attorney for the government, a search warrant authorized by this rule may be issued (1) by a federal magistrate, or a state court of record within the federal district, for a search of property or for a person within the district, (2) by a federal magistrate for a search of property or for a person either within or outside the district if the property or person is within the district when the warrant is sought but might move outside the district before the warrant is executed, and (3) by a federal magistrate for a search of property outside the United States if the property is lawfully subject to search and seizure by the United States and is relevant to a criminal investigation in the district in which the warrant is sought.

(b) **Property or Persons Which May Be Seized With a Warrant.** A warrant may be issued under this rule to search for and seize any (1) property that constitutes evidence of the commission of a criminal offense; or (2) contraband, the fruits of crime, or things otherwise criminally possessed; or (3) property designed or intended for use or which is or has been used as the means of committing a criminal offense; or (4) person for whose arrest there is probable cause, or who is unlawfully restrained.

(c) **Issuance and Contents.**

(1) **Warrant Upon Affidavit.** A warrant other than a warrant upon oral testimony under paragraph (2) of this subdivision shall issue only on an affidavit or affidavits sworn to before the federal magistrate or state judge and establishing the grounds for issuing the warrant. If the federal magistrate or state judge is satisfied that grounds for the application exist or that there is probable cause to believe that they exist, that magistrate or state judge shall issue a warrant identifying the property or person to be seized and naming or describing the person or place to be searched. The finding of probable cause may be based upon hearsay evidence in whole or in part. Before ruling on a request for a warrant the federal magistrate or state judge may require the affiant to appear personally and may examine under oath the affiant and any witnesses the affiant may produce, provided that such proceeding shall be taken down by a court reporter or recording equipment and made part of the affidavit. The warrant shall be directed to a civil officer of the United States authorized to enforce or assist in enforcing any law thereof or to a person so authorized by the President of the United States. It shall command the officer to search, within a specified period of time not to exceed 10 days, the person or place named for the property or person specified. The warrant shall be served in the daytime, unless the issuing authority, by appropriate provision in the warrant, and for reasonable cause shown, authorizes its execution at times other than daytime. It shall designate a federal magistrate to whom it shall be returned.

(2) **Warrant Upon Oral Testimony.**

(A) **General Rule.** If the circumstances make it reasonable to dispense with a written affidavit, a Federal magistrate may issue a warrant based upon sworn oral testimony communicated by telephone or other appropriate means.

---

[1] So in original.

(B) Application. The person who is requesting the warrant shall prepare a document to be known as a duplicate original warrant and shall read such duplicate original warrant, verbatim, to the Federal magistrate. The Federal magistrate shall enter, verbatim, what is so read to such magistrate on a document to be known as the original warrant. The Federal magistrate may direct that the warrant be modified.

(C) Issuance. If the Federal magistrate is satisfied that the circumstances are such as to make it reasonable to dispense with a written affidavit and that grounds for the application exist or that there is probable cause to believe that they exist, the Federal magistrate shall order the issuance of a warrant by directing the person requesting the warrant to sign the Federal magistrate's name on the duplicate original warrant. The Federal magistrate shall immediately sign the original warrant and enter on the face of the original warrant the exact time when the warrant was ordered to be issued. The finding of probable cause for a warrant upon oral testimony may be based on the same kind of evidence as is sufficient for a warrant upon affidavit.

(D) Recording and Certification of Testimony. When a caller informs the Federal magistrate that the purpose of the call is to request a warrant, the Federal magistrate shall immediately place under oath each person whose testimony forms a basis of the application and each person applying for that warrant. If a voice recording device is available, the Federal magistrate shall record by means of such device all of the call after the caller informs the Federal magistrate that the purpose of the call is to request a warrant. Otherwise a stenographic or longhand verbatim record shall be made. If a voice recording device is used or a stenographic record made, the Federal magistrate shall have the record transcribed, shall certify the accuracy of the transcription, and shall file a copy of the original record and the transcription with the court. If a longhand verbatim record is made, the Federal magistrate shall file a signed copy with the court.

(E) Contents. The contents of a warrant upon oral testimony shall be the same as the contents of a warrant upon affidavit.

(F) Additional Rule for Execution. The person who executes the warrant shall enter the exact time of execution on the face of the duplicate original warrant.

(G) Motion to Suppress Precluded. Absent a finding of bad faith, evidence obtained pursuant to a warrant issued under this paragraph is not subject to a motion to suppress on the ground that the circumstances were not such as to make it reasonable to dispense with a written affidavit.

(d) Execution and Return with Inventory. The officer taking property under the warrant shall give to the person from whom or from whose premises the property was taken a copy of the warrant and a receipt for the property taken or shall leave the copy and receipt at the place from which the property was taken. The return shall be made promptly and shall be accompanied by a written inventory of any property taken. The inventory shall be made in the presence of the applicant for the warrant and the person from whose possession or premises the property was taken, if they are present, or in the presence of at least one credible person other than the applicant for the warrant or the person from whose possession or premises the property was taken, and shall be verified by the officer. The federal magistrate shall upon request deliver a copy of the inventory to the person from whom or from whose premises the property was taken and to the applicant for the warrant.

(e) Motion for Return of Property. A person aggrieved by an unlawful search and seizure or by the deprivation of property may move the district court for the district in which the property was seized for the return of the property on the ground that such person is entitled to lawful possession of the property. The court shall receive evidence on any issue of fact necessary to the decision of the motion. If the motion is granted, the property shall be returned to the movant, although reasonable conditions may be imposed to protect access and use of the property in subsequent proceedings. If a motion for return of property is made or comes on for hearing in the district of trial after an indictment or information is filed, it shall be treated also as a motion to suppress under Rule 12.

(f) Motion to Suppress. A motion to suppress evidence may be made in the court of the district of trial as provided in Rule 12.

(g) Return of Papers to Clerk. The federal magistrate before whom the warrant is returned shall attach to the warrant a copy of the return, inventory and all other papers in connection therewith and shall file them with the clerk of the district court for the district in which the property was seized.

(h) Scope and Definition. This rule does not modify any act, inconsistent with it, regulating search, seizure and the issuance and execution of search warrants in circumstances for which special provision is made. The term "property" is used in this rule to include documents, books, papers and any other tangible objects. The term "daytime" is used in this rule to mean the hours from 6:00 a.m. to 10:00 p.m. according to local time. The phrase "federal law enforcement officer" is used in this rule to mean any government agent, other than an attorney for the government as defined in Rule 54(c), who is engaged in the enforcement of the criminal laws and is within any category of officers authorized by the Attorney General to request the issuance of a search warrant.

Rule 42. Criminal Contempt

(a) Summary Disposition. A criminal contempt may be punished summarily if the judge certifies that the judge saw or heard the conduct constituting the contempt and that it was committed in the actual presence of the court. The order of contempt shall recite the facts and shall be signed by the judge and entered of record.

(b) Disposition Upon Notice and Hearing. A criminal contempt except as provided in subdivision (a) of this rule shall be prosecuted on notice. The notice shall state the time and place of hearing, allowing a reasonable time for the preparation of the defense, and shall state the essential facts constituting the criminal contempt charged and describe it as such. The notice shall be given orally by the judge in open court in the presence of the defendant or, on application of the United States attorney or of an attorney appointed by the court for that purpose, by an order to show cause or an order of arrest. The defendant is entitled to a trial by jury in any case in which an act of Congress so provides. The defendant is entitled to admission to bail as provided in these rules. If the contempt charged involves disrespect to or criticism of a judge, that judge is disqualified from presiding at the trial or hearing except with the defendant's consent. Upon a verdict or finding of guilt the court shall enter an order fixing the punishment.

X.   GENERAL PROVISIONS

Rule 43.   Presence of the Defendant

(a) Presence Required. The defendant shall be present at the arraignment, at the time of the plea, at every stage of the trial including the impaneling of the jury and the return of the verdict, and at the imposition of sentence, except as otherwise provided by this rule.

(b) Continued Presence Not Required. The further progress of the trial to and including the return of the verdict shall not be prevented and the defendant shall be considered to have waived the right to be present whenever a defendant, initially present,

(1) is voluntarily absent after the trial has commenced (whether or not the defendant has been informed by the court of the obligation to remain during the trial), or

(2) after being warned by the court that disruptive conduct will cause the removal of the defendant from the courtroom, persists in conduct which is such as to justify exclusion from the courtroom.

(c) Presence Not Required. A defendant need not be present in the following situations:

(1) A corporation may appear by counsel for all purposes.

(2) In prosecutions for offenses punishable by fine or by imprisonment for not more than one year or both, the court, with the written consent of the defendant, may permit arraignment, plea, trial, and imposition of sentence in the defendant's absence.

(3) At a conference or argument upon a question of law.

(4) At a reduction of sentence under Rule 35.

Rule 44. Right to and Assignment of Counsel

(a) Right to Assigned Counsel. Every defendant who is unable to obtain counsel shall be entitled to have counsel assigned to represent that defendant at every stage of the proceedings from initial appearance before the federal magistrate or the court through appeal, unless that defendant waives such appointment.

(b) Assignment Procedure. The procedures for implementing the right set out in subdivision (a) shall be those provided by law and by local rules of court established pursuant thereto.

(c) Joint Representation. Whenever two or more defendants have been jointly charged pursuant to Rule 8(b) or have been joined for trial pursuant to Rule 13, and are represented by the same retained or assigned counsel or by retained or assigned counsel who are associated in the practice of law, the court shall promptly inquire with respect to such joint representation and shall personally advise each defendant of the right to the effective assistance of counsel, including separate representation. Unless it appears that there is good cause to believe no conflict of interest is likely to arise, the court shall take such measures as may be appropriate to protect each defendant's right to counsel.

Rule 45. Time

(a) Computation. In computing any period of time the day of the act or event from which the designated period of time begins to run shall not be included. The last day of the period so computed shall be included, unless it is a Saturday, a Sunday, or a legal holiday, or, when the act to be done is the filing of some paper in court, a day on which weather or other conditions have made the office of the clerk of the district court inaccessible, in which event the period runs until the end of the next day which is not one of the aforementioned days. When a period of time prescribed or allowed is less than 11 days, intermediate Saturdays, Sundays and legal holidays shall be excluded in the computation. As used in these rules, "legal holiday" includes New Year's Day, Birthday of Martin Luther King, Jr., Washington's Birthday, Memorial Day, Independence Day, Labor Day, Columbus Day, Veterans Day, Thanksgiving Day, Christmas Day, and any other day appointed as a holiday by the President or the Congress of the United States, or by the state in which the district court is held.

(b) Enlargement. When an act is required or allowed to be done at or within a specified time, the court for cause shown may at any time in its discretion (1) with or without motion or notice, order the period enlarged if request therefor is made before the expiration of the period originally prescribed or as extended by a previous order or (2) upon motion made after the expiration of the specified period permit the act to be done if the failure to act was the result of excusable neglect; but the court may not extend the time for taking any action under Rules 29, 33, 34 and 35, except to the extent and under the conditions stated in them.

[**(c) Unaffected by Expiration of Term.**] (Rescinded Feb. 28, 1966, eff. July 1, 1966.)

(d) For Motions; Affidavits. A written motion, other than one which may be heard *ex parte*, and notice of the hearing thereof shall be served not later than 5 days before the time specified for the hearing unless a different period is fixed by rule or order of the court. For cause shown such an order may be made on *ex parte* application. When a motion is supported by affidavit, the affidavit shall be served with the motion; and opposing affidavits may be served not less than 1 day before the hearing unless the court permits them to be served at a later time.

(e) Additional Time After Service by Mail. Whenever a party has the right or is required to do an act within a prescribed period after the service of a notice or other paper upon that party and the notice or other paper is served by mail, 3 days shall be added to the prescribed period.

Rule 46. Release From Custody

(a) Release Prior to Trial. Eligibility for release prior to trial shall be in accordance with 18 U.S.C. §§ 3142 and 3144.

(b) Release During Trial. A person released before trial shall continue on release during trial under the same terms and conditions as were previously imposed unless the court determines that other terms and conditions or termination of release are necessary to assure such person's presence during the trial or to assure that such person's conduct will not obstruct the orderly and expeditious progress of the trial.

(c) Pending Sentence and Notice of Appeal. Eligibility for release pending sentence or pending notice of appeal or expiration of the time allowed for filing notice of appeal, shall be in accordance with 18 U.S.C. § 3143. The burden of establishing that the defendant will not flee or pose a danger to any other person or to the community rests with the defendant.

(d) Justification of Sureties. Every surety, except a corporate surety which is approved as provided by law, shall justify by affidavit and may be required to describe in the affidavit the property by which the surety proposes to justify and the encumbrances thereon, the number and amount of other bonds and undertakings for bail entered into by the surety and remaining undischarged and all the other liabilities of the surety. No bond shall be approved unless the surety thereon appears to be qualified.

(e) Forfeiture.

(1) Declaration. If there is a breach of condition of a bond, the district court shall declare a forfeiture of the bail.

(2) Setting Aside. The court may direct that a forfeiture be set aside in whole or in part, upon such conditions as the court may impose, if a person released upon execution of an appearance bond with a surety is subsequently surrendered by the surety into custody or if it otherwise appears that justice does not require the forfeiture.

(3) **Enforcement.** When a forfeiture has not been set aside, the court shall on motion enter a judgment of default and execution may issue thereon. By entering into a bond the obligors submit to the jurisdiction of the district court and irrevocably appoint the clerk of the court as their agent upon whom any papers affecting their liability may be served. Their liability may be enforced on motion without the necessity of an independent action. The motion and such notice of the motion as the court prescribes may be served on the clerk of the court, who shall forthwith mail copies to the obligors to their last known addresses.

(4) **Remission.** After entry of such judgment, the court may remit it in whole or in part under the conditions applying to the setting aside of forfeiture in paragraph (2) of this subdivision.

(f) **Exoneration.** When the condition of the bond has been satisfied or the forfeiture thereof has been set aside or remitted, the court shall exonerate the obligors and release any bail. A surety may be exonerated by a deposit of cash in the amount of the bond or by a timely surrender of the defendant into custody.

(g) **Supervision of Detention Pending Trial.** The court shall exercise supervision over the detention of defendants and witnesses within the district pending trial for the purpose of eliminating all unnecessary detention. The attorney for the government shall make a biweekly report to the court listing each defendant and witness who has been held in custody pending indictment, arraignment or trial for a period in excess of ten days. As to each witness so listed the attorney for the government shall make a statement of the reasons why such witness should not be released with or without the taking of a deposition pursuant to Rule 15(a). As to each defendant so listed the attorney for the government shall make a statement of the reasons why the defendant is still held in custody.

(h) **Forfeiture of Property.** Nothing in this rule or in chapter 207 of title 18, United States Code, shall prevent the court from disposing of any charge by entering an order directing forfeiture of property pursuant to 18 U.S.C. 3142(c)(1)(B)(xi) if the value of the property is an amount that would be an appropriate sentence after conviction of the offense charged and if such forfeiture is authorized by statute or regulation.

Rule 47. Motions

An application to the court for an order shall be by motion. A motion other than one made during a trial or hearing shall be in writing unless the court permits it to be made orally. It shall state the grounds upon which it is made and shall set forth the relief or order sought. It may be supported by affidavit.

Rule 48. Dismissal

(a) **By Attorney for Government.** The Attorney General or the United States attorney may by leave of court file a dismissal of an indictment, information or complaint and the prosecution shall thereupon terminate. Such a dismissal may not be filed during the trial without the consent of the defendant.

(b) **By Court.** If there is unnecessary delay in presenting the charge to a grand jury or in filing an information against a defendant who has been held to answer to the district court, or if there is unnecessary delay in bringing a defendant to trial, the court may dismiss the indictment, information or complaint.

Rule 49. Service and Filing of Papers

(a) **Service: When Required.** Written motions other than those which are heard ex parte, written notices, designations of record on appeal and similar papers shall be served upon each of the parties.

(b) Service: How Made. Whenever under these rules or by an order of the court service is required or permitted to be made upon a party represented by an attorney, the service shall be made upon the attorney unless service upon the party personally is ordered by the court. Service upon the attorney or upon a party shall be made in the manner provided in civil actions.

(c) Notice of Orders. Immediately upon the entry of an order made on a written motion subsequent to arraignment the clerk shall mail to each party a notice thereof and shall make a note in the docket of the mailing. Lack of notice of the entry by the clerk does not affect the time to appeal or relieve or authorize the court to relieve a party for failure to appeal within the time allowed, except as permitted by Rule 4(b) of the Federal Rules of Appellate Procedure.

(d) Filing. Papers required to be served shall be filed with the court. Papers shall be filed in the manner provided in civil actions.

(e) Filing of Dangerous Offender Notice. A filing with the court pursuant to 18 U.S.C. § 3575(a) or 21 U.S.C. § 849(a) shall be made by filing the notice with the clerk of the court. The clerk shall transmit the notice to the chief judge or, if the chief judge is the presiding judge in the case, to another judge or United States magistrate in the district, except that in a district having a single judge and no United States magistrate, the clerk shall transmit the notice to the court only after the time for disclosure specified in the aforementioned statutes and shall seal the notice as permitted by local rule.

Rule 50. Calendars; Plan for Prompt Disposition

(a) Calendars. The district courts may provide for placing criminal proceedings upon appropriate calendars. Preference shall be given to criminal proceedings as far as practicable.

(b) Plans for Achieving Prompt Disposition of Criminal Cases. To minimize undue delay and to further the prompt disposition of criminal cases, each district court shall conduct a continuing study of the administration of criminal justice in the district court and before United States magistrates of the district and shall prepare plans for the prompt disposition of criminal cases in accordance with the provisions of Chapter 208 of Title 18, United States Code.

Rule 51. Exceptions Unnecessary

Exceptions to rulings or orders of the court are unnecessary and for all purposes for which an exception has heretofore been necessary it is sufficient that a party, at the time the ruling or order of the court is made or sought, makes known to the court the action which that party desires the court to take or that party's objection to the action of the court and the grounds therefor; but if a party has no opportunity to object to a ruling or order, the absence of an objection does not thereafter prejudice that party.

Rule 52. Harmless Error and Plain Error

(a) Harmless Error. Any error, defect, irregularity or variance which does not affect substantial rights shall be disregarded.

(b) Plain Error. Plain errors or defects affecting substantial rights may be noticed although they were not brought to the attention of the court.

Rule 53. Regulation of Conduct in the Court Room

The taking of photographs in the court room during the progress of judicial proceedings or radio broadcasting of judicial proceedings from the court room shall not be permitted by the court.

Rule 54. Application and Exception

(a) **Courts.** These rules apply to all criminal proceedings in the United States District Courts; in the District Court of Guam; in the District Court for the Northern Mariana Islands, except as otherwise provided in articles IV and V of the covenant provided by the Act of March 24, 1976 (90 Stat. 263); in the District Court of the Virgin Islands; and (except as otherwise provided in the Canal Zone Code) in the United States District Court for the District of the Canal Zone; in the United States Courts of Appeals; and in the Supreme Court of the United States; except that the prosecution of offenses in the District Court of the Virgin Islands shall be by indictment or information as otherwise provided by law.

(b) **Proceedings.**

(1) **Removed Proceedings.** These rules apply to criminal prosecutions removed to the United States district courts from state courts and govern all procedure after removal, except that dismissal by the attorney for the prosecution shall be governed by state law.

(2) **Offenses Outside a District or State.** These rules apply to proceedings for offenses committed upon the high seas or elsewhere out of the jurisdiction of any particular state or district, except that such proceedings may be had in any district authorized by 18 U.S.C. § 3238.

(3) **Peace Bonds.** These rules do not alter the power of judges of the United States or of United States magistrates to hold to security of the peace and for good behavior under Revised Statutes, § 4069, 50 U.S.C. § 23, but in such cases the procedure shall conform to these rules so far as they are applicable.

(4) **Proceedings Before United States Magistrates.** Proceedings involving misdemeanors and other petty offenses before United States magistrates are governed by Rule 58.

(5) **Other Proceedings.** These rules are not applicable to extradition and rendition of fugitives; civil forfeiture of property for violation of a statute of the United States; or the collection of fines and penalties. Except as provided in Rule 20(d) they do not apply to proceedings under 18 U.S.C., Chapter 403—Juvenile Delinquency—so far as they are inconsistent with that chapter. They do not apply to summary trials for offenses against the navigation laws under Revised Statutes §§ 4300–4305, 33 U.S.C. §§ 391–396, or to proceedings involving disputes between seamen under Revised Statutes, §§ 4079–4081, as amended, 22 U.S.C. §§ 256–258, or to proceedings for fishery offenses under the Act of June 28, 1937, c. 392, 50 Stat. 325–327, 16 U.S.C. §§ 772–772i, or to proceedings against a witness in a foreign country under 28 U.S.C. § 1784.

(c) **Application of Terms.** As used in these rules the following terms have the designated meanings.

"Act of Congress" includes any act of Congress locally applicable to and in force in the District of Columbia, in Puerto Rico, in a territory or in an insular possession.

"Attorney for the government" means the Attorney General, an authorized assistant of the Attorney General, a United States Attorney, an authorized assistant of a United States Attorney, when applicable to cases arising under the laws of Guam the Attorney General of Guam or such other person or persons as may be authorized by the laws of Guam to act therein, and when applicable to cases arising under the laws of the Northern Mariana Islands the Attorney General of the Northern Mariana Islands or any other person or persons as may be authorized by the laws of the Northern Marianas to act therein.

"Civil action" refers to a civil action in a district court.

The words "demurrer," "motion to quash," "plea in abatement," "plea in bar" and "special plea in bar," or words to the same effect, in any act of Congress shall be construed to mean the motion raising a defense or objection provided in Rule 12.

"District court" includes all district courts named in subdivision (a) of this rule.

"Federal magistrate" means a United States magistrate as defined in 28 U.S.C. §§ 631–639, a judge of the United States or another judge or judicial officer specifically empowered by statute in force in any territory or possession, the Commonwealth of Puerto Rico, or the District of Columbia, to perform a function to which a particular rule relates.

"Judge of the United States" includes a judge of a district court, court of appeals, or the Supreme Court.

"Law" includes statutes and judicial decisions.

"Magistrate" includes a United States magistrate as defined in 28 U.S.C. §§ 631–639, a judge of the United States, another judge or judicial officer specifically empowered by statute in force in any territory or possession, the Commonwealth of Puerto Rico, or the District of Columbia, to perform a function to which a particular rule relates, and a state or local judicial officer, authorized by 18 U.S.C. § 3041 to perform the functions prescribed in Rules 3, 4, and 5.

"Oath" includes affirmations.

"Petty offense" is defined in 18 U.S.C. § 19.

"State" includes District of Columbia, Puerto Rico, territory and insular possession.

"United States magistrate" means the officer authorized by 28 U.S.C. §§ 631–639.

Rule 55. Records

The clerk of the district court and each United States magistrate shall keep records in criminal proceedings in such form as the Director of the Administrative Office of the United States Courts may prescribe. The clerk shall enter in the records each order or judgment of the court and the date such entry is made.

Rule 56. Courts and Clerks

The district court shall be deemed always open for the purpose of filing any proper paper, of issuing and returning process and of making motions and orders. The clerk's office with the clerk or a deputy in attendance shall be open during business hours on all days except Saturdays, Sundays, and legal holidays, but a court may provide by local rule or order that its clerk's office shall be open for specified hours on Saturdays or particular legal holidays other than New Year's Day, Birthday of Martin Luther King, Jr., Washington's Birthday, Memorial Day, Independence Day, Labor Day, Columbus Day, Veterans Day, Thanksgiving Day, and Christmas Day.

Rule 57. Rules by District Courts

Each district court by action of a majority of the judges thereof may from time to time, after giving appropriate public notice and an opportunity to comment, make and amend rules governing its practice not inconsistent with these rules. A local rule so adopted shall take effect upon the date specified by the district court and shall remain in effect unless amended by the district court or abrogated by the judicial council of the circuit in which the district is located. Copies of the rules and amendments so made by any district court shall upon their promulgation be furnished to the judicial council and the Administrative Office of the United States Courts and be made available to the public. In all cases not provided for by rule, the district judges and magistrates may regulate their practice in any manner not inconsistent with these rules or those of the district in which they act.

Rule 58. Procedure for Misdemeanors and Other Petty Offenses

(a) Scope.

(1) In General. This rule governs the procedure and practice for the conduct of proceedings involving misdemeanors and other petty offenses, and for appeals to judges of the district courts in such cases tried by magistrates.

(2) Applicability of Other Federal Rules of Criminal Procedure. In proceedings concerning petty offenses for which no sentence of imprisonment will be imposed the court may follow such provisions of these rules as it deems appropriate, to the extent not inconsistent with this rule. In all other proceedings the other rules govern except as specifically provided in this rule.

(3) Definition. The term "petty offenses for which no sentence of imprisonment will be imposed" as used in this rule, means any petty offenses as defined in 18 U.S.C. § 19 as to which the court determines that, in the event of conviction, no sentence of imprisonment will actually be imposed.

(b) Pretrial Procedures.

(1) Trial Document. The trial of a misdemeanor may proceed on an indictment, information, or complaint or, in the case of a petty offense, on a citation or violation notice.

(2) Initial Appearance. At the defendant's initial appearance on a misdemeanor or other petty offense charge, the court shall inform the defendant of:

(A) the charge, and the maximum possible penalties provided by law, including payment of a special assessment under 18 U.S.C. § 3013, and restitution under 18 U.S.C. § 3663;

(B) the right to retain counsel;

(C) unless the charge is a petty offense for which appointment of counsel is not required, the right to request the assignment of counsel if the defendant is unable to obtain counsel;

(D) the right to remain silent and that any statement made by the defendant may be used against the defendant;

(E) the right to trial, judgment, and sentencing before a judge of the district court, unless the defendant consents to trial, judgment, and sentencing before a magistrate;

(F) unless the charge is a petty offense, the right to trial by jury before either a magistrate or a judge of the district court; and

(G) if the defendant is held in custody and charged with a misdemeanor other than a petty offense, the right to a preliminary examination in accordance with 18 U.S.C. § 3060, and the general circumstances under with the defendant may secure pretrial release.

(3) Consent and Arraignment.

(a) **Trial Before a Magistrate.** If the defendant signs a written consent to be tried before the magistrate which specifically waives trial before a judge of the district court, the magistrate shall take the defendant's plea. The defendant may plead not guilty, guilty or with the consent of the magistrate, nolo contendere.

(b) Failure to Consent. If the defendant does not consent to trial before the magistrate, the defendant shall be ordered to appear before a judge of the district court for futher proceedings on notice.

(c) Additional Procedures Applicable Only to Petty Offenses for Which No Sentence of Imprisonment Will be Imposed. With respect to petty offenses for which no sentence of imprisonment will be imposed, the following additional procedures are applicable:

(1) Plea of Guilty or Nolo Contendere. No plea of guilty or nolo contendere shall be accepted unless the court is satisfied that the defendant understands the nature of the charge and the maximum possible penalties provided by law.

(2) Waiver of Venue for Plea and Sentence. A defendant who is arrested, held, or present in a district other than that in which the indictment, information, complaint, citation or violation notice is pending against that defendant may state in writing a wish to plead guilty or nolo contendere, to waive venue and trial in the district in which the proceeding is pending, and to consent to disposition of the case in the district in which that defendant was arrested, is held, or is present. Unless the defendant thereafter pleads not guilty, the prosecution shall be had as if venue were in such district, and notice of the same shall be given to the magistrate in the district where the proceeding was originally commenced. The defendant's statement of a desire to plead guilty or nolo contendere is not admissible against the defendant.

(3) Sentence. The court shall afford the defendant an opportunity to be heard in mitigation. The court shall then immediately proceed to sentence the defendant, except that in the discretion of the court, sentencing may be continued to allow an investigation by the probation service or submission of additional information by either party.

(4) Notification of Right to Appeal After imposing sentence in a case which has gone to trial on a plea of not guilty, the court shall advise the defendant of the defendant's right to appeal including any right to appeal the sentence. There shall be no duty on the court to advise the defendant of any right of appeal after sentence is imposed following a plea of guilty or nolo contendere, except that the court shall advise the defendant of any right to appeal the sentence.

(d) Securing the Defendant's Appearance; Payment in Lieu of Appearance.

(1) Forfeiture of Collateral. When authorized by local rules of the district court, payment of a fixed sum may be accepted in suitable cases in lieu of appearance and as authorizing the termination of the proceedings. Local rules may make provision for increases in fixed sums not to exceed the maximum fine which could be imposed.

(2) Notice to Appear. If a defendant fails to pay a fixed sum, request a hearing, or appear in response to a citation or violation notice, the clerk or a magistrate may issue a notice for the defendant to appear before the court on a date certain. The notice may also afford the defendant an additional opportunity to pay a fixed sum in lieu of appearance, and shall be served upon the defendant by mailing a copy to the defendant's last known address.

(3) Summons or Warrant. Upon an indictment or a showing by one of the other documents specified in subdivision (b)(1) of probable cause to believe that an offense has been committed and that the defendant has committed it, the court may issue an arrest warrant or, if no warrant is requested by the attorney for the prosecution, a summons. The showing of probable cause shall be made in writing upon oath or under penalty for perjury, but the affiant need not appear before the court. If the defendant fails to appear before the court in response to a summons, the court may summarily issue a warrant for the defendant's immediate arrest and appearance before the court.

(e) Record. Proceedings under this rule shall be taken down by a reporter or recorded by suitable sound equipment.

(f) New Trial. The provisions of Rule 33 shall apply.

(g) Appeal.

(1) Decision, Order, Judgment or Sentence by a District Judge. An appeal from a decision, order, judgment or conviction or sentence by a judge of the district court shall be taken in accordance with the Federal Rules of Appellate Procedure.

(2) Decision, Order, Judgment or Sentence by a Magistrate.

(a) Interlocutory Appeal. A decision or order by a magistrate which, if made by a judge of the district court, could be appealed by the government or defendant under any provision of law, shall be subject to an appeal to a judge of the district court provided such appeal is taken within 10 days of the entry of the decision or order. An appeal shall be taken by filing with the clerk of court a statement specifying the decision or order from which an appeal is taken and by serving a copy of the statement upon the adverse party, personally or by mail, and by filing a copy with the magistrate.

(b) Appeal From Conviction or Sentence. An appeal from a judgment of conviction or sentence by a magistrate to a judge of the district court shall be taken within 10 days after entry of the judgment. An appeal shall be taken by filing with the clerk of court a statement specifying the judgment from which an appeal is taken, and by serving a copy of the statement upon the United States Attorney, personally or by mail, and by filing a copy with the magistrate.

(c) Record. The record shall consist of the original papers and exhibits in the case together with any transcript, tape, or other recording of the proceedings and a certified copy of the docket entries which shall be transmitted promptly to the clerk of court. For purposes of the appeal, a copy of the record of such proceedings shall be made available at the expense of the United States to a person who establishes by affidavit the inability to pay or give security therefor, and the expense of such copy shall be paid by the Director of the Administrative Office of the United States Courts.

(d) Scope of Appeal. The defendant shall not be entitled to a trial de novo by a judge of the district court. The scope of the appeal shall be the same as an appeal from a judgment of a district court to a court of appeals.

(3) Stay of Execution; Release Pending Appeal. The provisions of Rule 38 relating to stay of execution shall be applicable to a judgment of conviction or sentence. The defendant may be released pending appeal in accordance with the provisions of law relating to release pending appeal from a judgment of a district court to a court of appeals.

Rule 59. Effective Date

These rules take effect on the day which is 3 months subsequent to the adjournment of the first regular session of the 79th Congress, but if that day is prior to September 1, 1945, then they take effect on September 1, 1945. They govern all criminal proceedings thereafter commenced and so far as just and practicable all proceedings then pending.

Rule 60. Title

These rules may be known and cited as the Federal Rules of Criminal Procedure.

Appendix D

PROPOSED AMENDMENTS TO FEDERAL RULES OF CRIMINAL PROCEDURE

[New material is underlined; material to be deleted is lined through.]

Rule 12. Pleadings and Motions Before Trial; Defenses and Objections

* * *

(i) Production of Statements at Suppression Hearing. Except as herein provided, rule 26.2 shall apply at a hearing on a motion to suppress evidence under subdivision (b)(3) of this rule. For purposes of this subdivision, a law enforcement officer shall be deemed a witness called by the government ~~, and upon a claim of privilege the court shall excise the portions of the statement containing privileged matter~~.

Rule 16. Discovery and Inspection

(a) Disclosure of Evidence by the Government.

(1) Information Subject to Disclosure.

* * *

<u>**(E) Expert Witnesses.** Upon request of a defendant, the government shall disclose to the defendant any evidence which the government may present at trial under Rules 702, 703, or 705 of the Federal Rules of Evidence. This disclosure shall be in the form of a written report prepared and signed by the witness that includes a complete statement of all opinions to be expressed and the basis and reasons therefor, the data or other information relied upon in forming such opinions, any exhibits to be used as a summary of or support for such opinions, and the qualifications of the witness.</u>

(2) Information Not Subject to Disclosure. Except as provided in paragraphs (A), (B), ~~and~~ (D)<u>, and (E)</u> of subdivision (a)(1), this rule does not authorize the discovery or inspection of reports, memoranda, or other internal government documents made by the attorney for the government or other government agents in connection with the investigation or prosecution of the case, or of statements made by government witnesses or prospective government witnesses except as provided in 18 U.S.C. § 3500.

* * *

(b) Disclosure of Evidence by the Defendant.

(1) Information Subject to Disclosure.

* * *

<u>**(C) Expert Witnesses.** If the defendant requests disclosure under subdivision (a)(1)(E) of this rule, upon compliance with the request by the government, the defendant, on request of the government, shall provide the government with a written report prepared and signed by the witness that includes a complete statement of all opinions to be expressed and the basis and reasons therefor, the</u>

data or other information relied upon in forming such opinions, any exhibits to be used as a summary of or support for such opinions, and the qualifications of the witness.

Rule 26.2. Production of Statements of Witnesses

* * *

(c) Production of Excised Statement. If the other party claims that the statement contains privileged information or matter that does not relate to the subject matter concerning which the witness has testified, the court shall order that it be delivered to the court in camera. Upon inspection, the court shall excise the portions of the statement that are privileged or that do not relate to the subject matter concerning which the witness has testified, and shall order that the statement with such material excised, be delivered to the moving party. Any portion of the statement that is withheld from the defendant over the defendant's objection shall be preserved by the attorney for the government, and, in the event of a conviction and an appeal by the defendant, shall be made available to the appellate court for the purpose of determining the correctness of the decision to excise the portion of the statement.

(d) Recess for Examination of Statement. Upon delivery of the statement to the moving party, the court, upon application of that party, may recess the proceedings in the trial for the examination of such statement and for preparation for its use in the trial proceedings.

* * *

(g) Scope of Rule. Subdivisions (a)–(d) and (f) of this rule shall apply at a suppression hearing held pursuant to Rule 12, at trial pursuant to this rule, at sentencing pursuant to Rule 32(f), at hearings to revoke or modify probation or supervised release held pursuant to Rule 32.1(c), at detention hearings held pursuant to Rule 46(i), and at an evidentiary hearing held pursuant to Section 2255 of Title 28, United States Code.

Rule 26.3 Mistrial

Before ordering a mistrial, the court shall provide an opportunity for the government and for each defendant to comment on the propriety of the order, including whether each party consents or objects to a mistrial, and to suggest any alternatives.

Rule 32. Sentence and Judgment

* * *

(f) Production of Statements at Sentencing Hearing.

(1) In General. Rule 26.2 (a)–(d), (f) shall apply at a sentencing hearing under this rule.

(2) Sanctions for Failure to Produce Statement. If a party elects not to comply with an order pursuant to Rule 26.2(a) to deliver a statement to the moving party, the court shall not consider the affidavit or testimony of the witness in sentencing.

Rule 32.1. Revocation or Modification of Probation or Supervised Release

* * *

(c) Production of Statements.

(1) In General. Rule 26.2(a)–(d) and (f) shall apply at any hearing under this rule.

(2) **Sanctions for Failure to Produce Statement.** If a party elects not to comply with an order pursuant to Rule 26.2(a) to deliver a statement to the moving party, the court shall not consider the affidavit or testimony of the witness.

Rule 40.　Commitment to Another District

(a) **Appearance Before Federal Magistrate.** If a person is arrested in a district other than that in which the offense is alleged to have been committed, that person shall be taken without unnecessary delay before the nearest available federal magistrate. Preliminary proceedings concerning the defendant shall be conducted in accordance with Rules 5 and 5.1, except that if no preliminary examination is held because an indictment has been returned or an information filed or because the defendant elects to have the preliminary examination conducted in the district in which the prosecution is pending, the person shall be held to answer upon a finding that such person is the person named in the indictment, information or warrant. If held to answer, the defendant shall be held to answer in the district court in which the prosecution is pending, provided that a warrant is issued in that district if the arrest was made without a warrant, upon production of the warrant or a certified copy thereof. The warrant or certified copy may be produced by facsimile transmission.

* * *

Rule 41.　Search and Seizure

* * *

(c) **Issuance and Contents.**

* * *

(2) **Warrant Upon Oral Testimony.**

(A) **General Rule.** If the circumstances make it reasonable to dispense with a written affidavit, a Federal magistrate judge may issue a warrant based, in whole or in part, upon sworn oral testimony communicated by telephone or other appropriate means, including facsimile transmission.

* * *

Rule 46.　Release From Custody

* * *

(i) **Production of Statements.**

(1) **In General.** Rule 26.2(a)–(d) and (f) shall apply at a detention hearing held pursuant to 18 U.S.C. § 3144.

(2) **Sanctions for Failure to Produce Statement.** If a party elects not to comply with an order pursuant to Rule 26.2(a) to deliver a statement to the moving party, the court shall not consider the affidavit or testimony of witness at the detention hearing.

†